Politics and Government in Byzantium

Politics and Government in Byzantium

The Rise and Fall of the Bureaucrats

Jonathan Shea

I.B. TAURIS
LONDON • NEW YORK • OXFORD • NEW DELHI • SYDNEY

I.B. TAURIS
Bloomsbury Publishing Plc
50 Bedford Square, London, WC1B 3DP, UK
1385 Broadway, New York, NY 10018, USA

BLOOMSBURY, I.B. TAURIS and the I.B. Tauris logo are trademarks of
Bloomsbury Publishing Plc

First published in Great Britain 2020

Copyright © Jonathan Shea, 2020

Jonathan Shea has asserted his right under the Copyright, Designs and
Patents Act, 1988, to be identified as Author of this work.

For legal purposes the Acknowledgements on p. xii constitute an extension
of this copyright page.

Series design by Rebecca Heselton
Cover image: The Byzantine Emperor Nicephorus III and the chief four officials of
his court. (© Bibliothèque Nationale de France Manuscript Coislin 79 folio 2)

All rights reserved. No part of this publication may be reproduced or transmitted
in any form or by any means, electronic or mechanical, including photocopying,
recording, or any information storage or retrieval system, without prior
permission in writing from the publishers.

Bloomsbury Publishing Plc does not have any control over, or responsibility for, any
third-party websites referred to or in this book. All internet addresses given in this
book were correct at the time of going to press. The author and publisher regret any
inconvenience caused if addresses have changed or sites have ceased to exist,
but can accept no responsibility for any such changes.

A catalogue record for this book is available from the British Library.

A catalog record for this book is available from the Library of Congress.

ISBN: HB: 978-0-7556-0193-6
ePDF: 978-0-7556-0194-3
eBook: 978-0-7556-0195-0

Typeset by Deanta Global Publishing Services, Chennai, India
Printed and bound in Great Britain

To find out more about our authors and books visit www.bloomsbury.com and
sign up for our newsletters.

For Alexander, who came along just in time to help.
BNxcsaψχzbnzS3AA313sdωψωω

Contents

List of illustrations		viii
Acknowledgements		xii
1	Byzantium at the turning point	1
	1.1 Byzantium in the eleventh century	2
	1.2 Seals, coins and lists	6
2	The Byzantine bureaucrat	25
	2.1 Piety and seals	25
	2.2 Family names	29
	2.3 Career bureaucrats	33
3	The rise of the civilians, c. 966–c. 1066	39
	3.1 Changing with the times: The *logothesia* and the treasuries	41
	3.2 Slipping backwards: The imperial chancery	69
	3.3 Governing the capital	81
	3.4 A new bureaucratic elite: The judiciary	91
4	The collapse of civilian government, c. 1066–c. 1133	125
	4.1 Reform and consolidation: The *logothesia* and treasuries	126
	4.2 The chancery: A part of the imperial household?	136
	4.3 The administration of Constantinople: A steady decline	143
	4.4 Falling from Grace: The judiciary	147
	4.5 The end of civilian government	157
5	Changing priorities and an evolving government	161
	5.1 The Byzantine hierarchy in the eleventh century	161
	5.2 Increasing numbers and growing complexity	168
	5.3 Imperial priorities	173
Appendix – *chartoularioi*, *notarioi* and *logariastai*		179
Notes		186
Bibliography		232
Index		245

Illustrations

1.1 Nikephoros III Botaneiates (1078–1081) gold bulla. Dumbarton Oaks, Byzantine Collection, Washington, DC, BZS.1948.17.4296 — 4
2.1 Seal of John *patrikios*, imperial *notarios*, judge of the Velum and of the Kibyrraiotai. Dumbarton Oaks, Byzantine Collection, Washington, DC, BZS.1955.1.2420 — 26
2.2 Seal of Michael *vestes*, judge of the Velum and *epi tes basilikes sakelles*. Dumbarton Oaks, Byzantine Collection, Washington, DC, BZS.1958.106.4734 — 27
2.3 Seal of Michael Machetarios, *vestarches* and *eparch*. Dumbarton Oaks, Byzantine Collection, Washington, DC, BZS.1958.106.5704 — 30
2.4 Seal of George Kibyrraiotes, *proedros* and *protonotarios* of the *dromos*. Dumbarton Oaks, Byzantine Collection, Washington, DC, BZS.1947.2.1073 — 31
2.5 Seal of Basil Tzirithon, *protovestarches*, judge of the Velum and judge of the Kibyrraiotai. Harvard Art Museums/Arthur M. Sackler Museum, Bequest of Thomas Whittemore, 1951.31.5.781 — 34
3.1 Seal of Stephen *protovestes*, *oikistikos ton neon orthoseon* and judge of the Armeniakoi. Dumbarton Oaks, Byzantine Collection, Washington, DC, BZS.1955.1.2125. — 51
3.2 Seal of Nikephoros Laktentitzes, imperial *protopatharios epi tou Chrysotriklinou*, *mystographos* and *chartoularios* of the *stratiotikon logothesion*. Dumbarton Oaks, Byzantine Collection, Washington, DC, BZS.1958.106.5404. — 53
3.3 Seal of Niketas Xylinites, *proedros* and *logothetes tou dromou*. Dumbarton Oaks, Byzantine Collection, Washington, DC, BZS.1958.106.3238 — 56
3.4 Seal of Theodore *patrikios* and *ephoros*. Dumbarton Oaks, Byzantine Collection, Washington, DC, BZS.1955.1.2143 — 67
3.5 Seal of Nicholas, *protospatharios* and *asekretis*. Dumbarton Oaks, Byzantine Collection, Washington, DC, BZS.1958.106.3159 — 73
3.6 Seal of Nicholas *hypatos*, judge of the Hippodrome and *symponos*. Harvard Art Museums/Arthur M. Sackler Museum, Bequest of Thomas Whittemore, 1951.31.5.1348 — 87
3.7 Seal of Eustathios *magistros* and *droungarios tes viglas*. Dumbarton Oaks, Byzantine Collection, Washington, DC, BZS.1958.106.5598 — 97
3.8 Seal of Constantine *vestarches*, judge of the Velum and *megas kourator* of the *sekreton* of the Mangana. Dumbarton Oaks, Byzantine Collection, Washington, DC, BZS.1958.106.5709 — 104
3.9 Seal of Niketas *proedros* and *epi ton kriseon*. Harvard Art Museums/Arthur M. Sackler Museum, Bequest of Thomas Whittemore, 1951.31.5.340 — 111

3.10	Constantine IX Monomachos (1042–55) Miliaresion, 1042–55, Constantinople. Harvard Art Museums/Arthur M. Sackler Museum, Bequest of Thomas Whittemore, 1951.31.4.1581	119
4.1	Seal of John Beriotes, *vestes*, judge of the Velum, *megas chartoularios* of the *stratiotikon logothesion*, imperial *protonotarios* of the *sekreton* of the *sakelle*. Harvard Art Museums/Arthur M. Sackler Museum, Bequest of Thomas Whittemore, 1951.31.5.1267	133
4.2	Seal of Eustathios *epi tou kanikleiou*, *ethnarches* and grand *droungarios* of the fleet. Dumbarton Oaks, Byzantine Collection, Washington, DC, BZS.1955.1.4060	137
4.3	Seal of John Solomon, *protoproedros* and *epi ton deeseon*. Dumbarton Oaks, Byzantine Collection, Washington, DC, BZS.1955.1.3324	142
4.4	Seal of Nicholas Mermentoulos, *nobelissimos* and *eparch*. Dumbarton Oaks, Byzantine Collection, Washington, DC, BZS.1958.106.5531	144
4.5	Seal of Pekoules, judge and *koiaistor*. Dumbarton Oaks, Byzantine Collection, Washington, DC, BZS.1955.1.4040	148
4.6	Seal of Nikephoros *proedros* and 'first' of the judges. Dumbarton Oaks, Byzantine Collection, Washington, DC, BZS.1955.1.3734	150
5.1	Seal of Philaretos *illoustrios*, *exaktor* and judge of the East. Harvard Art Museums/Arthur M. Sackler Museum, Bequest of Thomas Whittemore, 1951.31.5.139	168
5.2	Basil II (976–1025) Nomisma Histamenon, 1005–25, Constantinople. Dumbarton Oaks, Byzantine Collection, Washington, DC, BZC.1948.17.3173	170
5.3	Romanos III Argyros (1028–34) Miliaresion, Constantinople. Harvard Art Museums/Arthur M. Sackler Museum, Bequest of Thomas Whittemore, 1951.31.4.1573	174
5.4	Alexios I (1081–1118) Aspron Trachy Nomisma, 1092–3, Constantinople. Dumbarton Oaks, Byzantine Collection, Washington, DC, BZC.1969.8	176
6.1	Seal of John *notarios*. Dumbarton Oaks, Byzantine Collection, Washington, DC, BZS.1958.106.4610 John notarios	181

Tables

1.1	The Byzantine Hierarchy of Titles in the Late Tenth and Eleventh Centuries	14
1.2	Relative Relation of Titles across the Eleventh Century	15
1.3	The Byzantine Hierarchy of Titles under Alexios I Komnenos (1081–1118)	16
1.4	Rogai as Recorded in the Chrysobull of 1074 (bold), and the Reconstructions of H. Ahrweiler (roman) and J.-C. Cheynet (italics)	19
1.5	An Example of Allocated Values	22
3.1	Normalized Seal Data, in Percentages, for the Titles of the *Sakellarios* c. 966–c. 1066	45
3.2	Normalized Seal Data, in Percentages, for the Titles of the *Logothetes tou Genikou* c. 966–c. 1066	47

3.3	Normalized Seal Data, in Percentages, for the Titles of the *Megas Chartoularios* of the *Genikon Logothesion* c. 966–c. 1066	49
3.4	Normalized Seal Data, in Percentages, for the Titles of the *Chartoularios* of the *Genikon Logothesion* c. 966–c. 1066	49
3.5	Normalized Seal Data, in Percentages, for the Titles of the *Asekretai* c. 966–c. 1066	73
3.6	Normalized Seal Data, in Percentages, for the Titles of the *Mystographoi* c. 966–c. 1066	78
3.7	Normalized Seal Data, in Percentages, for the Titles of the *Epi ton Deeseon* c. 966–c. 1066	79
3.8	Normalized Seal Data, in Percentages, for the Titles of the *Mystolektai* c. 966–c. 1066	80
3.9	Normalized Seal Data, in Percentages, for the Titles of *Eparchs* c. 966–c. 1066	84
3.10	Normalized Seal Data, in Percentages, for the Titles of *Symponoi* c. 966–c. 1066	87
3.11	Normalized Seal Data, in Percentages, for the Titles of *Koiaistores* c. 966–c. 1066	95
3.12	Normalized Seal Data, in Percentages, for the Titles of Judges of the Velum c. 966–c. 1066	103
3.13	Normalized Seal Data, in Percentages, for the Titles of Judges of the Hippodrome c. 966–c. 1066	106
3.14	Percentage of Judges of the Velum and Judges of the Hippodrome Who Served as Theme Judges c. 966–c. 1066	109
3.15	Normalized Seal Data, in Percentages, for the Titles of *Exaktores* c. 966–c. 1066	116
3.16	Normalized Seal Data, in Percentages, for the Titles of *Kensores* c. 966–c. 1066	117
4.1	Normalized Seal Data, in Percentages, for the Titles of *Sakellarioi* c. 1066–c. 1133	127
4.2	Normalized Seal Data, in Percentages, for the Titles of *Logothetai tou Genikou* c. 1066–c. 1133	129
4.3	Normalized Seal Data, in Percentages, for the Titles of the *Megaloi Chartoularioi tou Genikou* c. 1066–c. 1133	130
4.4	Normalized Seal Data, in Percentages, for the Titles of the *Chartoularioi tou Genikou* c. 1066–c. 1133	131
4.5	Normalized Seal Data, in Percentages, for the Titles of the *Asekretai* c. 1066–c. 1133	139
4.6	Normalized Seal Data, in Percentages, for the Titles of the *Mystographos* c. 1066–c. 1133	140
4.7	Normalized Seal Data, in Percentages, for the Titles of the *Epi ton Deeseon* c. 1066–c. 1133	141
4.8	Normalized Seal Data, in Percentages, for the Titles of the *Mystolektai* c. 1066–c. 1133	143

4.9	Normalized Seal Data, in Percentages, for the *Titles of the Eparchs* c. 1066–c. 1133	144
4.10	Normalized Seal Data, in Percentages, for the Titles of the *Symponoi* c. 1066–c. 1133	146
4.11	Normalized Seal Data, in Percentages, for the Titles of the *Koiaistores* c. 1066–c. 1133	148
4.12	Normalized Seal Data, in Percentages, for the Titles of the Judges of the Velum c. 1066–c. 1133	152
4.13	Normalized Seal Data, in Percentages, for the Titles of the Judges of the Hippodrome c. 1066–c. 1133	154
4.14	Normalized Seal Data, in Percentages, for the Titles of the *Exaktores* c. 1066–c. 1133	157
4.15	Normalized Seal Data, in Percentages, for the Titles of the *Kensores* c. 1066–c. 1133	157
5.1	Titles Found Together on Seals	162
5.2	Normalized Seal Data, in Percentages, for Highest Titles Held by Bureaucrats c. 966–c. 1133 with the Total Number of Holders in Parentheses	164
5.3	Number of Titles Awarded in Proportion by Period Based on an Initial Size of 200 Bureaucrats	165
6.1	Normalized Seal Data, in Percentages, for the Titles of *Megaloi Chartoularioi* c. 966–c. 1133	180
6.2	Normalized Seal Data, in Percentages, for the Titles of *Chartoularioi* c. 966–c. 1133	181
6.3	Normalized Seal Data, in Percentages, for the Titles of *Protonotarioi* c. 966–c. 1133	182
6.4	Normalized Seal Data, in Percentages, for the Titles of Imperial *Notarioi* c. 966–c. 1133	183
6.5	Normalized Seal Data, in Percentages, for the Titles of *Notarioi* c. 966–c. 1133	184
6.6	Normalized Seal Data, in Percentages, for the Titles of *Logariastai* c. 966–c. 1133	184
6.7	Normalized Seal Data, in Percentages, for the Titles of *Ek Prosopou* c. 966–c. 1133	185

Acknowledgements

It is with great pleasure, and a deep sense of relief that I find myself in a position to thank those who have helped during the preparation of this monograph. I am lucky enough to work at an institution with three friends who are not only sigillographers but also have an interest in the same period as me. This project began four years ago at the suggestion of John Nesbitt who told me that I might want to look at the seals of the judges of the Velum and judges of the Hippodrome as there could be something interesting there. The project has grown quite a bit since then, but John was right, as ever, and the judiciary forms in many ways the core of this study. I want to thank him not only for putting the idea into my head but for reading multiple drafts of the manuscript, helping me formulate ideas and arguments, and examining the odd tricky seal with me. Eric McGeer has been a constant source of good suggestions and kindly read through each chapter. His advice has been invaluable, and if you come across a sentence in this work that you think is particularly pleasingly written it was probably Eric's. John and Eric also kindly gave me access to their unpublished translation of Scylitzes Continuatus. Lain Wilson through virtue of proximity was the least able to avoid me when I needed to speak to someone about my work. He has been beyond generous with his time and insights sitting down and helping me thrash out arguments and develop theories. John, Eric and Lain have helped me refine my ideas, and their input has improved my work immensely.

I have been lucky enough to receive advice from many friends and colleagues while preparing this manuscript. My late friend Ruth Macrides nurtured my love of Byzantium, helped introduce me to Dumbarton Oaks and patiently pushed me every time I needed pushing. For reading early drafts of parts of this book I owe her my thanks, but even more so for shaping a significant part of my life and career. John Cotsonis gave generously of this time allowing me to exploit his expertise in seal iconography and personal piety. I would like to express my gratitude to Werner Seibt and Jean-Claude Cheynet with whom I was fortunate enough to discuss elements of this book during their visits to Dumbarton Oaks. I am very grateful to Anthony Kaldellis who read the entire manuscript and provided generous encouragement and feedback. Jan Ziolkowski has been a firm supporter of all things seals during my time at Dumbarton Oaks and has encouraged me during the writing of the present volume. Friends and former colleagues at Dumbarton Oaks Margaret Mullett and Michael Maas helped get this monograph started. Margaret brought me on to the seals project at Dumbarton Oaks and has always been unstintingly supportive of my work. Likewise, Michael has been a steady source of encouragement, and without him it is unlikely that anyone would have accepted my publication proposal. Accepted it was, and I would like to express my appreciation to the staff at I. B. Tauris, particularly Tom Stottor with whom I started this project and Rory Gormley who saw it through to completion.

The anonymous reviewers of my work deserve special thanks. Their comments and suggestions have immensely improved this book, and I am very grateful for their input.

The deepest debts of all are those I owe to my family. My mum has supported and encouraged me all of my life. From her comes my love of history which set me on the path to writing this book. Lisa has been endlessly patient and loving. She has not only worked through ideas with me for countless hours but also ensured that I remained as sane coming out of this project as I was going in. I could not ask for a better partner in life. Last but not least Alexander. He was born as I started writing and happily helped with the typing. He also, newly able to pull himself up, destroyed the first hardcopy that I made and unwisely left unattended on a coffee table. I can only hope that my book does not provoke a similar impulse in its readers.

1

Byzantium at the turning point

Power rested on three factors: the people, the senate, and the army. Yet while they [the emperors] minimized the influence of the military, imperial favours were granted to the other two as soon as a new sovereign acceded.[1]

The period between the ascendency of Nikephoros II Phokas (963–69), the 'White Death of the Saracens', and the death of Alexios I Komnenos (1081–1118) has long been viewed as both fascinating and puzzling. Beginning with Nikephoros's elevation to the post of *domestikos ton scholon* in 955 and accelerating after his rise to the throne in 963, the empire embarked on a remarkable series of conquests. Byzantium's borders expanded far beyond its Anatolian and Aegean core to the islands of Crete and Cyprus in the south, the mountains of Armenia and the Euphrates Valley in the east and the River Danube in the west. The majority of these conquests were completed by 1018, when the Bulgarian Empire fell to Basil II 'the Bulgar-slayer' (976–1025). However, the first half of the eleventh century saw continued expansion, albeit on a humbler scale, notably in the capture of Edessa in Mesopotamia in 1031 and Ani in Armenia in 1046. There were also setbacks, such as the abortive attempts to recover Sicily in the 1030s and 1040s. Byzantium's strength provided security for its people, a growing economy and a flowering of art and culture. Although it was never invincible, the Byzantine Empire of the early eleventh century was the most powerful and wealthy state in the Mediterranean. However, by the 1060s the world around Byzantium was changing rapidly with new threats arising in Italy, the Danube frontier and the Near East simultaneously. Under pressure from three sides the empire slowly gave ground in the west in the 1050s and 1060s and in the east in the 1070s and 1080s.[2] By the early 1090s the empire had lost not only all of its eastern conquests from the last century but also almost everything east of the Aegean Sea, as well as its Italian territory. In Europe, many provinces had been devastated by Norman and Pecheneg invasions. Byzantium managed a partial recovery in Asia, aided by the mixed blessing of the First Crusade. Although the Komnenian dynasty founded by Alexios I Komnenos went on to rule a powerful state, the empire was never again as strong as it had been in the preceding period. The Komnenian restoration was in many respects reactionary, yet in others startlingly revolutionary. Territorially, socially and administratively, the twelfth-century empire was very different to its eleventh-century self.

At the centre of the expansive imperial enterprise of the early eleventh century and its later collapse were the bureaucrats based in Constantinople. Although we tend to associate the great conquests of the tenth and eleventh centuries with Byzantium's armies and the soldier emperors who commanded them, professional administrators ensured that the imperial military was fed and supplied, that taxes were collected so that the soldiers were paid, that communications were able pass from the front lines to the core of the empire and that the empire continued to function while the emperors spent long periods away on campaign. Limiting the Constantinopolitan bureaucrats to a military support role, however, does not do them justice. The eleventh century was the period in which they were at their most powerful. After the period of conquest, it was the bureaucrats who consolidated the new acquisitions, bore most of the burden of running the newly enlarged empire, incorporated new territory into the *theme* system of provincial government, administered the now very large imperial estates, collected taxes and allocated spending, and ensured that the law was applied, ideally evenly. Today we tend to lionize conquerors, but, as the history of the eleventh century shows, keeping the enlarged Byzantine Empire functioning was an even greater challenge than recovering lost territory.[3] Yet for over two generations after the death of the last great conqueror Basil II in 1025 Byzantium rose to the challenge, thanks in no small part to the bureaucrats of Constantinople. These civil servants belonged to a tradition with its foundations in the late Roman administrative reforms of the Tetrarchic period, although it had evolved over the centuries, most notably following the Islamic conquests of the seventh century and the subsequent focusing of power and government in the capital.[4] The Byzantine Empire was administered by a group of educated lay officials appointed and paid by the emperor.[5] The aim of this study is to examine these officials: who they were, what they did and how that tied into imperial policy in the ever-changing eleventh-century world.

The story of the bureaucrats of Byzantium c. 966–1100 is one of a group who took the administration of empire in new directions, experimenting with the means through which the law could become an instrument of government, and who saw their capital transform around them, and adapted to that change in creative ways. It is the tale of a group of men who in a European and Mediterranean world dominated by warlords ruled the most powerful state in that world as civilians. They were a diverse group by the standards of the time. Labelling them as Constantinopolitan is an easy shorthand for their cultural and political alignment, but like all rich governments and major cities that of Byzantium in Constantinople attracted recruits from far and wide. Socially too they were a broad group, from long-established families to humble clerks an increasing number of men found inclusion in the expanded elite of Constantinople. At the height of their power the bureaucrats of Byzantium lost everything, the new Komnenian emperors had far less time for them than earlier rulers, and the rewards of empire were directed away from the bureaucracy. This book explores both the successes and the ultimate failure of the bureaucrats to maintain their paramount position in the empire, and Byzantium's primacy in its world.

1.1 Byzantium in the eleventh century

The look of woe was everywhere and the Reigning City was filled with despair. Those in power gave no thought to curbing the daily injustices and the unlawful trials and exactions, but freely carried on with their oppressive and wicked policies just as though there was nothing at all the matter with the Romans, no war with foreign enemies, no divine wrath, no indigence and violence taking their toll on the populace in their daily life.[6]

Recently Anthony Kaldellis has addressed the history of Byzantium in the period covered in the present study, successfully putting to rest the idea that it was one, long, Gibonian tale of easily manipulated emperors and their feeble civilian administrations sleepwalking towards a cliff while the Byzantine army stoutly fought on with no support from the capital until from their number the Komnenoi rode in on white chargers to save the day.[7] The rehabilitation of the imperial governments of the eleventh century has been a long-time coming, and while the situation may not have been as bad as stated in the first sentence of this section, the exaggeration is not too great. The only book to date to focus on the imperial administration in the eleventh century, G. Weiss's *Oströmische Beamte im Spiegel der Schriften des Michael Psellos*, relied heavily on the testimony of Michael Psellos and presented a conflicting picture of an educated, yet strangely ignorant group of men, operating a system so complex that it undermined the strength of the empire.[8] In his reassessment of the period as a whole Kaldellis has demonstrated that up until the 1060s at the earliest Byzantium was not appreciatively weaker than before, and that its emperors were not especially ineffectual. Constantine IX Monomachos, in many respects the most significant ruler of the period, has been rehabilitated, even as a military emperor. There is a good case to be made that the disasters which befell Byzantium at the end of the century were not rooted in long-standing systemic weaknesses. In short, the problems of the 1070s did not necessarily have their genesis in the 1040s.[9]

It is rarely in the nature of historians to accept such an answer; everyone ruling before a period of decline must in someway be responsible, at least in part, for what followed. This was certainly how the Byzantines felt, and the image of an imperial weakness leading the empire into disaster comes straight from the pages of Michael Psellos, Michael Attaleiates and John Skylitzes. Constantine IX usually comes in for particularly harsh criticism, he was militarily ineffectual, did not really understand, or had no interest in, the business of government and spent money recklessly. As John Skylitzes put it:

> I will say it: that it was from the time of this emperor and on account of his prodigality and pretentiousness that the fortunes of the Roman empire began to waste away. From that time until now it has regressed into an all-encompassing debility. He simply sought to be open-handed yet he ended up being utterly profligate.[10]

What was true for Monomachos, with the exception of Michael IV and Isaac I, was true for his fellow eleventh-century emperors, with a few variations to the tale. Romanos III was a vain glory seeker and Michael VI poured the rewards of empire onto his followers from the civilian party, while spurning the leader of the military faction.[11]

The simplistic explanation of the divisions in the period, between a military faction based largely in Anatolia and a civilian faction founded on control of the capital and the state machinery located there, has largely been shelved, alongside unhelpful questions of feudalism.[12] There was an ongoing struggle between shifting groups for access to imperial largesse, titles, offices and gifts, and eventually for control of the imperial office itself.[13] The key is that the forces involved and the alliances between them were constantly in flux. One of the simple truths of Byzantine history is that an emperor in firm control of Constantinople was unlikely to be dislodged from within the city, so all rebellions (as opposed to coups) were, of necessity, provincial in origin and, as the Byzantine capital was a formidable fortress, military in nature. This does not mean that there was a military faction ranged against the civilians of Constantinople, any more than it means that the various groups that made up the population of the capital were united behind their emperor. In fact, of all the emperors overthrown in the eleventh century only one, Nikephoros III Botaneiates, can be considered the victim of a military coup.[14] The rest were ousted by some subset of the population of their capital.[15] It is no surprise that the emperors should so heavily court the powerful of the capital, and in the eleventh century there was a shift in exactly who was included in this group.

There is evidence that in the eleventh century the guilds of Constantinople were gaining political influence in a way not seen before or afterwards.[16] The relationship between this phenomenon, the ruling style of Basil II, and the careers and origins of Romanos III, John the Orphanotrophos and his relatives Michael IV and Michael V, has been explored elsewhere and do not need repeating here.[17] What does seem obvious is that exactly the sort of men who were in the perfect place and wealthy enough to give their sons enough education to enter on a bureaucratic career were gaining in prominence in the eleventh century. Moreover, political power brought official recognition. Psellos famously recorded how Constantine IX opened the senate to the men of the market and the people of Constantinople.[18] While these new senators seem to have been of a new lower class than the more traditional elite, that they were elevated at all is a sign of both the changing nature of Byzantine politics and of a new way in which imperial authority had to account for, and include, the people of Constantinople.[19] What impact did this move by Constantine IX have on

Figure 1.1 Nikephoros III Botaneiates (1078–1081) gold bulla. Dumbarton Oaks, Byzantine Collection, Washington, DC, BZS.1948.17.4296.
This gold bulla of Nikephoros III depicts a bust of Christ on the obverse and the standing emperor with labarum and globus cruciger on the reverse. It was produced from the heavily debased coinage of the time and thus appears more silver than gold.
Rev. +ΝΙΚΗΦΔΕC-ΠΟΤΒΟΤΑΝΙΑΤ
Νικηφόρῳ δεσπότῃ τῷ Βοτανιάτῃ.
Nikephoros Botaneiates, despotes.

the bureaucrats of Constantinople? Did it diminish the standing of those already in the senate proper? What about those who had existed in the next tier down, the so-called sandal-wearing senators?[20] Is there any evidence of an increase in their number as the prospects of those from humbler backgrounds improved, or perhaps a push for promotion as their status became diluted or diminished by the influx of new senators? If Michael Hendy is correct, the same question can be asked later when Constantine X Doukas abolished the division between the two groups of senators making one unified senatorial order.[21] A further question arises, to what degree were the bureaucrats of Constantinople a part of a group which the emperors of the period courted?

The historians and commentators on the eleventh century not only tell us that the emperors of their time were bad; they tell us how, often in great detail. The two negative traits which concern us are the mismanagement of the empire's resources and of the system of titles, which, as title-holders drew an annual stipend from the treasury, amounted to much the same thing. With this in mind it is easy to see how enlarging the senate, and in so doing increasing the number of titled men receiving a stipend, could lead to a dangerous increase in government expenditure if not handled well. The most damning evidence of this sort of mismanagement comes from the reign of Nikephoros III Botaneiates (1078–81). As Nikephoros Bryennios records:

> He did not grant the highest honours to the most notable among the aristocracy, the military, or members of the senatorial class, or to those showing some favour towards him, but to all those who asked for them. He did the same with what the Romans called *offikia*, so that as a consequence expenditure exceeded revenue by several times. And so, for this reason, within a short space of time, money was lacking, the nomisma was debased and the gifts of money attached by the emperor to such honours and offices were brought to an end. For the influx of money which derived from Asia and which went to supply the treasury ceased because the whole of Asia fell into the possession of the Turks, and since that deriving from Europe also decreased drastically, because of its ill-use by earlier emperors, the imperial treasury found itself in the greatest want of money.[22]

Bryennios is clear that the policies of Nikephoros III brought about financial ruin, but explicitly links the economic crisis to the territorial collapse of Byzantium. Nikephoros III's great crime was to continue increasing the expenditure of the state at the same time that the revenues were declining. In this regard the 1070s were a unique period. Expenditure might have gone up in other periods, but the extent of the empire remained largely constant, especially in its Anatolian core, up until that point. Nikephoros III's reign falls over a century into the range covered by this study; what evidence is there among the bureaucrats of indiscriminate or universal promotions before Nikephoros III? As we will see the answer to this is that there is very little. There is certainly evidence of low-level title inflation, which we shall discuss further in the following pages, but nothing of the sort recorded in the late 1070s. Even the accessional promotion bonanzas indulged in by most eleventh-century emperors have left little record in the sources for the bureaucracy.

If the emperors of the eleventh century were not universally useless, and they were not lavishly rewarding their bureaucrats, how did they pass the time? One way was to reform their government. When we examine the lives of bureaucrats, we see that the administrative system of c. 966 had already undergone significant changes from that of a generation before, and the emperors of the eleventh century continued this work, helping to transform the fiscal structure of Byzantium, the judiciary and the government of the capital. It becomes clear that this was a system which rewarded its bureaucrats well, if they worked in an area of government currently in favour. They could become powerful, rich men. The emperors of the period had ideas about how to run their empire and acted upon them. Imperial priorities reveal a lot about the men on the throne based on the area they thought most in need of their attention, be it finance, land management, Constantinople or the judiciary. Government became more complex in the eleventh century, and there was a marked move towards standardization and centralization. It is difficult to determine whether an increase in the size and complexity of the bureaucracy helped inspire Psellos's bloated, diseased body metaphor when describing the Byzantine state, but more employees certainly meant more wages.[23] This is a far more interesting story than a century of incompetence and decline.

Before moving on to discuss the sources which will open up the world of the Byzantine Bureaucrat, a final word on the end of the period. In 1081, Alexios I Komnenos seized the throne of Byzantium and set about fundamentally changing the way that the empire ran. By the end of his reign the Byzantine Empire had a new elite, coinage, tax system and concept of status. We will examine these changes in the appropriate chapters and attempt to understand the place of the bureaucrats of Constantinople in the early days of the Komnenian system.

1.2 Seals, coins and lists

Δύο τοίνυν τούτων τὴν Ῥωμαίων συντηρούντων ἡγεμονίαν, ἀξιωμάτων φημὶ καὶ χρημάτων ...

Two things sustain the hegemony of the Romans, their system of titles and their money ...[24]

The overall question of decline – encompassing the actions of the Byzantine military, changing geopolitics and political machinations – lies outside the scope of this study. Instead, in the following chapters I aim to address the question of how the Byzantine Empire of the late tenth century through to the end of the eleventh century was administered, by whom, and the influence that this system had on the fortunes of the state that created it. In doing so I will build a picture of the bureaucratic element within the civilian elite of the capital. I use the terms 'bureaucrat' and 'bureaucracy' throughout this study, and as such they deserve a little more discussion. By 'bureaucrat' I mean an individual who undertook administrative functions as a part of the imperial government, in return for compensation – what we might today term a state employee or civil servant. These individuals were from a variety of social, economic and geographical backgrounds, but I am primarily concerned with those who worked in Constantinople, wherever they originated. Not included in the following analysis are those employed by the state in other areas, specifically the Byzantine military, the imperially funded parts of the church, and the provincial administrators with no demonstrable link to a metropolitan office. I also do not consider those individuals who possessed a title, and therefore a place within the Byzantine court hierarchy, but no office.[25]

By bureaucracy I mean the aggregate of these state office-holders, working in Constantinople, keeping the government of Byzantium operating. The term 'bureaucracy' brings to mind contemporary organizations, and the Byzantine system, with salaried officials, is at first sight deceptively modern.[26] Different departments oversaw different areas of the state; for instance, the *stratiotikon* was responsible for the military administration, and the tribunal of the judges of the Velum operated in some ways like a modern supreme court. However, the image of bureaus and bureaucrats with tightly defined responsibilities is a mirage. The final arbiter of who performed which function was the reigning emperor or empress, and they could appoint anyone to do anything. And so it was that the empire, under Basil II, could dispatch the *epi tou kanikleiou*, the keeper of the imperial inkstand, as ambassador to Baghdad, and later to command an army. The direct link between imperial favour and power was also demonstrated when Romanos Skleros, brother of Constantine IX's mistress Maria, was appointed *magistros* and *protostrator* on account of his link to the emperor.[27] A final example comes from the life of Michael Psellos, who asked Empress Theodora to adjudicate a case concerning his family. Rather than do so herself or refer the case to one of the existing tribunals in the capital, she created an ad hoc court consisting of the *protoasekretis*, the *epi ton kriseon*, the *nomophylax* and the *skribas*, none of whom were actually professional judges.[28]

In a similar vein, when I speak of an elite, I refer to a status granted by the emperor. This simple fact helps to distinguish Byzantium, with its service elite reliant on imperial favour, from that found in the kingdoms of Western Europe with their hereditary nobilities.[29] Proximity to imperial power was really all that mattered, but obviously the bureaucracy was not solely composed of individuals who had access to the rulers or would catch their eye. Even outside this charmed circle, among the humbler bureaucrats, there is ample evidence, often to an even greater degree than among senior office-holders, of an almost chaotic administration with blurred boundaries between various departments, and no clearly defined career structure in place. Byzantine bureaucrats, and the system within which they worked, often seem precociously modern, but for all its superficial similarities they worked in a very different environment to our own. Although the Byzantine bureaucracy extended far into the provinces, I will focus on the capital because, in contrast to the other powers of Christendom, Constantinople was at the centre of the empire, in almost every sense. No matter how directly or often we might think that the imperial government intervened in the lives of its provincial subjects, it could and did so when it wished, and the rhythms of provincial life must have been greatly influenced by the need to pay taxes. Imperial law came from Constantinople, taxes were assessed from, and sent to, the capital, and this was where the socially ambitious went to pursue their dreams. Constantinople was the centre of gravity around which the empire revolved, and at the heart of Constantinople was the imperial court and its attached bureaucracy, which through the actions of its members bound a large, sprawling and far-flung empire together.

The Constantinople-based bureaucracy had been at the centre of Byzantine government for centuries. However, what had been true earlier was doubly true in this period, when, as we shall see, the sigillographic evidence shows that the administration was growing in size and complexity. It was also a period when the emperors rarely left their capital. Proximity to the ruler, no matter the rank or position of the individual concerned was a reliable route to power, influence and wealth. While elements of the provincial administration of the period, and the relationship between the centre and the provinces, have been the focus of a number of works, the question of what was happening at the heart of the bureaucratic machine in the capital of Constantinople has gone largely unstudied.[30] One of the reasons for this general omission is the nature and paucity of source material. Each of the authors who cover part or all of the period in their works are unreliable sources. Anna Komnene eulogizes her father in the *Alexiad*, praising him and criticizing his predecessor, and the work of her husband, Nikephoros Bryennios, does much the same. John Zonaras who disliked Alexios is much more critical of that emperor's actions, including his treatment of the very groups that staffed the imperial bureaucracy. All three are thus imperfect sources for our needs. Michael Psellos, Michael Attaleiates and John Skylitzes likewise have an emperor over whom they fawn and one, Constantine IX, whom they blame for the empire's later ills.[31] Despite most of these sources being written by civilian bureaucrats, they are complimentary to the empire's military rulers and critical of the emperors who rose up from the capital. The surviving legal documents are far too few in number to be of more than superficial, or very specific, use.[32]

There is a source, however, that exists outside of the partisan politics and ideological squabbles of the time, and in numbers large enough to be reliable and revealing. Thousands of lead seals survive from this period, made for the very administrators whose numbers, promotion, pay and incompetence are supposed to have helped to ruin the empire. These small lead discs were designed to identify their owner and authenticate and protect their acts and writings. To these ends they include identifying inscriptions usually including the name, court title and office of the owner, and often a pious invocation frequently accompanied by a religious image. Seals were attached by bureaucrats to a wide range of items – letters (both official and private), wills, land deeds, tax documents, commercial transactions, legal decisions, dissents from legal decisions, official weighing apparatus and traded commodities, among a host of other forms of paperwork.[33] For our purposes it should be noted that the seals do not just represent paperwork and government documents, but people. Each seal is the record of an individual – what he did in life, how he fit into wider society – and often includes a profession of his personal piety. The vast majority of these men left no other record of their existence, and hence their seals are the only means by which we can attempt to see them and their place in the Byzantine world. In many respects seals give a voice to the civilian class woefully underrepresented in the narratives of the eleventh century. When we collect enough individuals together we can begin to see how the various departments of the government operated.

For this study I have collected data from all major published collections as well as unpublished seals from the Dumbarton Oaks and Harvard Art Museums' Collection. A full list of publications and collections can be found in the bibliography for this volume. While seals are an excellent source for administrative history there are a few problems with using them. The first is provenance; apart from a few specific publications, most notably the corpus of seals found in Bulgaria, the seals that exist in the world's major collections have no archaeological context. While we know that the seals used for this study were produced in Constantinople, we have no idea where the recipient of whatever the seal was affixed to lived and worked. Interestingly, the Bulgaria corpus presents almost the complete range of Constantinopolitan offices with which we are concerned, and for which we have evidence from other collections. This allows the tentative conclusion that, unless the world's seals all come from Bulgaria, geographical bias does not skew our results noticeably. This makes a certain sense as the capital was likely in frequent contact with all of the provinces, the difference being one of scale rather than substance. The second issue is rate of production and therefore chance of survival. Some offices likely produced more seals than others by virtue of issuing more paperwork, validating more documents or writing more letters. As the reader will see there is an underrepresentation of certain low-ranking officials in the seals record, usually minor clerical officials who might not have been required to validate documents or who might have sealed in fragile wax rather than lead. However, almost every office of which we are aware has left behind some sigillographic relic, as the bureaucrats in these offices were all involved to some degree in the creation of paperwork. They might not exist in the numbers required to assess the fortunes of that particular job, but they can contribute to a discussion of the department in which they worked and to an assessment of the bureaucracy as a whole. The third and final issue is that some offices likely produced documents that were more likely to be saved. It is entirely possible, although we can never be sure, that a seal of the *eparch* of Constantinople was more likely to be preserved than one of a lowly *notarios*. However, there was only one *eparch* at any one time, whereas there were hundreds of *notarioi*, and the sigillographic record reflects this fact, particularly as this study deals with the people that the seals represent, not individual seals. For our purposes a *notarios* known from one seal is as valuable as an *eparch* known from five.

When a bureaucrat appears in a written source he is brought in as a mover of events, a character in a story. What the reader is presented with is thus as much, if not more so, the creation of the author as an accurate portrait of the person in question. This distorted, second-hand image is somewhat corrected when we take seals as the foundation of our study rather than the written material. Seals were the personal commissions of the civilian bureaucrats in question: they tell us how that person chose to describe and represent himself, and they form a direct link between us and the Byzantine who owned them. By their very nature seals had to present an accurate picture of their owner. Any deviation from the truth on a seal only served to undermine the very functions that it was created to perform, to identify, authenticate and guarantee. As one eleventh-century inscription put it, Γραφῶν ἐπισφράγισμα πρακτέων κῦρος τυποῖ Μιχαὴλ τοῦ δρόμου λογοθέτης (Michael, *logothetes* of the *dromos*, marks the sealing of his writings and the validity of his acts).[34] Aside from the three uses mentioned earlier, seals also provided their owner with a medium through which to engage in self-promotion or self-identity creation, which it might be argued could undermine their usefulness as a source. However, in the period from c. 966 to 1100 this very personal and promotional aspect of seal design actually plays into our hands, as the self-identity/promotion in question was entirely influenced by a person's participation in the workings of the Byzantine state. In spite of the rising importance of family and pedigree, the only accepted mark of social status remained the honorific titles granted by the imperial court, and the surest source of wealth and power was imperial service through the holding of an office.[35] Thus, the very desire to use seals to promote oneself, in our period, actually increases the value of seals as a source for the administrative history of Byzantium and for the lives and careers of its bureaucrats.

Seals were more than just a means of securing correspondence and official documents; they were a way of establishing the authority and identity of the individual who struck them. This resulted in Byzantine seals of this period having much in common with a modern business card. While there are exceptions, the standard seal of the period under consideration had an inscription recording the name and family name should the owner possess one and wish to include it, dignity and office of the owner.[36] Dignities and offices were separate, though often linked. It was possible for an individual to possess a dignity and no office, or an office and no dignity. These two terms, office and dignity, deserve exploring before we continue further, as exploring how and when one paired with the other is crucial to our understanding of the Byzantine government. *Axiai dia logou*, positions conferred by nomination, were what we would today term offices. They were occupations, for example judge or clerk. They were held at the pleasure of the ruler, and he or she could nominate someone else to fulfil that role whenever they so pleased.[37] *Axiai dia brabeion*, granted by insignia, are what we call titles or dignities, and I shall use the two terms interchangeably.[38] They were divided into senatorial and processional, but the distinction was largely meaningless in our period, as the two groups formed one unified hierarchy. Their insignia ranged from ivory diplomas to official costumes. At least in the ninth century, once granted, *axiai dia brabeion* could not be taken back. Dignities were a mark of imperial favour, a title that indicated where the holder fell in the court hierarchy, and they could also come with an annual salary, a *roga*. Sometimes offices, but particularly dignities, were given out as marks of favour by the monarch. The indiscriminate granting and creation of dignities was much criticized by contemporary writers and blamed for undermining the whole imperial system. An understanding of the Byzantine hierarchy of dignities, and the financial rewards attached to them, is key to interpreting the seals belonging to Byzantine bureaucrats and using them to tackle questions about the functioning, and collapse, of the Byzantine state. In the remainder of this chapter we will explore these factors to set the framework for our analysis of the sigillographic evidence.

1.2.1 Reconstructing the court hierarchy

> But it cannot be seen by the unworthy,
> nor can it be heard by the boorish.
> Thus the golden guardian placed at the bottom
> will preserve its hidden grace,
> showing it only to the worthy,
> having received the signature of a noble hand.[39]

We shall take three documents: the *Escorial Taktikon*, a *chrysoboullos logos* issued by Michael VII Doukas and the account of the Blachernai Synod of 1094 to create hierarchy lists at fixed points in our story. The genre of two of these texts requires further comment. The *taktika* are a series of lists which describe the Byzantine hierarchy of offices and dignities at the time in which they were written. Four such lists survive from the ninth and tenth centuries (see below) and their primary function was to help with the organization of formal occasions (particularly banquets) by creating a list of precedence of all imperial and ecclesiastical officials who could possibly be in attendance. The various *taktika* contain varying amounts of detail, and none of them present a complete list of the officers of the empire.[40] *Chrysobull* is a general term for an imperial document secured by the emperor's gold bulla or seal. The example under discussion was the most prestigious of the three types issued in the eleventh century, the *chrysoboullos logos*. These were used for treaties with foreign powers (as in this case), and also for grants of privileges and more significant government business, such as issuing laws.[41]

The *Taktikon Escorial* presents a partial outline of the rankings of the *axiai dia logou* (offices) at the beginning of the period under consideration, and this text will form the jumping-off point for our analysis of each office. However, there are no such documents for the eleventh century, so we must look elsewhere for tools to reconstruct the Byzantine bureaucracy. In the absence of a clear hierarchy of offices detailing where functionaries fell in the ranks during the eleventh century, and which departments of state were privileged above others, it is the dignities, *axiai dia brabeion*, granted to individual bureaucrats, when combined with information about others who held the same office in the same period, that can reveal the relative importance of each position and bureau. What we need to proceed, then, is a series of reconstructions of the Byzantine hierarchy at regular intervals from c. 966 to c. 1118. Once these are established, the gaps can be filled in with a mixture of sigillographic and documentary evidence.

A partial outline of the imperial system of dignities at the beginning of our period is also presented in the *Escorial Taktikon*, dated c. 971–5.[42] As noted by its editor, Nicolas Oikonomides, the document is a rather plain list of dignities and titles, with little embellishment or description. It is also likely that in terms of dignities the *Taktikon Escorial* does not present a complete list. It was the last in a series of lists of precedence produced in the ninth and tenth century, beginning with the *Taktikon Uspenskij* dated to c. 811–13 or 842–3, then the *Kletorologion of Philotheos*, 899, and then the *Taktikon Beneševič* of 934–44.[43] The *Taktikon Uspenskij* and the *Kletorologion of Philotheos* both list 18 dignities, the *Taktikon Beneševič* 9, and the *Taktikon Escorial* only 8. All four agree on the rankings of the first five dignities in the hierarchy: *kaisar*, *nobelissimos*, *kouropalates*, *zoste patrikia* and *magistros*.[44] It is at this point that the *Escorial Taktikon* diverges from the three earlier texts, by adding in the new title *vestes* in the sixth position, a place taken by the rank of *anthypatos* in the other lists, which is itself absent from the 971–5 work.[45] All four lists place the titles of *patrikios* and *protospatharios* in the seventh and eighth positions. The list of dignities in the *Taktikon Escorial* ends with *protospatharios*, the *Taktikon Beneševič* continues on to the title of *spatharokandidatos*, while the *Taktikon Uspenskij* and the *Kletorologion of Philotheos* list a further nine dignities of descending rank: *dishypatos*, *spatharios*, *hypatos*, *strator*, *kandidatos*, *mandator*, *vestitor*, *silentiarios*, *kandidatoi pezon* and *apo eparchon-stratelates*.⁴⁶ It is tempting to conclude that the dignities missing from the two tenth-century texts were omitted because they were no longer awarded. However, sigillographic evidence proves that ranks below that of *spatharokandidatos* continued to be granted by the imperial court into the late tenth and eleventh century. What seems to have happened is that the authors of the two tenth-century *taktika* did not aim to create comprehensive lists of every dignity and office in the whole empire. Each of the four texts was created for a variety of specific purposes, none of which was to aid those researching the imperial system over one thousand years after their composition. The *Taktikon Escorial* almost certainly omitted the lower half of the hierarchy. Similarly, the fact that *zoste patrikia* and *anthypatos*, both attested in other sources in the late tenth century, are not included in the *Taktikon Escorial* is probably an omission on the part of the author, or later scribe, rather than an indication that these dignities were no longer in use. Using a slightly modified version of the *Taktikon Escorial* to account for its omissions, it is possible to recreate the hierarchy of court dignities as it existed at the beginning of our period, in the last third of the tenth century.

The *chrysoboullos logos*, or *chrysobull*, issued as a part of the marriage alliance between the Byzantine Emperor Michael VII Doukas's son Constantine and the Norman Duke Robert Guiscard's daughter Helena, allows us to recreate substantial parts of the hierarchy as it existed a century after the *Taktikon Escorial* was written.⁴⁷ In this document, Michael gave Robert the right to appoint one *kouropalates*, one *proedros*, ten *magistroi*, ten *vestarchai*, ten *vestai*, one *anthypatos*, four *patrikioi*, six *hypatoi*, fifteen *protospatharioi* and ten *spatharokandidatoi*. Unfortunately, this is only a partial list, although it does place over half of the titles known to exist at this time in order from highest to lowest. We know from accounts in other documents, and on seals, that there were other dignities at this time. However, with the exception of the title of *illoustrios*, all of the dignities not recorded in Robert Guiscard's *chrysobull* were modifications of those that are recorded.

The next step is to create hierarchies in the intermediate period. As noted earlier, the eleventh century was a period of title inflation. As the number of individuals with each dignity increased, so the value of each title decreased. The two means by which the imperial government could continue to reward its servants were either to grant an individual multiple titles, a phenomenon to which we will return shortly, or to promote him to a higher rank. We have seen how the historians of the eleventh century criticized the impulse to promote broadly, correctly identifying the damage that this could do to the Byzantine state. To make matters worse promotion was only a temporary solution to the problem of title inflation. Once enough people had been promoted, the higher title itself became degraded, and a new round of promotions would be required to maintain support for the emperor on the part of the service class. The Byzantines attempted to solve this problem by increasing the number of titles open to those serving the empire. By c. 1042–55 two titles previously reserved for eunuchs, *proedros* and *vestarches*, had been added to the general hierarchy.⁴⁸ Similarly, the dignities of *nobelissimos* and *kouropalates*, once reserved for members of the imperial family were being granted to those in imperial employ by the 1050s, as was *sebastos*, an imperial title, after 1078.⁴⁹ The emperors eventually moved beyond extending eligibility to certain titles, instead creating inflated versions of existing titles by adding the prefix *proto* from around 1059.⁵⁰ These inflated versions of existing titles were located in the hierarchy above their original selves, and below the next dignity in the chain. Thus, *protovestarches* ranked above *vestarches* and below *magistros*. The dignities of *protonobelissimos, protokouropalates, protoproedros, protovestarches, protovestes* and *protoanthypatos* are attested by 1060–70.[51] Piecing this together, Jean-Claude Cheynet has created the court hierarchy as it likely was by the beginning of the reign of Alexios I Komnenos in 1081; *kaisar, sebastos, protonobelissimos, nobelissimos, protokouropalates, kouropalates, protoproedros, proedros, magistros, protovestarches, vestarches, protovestes, vestes, protoanthypatos, anthypatos, illoustrios, patrikios, dishyptos, hypatos, protospatharios* and *spatharokandidatos*.[52]

This list contains a few anomalies, such as the titles of *illoustrios, hypatos* and *dishypatos*. The dignity of *illoustrios* is not found in any earlier list, nor is it a modification of an existing title, whereas *hypatos* and *dishypatos* are found on the ninth-century lists, but in positions below *protospatharios*, not above it. By the middle of the eleventh century, at the latest, sigillographic evidence points to all of these titles outranking *protospatharios*, and I suspect that a similar piece of very Byzantine reasoning might explain the creation of the dignity of *illoustrios* and the elevation of those of *hypatos* and *dishypatos*. In both cases the Byzantines, in need of new titles to add to the hierarchy, looked to the past. In the case of *hypatos* and *dishypatos* they looked to a century earlier, found two titles that had become so devalued in the intervening one hundred years as to be worthless, dusted them off, rebranded them and inserted them into the hierarchy. At some point in the tenth century, *hypatos* had transformed from a dignity into an office, changing back again in c. 1040, a process which must have helped distinguish the old dignity from its eleventh-century incarnation. With *hypatos* in a new elevated position, it is not difficult to image *dishypatos, hypatos* times two, coming in to fulfil the same role as *provestes* did for *vestes*. For *illoustrios*, the Byzantines looked back even further into their history where it had been the highest of the three grades of senator in the late Roman Empire.[53] Thus, what appears as a discrepancy was actually an example of antiquarian titular recycling: an interesting demonstration of how resourceful the Byzantines could be, and how pliant and inventive the 'static' Byzantine *taxis* was when the situation required.

Table 1.1 presents the evolving hierarchy up to the beginning of the reign of Alexios I Komnenos in 1081. There is no one satisfactory way of representing these titles as a changing system over a century. Certain titles, underlined, were reserved for the imperial family. Thus, a *magistros* of c. 1000 fell in fourth place overall, but occupied the highest rank available to a bureaucrat. By contrast in c. 1060 only *kaisar* remained out of bounds, so the second place in the hierarchy was now up for grabs, and *magistros*, though only slipping one place overall, had dropped three places in the hierarchy of generally available titles. Even if we discount those dignities reserved for the imperial family, we cannot just number the positions in the remaining hierarchy and use this for meaningful comparisons. The fifth place would be occupied successively by *protospatharios, anthypatos, vestarches, protoproedros* and finally *kouropalates*. However, this is again misleading as a *protospatharios* of c. 1000 and a *kouropalates* of c. 1081 were in no way equivalent just because they both came fifth in the rankings. At the very least, fifth of eight and fifth of twenty are clearly not the same thing: one is in the middle of the hierarchy, the other near the top. This brings me to Table 1.2, where the hierarchy has been divided into thirds signified by a different shade of grey.

Table 1.1 The Byzantine Hierarchy of Titles in the Late Tenth and Eleventh Centuries

	c. 1000		c. 1050		c. 1060		c. 1070		c. 1081
1	*Kaisar*	1	*Kaisar*	1	*Kaisar*	1	*Kaisar*	1	*Kaisar*
2	*Nobelissimos*	2	*Nobelissimos*	2	*Nobelissimos*	2	*Protonobelissimos*	2	*Sebastos*
3	*Kouropalates*	3	*Kouropalates*	3	*Kouropalates*	3	*Nobelissimos*	3	*Protonobelissimos*
4	*Magistros*	4	*Proedros*	4	*Proedros*	4	*Protokouropalates*	4	*Nobelissimos*
5	*Vestes*	5	*Magistros*	5	*Magistros*	5	*Kouropalates*	5	*Protokouropalates*
6	*Anthypatos*	6	*Vestarches*	6	*Vestarches*	6	*Protoproedros*	6	*Kouropalates*
7	*Patrikios*	7	*Vestes*	7	*Vestes*	7	*Proedros*	7	*Protoproedros*
8	*Protospatharios*	8	*Anthypatos*	8	*Anthypatos*	8	*Magistros*	8	*Proedros*
9	*Spatharokandidatos*	9	*Illoustrios*	9	*Illoustrios*	9	*Protovestarches*	9	*Magistros*
10	*Spatharios*	10	*Patrikios*	10	*Patrikios*	10	*Vestarches*	10	*Protovestarches*
11	*Mandator*	11	*Dishypatos*	11	*Dishypatos*	11	*Protovestes*	11	*Vestarches*
		12	*Hypatos*	12	*Hypatos*	12	*Vestes*	12	*Protovestes*
		13	*Protospatharios*	13	*Protospatharios*	13	*Protoanthypatos*	13	*Vestes*
		14	*Spatharokandidatos*	14	*Spatharokandidatos*	14	*Anthypatos*	14	*Protoanthypatos*
		15	*Spatharios*			15	*Illoustrios*	15	*Anthypatos*
						16	*Patrikios*	16	*Illoustrios*
						17	*Dishypatos*	17	*Patrikios*
						18	*Hypatos*	18	*Dishypatos*
						19	*Protospatharios*	19	*Hypatos*
						20	*Spatharokandidatos*	20	*Protospatharios*
								21	*Spatharokandidatos*

Byzantium at the Turning Point   15

Table 1.2 Relative Relation of Titles across the Eleventh Century

c. 1000		c. 1050		c. 1060		c. 1070		c. 1081	
1	Magistros	1	Proedros	1	Nobelissimos	1	Protonobelissimos	1	Sebastos
2	Vestes	2	Magistros	2	Kouropalates	2	Nobelissimos	2	Protonobelissimos
3	Anthypatos	3	Vestarches	3	Proedros	3	Protokouropalates	3	Nobelissimos
4	Patrikios	4	Vestes	4	Magistros	4	Kouropalates	4	Protokouropalates
5	Protospatharios	5	Anthypatos	5	Vestarches	5	Protoproedros	5	Kouropalates
6	Spatharokandidatos	6	Illoustrios	6	Vestes	6	Proedros	6	Protoproedros
7	Spatharios	7	Patrikios	7	Anthypatos	7	Magistros	7	Proedros
8	Mandator	8	Dishypatos	8	Illoustrios	8	Protovestarches	8	Magistros
		9	Hypatos	9	Patrikios	9	Vestarches	9	Protovestarches
		10	Protospatharios	10	Dishypatos	10	Protovestes	10	Vestarches
		11	Spatharokandidatos	11	Hypatos	11	Vestes	11	Protovestes
		12	Spatharios	12	Protospatharios	12	Protoanthypatos	12	Vestes
				13	Spatharokandidatos	13	Anthypatos	13	Protoanthypatos
						14	Illoustrios	14	Anthypatos
						15	Patrikios	15	Illoustrios
						16	Dishypatos	16	Patrikios
						17	Hypatos	17	Dishypatos
						18	Protospatharios	18	Hypatos
						19	Spatharokandidatos	19	Protospatharios
								20	Spatharokandidatos

As the number of titles is only once divisible by three it is possible to quibble about exactly where the dividing line should fall, but this tripartite structure is useful for visualizing the place not only of different titles over the eleventh century but also of seeing where they fit into the overall structure of the Byzantine court.

This takes us to c. 1081, roughly forty years before the end of the period covered by this study. During the 1080s, Emperor Alexios I Komnenos began an overhaul of the titles of the Byzantine Empire, creating a new system which placed his family and allies over everyone else. It took decades for this new system to reach maturity, but the essentials were put in place during the 1080s. To some degree the old system continued to exist into the twelfth century, but as a second-class set of dignities for those without imperial connections. We can account for this when assessing status, but it must be borne in mind that the hierarchy under the Komnenoi was completely different from that under their predecessors, and that direct comparisons might be misleading.

The new system mixed elements of the old hierarchy with new dignities based around the imperial title *sebastos*, the Greek for *augustus*.[54] Immediately after his accession in 1081, Alexios created the titles of *sebastokrator* and *protosebastos* and granted the title of *sebastos* itself as well.[55] Soon after the title of *panhypersebastos* appeared.[56] The titles not incorporated into the new Komnenian hierarchy were

Table 1.3 The Byzantine Hierarchy of Titles under Alexios I Komnenos (1081–1118)

c. 1094	c. 1118
Sebastokrator	*Sebastokrator*
Kaisar	*Kaisar*
Panhypersebastos	*Panhypersebastos*
Sebastohypertatos	*Sebastohypertatos*
Protosebastos	*Protosebastos*
Pansebastos	*Pansebastos*
Sebastos	*Sebastos*
Protonobelissimos	*Protonobelissimos*
nobelissimos	*nobelissimos*
Protokouropalates	*Protokouropalates*
Kouropalates	*Kouropalates*
Protoproedros	*Protoproedros*
Proedros	*Proedros*
Magistros	
Protovestarches	
Vestarches	
Protovestes	
Vestes	
Protoanthypatos	
Anthypatos	
Illoustrios	
Patrikios	
Dishypatos	
Hypatos	
Protospatharios	
Spatharokandidatos	

handed out to minor officials and provincial elites.⁵⁷ The early Komnenian system is difficult to recreate because there is no firm date for the abandonment of the older title structure. There is some evidence that many titles continued in use into the 1090s, and for the sake of argument I have chosen the date 1094, because this is when we can see the upper echelons of Alexios's new system in detail, recorded in the proceedings of the Blachernai Synod held in that year.

By the end of the reign of Alexios I, and after over a century of increasing complexity, the hierarchy had been reset and simplified around a different set of assumptions and priorities. Dignities under the Komnenoi had more to do with an individual's relationship with the imperial ruling elite rather than their service to the state. As such the reign of Alexios I makes a logical end point for our study. Using these lists, it is possible to place title holders on the imperial hierarchy over a century and a half. This allows an assessment of the fortunes of the office that they held and provides a window through which to view imperial priorities and the functioning of government.

1.2.2 Payments and income

*He spent some time there looking after political affairs, as well as he could, according honours and receptions to members of the Senate, and distributing the yearly gifts.*⁵⁸

Holders of offices or titles received an annual stipend known as a *roga*. This was a payment in gold coins, sometimes supplemented with and occasionally replaced by cloth. The annual salary, so to speak, of an individual was made up of the payment associated with their office and that attached to their title. The records of many of the reigns of the period begin with an account of the new ruler's generosity in giving out promotions and also gifts of cash.⁵⁹ Isaac I Komnenos (1057–9) meanwhile generously distributed honours and gifts upon taking the throne, but then cut the *rogai* given to office-holders as a cost-cutting measure.⁶⁰ The most novel take on this practice was that of the Empress Theodora in 1055. Theodora proclaimed that she did not need to dole out honours and gifts because this was not the first time that she had inherited the throne.⁶¹ These texts are not just referring to the monetary donatives given out at the beginning of a new reign but also to the payments attached to the offices and titles doled out by the emperors to their supporters. Understanding these payments can provide interesting evidence for the processes behind the rise and fall of the eleventh-century bureaucracy, as the *roga*, a means of distributing wealth, was fundamental to the maintenance of imperial control. No record of the salaries for bureaucratic offices has survived for the eleventh century, but we have estimates for the *roga* associated with titles. Even approximate figures for the amounts paid out by the Byzantine state to its bureaucrats can shed light on the cost of the administration and perhaps, by comparing department to department over time compliment the assessment of status through titles.

The values of some of the *rogai* paid to Byzantine dignity holders are recorded in a number of sources. The most impressive account is that of Liutprand Bishop of Cremona, who as ambassador to Constantinople for Berengar II of Italy (950–61) witnessed the distribution of *rogai* by the emperor Constantine VII in the Great Palace in Constantinople on Palm Sunday 950.⁶² Liutprand records the *rogai* of two dignities, *magistros*, at 24 pounds of gold coins and two silk *skaramangia*, and *patrikios*, as 12 pounds of gold coins and one silk *skaramangion*. Liutprand goes on to list a mixture of dignities and offices – *protospatharum, spathariorum, spatharocandidatorum, kitonitarum, manglavitarum* and *protocaravorum* – and the amounts that they received: 7, 6, 5, 4, 3, 2 and 1 pounds of gold.⁶³ Unfortunately, Liutprand gives seven grades of payment for six dignities and offices. I would suggest that this discrepancy stems from two sources: the bishop of Cremona was not aiming to accurately portray the salaries of the Byzantine court, but to present the court of Constantine VII to his readers in a way that suited his own ends, and that there is a good chance that Liutprand did not fully understand the ceremony he witnessed, or perhaps that he understood exactly what Constantine VII wanted him to, that Byzantium was far wealthier, and with an infinitely more complex government, than his native land. The nuances of who received what payment, and at how the amount given by the emperor, a combination of the *roga* for title and office, was calculated, were likely not explained by Constantine or his officials, nor sought by Liutprand himself. As such, I would propose that his account of the *rogai* for the eight groups for which he gives figures cannot be taken as entirely accurate. It is also unclear from Liutprand's account, and other testimony whether a man received a payment for all of the titles he held or just the senior one. As will be discussed later some titles, those at the top and bottom of the hierarchy, superseded one another so it is highly unlikely that their stipends were added together. I would suggest that the same was true for all other titles as well. In my assessment of office-holders I will give the figure for the *roga* attached to their highest ranked title. At the very least this will give a minimum payment received by the bureaucrat in question.

The first firm figure for a *roga* from our period comes from a court document dated to 1056, which records a legal dispute between Michael Psellos and his son-in-law to be, Elpidios Kenchres.⁶⁴ Psellos wished not only to break the engagement but also to recover his investment in the title of *protospatharios*, with an attached annual *roga* of 1 pound of gold coins, which he had purchased for Elpidios as a part of his daughter's dowry. Another piece of evidence for the payments attached to dignities in Byzantium is the aforementioned *chrysobull* granted by Michael VII Doukas to the Robert Guiscard in 1074.⁶⁵ The *chrysobull* records the *rogai* for the *hypatoi* as 2 pounds of gold coins, the *protospatharioi* as 1 pound of gold coins and the *spatharokandidatoi* as half a pound of gold coins. While the *rogai* of the titles above *hypatos* are not recorded in the *chrysobull*, the document does provide the total payment due to the forty-four title holders whom Guiscard was permitted to appoint as 200 pounds of gold coins. Hélène Ahrweiler proposed that the *rogai* for the older titles doubled with each step up the hierarchy; this is clearly visible in the figures given in the 1074 *chrysobull* for *spatharokandidatos*, half a pound of coins, *protospatharios*, 1 pound, and *hypatos*, 2 pounds. If this progression continued up the hierarchy, a *patrikios* would receive four pounds of coins annually, an *anthypatos* 8 pounds, a *magistros* 16 pounds, and a *kouropalates* 32 pounds. Ahrweiler then slotted in the newer titles – *vestes, vestarches* and *proedros* – into the existing scale of payments, with the resulting figure adding up to the 200 pounds of gold allocated by Michael VII.⁶⁶ Building on this foundation, Jean-Claude Cheynet added in all of the

Table 1.4 Rogai as Recorded in the Chrysobull of 1074 (bold), and the Reconstructions of H. Ahrweiler (roman) and J.-C. Cheynet (italics)

Dignity	Roga
Kouropalates	32lbs, 2,304 nomismata
Protoproedros	*30lbs, 2,160 nomismata*
Proedros	28lbs, 2,016 nomismata
Magistros	16lbs, 1,152 nomismata
Protovestarches	*15lbs, 1,080 nomismata*
Vestarches	14lbs, 1,008 nomismata
Protovestes	*13lbs, 936 nomismata*
Vestes	12lbs, 864 nomismata
Protoanthypatos	*10lbs, 720 nomismata*
Anthypatos	8lbs, 576 nomismata
Illoustrios	*6lbs, 432 nomismata*
Patrikios	4lbs, 288 nomismata
Dishypatos	*3lbs, 216 nomismata*
Hypatos	**2lbs, 144 nomismata**
Protospatharios	**1lb, 72 nomismata**
Spatharokandidatos	**0.5lb, 36 nomismata**

remaining new titles created in the eleventh century, generating not only a complete hierarchy but also a full list of the *rogai* attached to each dignity.[67]

Although the resulting scale of payments is somewhat conjectural it is probably fairly close to the actuality. What started out as an ordered system became more complex and idiosyncratic as new titles were added. That the system was amended rather than redesigned completely is suggested by the *roga* attached to the dignity of *protospatharios*, a key title, being the gateway to membership of the senate. Paul Lemerle demonstrated the remarkable consistency in the *roga* attached to this dignity from the late ninth to the end of the eleventh century, by highlighting evidence from the reigns of Leo VI (886–912), Constantine IX Monomachos and Nikephoros III Botaneiates.[68] Before our period, in the reign of Leo VI, the *roga* for a *protospatharios* was recorded as 1 pound of gold coins.[69] In 1045, when the emperor Constantine IX Monomachos established his monastery of Nea Mone on Chios, he wished to grant the institution an annual *roga* of one pound of coins in perpetuity, and the method that he chose was to grant the monastery a *protospatharaton*, the payment due to a *protospatharios*.[70] As we have seen, nine years later Psellos's proposed son-in-law received the same income from the same title. When payments to the Nea Mone were discussed by Nikephoros III Botaneiates in June 1079, the arrangement is still phrased in terms of the payment to a *protospatharios*. As suggested by Lemerle, a 1 pound of coins payment was so attached to the concept of a *protospatharios* that the term *protospatharaton* may have become akin to a unit of account.[71] Taken together, these pieces of evidence show that the salary of a *protospatharios* remained constant throughout almost two centuries of changes to the hierarchy, title inflation and currency devaluation. That the same was true of the other titles, and that newer additions to the hierarchy were inserted into the existing pay scale, just as they had been into the established *cursus honorum*, as argued by Ahrweiler and Cheynet, seems entirely in keeping with the evidence that we possess. *Roga* payments held steady until the reign of Nikephoros III Botaneiates (1078–81). The strains of running the empire, fighting civil wars and trying, and failing, to defend Anatolia from the Turks led the emperor to suspend *roga* payments. His successor Alexios I Komnenos (1081–1118) soon decided to cancel them altogether.

The cash payments outlined earlier might be augmented in two ways: with silks and by making an extra payment. As mentioned earlier in the discussion of the testimony of Liutprand certain officials received silk garments in addition to gold coins. Calculating the amount that this added to the value of the *roga* of officials is impossible. Even if we knew what type of garment was being distributed we do not have any prices for such clothing and we have no idea which dignities were entitled to receive silk as a part of their *roga*. For certain ranks at certain times it was possible to make a payment to the government in return for an increased *roga*. The rate of return was 9.72 per cent on the supplementary payment, or 7 *nomismata* for every 72 paid to the state. By the middle of the eleventh century the rate of return had dropped to 6 *nomismata* per extra 72 handed over to the government.[72] As Lemerle makes clear these figures are only applicable to the 'augmented *roga*', not the base payments associated with titles which, as we have seen, remained remarkably steady throughout the tenth and eleventh centuries.[73] As it is impossible to know whether an individual had negotiated such extra payments and whether they received silk garments these will not be considered further in this study.

The next question is how much were *rogai* worth? This is a much more problematic issue. It is impossible to assess the buying power of, say, 1 pound of gold coins over the century and a half under consideration. It is likely that the *nomisma* from 959 into the eleventh century was still considered to be the equal of the old pure gold version of the coin. Contemporary Byzantine authors did not directly mention the ongoing reduction of the gold content of the coinage until the very end of the period, when, as Michael Hendy noted, Nikephoros Bryennios and George Kedrenos both used it as the backdrop for a laudatory description of the coinage reforms of Alexios I Komnenos in 1092.[74] By the time Alexios stabilized the coinage the *nomisma histamenon* was only 8 carats of gold. That such extreme debasement would have been noted is not surprising, that it was only deemed worthy of comment at the point that it was being reversed is perplexing. The usual assumption is that there was no outcry because those in a position to complain were compensated in the form of promotion to a higher rank. Another possibility is that recipients of these payments were compensated in other ways, most notably with cloth. A further option is that until the financial collapse of the 1070s there might not have been anything about which to complain. Just because of the gold content of the *histamenon* dropped does not mean that the purchasing power of the coin fell with it. For the majority of the eleventh century, at least as late as 1068, perhaps 1075, there is evidence that prices remained stable.[75] Even after that the evidence we have for price rises is limited in scope to a few select places and times, most notably Constantinople at a time of an influx of refugees which coincided with a ham-fisted attempt by the government to set up a monopoly for the supply of Thracian grain to the capital.[76] There are enough factors here to explain away increasing wheat prices which might have caused general inflation (and it is by no means certain that there was any in the long term) without needing to blame the debasement of the coinage. Certainly there is no ground to take the evidence we have and extrapolate back into the eleventh century. It is also possible that until the 1070s the rate of debasement was so gentle, and that the silver used in place of gold in the *histamenon* was not enough to change the colour of the coin to any noticeable degree, making it conceivable that the effects of debasement were minimal.[77] This interpretation could be countered by reference to the fact that documentary sources reference coins of the period by names intended to distinguish one issue from another, a new development in the period. Terms such as *romanaton*, *monomachaton*, *doukaton* and *michaelaton* were used, referring to the issuing emperor, Romanos III Argyros (1028–34), Constantine IX Monomachos (1042–55), Constantine X Doukas (1059–67) and Michael VII Doukas (1071–8).[78] Also seen are *skeptatron*, *helioselenaton* and *stellatus* describing a particular iconography.[79] In short, we do not know what *rogai* were worth, but we can be reasonably confident that their value held steady for most of the eleventh century.

Taking into account these factors I believe that a consideration of *roga* payments is valid for a number of reasons. On a government level it is illustrative to see the official, on paper, expenditure in both pounds of gold and number of coins that maintaining the bureaucrats' titles took. As stated earlier the empire might have substituted gold for cloth or other materials at times, but in theory the *rogai* of the officials were paid in gold coins. Even a rough estimate of the cost in coins and gold will provide insight into the workings and actions of the imperial government in the eleventh century. Furthermore, for anyone more convinced than I of the inflationary effects of the debasement of the eleventh century, the figures will provide an interesting accompaniment to the discussion of the status of titles.

1.2.3 Dating and data

> Κύριε βοήθει τῷ σῷ δούλῳ Βασιλείῳ βασιλικῷ πρωτοσπαθαρίῳ καὶ κριτῇ.
> Σφραγὶς, φύλαξ πέφυκας, Λόγε, γραφῶν κε λόγων.
>
> Lord, help your servant Basil, imperial protospatharios and judge. Divine Word, you have become the seal and guardian of my letters and documents.[80]

This, then, is the framework for titles and *rogai* within which my analysis of the sigillographic evidence for the development of the Constantinopolitan bureaucracy will take place. A word of caution: very few seals can be dated exactly and equal date ranges cannot be applied to every specimen. At one end of the spectrum, where it is possible to identify the owner of a seal, and match the phase of their career recorded on the seal to a specific episode in a history or a dated document, we can assign narrow dates of a handful of years to a seal. At the far end of the spectrum, seals with few specific dating criteria might be reasonably dated to the entire eleventh century.[81] By dating criteria, I mean the presence on a seal of certain letter forms, decorations, titles and offices for which we have a terminus post quem or terminus ante quem, and iconographic choices, any of which, alone or in conjunction with others, could provide a reasonably sure date for the seal. To overcome the differences in dating in a way that

Table 1.5 An Example of Allocated Values

	Tenth Century Final Third	Eleventh Century			Twelfth Century First Third
		First Third	Middle Third	Final Third	
Seal 1		1	1	1	
Seal 2				3	
Seal 3	1.5	1.5			
Seal 4			1	2	
Total	1.5	2.5	2	6	

gives equal weight to each seal, I will normalize the data from the seals. To do so, I must balance the largest and smallest date ranges applied to seals in this study, one century and one-third of a century, respectively. Each seal will be assigned a value of three points, and these will be awarded to the third-of-a-century units encompassing the date of the seal in a fashion weighted in favour of the more finely dated seal. For example, a seal dated to the entire eleventh century would give one point to each third of that century, while a seal dated to the central third of the century would give all three points to that period. In the following example, seal 1 is dated to the eleventh century, so assigns one point to each third, seal 2 is dated to the final third of the eleventh century, which is where all three of its points are placed, while seal 3 is dated to the tenth/eleventh century, splitting its three points between the final and first thirds of the centuries respectively, and seal 4 is dated to the second half of the eleventh century and spends its points accordingly.

The division into thirds of a century will set the pattern for analysis moving forwards. Division of the period this way is not only a reflection of the need to gather sufficient data for analysis or the limitations of seal dating; it is a useful means of mapping the seals onto wider Byzantine history. The period c. 966–1000 provides a prologue to the story of the eleventh century. These years marked the early phase of reconquest in the east and the beginning of the reign of Basil II during which the processes that led to the transformation of the bureaucracy began. The first third of the eleventh century saw the second phase of these developments and ends roughly with the death of Basil II's immediate successors. The years between c. 1033 and c. 1066 saw the new bureaucratic machinery of the empire take shape and begin to be challenged, just as they saw the enlarged Byzantium tested on a number of fronts. The fourth period, c. 1066–1100, was one of collapse and rebirth for the empire, and readjustment for its administrative apparatus. The early twelfth century gives us a picture of the state following the Komnenian takeover, the epilogue of our eleventh-century story.

This level of analysis is made possible by the large numbers of surviving seals. My study incorporates 2,497 seals from museums across the world, archives and auction catalogues.[82] I will apply the type of analysis outlined earlier to any office for which we have evidence of individual bureaucrats numbering thirty or more.[83] This embraces a wide range of offices from across the central bureaucracy, but unfortunately not all. For the offices which are not as widely represented in the sigillographic record, this style of analysis is not appropriate. These seals, often belonging to those with an office filled by a single individual, will be discussed on a case-by-case basis.

By looking at how dignities and offices were paired on seals across the approximately 160 years under consideration, it is possible to use the seals to trace the fortunes of the empire's civilian officials. The picture that emerges is far more nuanced than that provided by the written material; in fact, seals are the only means we have of exploring an administrative system in flux. We can clearly see how the relatively peaceful and prosperous days of the early eleventh century saw an expansion of the civilian arm of government and a rise in its status to the point that we can hypothesize that a new form of government with educated Constantinopolitan officials, whether by birth or inclination, and the law at its heart took shape. Members of the administration were promoted, stipends granted, and above all the legal profession rose to a position of prominence that it had not held before, and would not again. The advancement of the legal profession is commented on by Psellos, a politician involved with legal education and Attaleiates, a judge, but through the use of seals we can both assess the reliability of their statements and also compare the fortunes of legal officials to other groups of civilian bureaucrats, gaining an understanding of their relative positions over time within the Byzantine system. Here we move from the hardly impartial nebulous generalities of the written sources to a more detailed and nuanced picture. Questions can also be asked here about the means through which the emperors sought to control their empire. An obvious though overlooked point is that the Constantinopolitan government of the eleventh century was strong. Attempts were made by interests from outside the capital to overthrow it on numerous occasions in the first-half of the eleventh century, yet, with the exception of Isaac Komnenos, all such rebels were defeated.[84] When the economic and political situation in Byzantium changed after c. 1050 we can see exactly which groups were cast aside by the emperor, which received some protection from the economic hardship of the times, and who was sheltered. The seals allow us a glimpse into the realities of government in a beleaguered empire struggling to keep itself afloat, and help us understand the process by which the civilian government of the eleventh century collapsed.

In this study we will consider only the seals of bureaucrats. Those struck by men serving in the army and navy will not be studied. Nor will the thousands of seals presenting a man with a court title but no office. Apart from falling outside of the scope of this study the last group are also difficult to assess; are we dealing with men who did not have an office, or who commissioned a *boulloterion* for use outside of their official capacities? The conclusions presented later are valid for the bureaucracy and speak to its role in the eleventh-century empire. When I speak of title inflation and *roga* grants, of the cost of titles to the state it is to this group that I am referring.

Seals allow us to see imperial policy on a grand scale and present us with a new means of understanding a century during which the old Roman order of Byzantium gave way to something noticeably more aristocratic and medieval. They also allow us to look at the civilian officials themselves, those men so maligned by the historians and writers of the period. We can see their social class not only through their titles but through the images of the saints that they chose to place on their seals. We can follow their career paths, both within Constantinople and between Constantinople and the provinces, and see generations of the same family entering imperial service. Furthermore, we can ask what it meant to be a bureaucrat in Byzantium and address some of the ideas that still pervade Byzantine studies of the rigid imperial administration with its various departments each with their own responsibility. Thus, we use seals not only to understand the mechanics of imperial government but also to bring to the fore hundreds of individual Byzantines who were responsible for ensuring that the empire ran from day to day.

2

The Byzantine bureaucrat

Κύριε βοήθει Βασιλείῳ πρωτοσπαθαρίῳ ἐπὶ τοῦ Χρυσοτρικλίνου, κριτῇ ἐπὶ τοῦ Ἱπποδρόμου, τοῦ Βήλου, νοταρίῳ τῆς βασιλικῆς σακέλλης καὶ μυστογράφῳ τῷ Χαλκούτζῃ.

Basil Chalkoutzes, imperial protospatharios epi tou Chrysotriklinou, judge of the Hippodrome, judge of the Velum, epi tes basilikes sakelles, and mystographos.[1]

Before moving into the history of the Byzantine administration in the late tenth to early twelfth centuries, let us take a brief moment to look at the men who worked in the bureaucracy. While there are some textual references, and we will return to these throughout this chapter, most of the people involved are known to us only through what they leave behind, their seals. While these do not allow us to explore many areas of their lives, they do provide certain pieces of information which allow us to create a partial picture of the bureaucrats of Byzantium. By examining the images of holy figures on their seals we can explore their personal piety and perhaps their social standing. We can see to which families they belonged, and perhaps get a sense of their geographical origins by tabulating the surnames of bureaucrats. Finally, we can explore their career progression through the few individuals for which we have multiple seals from different periods in their lives.

2.1 Piety and seals

Λέοντα, πανύμνητε, τὸν σὸν οἰκέτην πρωτοπροέδρῳ καὶ κοιαίστωρι σκέποις.

'All-Hymned One, protect Leo, your servant, protoproedros and koiaistor.'[2]

Of the 2,497 seals belonging to bureaucrats in our period, 1,833 have some sort of image on at least one side of the seal. Not all of these are of holy figures. Included in this total are a star, a lion, two peacocks and a boxer among other interesting designs. In total there are 31 seals with non-religious images on one side, with a further 220 with a cross, two showing the Manus Dei, and 11 depicting a bust that is not obviously a holy figure. Removing these from the total leaves 1,569 seals depicting Christ, the Virgin and one or more saints.[3] The percentage of seals depicting a holy figure is 62.8, slightly below the 70 per cent recorded by John Cotsonis in his study of all published seals across the same period.[4] The difference is to no small part made up by the increased percentage of bilateral inscriptions found on the seals of bureaucrats. There are a few other discrepancies between the figures presented for all seals and those which belonged to bureaucrats. In Cotsonis's rankings the top ten holy figures in this period by frequency of depiction were: the Virgin (35.6%), Nicholas (13%), Michael (8.5%), George (6.9%), Theodore (6.4%), John Prodromos (3.7%), Demetrios (3.5%), John Chrysostom (1.6%), Basil (1.6%), and Panteleimon (1.2%). Turning to the data used for the present study we see that nine of the same ten holy figures remain the most frequently depicted, but they appear in a different order, and with varying frequency: the Virgin (40.1%), Nicholas (17.3%), Michael (9.8%), George (5.7%), John Prodromos (3.8%), Theodore (3.1%), Panteleimon (2.1%), Mark (2.1%), John Chrysostom (2%), Basil (1.7%) and Demetrios (1.5%). Some of the discrepancy between the two sets of percentages is likely due to the number of unidentifiable saints in the corpus, and also to the fact that in the thirteen years since Cotsonis's article appeared many new seals have been published, enough to move the needle when it comes to the relatively small number of examples that we are dealing with once we move down the list of holy figures.

The most notable differences between the conclusions reached from Cotsonis' total corpus and those for the Constantinopolitan bureaucrats alone is that the top ten most popular saints appear in a different order and that St. Demetrios does not make an appearance but St. Mark does. This is not as potentially radical a change as it seems at first. Every seal depicting St. Mark belonged to a member of the Xeros family, known for their devotion to the Evangelist.[5] Without the Xeroi the ten most frequently depicted saints are the same for Cotsonis' general corpus and for Constantinopolitan bureaucrats alone, but the order in which they appear, their relative popularity, is quite different.

The three most popular holy figures are the same in both groups: the Virgin, St. Nicholas and St. Michael. All three were more popular, the Virgin and Nicholas significantly so, among Constantinopolitan bureaucrats than the seal owning population in general. A further difference can be seen in the next group of saints, which in Cotsonis's list are St. George, St. Theodore, St. John Prodromos and St. Demetrios. These rankings were different among the bureaucrats; St. Demetrios is right at the bottom of the list, switching places with St. Panteleimon while St. John supplants St. Theodore in fifth place. All of the military saints were less frequently depicted on seals belonging to

Figure 2.1 Seal of John *patrikios*, imperial *notarios*, judge of the Velum and of the Kibyrraiotai. Dumbarton Oaks, Byzantine Collection, Washington, DC, BZS.1955.1.2420. The obverse shows an image of St. John Chrysostom.
Ⓐ|IW̅|O-⚡|CTO|M,
Ὁ ἅγιος Ἰωάννης ὁ Χρυσόστομος.

Figure 2.2 Seal of Michael *vestes*, judge of the Velum and *epi tes basilikes sakelles*. Dumbarton Oaks, Byzantine Collection, Washington, DC, BZS.1958.106.4734.
The obverse shows an image of St. Michael in imperial garb. The metrical inscription beseeches Michael alongside his fellow angels to aid the seal's owner.
Obv. ΔΥΛ,ΡΟΗΘ,ϹѠΓΕΝ,ϹΤΡ.Τ,Γ,Τ
Rev. +ΜΙΧ..Λ|ΡΕϹΤ.ΚΡΙ|ΤΗΤΥΡΗΛΥ|ΚΑΙΕΠΙΤΗϹ|ΡΑϹΙΛΙΚΗϹ|ϹΑΚΕΛΛΗϹ
Δούλῳ βοήθει σῷ γένει στρατηγέτα Μιχαὴλ βέστῃ, κριτῇ τοῦ βήλου καὶ ἐπὶ τῆς βασιλικῆς σακέλλης.
Commander of the heavenly host, with your kind come to the aid of your servant Michael *vestes*, judge of the Velum and *epi tes basilikes sakelles*.

Constantinopolitan bureaucrats than by the population in general, the difference ranges from a drop of a fifth for St. George to over half for Sts. Theodore and Demetrios. Even though the figures for St. John Prodromos are the same in both bodies of seals the relative unpopularity of the military saints apart from St. George was enough to move him up the rankings. At the bottom of the list we can see that St. John Chrysostom was more popular in Constantinople than in the general corpus, St. Basil equally so in both, and St. Demetrios significantly less so in the capital than the empire as a whole.[6]

How to account for these differences? There are relatively straightforward explanations for some of the differences. Cotsonis comments on the frequency with which the owners of seals depicting St. Demetrios had some association with either the Balkans or Thessaloniki, the city of which he was patron.[7] None of the families represented in the present study are known to have originated in Thessaloniki, and obviously that was not where these particular bureaucrats worked. Perhaps the discrepancy between the figures presented by Cotsonis and those from my data is due to the fact that the inhabitants of Thessaloniki and its environs played little part in the administration of the empire as a whole. The same might be true on a lesser scale for St. Theodore who was a popular object of devotion for men from the eastern regions of the empire.[8] The point is emphasized by the fact that St. George saw the smallest drop in frequency of depiction of the military saints with Constantinopolitan bureaucrats compared to the general corpus. Cotsonis found no particular geographic concentration of sigilants using St. George for seals; he was popular across the empire.[9] He was also the subject of devotion in the capital and a particular focus of devotion of the Monomachos family, including Emperor Constantine IX.[10]

While military saints were less popular among Constantinopolitan bureaucrats than among the population in general other holy figures show the opposite trend.

The eleventh century was a period of increasing devotion to the Virgin. As a powerful intercessor and divine guardian of Constantinople it should come as no surprise that not only was the Virgin the most frequently depicted holy figure on the seals of Constantinopolitan bureaucrats, but that she was more popular in the capital than among the general population. The particular devotion to St. John Prodromos among the civil bureaucracy has been commented upon by John Cotsonis, and related to his significant role in the Bible and powers as an intercessor.[11] The general reasons for Michael's popularity, his association with the emperor, his gifts as a healer, and his important shrines in Constantinople and elsewhere, are well documented.[12] We have no reason to assume that the bureaucrats of Constantinople had extra reasons to favour St. Michael beyond those already listed – perhaps they just took them more seriously. In spite of being classed often as a military saint (he is after all commander of the Heavenly host) this does not seem to have been his main appeal when we come to seal design. In the general corpus Michael was almost four times more prevalent on seals of civilian administrators than on those of military men, so he clearly did not have a special place in hearts of the soldiers.[13] He is almost never depicted in military costume on seals, and his usual dress is that of a Byzantine emperor.[14] Of all of the possible reasons one might see for Michael's image being chosen for the seals of Constantinopolitan bureaucrats, his association with the emperor seems most obvious. Many in the bureaucracy stood a better chance of seeing and meeting an emperor in the eleventh century than anyone else in the empire. Furthermore, they must have been more aware than most just how much of their lives revolved around imperial ceremonial, decisions and whims. Who better to place on their seals than the emperor's divine counterpart? St. Panteleimon is by far the most popular martyr saint in Cotsonis's general corpus.[15] He appears twice as frequently on bureaucrats' seals as in the general corpus. He had no particular link to the capital; his role as physician and healer made him generally popular. It is likely that the difference in the frequency of his depictions between the two groups of seals is the result of the lower popularity of Sts. Theodore and Demetrios in the capital. St. John Chrysostom is an interesting case. In the general corpus he was found most commonly on seals of civilian administrators, then on high-ranking church officials, but never on seals belonging to the military. The other hierarch to make it into the top ten, St. Basil, was particularly popular with the ecclesiastical elite, but also the tenth most commonly chosen saint for the seals of Constantinopolitan bureaucrats. St. Basil and St. John were the authors of the two chief liturgies of the Byzantine Empire and thus were certainly well known to the general population.[16] St. John's mosaic was, and is, featured prominently in Hagia Sophia, and he was strongly associated with the Byzantine capital of which he had been archbishop and where his relics resided. Whether any of this mattered to bureaucrats looking for a divine protector for their seals is unknown. His strongly Constantinopolitan credentials might have been enough to make him appeal to bureaucrats, but he was almost exactly equally popular among the general population, and there is no sense that his popularity was limited to sigilants from or working in the capital.

An assessment of the seals of Constantinopolitan bureaucrats supports the conclusions made by John Cotsonis with respect to family and homonymous saints.[17] Aside from the aforementioned Xeroi there is no evidence of families favouring one particular saint over another. Nor is there any evidence of bureaucrats choosing their namesake in numbers that would indicate a pattern. What we do have is a group with the usual devotion to the Virgin, St. Nicholas, and St. Michael, although in the case of the Mother of God and the Archangel to a greater degree than seen in the general population. They were also more even in the foci of their piety. The fifty-seven saints present on their seals feature in a more even distribution than that seen in the general corpus. At the same time strongly regional saints, especially St. Demetrios, were less important to the bureaucrats of the capital than to their fellow Byzantines. While this is very likely a sign that the people of Thessaloniki and its region did not contribute members to the central administration in the same way that they did to that of the Balkan provinces or the western armies, with the exception of the Virgin, guardian of the city, there is no corresponding increase in the presence of traditionally Constantinopolitan saints, such as St. John Chrysostom. While the total number of saints featuring on the seals in question is about half of that found in Cotsonis's corpus the more even distribution in the seals of bureaucrats suggests a more widespread piety than among the population as a whole.

2.2 Family names

Σφραγὶς ἐπάρχου Μιχαὴλ τοῦ βεστάρχου Μαχηταρίων ἐκ γένους παρηγμένου.

Seal of the eparch and vestarches Michael, a man brought forth from the Machetarios family.[18]

A study of every family known to have worked in the Constantinopolitan bureaucracy in the late tenth and eleventh centuries could be the subject of a book of this size in itself, and as such is not my intent here. Instead I wish to present a few of the more interesting families represented on the seals and draw a few general conclusions about them, their origins and their connections to the central administration. In general, family names appear on seals of individuals associated with the bureaucracy only in the eleventh century, sometime after their debut on seals belonging to the military families of the eastern border in the tenth century.[19] In total 808 seals (32.4%) were struck by someone with a family name, of which 731 struck by 331 men from 203 different families are more or less firmly identified.

Family names derived from a toponym are common, at least thirty, and represent men from across the empire. A number of names indicate that the men in question were either themselves not of Constantinopolitan origin or that their families had moved to the capital recently enough for family names to be in fashion. Possible toponyms include the following: Abydinos (Abydos in the theme of the Aegean Sea), Adramytenos (Atramyttion in the theme of Samos), Antiochites (from an Antioch, although possible resident in Constantinople long before the eleventh century),[20] Arabantenos (likely from al-Rāwandān in Syria), Beriotes (from Bera in Thrace),[21] Charsianites (from the theme Charsianon in eastern Anatolia), Chersonites (Cherson in the Crimea), Chiotes (Chios in the Aegean), Galaton (Galatia in Paphlagonia),[22] Helladikos (from the theme of Hellas), Karianites (possibly from Caria, Aphrodisias, or Karin in Armenia), Kastamonites (from Kastamon in Paphlagonia), Kephallonites

Figure 2.3 Seal of Michael Machetarios, *vestarches* and *eparch*. Dumbarton Oaks, Byzantine Collection, Washington, DC, BZS.1958.106.5704.

The metrical inscription which occupies both sides of Michael's seal is divided equally between his office and title on the obverse and his family on the reverse.

Obv. CΦΡΑ|ΓΙCΕΠΑΡ|ΧΟΥΜΙΧΑ|ΗΛΤΟΥΒΕ|CΤΑΡΧ'
Rev. ΜΑΧΗ|ΤΑΡΙШΝ|ΕΚΓΕΝΟΥC|ΠΑΡΗΓ|ΜΕΝΟΥ
σφραγὶς ἐπάρχου Μιχαὴλ τοῦ βεστάρχου Μαχηταρίων ἐκ γένους παρηγμένου.
Seal of the eparch and *vestarches* Michael, a man brought forth from the Machetarios family.

(from the theme of Kephallenia), Kibyrraiotes (from Kibyrraiotai theme), Mytilenaios (from Mytilene on the island of Lesbos), Pamphilos (from Pamphylia in the Kibyrraiotai theme), Radenos (possibly from the town of Rade in the Anatolikon theme),[23] Romaios (possibly from Italy, although Romaios may also indicate a legal professional),[24] and Smyrnaios (from Smyrna in the theme of Samos). These names cover a wide geographical range, from towns close to Constantinople to Greece, the Aegean shore, and from the southern coast of Anatolia to Syria, the Ionian Islands to the Crimea, and perhaps even Italy. Many of these regions are also represented by members of families whose names do not mention a specific place, but hint at a non-Greek origin, such as Artabasdos (Armenian),[25] Chryselios (probably of Slavic origin),[26] Chrysos (maybe Greek, Turkish, Slavic, Arabic, or Armenian),[27] Diabatenos (likely Armenian), Iasites (Armenian),[28] Machetarios (Armenian)[29] and Tornikios (Armenian or Georgian). Furthermore, there were members of families with known provincial origins: Phokas, Skleros, Maleinos and Mousele, all families from Anatolia that had lost prominence in the tenth century and at least one branch of which migrated to the capital, and Botaneiates, Gymnos,[30] Hikanatos[31] and Kekaumenos. The well-known Xiphilinos family were from Trebizond, and the Philokales family might have been descended from the upwardly mobile Anatolian peasant shamed, and ruined, by Basil II in 996.[32] Approximately half of the families for whom origins can be proposed either originated in Constantinople or had been resident there for generations by the eleventh century. Many were named for regions of the city, such as Akropolites, Anthemiotes, Areobindos/enos, Blachernites, Makrembolites, Promoundenos and Vlangas, and possibly Chalkoprateites, Katakalon and Kyparissiotes.[33] Others were not, such as the Alopos, Choirosphaktes, Garidas, Saronites, Bringas, Monomachos and Chrysoberges families, which even if they had originated and maintained a presence in the provinces, had been established in the capital for some time.[34]

Figure 2.4 Seal of George Kibyrraiotes, *proedros* and *protonotarios* of the *dromos*. Dumbarton Oaks, Byzantine Collection, Washington, DC, BZS.1947.2.1073.
George's family originated from the south coast of Asia Minor. The genitive inscription usually implies 'seal of …'.
Obv. + ΓΕШΡ|ΓΙȢΠΡΟΕ|ΔΡȢSĀΝΟ|ΤΑΡΙȢ
Rev. ΤȢΔΡΟ|ΜȢΤȢΚΙ|ΡΥΡΡΑΙ|ШΤΟV
Γεωργίου προέδρου καὶ πρωτονοταρίου τοῦ δρόμου τοῦ Κιβυρραιώτου.
George Kibyrrauites, *proedros* and *protonotarios* of the *dromos*.

No matter their origins, every Byzantine considered in this study worked for at least part of his life in Constantinople. Possibly the longest resident family in the city discussed in this study was the Xylinites family. Three different men named Niketas Xylinites rose to prominence in capital: the first backed the unsuccessful rebellion of Anastasios II against Leo III in 719, the second was forced to enter a monastery after an affair with Eudokia the wife of Basil I, and the third was a close supporter of Empress Theodora. This was an incredibly long time for a family to remain among the elite of Constantinople, especially considering the reasons for which two of them are known to history. Most of the other families for whom histories can be constructed were of far more recent origins. Of almost comparable antiquity were the Kamateroi, who served in the bureaucracy from the ninth century. The Tzirithon family made their debut in Byzantine history by joining a failed plot against Leo VI.[35] Comparatively old were the Saronitai, who were prominent in the early tenth century at the court of Romanos I.[36] Of a similar age was the Garidas family, also from the capital, and the Varys family, supporters of the failed contender for the throne Leo Phokas in 919.[37] Others only appeared in the eleventh century, such as the Promoundenos[38] and Machetarios[39] families, some not until the second half of the century, such as the Serblias family, or the Mermentoulos family, about whom more later.[40]

For some families we have sigillographic evidence of multiple members of the family, even multiple generations, serving in the bureaucracy. Seals of three Alopoi – Constantine, Leo and Niketas – are known from the mid- and late eleventh century, for instance. The story of the members of the Anzas family has been traced by Nesbitt and Seibt, who documented generations of men over three centuries working mostly in the Constantinopolitan judiciary.[41] A similar picture has emerged from an exploration of the Hexamilites family.[42] Of the 202 families known from their seals, 52 are represented by more than one man. This is a high percentage, and it makes one wonder how many of the significantly larger group of bureaucrats which did not have a family name, or who chose not to use it on their seals, were related to one another. That service in the bureaucracy ran in families should not surprise us. We see similar patterns in the Byzantine military. The rewards of serving in Constantinople could be great, enough to keep a family in the elite for decades if not centuries, as long as each subsequent generation continued to serve. Many of the men holding office in Constantinople in the eleventh century were followed by their descendants into the twelfth century, and some, such as the Pepgomenoi, continued doing so into the fifteenth century.[43] The main qualifications for success in the bureaucracy, aside from the perpetual presence of patronage, were an education and the brains to use it. Being the son of a bureaucrat would improve a young man's chance of getting the required education for an administrative post and provide him with a foot in the door as well.

We could be forgiven for seeing how insider status and an economically and geographically privileged position might create a closed system. However, this was clearly not the case. Most of the family names on seals belong to new families, not the traditional elite, and as we have seen many of these new families originated outside of the capital. Constantinople itself acted as a magnet pulling in people from the provinces, and it is not surprising that many of those who could afford an education found their way into the state bureaucracy. We know that this is exactly what happened with Michael Attaleiates and also John Xiphilinos, and the seals suggest the same story would likely be seen over again with Theodore Smyrnaios, Niketas Galaton or one of the other men who either originated outside of the capital or came from a family that did if only we had more evidence. There is ample proof that access to the bureaucracy, and the chance to rise to the very top, was not limited to a few elite families from Constantinople. Within the limits of a medieval government, we might almost call the system meritocratic, at least in its hiring practices. The bureaucracy was also rather more open than not when it came to families with a military pedigree. There is still somewhat of an impression that there were military families and civilian families. However, it is clear that there was a significant amount of crossover between the two within some families. The Argyroi were a long-standing military family appearing in the Charsianon theme in the mid-ninth century.[44] Despite their continued presence in the Byzantine army Argyroi joined the bureaucracy in the eleventh century. John Argyros was an imperial *notarios* in the *sekreton* of the *ephoros*, concerned with crownlands, while Niketas Argyros was *praitor* of Constantinople.[45] The most famous member of the family was Romanos Argyros who served as *eparch* of Constantinople before marrying Zoe, daughter of Constantine VIII and soon after ascending the throne as Romanos III. The Artabasdos family had served in the Byzantine army since the ninth century but are increasingly found in the civilian arm of government in the eleventh century.[46] The same was true of the Chalkoutzes family who first appear in the sources in the second half of the tenth century. Prominent soldiers for decades, one branch of the family became bureaucrats in the eleventh century.[47] These men and many more from other traditionally military families who found their way into the civilian administration were not the first to tread this path. The Choirosphaktes family had begun as soldiers from the Peloponnese, but by the tenth century were members of the elite of the capital.[48] It is impossible to know whether this was a case of brothers choosing radically different careers, sons breaking away from the family path well-trodden or distant cousins with different occupations. What is clear is that there was not always a firm distinction between civilian and military families.

We will conclude this section on family names with two interesting cases which point to a completely different origin from those seen until now. The Chrysobalantites family name proclaimed that they were the ones who had become rich in the market, while that of the Sapanopolos family advertised their past as soap merchants. This family was unknown before the eleventh century.[49] One is tempted to see the results of the policies of Constantine IX in admitting men from guild backgrounds into the senate, but we know from the career of Michael Psellos that men from craft and mercantile backgrounds were already entering the bureaucracy before that point, and here we have suitably named examples.[50]

The family names of bureaucrats in Constantinople show a great variety in place of origin, both within and outside Byzantium, social background and family traditions. They allow us to glimpse the more meritocratic side of the bureaucracy, with men from new families rising to the top of the hierarchy as *eparch* while someone from one of the oldest families in the capital worked as a humble imperial *notarios*.[51] While they do not account for the majority of the seals used for this study, and therefore represent a minority of the men we will discuss in the following pages, I see no reason why they should not be representative of the wider body of bureaucrats in terms of the picture that they paint of a group of state servants drawn from a wide range of imperial subjects.

2.3 Career bureaucrats

This noble youth was yesterday a clerk [mystographos]
and is today newly made a tax collector [exactor].
The former is gone; the latter came of a sudden,
And this, in turn, will not last for long.[52]

As we have seen the family names of bureaucrats suggest that the administration in Constantinople attracted men from a wide variety of backgrounds. For an educated man the promise of a regular salary, access to promotion, the possibility of titles, and therefore a place at court with all of the perks that brought must have made the life of a career bureaucrat an appealing one. There were few other options that could provide the same sort of stability. The life of a soldier offered many of the same perks, but with much more risk, and there was always the church. How did a bureaucratic career begin? Patronage was a factor. Psellos arranged for the fiancé of his adopted daughter to become a *protospatharios* and an imperial *notarios* at the charitable foundation of the Antiphonetes, and later engineered Elpidios's appointment as judge of the Hippodrome.[53] In the following years Psellos lobbied the emperor to grant ever more offices to Elpidios. He was promoted to the tribunal of the Velum and given the further offices of *thesmographos*, then *mystographos* and eventually *exaktor*. He was

Figure 2.5 Seal of Basil Tzirithon, *protovestarches*, judge of the Velum and judge of the Kibyrraiotai. Harvard Art Museums/Arthur M. Sackler Museum, Bequest of Thomas Whittemore, 1951.31.5.781.
This seal was struck at the mid-point of Basil's successful career.
Rev. + KĒR,Θ,|RACIΛEIW|ĀRECTAPXH|KPITHTꞪRHΛ,|STWNKIRVP|PAIWT,TWT·I|PIΘWNI
Κύριε βοήθει Βασιλείῳ πρωτοβεστάρχῃ, κριτῇ τοῦ βήλου καὶ τῶν Κιβυρραιωτῶν τῷ Τζιρίθωνι.
Lord, help Basil Tzirithon, *protovestarches*, judge of the Velum and of the Kibyrraiotai.

even granted the dignity of *patrikios* after Psellos lobbied on his behalf.[54] Even with Psellos's help he started his career with the low title of *protospatharios* and two far from prestigious offices. However, he rose quickly due to the patronage of Psellos, and we must wonder how long it would have taken Kenchres to attain the offices that he did, or the rank of *patrikios*, without a powerful benefactor.

A similarly exceptional story of patronage can be seen in the story of Constantine nephew of the patriarch Michael Keroularios.[55] He also attained high rank and office at a young age, sponsored first by his powerful uncle, and then by Isaac I Komnenos as a form of penance for his mistreatment of the old patriarch.[56] Although unusual in terms of the characters involved, not every young aspiring bureaucrat had the backing of influential ministers, the patriarch and the emperor; it must have helped to know someone already in the bureaucracy. For others raw talent might have been enough. It worked for Psellos and his friends, none of whom was from a wealthy or powerful family. Elpidios Kenchres began somewhere near the bottom of the judicial hierarchy and moved up. Was this common, or did people jump in the middle? Unfortunately, we have fewer sources reliably attributed to low-ranking men than their more fortunate contemporaries. However, there is some evidence that men did start at the bottom and move up. Basil Tzirithon's first appearance was as a *protospatharios* and judge of the Hippodrome and imperial *notarios* in the treasury of the *eidikon*. He ended his career as a *protoproedros* and *eparch*.[57] A final example, Nicholas Akapnes, began his career as an *asekretis*, before becoming at two different points in his career judge of Hellas and *mystolektes*, and *kensor* and judge of Tarsos and Seleukeia.[58] While not at the top of the hierarchy, Nicholas had managed to move from a minor secretarial position into a more important position at the chancery, a judicial position and two important provincial governorships.

The almost modern nature of the organization of the Byzantine state, on paper at least, might lead us to assume that career paths followed if not exactly the same logic that they do in modern bureaucracies, at least something similar. When we explore the evidence of careers, much of which comes from the sigillographic record, we see that this was not the case at all. A few notes first on the nature of our evidence. Mostly we are reliant on seals, especially if we wish to see the more elusive lower ends of the bureaucracy, though these can be supplemented with documentary and narrative sources where available. The problem is that we do not know for certain that we are dealing with one individual when we are presented with multiple seals from different stages in a career. It is possible that there might have been two Constantine Promoundenoi who were cousins living at the same time and named after their grandfather, for example. However, the seals we have layout what seems to be a logical career for a man working in the judiciary at that time with gradual advancement up the ranks over a few decades accompanying multiple provincial assignments. Family names certainly help as a first step in identifying an individual owner of multiple seals. Out of the 384 seals struck by a bureaucrat named John between c. 966 and c. 1120, it helps that five of them, of two different types, bear the surname Hexamilites. The next step is to assess whether the seal inscriptions present a plausible career path. In the case of John Hexamilites they do, allowing us to assign them to the same individual.[59]

Without a family name it is hard to be certain that multiple seals represent the same man. To stick with the name John, twenty seals of men so named record the sole office of *notarios*. Do we have twenty men with one surviving seal apiece, one man with twenty seals, or something in between? Dating helps narrow things down, but often not greatly. If an individual had a particularly rare or unusual design for his seal, either in the composition of the inscription or the iconography, we can more confidently assign them to the same person. With our test case of Johns *notarioi*, none had an interesting inscription, and in terms of iconography there are six St. Johns (three Prodromos and two Chrysostom), two Theodores, three Nicholases, a cross, a peacock, two unidentifiable busts, two bilateral inscriptions and two St. Michaels. As noted earlier the saints represented all fall into the category of top ten most popular holy figures to depict on seals. As neither side of any seal was struck with the same *boulloterion* as any of the others, we must conclude that we have nineteen different men. Such limitations of evidence, however, should not be an excuse for paralysis, merely a reason for caution. It unfortunately does mean that we are on far firmer ground when discussing men with family names, who unfortunately make up a minority of the total of known bureaucrats. However, I see little reason why they should not be largely representative of those without family names.

Some bureaucrats spent virtually their entire career in Constantinople. Apart from one stint in the Thrakesion theme as a judge, Sergios Hexamilites spent his entire known career, 1066–85, through the reigns of five emperors, in the capital, during which he rose from *vestes* and judge, to *vestes* and judge of the Velum, keeping that office as *vestarches* and *protoproedros* before becoming *dikaiophylax* and *eparch*, and finally *logothetes ton sekreton*.[60] There is less evidence for the career of Michael Philokales, *mystikos* with the title of *proedros*, and later under Alexios I, as *protoproedros*, *mystikos*, and *eparch* of Constantinople.[61] We do not know for how long he was *mystikos* before his promotion, and it is possible that these two seals represent a significant period of Michael's life. Many bureaucrats spent considerable time in the provinces yet continued to hold positions in Constantinople. A good example is George Makrembolites. Early in his career he held the rather modest title of *spatharokandidatos* while serving as judge of Chaldia on the eastern edge of the empire.[62] Later we see him with two Constantinopolitan positions, judge of the Hippodrome and judge of the Velum, while also serving as judge of the Anatolikon in central Asia Minor.[63] How did George manage to be both a judge in Constantinople and effectively the governor of a province hundreds of miles from the capital? There are two options that seem viable to me. Firstly, John sent underlings to do the majority of the provincial work. While this might have worked for certain officials, tax assessors for instance, it is difficult to imagine a long-term absentee provincial governor. Secondly, that he took a hiatus from his Constantinopolitan duties, without giving up his position, and resumed them on his return to the capital. Eustathios Romaios did just this after his period as an *anagrapheus*. It is even possible that his position as a senior Constantinopolitan judge might have helped him in his provincial assignment. It is certainly easier to imagine men being more willing to sign up for provincial service if they knew that they had a position waiting for them on their return.

One thing that becomes immediately obvious is that for many bureaucrats, if they wanted to discharge their duties in person, they had to move around a lot. Take for example John Elesbaam. He first appears in the sigillographic record as judge of the Hippodrome and judge of the Anatolikon theme in central Anatolia, with the dignity of *patrikios*. He was later promoted to *anthypatos* and *patrikios* as judge of the theme of Drougoubiteia in the central Balkans, and then *vestes* and judges of the Velum and judge of Thrace and Macedonia in the eastern Balkans.[64] Equally mobile was Basil Tzirithon, who began his career as a lowly *protospatharios*, judge of the Hippodrome, and imperial *notarios* of the *eidikos*, all in Constantinople, was promoted to *anthypatos* and *patrikios* when he became judge of the Velum, and held these titles and his position as judge as *antiprosopon* of the *epi ton oikeiakon* and during a stint as judge of Drougoubiteia after 1050.[65] He was promoted to *protovestarches* for his next provincial assignment as judge of the Kibyrraiotai on the southern coast of Asia Minor, likely in the 1060s or early 1070s, before returning to the capital as *dikaiophylax* and *exisotes* of the West, before a final promotion to *eparch* of Constantinople after 1080.[66] He held the dignity of *protoproedros* alongside his Constantinopolitan offices.

Perhaps the most mobile bureaucrat I have come across was Constantine from the Constantinopolitan family of the Promoundenoi.[67] Constantine appears in the sources as *mystographos*, *megas chartoularios tou genikou*, and judge of the Cycladic Islands, a mixture of provincial and Constantinopolitan posts, with the title of *protospatharios*, possibly as early as 1040.[68] The next phase in his career saw him joining the judges of the Velum, an office which he would keep for the rest of his career, and also serving as judge of the Anatolikon, during which assignment he received promotion to *vestes* and *patrikios*.[69] As *vestarches* he acted at different times as judge of the Anatolikon and Armeniakon, and *praitor* of the Boukellarion, all in the 1050s and 1060s.[70] It is likely that he served in the Anatolikon twice, for he is recorded as *magistros* and judge of the theme, and if so two of his promotions happened during different tenures in that province.[71] His final seal records the office of judge of the Thrakesion on the Aegean coast of Anatolia, with the titles *magistros* and *vestes* likely in the late 1060s.[72] In an admittedly interesting career, Constantine had moved from the capital to the Aegean islands, back to Constantinople, then to central (twice), northern, eastern and then western Anatolia, with possible periods in the capital in between. Although he never went to the Balkans or the eastern frontier, he served in some of the largest and most important of the empire's core Asian provinces.

Constantine Promoundenos also exemplifies another element of the bureaucratic career, the frequency with which people switched or mixed apparent specializations. Although he spent most of his career as a judge of one place or another, it must be remembered that theme judges were more civilian governors than strictly judicial officials. However, as judge of the Velum he was a member of an important tribunal in the capital. Although he never returned to either area, this long career in provincial administration and the judiciary grew out of a secretarial position, *mystographos*, and as a record keeper in the department charged with collecting general taxation. John Beriotes had a similarly diverse career. As *vestes* after 1060, Beriotes served as a judge of the Hippodrome (judicial), *megas logothetes tou stratiotikou* (military administration), and imperial *protonotarios* of the *sakellion* (a treasury).[73] It is possible that some or all of the seals bearing the same name recording the offices of judge of the Velum (judicial), and *eparch* of Constantinople with jurisdiction over the life of the capital, and later *epi ton oikeiakon* (manager of fiscal lands) belonged to the same man.[74] Even if we believe that these seals belonged to three different men between them they worked in six different departments each with its own remit and presumably different requirements from its employees. The same was true of a certain Pothos who was a judge of the Velum at every known point in his career, but was also at different times *megas chartoularios tou genikou*, judge of Paphlagonia and *epi tou vestiariou* (chief of the *vestiarion* treasury).[75] Particularly lower down the ladder we see numerous men holding multiple positions at the same time, often with overlapping requirements, a *notarios* and a *chartoularios*, or *asekretis* and a *notarios*, for example, all of which required basic literacy and some skill with numbers, but not always. It was clearly not unusual to work in multiple branches of Byzantine government at once. The exception was when a man rose to become one of the chief officials of the state. Once they attained a certain position the Byzantines were far less likely to hold another office than earlier in their careers, but it still happened on occasion.

I find it necessary to return to the question of seals as résumé rather than accurate representations of their owner at the point in time when they were created. In all the careers listed above, there is not a single seal which records all of the offices that we know the man in question held from the testimony of his other seals. Theodore Proteuon, for example, is known from four stages of his career.[76] In three he was a *protospatharios*: as judge of the Kibyrraiotai, as judge of the Armeniakon and as judge of the Velum and *koiaistor*. Later, as *patrikios* he was only a judge of the Velum. No single stage of his career appears on more than one of his seals, and the office of *koiaistor* was removed from his final seal. His seals are a handful among many which demonstrate that the Byzantines did not place their résumé on their seals. To assume so requires us to accept that only certain former positions were listed, that one type of *judge* drove out another, or that different provincial judgeships, which are never recorded together on seals, superseded one another. To do so is to set sail into an ocean of caveats that can be extended or ignored to shape the evidence as we see fit and to ignore a pattern in the composition of seal inscriptions going back to the sixth century. The simplest explanation is that the Byzantines inscribed on their seals a description of themselves and the authority and position they currently held, that would allow them to be identified and to give validity to whatever they had secured.

From our exploration of family names and careers, a further question presents itself: Do we disproportionately find members of elite families in the most important offices? The short answer is no. Of the *eparchs* who lived in our period three came from families that are well-known, Argyros, Hexamilites and Kamateros, and the last one was in the process of joining the Komnenian elite when its member was in office, but the rest were either from families that were either less distinguished, such as the Machetarioi or Mermentouloi, or possessed no family name, this last group making up the majority of the *eparchs*. It is a similar story for the *droungarios tes viglas*. Apart from Constantine nephew of the patriarch and one Makrembolites, the elite families of Constantinople are not present in the roster of *droungarioi*. Even the *logothetes tou dromou*, an office given to some of the most important members of the Byzantine administration, was held by one Phokas, brother of the emperor, and one Xylinites in our period. The *logothetai tou genikou* were a more refined bunch, with multiple Xeroi, a Promoundenos, and a Monomachos among their number, but this still leaves the majority of the holders of the office from less renowned families or no known family at all. Among all of the heads of department I can see no evidence that established Constantinopolitan families dominated or were even more than occasional holders of offices.

3

The rise of the civilians, c. 966–c. 1066

Romanos, protospatharios epi tou theophylaktou koitonos and kensor, Michael, protospatharios, judge of the Velum, and epi ton oikeiakon, Nikephoros, protospatharios, judge of the Hippodrome, and mystographos, Leontios, protospatharios, judge of the Hippodrome, and epi ton deeseon.[1]

Byzantium's emperors said a lot about government and particularly their personal approach to ruling. They promulgated laws, issued statements and wrote speeches and books on the subject. Shortly before the beginning of our period Constantine VII produced three books on governance: one on the provinces of the empire, *De Thematibus*; one on foreign policy, *De Administrando Imperio*; and one on palace ceremony, *De Ceremoniis*. In the introduction to the last text, Constantine VII wrote that 'through praiseworthy ceremonial the imperial rule appears more beautiful and acquires more nobility and so is a cause of wonder to both foreigners and our own people', and ceremony was codified as 'befits the imperial rule and what is worthy of the senatorial order, so that the reins of power will be managed with order and beauty', and also that 'the imperial power will have more measure and order, reflecting the harmony and movement of the creator in relation to the whole, and it will appear to those subject to it to be more dignified and for this reason both sweeter and more wonderful'.[2] Constantine understood, quite rightly, that ceremony was an integral part of government. Bureaucrats were many of the actors in Constantine's performances. A later Constantine, Monomachos obsessed over the legal apparatus of the empire. He saw the law, much as the earlier emperor had seen ceremony, as an expression of the emperor's authority. The correct and consistent application of that law assumed paramount importance.[3] All of the emperors of the eleventh century presented the functions of imperial government to suit their personal agenda and style of rule. It can be tricky to get behind the rhetoric. Was Constantine VII really an antiquarian obsessed with ceremony and beautifying imperial power? Can we be sure that Basil II was an aloof autocrat forced to micromanage the empire to combat corruption? Did Monomachos really care deeply about the law? They wanted us to think so, but that tells us little about the realities of government.

Sigillographic data cuts through the fog of rhetoric and reveals the actions of government. A speech about autocratic government is an exercise in creating an image, a necessary part of being a ruler, but what does it mean then, if government expands vastly under your rule, with power delegated to ever more people? Speaking about your subjects' access to the law is all well and good, but more meaningful is an increase in the number and the status of the judiciary. What could it mean that the emperors of the eleventh century rarely spoke about the smooth operation of the apparatus which assessed, collected and distributed the empire's resources?

Government is about priorities, and every emperor tried to some degree to remake Byzantine government in his image. His success largely dictated his chances of keeping the throne.[4] The government of the empire was ever evolving. Beneath Constantine VII's ceremonies and the static facade that the empire presented to the world as part of the imperial show, the bureaucracy was constantly adapting to an ever-changing world and to the priorities of every new regime. In this chapter, we shall explore what seals tell us about the priorities of imperial government in the first century of our period, c. 966–c. 1066. The starting point will be the *Taktikon Escorial* of 971–5. Each assessment of an office will begin with a statement of where it fell in the final list of precedence. In doing so I will partly follow in the footsteps of Nicolas Oikonomides by giving an office's position among the *axiai dia logou*, ignoring the purely honorific positions along with those belonging to retired officials, ecclesiastical positions outside of the imperial system, and palace flunkies, and thus its place in the total list. Each office will thus be given two rankings, one placing this bureaucratic position into the context of the wider Byzantine court establishment, and another to present a more accurate view of where the office fell in the rankings of individuals appointed by the emperor to perform a task paid by the state. For example, the *sakellarios* was in 120th position in the whole hierarchy, but 102nd place in the list of offices.

This chapter largely covers the period of Byzantine history when the empire was strong. Even when not expanding territorially, internally, in terms of the economy, the population, urbanization, Byzantium was growing and becoming more complex. One of our aims is to begin to write the story of how the government of the empire adapted to developments elsewhere in the empire. Usually data from seals cannot tell us much about individual emperors, because we are not able to date them narrowly enough. However, due to his long reign, the first two periods into which this study is split, namely the final third of the tenth century and the first third of the eleventh, almost exactly coincide with the reign of Basil II. In the following pages, we will create a picture of government under this most enigmatic of emperors, and then compare it to that created by the succeeding generation.

For ease of analysis I have divided my investigation of the Byzantine government into four major blocks, first, the administrative bureaus of a mainly financial nature, including the treasuries, then second, the various departments which could be loosely termed the chancery, responsible for drafting imperial documents, followed, third, by the bureaucrats who administered the capital, and finally, fourth, the judiciary working in Constantinople. These divisions seem neat and orderly, a misleading impression, which is not my intent. However, we must divide the government somehow before diving into the evidence for its evolution over the century which is the subject of this chapter, and these four groups are as good an option as any other.[5] Furthermore, two of these divisions, between the *sekreta*, roughly speaking the first two of my groups, and the judiciary, were considered significant enough by Philotheos that the distinction between the two found its way into the structure of his *Kletorologion*, putting us in his good company. The four divisions will be presented in the order outlined earlier as this order represents the great variety of reforms undertaken by the Byzantines in this period. In the administration, finance and chancery we can see departments where the vast majority of state employees saw their status fall into one of three categories, gentle decline, stagnation or inflation level advancement depending, usually, on how important their office was to begin with. When we turn to Constantinople we will see a system evolving to meet the needs of the imperial capital. Finally, with the judiciary, we will explore some of the most interesting and far-reaching government reforms of the Middle Byzantine period.

Before jumping into the offices themselves, a few issues of vocabulary must be addressed. As has been mentioned before, we are piecing together the Byzantine administration from a wide variety of sources, none of which were created with our current goals in mind. In a similar vein, there is no official list of terms used by the Byzantines to describe their government structure. Thus, bureaus were termed *sekreta* by Philotheos, and derived from this, some, but not all, of their heads were *sekretikoi*.[6] Some of the *sekretikoi* held the office of *logothetes* (director), and their department might be dubbed a *sekreton* or a *logothesion*, the latter simply being a bureau the head of which was a *logothetes*. In the eleventh century, *logothesion* was dropping out of fashion in favour of *sekreton* in documents but was still a popular term on seals. Similarly, while Philotheos reserved the term *sekretikoi* for the great offices of state, other sources, for example Constantine VII's *De Ceremoniis*, applied the term much more broadly to mean bureaucrat. Likewise, the Byzantine word for judge, *krites*, was the name of a provincial officer, who had administrative, financial and judicial powers. The theme judges will appear in this study infrequently, so there should be little room for confusion.

3.1 Changing with the times: The *logothesia* and the treasuries

Tribute-levying manikins who contribute absolutely nothing to the common good, but whose sole intent is to wear down and squeeze dry the poor, and from their injustice and abundant shedding of the blood of the poor they store up many talents of gold.[7]

We begin our exploration of the Byzantine government with a group of officials who perhaps fit the modern idea of bureaucrats better than any others we shall consider in this book, those men involved with the collection and distribution of state resources and the basic administration of the empire. As the quotation just provided, written by a disgruntled military officer, demonstrates, the personnel of the departments associated with tax assessment, collection, military administration and communications were not always regarded fondly by their fellow Byzantines. As a group, they are rarely mentioned in the sources, and when they are it is often as a grey faceless mass, the Vogons of Byzantium. They were rarely the star of the show, except for a few *logothetai tou dromou*, and they were never involved in anything dramatic. But they made sure that taxes were assessed, collected and spent, that the army was paid and supplied and that letters, people and goods could move from one end of the empire to the other, and beyond. In many ways, they held the empire together as much as any cultural or religious force.

Most of the departments of the tenth- and eleventh-century Byzantine central administration had their origins in the *scrinia* of the late Roman *praefectura praetorio per Orientem*, the praetorian prefecture of the East, while others derived from the *comitiva sacarum largitionum* and the *res privata*, the central financial departments based in the capital.[8] Over time they broke away from the prefecture, and alongside a number of palatine bureaus became independent government departments, eventually displacing their former superiors. Philotheos used the term *sekreton* to designate the great bureaus of the empire of his time, with department heads usually termed *sekretikoi*. In the *Kletorologion*, subordinate officials are often described as 'of the *sekreton*', a term which also frequently appears on seals. The *sekreta*, listed in the order in which their department head appears in the later *Escorial Taktikon*, and the order in which they will be considered in this chapter, are the *genikon* (general taxation and some land management), *stratiotikon* (military finance, recruitment, and muster-rolls), *dromos* (internal communications and foreign relations), *sakellion* (a treasury), *vestiarion* (a treasury), *eidikon* (a treasury), and finally those departments involved in the management of the estates owned by the government, the *megale kouratoreia* (all state lands) and the departments of the *epi ton oikeiakon* (fiscal lands), *ephoros* (crown lands) and of the *euageis oikoi* (charitable foundations). The *genikon*, *stratiotikon* and *dromos* were led by a *logothetes* (director). The early *logothetai* were minor fiscal officials but, following the restructuring of the empire's government between the sixth and eighth centuries, rose to become heads of their own bureau, named *logothesia* after their chief. This situation was fully in place by the time that Philotheos was writing at the end of the ninth century, but it had likely existed in that form for some time by that point.[9] The *sakellion* and the *vestiarion* fell under the authority of a *chartoularios* (recordkeeper), while the *eidikon*, *megale kouratoreia*, and the departments of the *epi ton oikeiakon* and *ephoros* were led by an eponymous official, the *eidikos*, *megas kourator* (the great curator), *epi ton oikeiakon* (lit. of the household) and the *ephoros* (lit. the overseer) respectively. The exception to both was the *oikonomos* of the *euageis oikoi* (manager of the charitable foundations). We will take each of these *sekreta* in turn, list the officials who worked in that department, and examine their duties. There are a number of officials who are found in multiple departments, such as the *chartoularioi*, *notarioi*, *kankellarioi*, *mandatories*, *kouratores* and *logariastes*. To avoid unnecessary repetition, we will talk about them here before turning to the more specific exploration of the *sekreta*.

Chartoularioi and sometimes also *megaloi chartoularioi* were found in the *logothesia* of the *genikon*, *stratiotikon* and *dromos* and in the treasuries of the *sakellion* and the *vestiarion*.[10] The *chartoularioi* derived their name from their primary function, which was to handle and keep official documents, *chartes*. Alongside general *chartoularioi* we encounter *chartoularioi* with specific geographical or departmental responsibilities and others who cared for specific archives or treasuries. Similar to the *chartoularioi* were the *protonotarioi*, imperial *notarioi* and *notarioi*, who generally acted as clerks. They were found in the *dromos*, *sakellion*, *vestiarion* and the *eidikon*. Like the *chartoularioi* they were a diverse group. The *protonotarios* of the *dromos* was the second in command of the *sekreton*, while other *protonotarioi* (first *notarios*) simply led a group of regular *notarioi* in their sectretarial duties. Others worked in the themes, or in a similar capacity to the *chartoularioi* in the central bureaus. *Protokankellarioi* and *kankellarioi* are found in the *logothesia* of the *genikon* and *stratiotikon*, and the treasuries of the *sakellion*, *vestiarion* and *eidikon*, and in the departments of the *eparch* and *koiaistor*. In Philotheos's breakdown of departments they are listed as minor officials, probably engaged in secretarial work.[11] *Mandatores* were employed by the *stratiotikon*, *dromos* and *vestiarion*, with the latter also including *protomandatores* on its staff. They had diverse and probably ad hoc functions, acting as their superior's representative or messengers as need dictated. The *dromos*, *vestiarion* and *megale kouratoreia* employed *kouratores*, (curators). In general, they were in charge of a piece of state land, whether rural or urban, palace or an imperial workshop.

The final office common to a number of departments, the *logariastes*, deserves special mention. The term means accountant, and if we are to understand the name as applying to the duties of the office, it marks a thought-provoking addition to the staff of the majority of the *sekreta*. Interestingly, considering that all of the *sekreta* listed earlier had duties that included some amount of revenue or resource collection, storage and distribution, a dedicated accountant is not listed as a part of their staffs in the *Kletorologion of Philotheos* or the *Escorial Taktikon*, although the limited nature of the latter list makes this less surprising than it might seem at first. Documentary evidence and the surviving seals make it clear that the *logariastes* appeared in the eleventh century.[12] The first documentary evidence for a *logariastes* in one of the *sekreta* in Constantinople dates to 1012.[13] As has been noted, the appearance of specialized accountants across the government, in the financial bureaus, treasuries and departments concerned with estate management, and in private households, could be taken as evidence of a new interest in efficient and accurate exploitation of resources.[14]

Due to the imbalance of the surviving evidence we will more often than not focus on the heads of the *sekreta* rather than their deputies and lower level bureaucrats. However, for certain *sekreta* large amounts of evidence survive from men with more humble positions. For no department do we have a large body of evidence for every known office within it. Many positions are represented by a single seal, or, less frequently, a single mention in a written source. Beyond the fact that the office continued to exist, these sources provide little information on the *sekreton* as a whole or on the roles of the men who worked within it. I will mention them as we proceed *sekreton* by *sekreton*, but they will contribute little to our discussion of the mechanics of government.

Before we begin there is one further group of seals which must be discussed. Of the lower offices mentioned earlier, where more than one person held it at once, the vast majority of the surviving sigillographic evidence is sadly unspecific. By this I mean that of the numerous types of clerical and accounting offices – the *chartoularioi*, *notarioi*, *kankellarioi*, *mandatores*, *kouratores* and *logariastai* – very few seals bothered to be specific. The number of seals which record the office of *chartoularios*, for example, dwarfs those which specify *chartoularios tou genikou*. The same is true for all of the other offices as well. This presents a few obvious problems: firstly, it is impossible to assign the owners of such seals to a particular department; secondly, for some offices it is difficult to distinguish between those who served in the capital and those stationed in the provinces, although it is a fair assumption to assume that if no place is mentioned then they worked in the more prestigious locale, in this case Constantinople; and thirdly, and this is a problem specific to the *mandatores*, it is often impossible to know whether the individual concerned was referring to a dignity, civilian office or military rank. As such, while I am comfortable in assigning the majority of these seals to the central bureaucracy, those of the *mandatores* will largely be left outside of the present study. For the rest, they cannot be used here except to offer a general sense on the fortunes of lower-level administrators.

We shall now turn to the departments themselves. I will argue that, with a few exceptions, the evidence points to a promotion for the elite members of the *sekreta* in line with title inflation, and for the lower-level staff a flattening out of titles around the rank of *protospatharios*, which for many meant a loss of status. These *sekreta* are therefore a good place to begin our exploration of the Byzantine bureaucracy, as their staff were not the over-promoted leeches feeding of the public purse of the account of Psellos:they are in some senses a good control group, for their fortunes were average. However, this does not mean that they are not interesting. The relative rankings of the various *sekreta* reveal glimpses of imperial priorities in this period, as does the creation of new departments and the place which they came to occupy in the existing system.

3.1.1 The *logothesia*

> *The offices of the sekreta, these are eleven in number, the sakellarios, the logothetes tou genikou, the logothetes tou stratiotikou, the logothetes tou dromou. ...*[15]

3.1.1.1 *The* sakellarios

> Ἅγιε Γεόργε βοήθει τῷ σῷ δούλῳ Νικολάῳ βασιλικῷ πρωτοσπαθαρίῳ ἐπὶ τοῦ Χρυσοτρικλίνου καὶ βασιλικῷ σακελλαρίο το Ἀνγούρῃ.

> Saint George, help your servant Nicholas Anagoures imperial protospatharios epi tou Chrysotriklinou and imperial sakellarios.[16]

We will begin with the *sakellarios* who was different from the other *sekretikoi* (heads of department) as by the period covered in this study he was no longer the chief of his original *sekreton* but was the overseer of all the empire's financial departments. The *sakellarios* is first heard of in the fifth century, as an official of the *sacellum*, the emperor's private treasury.[17] However, at some point in the fifth or early sixth century he had become the most important treasury official in the empire. At this point the *sakellarios* was head of the treasury known as the *sakellion*, but by the early seventh century the *sakellarios* had left his old department behind to act as overall head of the state finances, with oversight of the financial dealings of the *sekreta*. It is in this exalted position in which position we find him in c. 966.[18] The *sakellarios* was served by *notarioi* in each department as well as *mandatores*. Philotheos tells us that it was through the *notarioi* that the *sakellarios* performed his supervisory duties over the *offikia*.[19]

The *sakellarios* was, as we would expect from his duties, an important man with a high status within the hierarchy. In the *Escorial Taktikon* he ranks second among the bureaucrats behind the *eparch*, in 120 (total hierarchy), 102 (offices) in the list of precedence.[20] In the earlier *Taktikon Beneševič* he is listed among the *protospatharioi*, but the sigillographic evidence proves that times had changed when the *Escorial Taktikon* was written. There are eighty-seven seals belonging to fifty-three *sakellarioi* in the database used for this study, the normalized data can be seen in Table 3.1.

The data available on the *sakellarioi* is chronologically limited. Almost all of the seals considered here belonged to individuals who lived c. 966–1033. There are very few seals of *sakellarioi* dated after c. 1033, and equally few mentions in the written sources. This is rather unusual. The office of *sakellarios* is one of a small number of positions which has left an increasingly small imprint in the seals record. For most offices, evidence is somewhat sparse for the end of the tenth century, then increases into the middle of the eleventh century. For the *sakellarioi* we see the exact opposite pattern, a large number of seals, and individuals, for the tenth century, with dwindling numbers into the mid-eleventh century.[21] The inescapable conclusion is that in terms of their role in the running of the state, the *sakellarioi* did not fare well in the eleventh century. This conclusion is supported by the data presented in Table 3.1. It shows that the titles of the *sakellarioi* held steady in the final third of the tenth century and the opening decades of the eleventh century. The most common title held by the *sakellarioi* was that of *anthypatos*, paired with *patrikios* or *patrikios* and *protospatharios*. They held a relatively exalted position in the tenth century, third in the hierarchy, the lowest of the upper-level titles, possibly slipping to the highest of the lower grade dignities by the time that our evidence dries up. But their position became far less important as time went on, and to some degree ceased functioning in the same way by the middle decades of the eleventh century. Why this should have happened is not immediately apparent. Perhaps it is linked to the appearance of the *logariastai*. With dedicated accountants monitoring the finances of the *sekreta* the *sakellarios* might not have been as useful.

Table 3.1 Normalized Seal Data, in Percentages, for the Titles of the *Sakellarios* c. 966–c. 1066

Title/Period	Tenth Century Final Third	Eleventh Century First Third	Eleventh Century Middle Third
Magistros	8.5	5.9	
Vestes and *Patrikios*	5.1	5.9	
Anthypatos, *Patrikios* and *Protospatharios*	35.6	41.2	
Anthypatos and *Patrikios*	5.1	5.9	
Patrikios and *Protospatharios*	3.4		
Protospatharios	18.6	17.6	100
None	23.7	23.5	

3.1.1.2 *The* sekreton tou genikou

> Subject to the logothetes tou genikou are twelve kinds of titles: great chartoularioi of the sekreton, chartoularioi of the chests, epoptai of the themes, kometes of the water, the oikistikos, kommerkiarioi, the kourator, the komes of the lamia, dioiketai, kommentianos, protokankellarios, kankellarioi.[22]

The *sekreton tou genikou*, the general financial department, was a fiscal department that first appears in the sources in the person of the *logothetes tou genikou* in 692.[23] However, its origin was much older in the general treasury, the *genike trapeza* and related *scrinia*, of the praetorian prefecture of the East.[24] Just like its earlier incarnation the *genikon* was responsible for the assessment and collection of the basic land tax throughout the empire.[25] Up until the eleventh century it had also controlled the fiscal lands of the empire, about which more can be found in the following pages, but increasingly lost this role to the *epi ton oikeiakon*.

In descending order the officials serving in the *genikon* mentioned by Philotheos were the *logothetes* (director); the *megaloi chartoularioi tou sekretou* (great recordkeepers of the department), who kept the tax registers of the empire; the *chartoularioi ton arklon*, 'of the chests', possibly the officials in charge of provincial treasuries and likely the local land registers (*kodikes tou genikou*); the *epoptai ton thematon*, the men who revised the tax registers; the *kometes hydaton* (counts of the water), possibly in charge of access to water supplies such as aqueducts and related charges; the *oikistikos* (on whom see below); the *kommerkiarioi*, collectors of the commercial tax, *o tes kouratias*, an official involved with the crown estates which had originally belonged to imperial subjects; *o komes tes lamias*, a count responsible for either the imperial mines or the granaries of Constantinople; *dioiketai*, tax collectors; the *komentianos*, function unknown; the *protokankellarios*; and the *kankellarios* (clerical staff).[26] Of all of the officials listed by Philotheos in the *sekreton* of the *genikon*, only the *logothetes* and the *oikistikos* were included in the *Escorial Taktikon*. This was likely because the *oikistikos*, though rather low down on the list in the rankings of Philotheos, had by this time evolved into an independent position of which we shall say more in the following pages. The sigillographic material provides evidence of officials not included in the list of Philotheos, such as *protonotarioi*, imperial *notarioi*, *notarioi*, *logariastai* and the office of the *antiprosopon*. In total there is evidence for staff in eighteen different positions.

Among all the *sekreta*, that of the *genikon* has left behind the largest number of seals both in terms of absolute number and individual office-holders. Having said that, when we examine which offices have left a statistically useable amount of evidence, the list is just as limited as with the other *sekreta*: the *logothetes*, the *megaloi chartoularioi* and the *chartoularioi*. Although there are also seals for the *komes tes lamias*, imperial *notarioi*, *epoptai*, the *chartoularioi* of various *arkla*, the *dioiketai* and the *kommerkiarioi*, only the first two of these lived and worked in Constantinople, and only those belonging to the provincial *kommerkiarioi* have survived in large enough numbers to be useful here.

3.1.1.2.1 The logothetes tou genikou

Θεοτόκε βοήθει τῷ σῷ δούλῳ Νικήτᾳ ἀνθυπάτῳ πατρικίῳ βασιλικῷ πρωτοσπαθαρίῳ καὶ γενικῷ λογοθέτῃ.

Theotokos, help your servant Niketas, anthypatos patrikios imperial protospatharios and genikos logothetes.[27]

The *logothetes tou genikou*, the director of the *sekreton*, is known from fifty-four seals which belonged to thirty-four *logothetai*.

The *logothetes tou genikou* was one of the highest-ranking civilian officials at the time of the composition of the *Escorial Taktikon*, coming in third place behind the *eparch* and the *sakellarios*, ranking 124 (total hierarchy) 103 (offices) among the secular *axiai dia logou*.[28] The sigillographic evidence presents a rather complex picture for the final third of the tenth century, with roughly the same percentage holding the titles of *magistros* and *protospatharios*. In all periods, almost everyone concerned was only *logothetes tou genikou* (we will deal with the few exceptions later), so the answer for this unusual spread cannot be that their titles were influenced by other offices. The range of *rogai* paid in the final third of the tenth century was thus incredibly broad, 1–16 pounds of *nomismata*, and in terms of status they were either in the middle of the *cursus honorum* or at the top. It is difficult to account for this huge range in both status and income in the final third of the tenth century. Could it be the result of the individuals who held the office and either their career history or their relationship to the emperor? Or perhaps the result of the value different emperors placed in the office itself? Sadly, without more evidence it is impossible to know for sure. What can be said is that the picture shifted radically in the first

Table 3.2 Normalized Seal Data, in Percentages, for the Titles of the *Logothetes tou Genikou* c. 966–c. 1066

Title/Period	Tenth Century Final Third	Eleventh Century First Third	Eleventh Century Middle Third
Proedros			16.4
Magistros, Anthypatos, Patrikios and *Protospatharios*	4.8	7.7	
Magistros, Anthypatos and *Patrikios*	9.5		
Magistros	19.1		
Vestarches and *Patrikios*			5.5
Vestarches			8
Vestes			10.9
Anthypatos, Patrikios and *Protospatharios*	9.5	15.4	
Anthypatos and *Patrikios*	12.7	30.7	10.8
Patrikios and *Protospatharios*	3.2		
Patrikios	3.2	5.1	21.4
Protospatharios	31.7	41	21.5
None	6.3		5.5

third of the eleventh century. The percentage of *protospatharioi* increased by a third to 41, and that of *magistroi* dropped considerably to 7.7. The difference was caused by men for whom *anthypatos* was their highest title, who make up 46.1 per cent of the whole. The range of *rogai* payments remained wide, 1 pound to 16 pounds of coins; however, the most common salary had become that of the *protospatharioi* at the bottom of the range. The mean average *roga* in the first third of the eleventh century was 4.45 pounds of coins. In terms of status the *protospatharioi* retained their position in the middle of the pack, but the large number of *anthypatoi* broke into the upper levels of the hierarchy. The seals from the middle third of the eleventh century present yet another different picture. The range of titles this time is from *protospatharios* up to *proedros*, with a corresponding *roga* range of 1 to 28 pounds of gold. In terms of percentages the number of *protospatharioi* halved, there was a fourfold increase in the number of *patrikioi*, and a similar decrease in the proportion of *anthypatoi*. The difference was made up through the appearance of *vestai* and *vestarchai*. The most common *rogai* payments remained that for the *protospatharioi*, 1 pound of coins, joined by those for the *patrikioi*, 4 pounds. The average payment in this period rose to 9 pounds, due largely to the few *proedroi* who had joined the ranks of *logothetes*.

The seals present a rather confused picture of the fortunes of the *logothetes tou genikou*. Which image is accurate, that of the *protospatharios* or the *magistros* and *proedros*? It seems that there was a decrease in the fortunes of the office in the first third of the eleventh century, with the vast majority, all but 7.7 per cent, with titles between *protospatharios* and *anthypatos*. This put them firmly in the middle of the hierarchy as it existed at that time. In the middle third of the eleventh century, we see a progression that is much more familiar from our examinations of other offices. The percentage of *protospatharioi*, now in the lower third of the hierarchy, decreased, as did that of *anthypatoi*, upper-middle, although they still accounted for a third of the total. The difference was mostly made up by an increase in lowly *patrikioi*, bottom third, and *vestai* and *vestarchai*, either at the bottom of the top third or the top of the middle third depending on the date. Either way the only individuals who maintained the earlier generation's place in the hierarchy were the *vestarchai*, who accounted for only 13.5 per cent of the whole, while the remainder saw a drop in their status. This rather grim picture does not account for the 16.4 per cent of *logothetai* who, as *proedroi*, had reached the highest rank available to men not of the imperial family at that time.

3.1.1.2.2 *The subordinates of the* logothetes tou genikou

> Κωνσταντῖνος σπαθαροκανδιδᾶτος ἐπὶ τοῦ Χρυσοτρικλίνου, βασιλικὸς νοτάριος εἰς τὸ γενικὸν ὁ Ἀρεοβινδηνός.

> Constantine Areobindenos, spatharokandidatos epi tou Chrysotriklinou, imperial notarios of the genikon.[29]

Although the *megaloi chartoularioi* (great *chartoularioi*) were not important enough for an entry in the *Escorial Taktikon*, they have left behind even more sigillographic evidence than their superiors, seventy-eight seals struck by thirty-five men. The data from these seals is normalized in Table 3.3, and clearly demonstrates that for all three periods under consideration the dominant dignity attached to this office was that of *protospatharios*. While the seals show a drop in the percentage of *protospatharioi* in the middle third of the eleventh century, by a third, it is important to remember that there is not a single known *megas chartoularios* who held just that office who was ranked higher than *protospatharios* between c. 966 and c. 1066. The men who held higher titles (*vestarches*, *vestes* and *hypatos*) performed other functions which likely explain their ranks, such as judge of the Velum, *kouratores*, or theme judges. There were, however, *megaloi chartoularioi* who were *protospatharioi* and also performed other functions. It is reasonable to conclude that a *megas chartoularios* of the *genikon* was almost certainly a *protospatharios* in c. 966–c. 1066, and that as a result their status and income would have decreased notably over time.

The next rung down the ladder at the *genikon*, the *chartoularioi*, have left behind evidence from twenty-nine men in the form of forty-four seals. Although *protospatharios* remained the most common dignity for the *chartoularioi* throughout the late tenth to the mid-eleventh century, the overall proportion dropped over time, and the percentage of lower-ranking *spatharokandidatoi* rose until, by the middle third of the eleventh century, the two titles accounted for an equal number of men. As with the *megaloi chartoularioi*, the apparent upswing in the status of the *chartoularioi* in the

Table 3.3 Normalized Seal Data, in Percentages, for the Titles of the *Megas Chartoularios* of the *Genikon Logothesion* c. 966–c. 1066

Title/Period	Tenth Century Final Third	Eleventh Century	
		First Third	Middle Third
Vestarches			4.8
Vestes			9.5
Hypatos and *Protospatharios*			7.1
Protospatharios	93.5	91.4	66.7
Spatharokandidatos	6.5	5.2	7.1
None		3.3	4.8

Table 3.4 Normalized Seal Data, in Percentages, for the Titles of the *Chartoularios* of the *Genikon Logothesion* c. 966–c. 1066

Title/Period	Tenth Century Final Third	Eleventh Century	
		First Third	Middle Third
Anthypatos and *Patrikios*		9.5	4.7
Patikios and *Protospatharios*			13.8
Patrikios			6.9
Protospatharios	49.9	42.7	37.5
Spatharokandidatos	13.9	26.2	37.1
Spatharios	11		
None	25.1	21.6	

middle third of the eleventh century, with a significant percentage of men holding the rank of *patrikios* either alone or in conjunction with the higher *anthypatos* or lower *protospatharios*, is deceptive. All of the individuals with titles above *protospatharios* also performed other functions such as *megas kourator*, judge of the Hippodrome, or theme judge, and occasionally a combination of the two.[30] Here we see a relative decline in the status and income of the position of *chartoularios* of the *genikon* on a greater scale than that observed for the *megas chartoularios*, though some few men escaped this fate by accumulating more offices.

There is little evidence for *notarioi* of any level working for the *logothetes tou genikou*. From the period under consideration here we know of two *protonotarioi* (first clerks), from one seal and the *Peira*.[31] A further eight imperial *notarioi* and *notarioi* are known from nine seals, all dated c. 966–c. 1060. Three displayed no titles on their seals, one was a *spatharios*, two were *spatharokandidatoi*, and two were *protospatharioi*.[32]

3.1.1.3 The oikistikos

> Κύριε βοήθει τῷ σῷ δούλῳ Στεφάνῳ πρωτοβέστῃ, οἰκιστικῷ τῶν νέων ὀρθώσεων καὶ κριτῇ τῶν Ἀρμενιακῶν.

> Lord, help your servant Stephen, protovestes, oikistikos ton neon orthoseon and judge of the Armeniakoi.[33]

The *oikistikos* first appears in the *Kletorologion of Philotheos* as a subordinate of the *logothetes tou genikou*.[34] The office was also mentioned in the *Escorial Taktikon*, where it occupied the 187th (total hierarchy) 164th (offices) place.[35] In the eleventh century, seals of support staff appear, indicating that the *oikistikos* was now the head of his own department.[36] He is listed last among the chiefs of bureaus in a number of documents issued in favour of monastic foundations, a further indication of his new status.[37] Nesbitt argues convincingly that the remit of the *oikistikos* and his department expanded over time from recording the properties benefitting from tax exemptions, to lands which did not produce revenue for any reason, to overseeing the reimposition of taxes on lands being brought back into the fiscal system, or *orthosis*.[38]

The limited sigillographic evidence (so limited that I will discuss it all here although three of the seals belong in the following section) consists of nine seals of eight men and supports Nesbitt's argument. We see the *oikistikoi* with no title in the late tenth century, advancing to *spatharios* and *protospatharios* in the early eleventh, with a *vestes* and *protovestes* in the second half of the century.[39] Only one seal is out of place with the idea of the *oikistikos* growing in importance and becoming independent. Dated to the tenth/eleventh century, it records that its owner, Constantine, held the titles of *anthypatos*, *patrikios* and *protospatharios*.[40] The *oikistikos* begins to be listed in documents among the heads of departments in 1045, a date which tallies with the boost in status from *protospatharios* to *vestes* in the seals. Might this be the point at which the office became independent? At least one subordinate is known earlier than this, from the tenth/eleventh century, a *notarios tou oikistikou*.[41] It is possible that the *oikistikos* had his own subordinates while still reporting to the *logothetes tou genikou*,

Figure 3.1 Seal of Stephen *protovestes, oikistikos ton neon orthoseon* and judge of the Armeniakoi. Dumbarton Oaks, Byzantine Collection, Washington, DC, BZS.1955.1.2125.
Obv. +K̄ERΘ|TWCWΔΥΛ,|.TEΦANWĀ|RECTHOIKI|CTIKW
Rev. TWNNE|WNOPΘW|CEWNSKPI|THTWNAP|MENIAK,
Κύριε βοήθει τῷ σῷ δούλῳ Στεφάνῳ πρωτοβέστῃ, οἰκιστικῷ τῶν νέων ὀρθώσεων καὶ κριτῇ τῶν Ἀρμενιακῶν.
Lord, help your servant Stephen, *protovestes, oikistikos ton neon orthoseon* and judge of the Armeniakoi.

but impossible to prove. If independent early, as a *protospatharios*, he was rather low ranking. Regardless of when the *oikistikos* became independent, the sigillographic evidence is consistent with Nesbitt's argument concerning mission creep in terms of duties, which could certainly explain the gradual increase in status in the mid- and later eleventh century. There are three other pieces of information which speak to this point, all of which suggest that in the second half of the eleventh century there were multiple *oikistikoi*. Firstly, the seal of Theophylaktos *vestarches*, judge, *megas oikistikos* and *gerokomos*. Generally speaking the addition of *megas* (great) to an office meant it was important, or that multiple men held the same position and one was being distinguished as the leader of the group, an alternative to the prefix *proto*.[42] That the latter was meant in this case is indicated by the other two pieces of evidence, the seals of Stephen *protovestes, oikistikos ton neon orthoseon* and *krites ton Armeniakon*, and Michael *proedros* and *logariastes ton oikistikon* (accountant in the department of the *oikistikoi*).[43] Michael's seal specifically mentions that he works for multiple *oikistikoi*, while Stephen's seal specifies that he was the *oikistikos* with responsibility for a new type of reimplementing taxes on property, which itself implies that there were *oikistikoi* responsible for the other areas of the department's jurisdiction.

What we have here are indications of a department with a gradually swelling remit which led to the appointment of more than one *oikistikos*, under a *megas oikistikos*, with a staff of supporting *notarioi* and *logariastai*. It seems to suggest both a bureaucracy becoming larger and more specialized, and also a more complex economy, with exemptions being more closely registered on the one hand, but also surveys of non-productive land in general being made on the other, and new tactics adopted to bring that land back onto the tax registers.

3.1.1.4 *The* sekreton tou stratiotikou

> Subject to the logothetes tou stratiotikou are seven kinds of titles, namely: chartoularioi of the sekreton, chartoularioi of the themes, chartoularioi of the tagmata, legatarioi, optiones, protokankellarios, mandatores.[44]

The *sekreton tou stratiotikou* (department for military affairs) was likely an evolution of the old, similarly named, department of the praetorian prefecture of the East concerned with military pay.[45] We know little for sure about the jurisdiction of the *sekreton* of the *stratiotikon*. The only textual mention of the duties of the department speaks of how the *logothetes* (director) was responsible for the monitoring and cancelling the tax exemptions applied to soldiers.[46] This has led to theories about the overall remit of the *stratiotikon* that range from the purely financial, not just monitoring the privileges of soldiers, but handling their pay as well, to oversight of the registers of *strateia* (military obligations), to responsibilities that today would be in the remit of a department of defence.[47] As officials under his control were responsible for keeping the military registers in order and distributing soldiers pay, it seems likely that the *sekreton tou stratiotikou* was concerned with all elements of supplying and registering the soldiers of the empire and their military obligations.[48] The *Kletorologion of Philotheos* records the staff of the *sekreton* as the *logothetes* (director); the *chartoularioi tou sekretou* (recordkeepers of the department), working in the capital; the *chartoularioi ton thematon* (recordkeeprs of the *themes*), working in the provinces and likely making sure that the military registers were up-to-date; the *chartoularioi ton tagmaton* (recordkeepers of the regiments), assigned to the *tagmata*; *legatarioi* (legates) their exact function is unclear (elsewhere we find military *legatarioi* in the *tagmata*, and *legetarioi* with policing duties in the office of the *eparch*); *optiones*, who distributed the soldiers salaries; *protokankellarioi*; and *mandatores*.[49] As with the other *sekreta*, only a limited number of these offices (the *megas chartoularios*, the *chartoularios* and the *protonotarios*, all clerical officials) have left behind evidence that is both substantive and firmly identifiable as belonging to men who worked for the *sekreton tou stratiotikou*.

3.1.1.4.1 *The* logothetes tou stratiotikou

> Κύριε βοήθει τῷ σῷ δούλῳ Νικήτᾳ ἀνθυπάτῳ, πατρικίῳ, βασιλικῷ πρωτοσπαθαρίῳ καὶ στρατιωτικῷ λογοθέτῃ.

> Lord, help your servant Niketas, anthypatos, patrikios, imperial protospatharios and stratiotikos logothetes.[50]

It is possible that the *logothetes tou stratiotikou* was the first of the *logothetai* to be mentioned in a source, appearing in the *Chronicon Paschale* in an entry dated to 626.[51] The *logothetes tou stratiotikou* appeared in the *Escorial Taktikon* in the 127th (total hierarchy) 105th (offices) place, above the *logothetes tou dromou*, and just below the *koiaistor*. When we come to the sigillographic evidence, there is sadly too little for statistical analysis, only twenty-seven seals, representing eighteen men. Although not all of these seals can be narrowly dated, a rough pattern emerges from those that can. In the latter half of the tenth century the *logothetai tou stratiotikou* likely held the rank of *protospatharios*. Half of the known men were *anthypatoi* and/or *patrikioi* in the last decades of the century, the other half remained *protospatharioi*. With one exception, a *protospatharios*, all of the *logothetai* with seals dated to the end of the period covered in this chapter, c. 1066, held both the dignity of *anthypatos* and that of *patrikios*. The pattern seems to be a gradual transition from the majority of *logothetes* having the rank of *protospatharios*, with its *roga* of seventy-two *nomismata*, in the final third of the tenth century, to *patrikios*, either alone or in conjunction with *protospatharios*, or *anthypatos*, after c. 1000. As we have seen with other administrators of roughly the same level, the promotion evident in the seals was relatively modest in terms of status, with most of the *logothetai* holding their rank level until c. 1060, and somewhat more generous in terms of *rogai*.

3.1.1.4.2 The subordinates of the logothetes tou stratiotikou

> Κύριε βοήθει Θεοδώρῳ σπαθαροκανδιδάτῳ καὶ μεγάλῳ χαρτουλαρίῳ τοῦ στρατιωτικοῦ τῷ Τζουμένῃ.

> Lord, help Theodore Tzoumenes, spatharokandidatos and megas chartoularios of the stratiotikon.[52]

The staff of the *sekreton* have left behind varying amounts of evidence. For the period c. 966–c. 1066, we know of six *megaloi* (great) *chartoularioi* from seven seals, twenty-one *chartoularioi* from twenty-five seals, and two *protonotarioi* from two seals. For all but the *chartoularioi* this is too little evidence on which to build much of an argument. One interesting point about the *megaloi chartoularioi* is that the two titles recorded, *spatharokandidatos* and *protospatharios*, are matched in their dating, meaning that there is no evidence for an upward progression in dignities for this office. Both *protonotarioi* lived at the end of the tenth to the beginning of the eleventh century, and both were *protospatharioi*. With the *chartoularioi* we are on moderately firmer ground and can

Figure 3.2 Seal of Nikephoros Laktentitzes, imperial *protopatharios epi tou Chrysotriklinou*, *mystographos* and *chartoularios* of the *stratiotikon logothesion*. Dumbarton Oaks, Byzantine Collection, Washington, DC, BZS.1958.106.5404.
The obverse shows an image of a standing St. Michael, holding the labarum and globus cruciger.
Rev. +ΝΙΚΗΦ|Ρ,ĀСΠΑΘΑΡ,|ΕΠΙΤΉⲶΓΚΛ̄|ΜVСΤΟΓΡΑΦ,S|ΧΑΡΤΉΛΑΡ,ΤΉ|СΤΡΑΤΙѠΤ, ΚΉ|ΛΟΓΟΘΕСΙΉ|ΟΛΑΚΤΕΝΤ,|-ΤƩΗС-
Νικηφόρος πρωτοσπαθάριος ἐπὶ τοῦ Χρυσοτριγκλίνου, μυστογράφος καὶ χαρτουλάριος τοῦ στρατιωτικοῦ λογοθεσίου ὁ Λακτεντίτζης.

see the outlines of a shift from an equal number of *spatharioi, spatharokandidatoi* and *protospatharioi* in the second half of the tenth century, to an almost equal split of *spatharokandidatoi* and *protospatharioi* by c. 1000, to a majority of *protospatharioi*, five out of nine men, with just a single *spatharokandidatos* and three with no title c. 1000–c. 1066. Even with this progression the *chartoularioi* would have moved down the hierarchy as a whole from mostly the middle range until c. 1033 to the lowest levels by c. 1066.

It seems fair to say that the subordinates of the *logothetes tou stratiotikou* were largely *spatharokandidatoi* or *protospatharioi* by c. 1066, with most holding the latter title. While this looks like an upward move at first glance, when we take into account the changes underway in the system of titles, it was actually a demotion. Moreover, even for the *chartoularioi*, in the century after c. 966 there was no change in the upper dignity awarded to the personnel of the *sekreton*, which in an era of government reorganization and potential title inflation must be considered deterioration in their status.

3.1.1.5 *The* sekreton tou dromou

Σφραγὶς προέδρου καὶ κριτοῦ Κωνσταντίνου ᾧ φροντίς ἐστιν ἀκριτῶν καὶ τῶν δρόμων.

Seal of the proedros and judge Constantine whose duty it is to supervise the frontier dwellers and the highways.[53]

The *sekreton* of the *dromos* was one of the most important departments in the empire. The first mention of the *logothetes tou dromou* dates to 760 by which point he had taken over a large number of the duties that had once belonged to the bureau of the *magister officiorum* and the praetorian prefect, namely control of the *cursus publicus*, the public post, or *dromos* after which the department was named. The *logothetes* (director) was thus responsible for communication within the empire, including messengers and hostels, as well as foreign relations, from sending and receiving ambassadors, to accommodations for envoys and interpreters to help them once they reached Constantinople.[54] Oikonomides was of the opinion that the role of the public post, and the financial elements of the *sekreton tou dromou* involved with this, declined in the eleventh century, but that the *dromos* remained important because of its involvement with foreign relations.[55] Some confusion has arisen because of the inclusion on certain seals of the term *oxeis dromos*, rapid or fast post, as opposed to the slow post, *platys dromos*. Laurent considered that there were two separate departments: an ordinary and a rapid *dromos*.[56] However, I am inclined to agree with Nicolas Oikonomides, Werner Seibt and Michael Hendy in dismissing this idea.[57] There is no evidence, sigillographic or documentary, to indicate that *oxeis* was anything more than an epithet applied to the *sekreton* of the *dromos*, and infrequently at that. Moreover, as Hendy observed, there is no record of the *platys dromos* on seals, which there surely would have been had the distinction between the two services survived into the middle Byzantine period.[58]

Philotheos lists the staff of the *dromos* in descending order as the *logothetes* (director); the *protonotarios tou dromou*, literally the first clerk, but clearly more than this as he acted as the deputy of the *logothetes*; the *chartoularioi tou dromou* (recordkeepers of the post/department), fiscal and clerical officials; *episkeptitai* (inspector), who managed property attached to the *sekreton*; the *ermeneutai* (interpreters); *o kouratores tou apokrisiarikiou* (curators), the men who were responsible for the buildings reserved for ambassadors and messengers; *diatrechontes*; and *mandatores*.[59] That the *dromos* was an important, and in some ways unique, department, is demonstrated by the fact that more members of this *sekreton* were included in the *Escorial Taktikon* than any other. The *protonotarios* of the *dromos* is, in fact, the only *protonotarios* included in that work, which also records the position of the *chartoularios* of the *oxys dromos* as well.[60] Evidence for many of these officials is lacking, although it exists for some not found in the *taktika*, namely the *protomandator* and the *ek prosopou* (representative of the *dromos*). In the following section we will explore the status trajectories of the *logothetes*, the *protonotarios*, the *chartoularioi* and *notarioi*.

3.1.1.5.1 The logothetes tou dromou

> Θεοτόκε βοήθει τῷ σῷ δούλῳ Νικήτᾳ προέδρῳ καὶ λογοθέτῃ τοῦ δρόμου τῷ Ξυλινίτῃ.
>
> Theotokos, help your servant Niketas Xylinites, proedros and logothetes of the dromos.[61]

The *logothetai tou dromou* first appear in a source in 760 and were frequently the most important civil official in the empire.[62] According to *De Ceremoniis* the *logothetes* (director) met the emperor every morning in the throne room of the *Chrysotriklinos*.[63] As we would expect from the head of the *sekreton* involved with foreign relations, he was also involved in the reception of ambassadors and present when they met the emperor.[64] The evidence regarding the status of the *logothetes tou dromou* is not particularly abundant. He appears in a small number of written records, few of which preserve much information at all beyond a name. The exceptions are when a particularly powerful or important individual held the office, which we shall discuss shortly. There are only thirty-five seals which belonged to nineteen men from our period. Nonetheless, if we start with the *Escorial Taktikon*, then progress to the seals, a pattern does emerge of an office whose status was shaped by a few of the men who held it.

Determining the status of the *logothetes tou dromou* from any source is difficult, largely because a number of the men concerned were important before they filled the office, and their status did not come from their post but shaped the position of *logothetes tou dromou* for their successors. In this vein, we must see the late-ninth-century Stylianos Zaoutzes, who was father of the second wife of Leo VI and who was granted the title of *magistros*, and Leo Phokas, brother of Emperor Nikephoros II Phokas and *logothetes tou dromou* in the 960s. These were powerful men, and we can perhaps add Niketas Xylinites, given the post by Empress Theodora, who were of high-rank independent of their office. When we combine this issue with the unfortunately small number of seals of known office-holders, we must accept that any single individual can skew our understanding of the office and its place in the Byzantine system. On the other hand, that such important men were trusted with this office strongly suggests that it was crucial to the functioning of the government.

Figure 3.3 Seal of Niketas Xylinites, *proedros* and *logothetes tou dromou*. Dumbarton Oaks, Byzantine Collection, Washington, DC, BZS.1958.106.3238.
Niketas Xylinites belonged to one of the oldest families in Constantinople and was granted the office of logothetes tou dromou for his support of the Empress Theodora.
Rev. ΘΚΕROH.|ΤШCШΔΨ..|ΝΙΚΗΤΑΠ...|ΔΡШΣΛΟΓΟ.Є|ΤΗΤΟVΔΡΟ.|ΤШΙVΛΙΝΙ|ΤΗ
Θεοτόκε βοήθει τῷ σῷ δούλῳ Νικήτᾳ προέδρῳ λογοθέτῃ τοῦ δρόμου τῷ Ξυλινίτῃ.
Theotokos, help your servant Niketas Xylinites, *proedros* and *logothetes tou dromou*.

This impression is contradicted by the place of the *logothetes tou dromou* in the *Escorial Taktikon* where he is 132nd (total hierarchy) 109th (offices) in the hierarchy of the *axiai dia logou*, behind the *eparch* of Constantinople, the *sakellarios*, the *logothetes tou genikou* and *tou stratiotikou*, and the *koiaistor*. This is an odd position for an office so often given to men assumed either to be the power behind the throne or to have been in charge of the entire administrative structure of the empire. It is possible that the *Escorial Taktikon* is itself an inaccurate representation of the office. Two possible reasons for this inaccuracy are apparent: firstly, it was produced during the reign of John I Tzimiskes, who had usurped the throne of the brother of the *logothetes tou dromou*, Leo Phokas, and so perhaps the office was being humbled in the 970s; secondly, that the *Escorial Taktikon* presents the official hierarchy, but emperors could always grant powers to an official regardless of their supposed place in the system, and that for some reason the *logothetes tou dromou* was often their chosen means for creating a chief bureaucrat. Unfortunately, both of these possibilities lead us to the obvious question, why was the *logothetes* so powerful that he was the natural choice for 'prime minister' in the first place? The answer almost certainly lies in his position as a virtual foreign minister who also had control over the official lines of communication within the empire.

What is obvious from the seals is that the *logothetai tou dromou* were important throughout the period in question. In the early and mid-tenth century, seals record them holding the title of *patrikios*, at the time an important dignity at the top end of the hierarchy, sometimes in conjunction with the even more exalted title of *anthypatos*, or *anthypatos* and *protospatharios*, although a few individuals were *magistroi*. By the last third of the tenth century, the *logothetai* were usually *magistroi*. It seems like the first *logothetes* to be honoured with this high rank was the rather exceptional Leo Phokas. However, once the position of *logothetes tou dromou* was associated with the dignity of *magistros*, the two were linked. The well-known Symeon Logothetes was a *magistros*, as was a certain Lykastos, *magistros* and *vestes*, and John, *magistros*, *anthypatos*, *patrikios*, and imperial *spatharios*. Seals from the first third of the eleventh century confirm this transition to predominantly *magistroi*, although, Eustathios

Romaios, who attended the Synod of Patriarch Alexios Stoudites, held only the lower titles of *vestes*, *anthypatos* and *patrikios*.⁶⁵ Similarly, in 1055, the *logothetes* John was only a *vestarches*; however, his successor Niketas Xylinites, one of the men placed into a position of importance by Empress Theodora, and thus another special case in the mould of Leo Phokas, held the higher title of *proedros*.⁶⁶ As had happened with Leo, the appointment of an important imperial favourite to the office of *logothetes tou dromou* brought with it a new standard title, *proedros*, which was common for the remainder of the middle third of the century, when it was usually the highest title available to those outside of the imperial family.⁶⁷

Earlier we see a gradual promotion once the level of *magistros* had been attained. Leo Phokas and Symeon and their successors should have received *rogai* of 16 pounds of *nomismata*. John *vestarches* was given a *roga* of 14 pounds, which seems like the beginning of a decline, although Niketas Xylinites, as *proedros*, received 28 pounds of gold. While we should remember that Xylinites was particularly close to Theodora, and thus may have been given a title that reflected more than the importance of his office, *proedros* became, as far as we can tell from our limited material, the usual dignity attached to the office of *logothetes tou dromou* for the rest of the period. Just as the appointment of Leo Phokas had seen a permanent jump in the titles attached to the office in the 960s, so too, apparently, did the rise of Niketas Xylinites nearly a century later. Until his appearance on the scene, in 1055, the position of *logothetes tou dromou* had been rather steady in terms of both status and income, being damaged slightly financially by the devaluations which occurred in the 1040s and 1050s. By moving from *magistros* to *proedros*, Xylinites not only wiped away these losses; he vastly increased his income. In terms of status little changed, the move from *magistros* to *proedros* was a promotion of but one step in the hierarchy. The *logothetes tou dromou* was, and remained, an important man c. 966–c. 1066, but although his income increased greatly after 1055, his status did not. There appears to have been a certain stability to his position in the bureaucratic hierarchy, as well as the imperial one. Having said this, time and again the *logothetei tou dromou* were involved in decisions that would seem to have been above their level or influence based on their titles and the position of their office in the hierarchy. This was certainly the case with Leo Phokas acting as prime minister, John, who was a member of the deathbed discussion with Constantine IX about who should succeed him to the throne, and Niketas Xylinites, who not only was rewarded for helping Theodora come to the throne, but was one of the five men who met to choose her successor in 1056.⁶⁸

3.1.1.5.2 The subordinates of the logothetes tou dromou

> Κύριε βοήθει τῷ σῷ δούλῳ Ἀνδρέᾳ βασιλικῷ πρωτοσπαθαρίῳ καὶ ἐπὶ τοῦ χρυσοτρικλίνου καὶ χαρτουλαρίῳ τοῦ ὀξέου δρόμου.

> Lord, help your servant Andreas, imperial protospatharios and epi tou chrysotriklinou and chartoularios of the oxys dromos.⁶⁹

Few seals have survived which belonged to the men who worked under the *logothetes tou dromou*, and even fewer where a particular office is represented by more than one or two seals. For instance the *protonotarios* of the *dromos*, deputy of the *logothetes*, who appeared in the *Escorial Taktikon* in 172nd (total hierarchy) 149th (offices) place, is represented by only five seals belonging to five men dated c. 966–c. 1066; three were *protospatharioi*, two recorded no title. Their juniors, the *imperial notarioi tou dromou* are even more sparsely represented, with three seals belonging to three men, one *protospatharios* and one *patrikios* from the first half of the eleventh century, and one with no title from the middle third of the century. The *chartoularioi* of the *dromos*, *Escorial Taktikon* 176th (total hierarchy) 153rd (offices), have left behind slightly more evidence of their work, fourteen seals owned by thirteen men, displaying a quite consistent pattern of titles: three *protospatharioi* and two *spatharokandidatoi* dated to the last third of the tenth century, a *spatharokandidatos*, two *protospatharioi*, and a *patrikios* dated to the decades around the year 1000, and a *protospatharios* and an *anthypatos*, *patrikios*, and *protospatharios* from the first third of the eleventh century. The impression that these seals give is that the clerical positions in the department of the *dromos* were rather consistently *protospatharioi* in c. 966–c. 1066, with some few individuals falling slightly lower in the hierarchy, *spatharokandidatoi*, or slightly higher, *patrikioi*, but with little change in their status across the century covered by this chapter.

3.1.2 The treasuries

> What was given as extra items from the department of the Vestiarion to the droung-garios of the fleet for the Cretan expedition.
>
> 150 crowbars, 130 bolts/lynch-pins for the chelandia, 12 iron slings, 240 mallets, 300 mattocks.[70]

3.1.2.1 *The* sakellion

> Subject to the chartoularios of the sakellion are ten kinds of titles, namely: impe-rial notarioi of the sekreton, protonotarioi of the themes, xendochoi, the zygostates, metretai, gerokomoi, chartoularioi of the oikon, protokankellarios, kankellarioi, and the domestikos of the Thymeles.[71]

By the end of the ninth century at the latest, the *sakellion* was a department with diverse functions. It had begun life as the *sacellum*, a part of the *sacrum cubiculum*, and like all of the other *sekreta* discussed in this chapter had evolved in the seventh or eighth centuries into an independent department with expanded responsibilities and increased status.[72] The earliest descriptions of the new department date to the seventh century and describe the *sakellion* as a treasury for coins. However, the staff listed as working at the *sakellion* by Philotheos include more than just treasury officials, indicating the broad responsibilities of the department by the end of the ninth century. In descending order underneath the *chartoularios* (recordkeeper) of the *sakellion*, Philotheos listed the imperial *notarioi* (clerks) of the *sekreton*; the *protonotarioi* (first clerks) of the themes; the *xenodochoi* (guest house director), officials in charge of hostels and hospitals for travellers, the sick and the poor; a *zygostates* (lit. weigher with a balance), a man in charge of the weight of coins; *metretai*, men responsible for measures; *gerokomoi*, responsible for charitable institutions caring for the elderly and infirm poor; *chartoularioi* of the *oikon*; a *protokankellarios*; *kankellarioi*; and a *domestikos tes Thymeles*, a financial official in charge of payments for public entertainment.[73] Between the composition of the *Kletorologion of Philotheos* and the *Escorial Taktikon* the vocabulary used for the head of the *sakellion* changed. Where Philotheos recorded a *chartoularios tou sakelliou*, the *Taktikon* mentions the *ho tou sakelliou*, which appears on the seals in various guises as *epi tes sakelles*, *sakelles* and *epi tou basilikes sakelles*.[74] There is no reason to think that this was anything more than a change in terminology, which, as noted earlier, can be observed in a number of departments.

3.1.2.1.1 The epi tes sakelles

Δούλῳ βοήθει σῷ γένει στρατηγέτα Μιχαὴλ βέστῃ, κριτῇ τοῦ βήλου καὶ ἐπὶ τῆς βασιλικῆς σακέλλης.

Commander of the heavenly host, with your kind come to the aid of your servant Michael vestes, judge of the Velum, and epi tes imperial sakelles.[75]

In the *Escorial Taktikon*, the *epi tes sakelles* (lit. of the *sakellion*) occupied the 140th (total hierarchy) 117th (offices) position, making him the eighth highest-ranking bureaucrat, and the highest placed of the three heads of treasuries. Too few seals of the chief of the *sakellion* survive for the data to be normalized. There are only twenty-six seals belonging to seventeen men. Nonetheless a pattern emerges from the inscriptions on the few surviving seals. Of the nine men who lived wholly or partly between c. 966 and c. 1033 the seals of all but three records that their highest title was that of *anthypatos*, usually, but not always, paired with *patrikios*, and more often than not also with *protospatharios*. Of the exceptions, two were *protospatharioi*, and two chose not to include their titles on their seals. For the middle third of the eleventh century two of the five known *epi tes sakelles* were *vestarchai*, one a *vestes*, one a *protospathrios*, and one a *magistros* and *vestes*. In terms of status, the *epi tes sakelles* who were *anthypatoi* occupied the lowest position in the top third of the hierarchy in the late-tenth- and early-eleventh-century hierarchy, exactly the same place as the mid-eleventh century *vestarchai*. From c. 966 to c. 1033 the range of *roga* payments was 1 pound of *nomismata* for a *protospatharios* up to 8 pounds for an *anthypatos*. In the middle of the century the range was from 1 pound to 28, but with the most common *roga* being 14 pounds for the *vestarchai*, figures similar to those for the earlier period. Although we are dealing with fewer pieces of evidence than is ideal, the case of the *epi tes sakelles* looks like a textbook example of an office responding to title inflation and currency debasement. The changes in the dignities attached to the office, and the corresponding *roga* payments, meant that successive generations of office-holders held their place in the hierarchy and kept their income steady.

3.1.2.1.2 *The subordinates of the* epi tes sakelles

> Κύριε βοήθει τῷ σῷ δούλῳ Βασιλείῳ σπαθαροκανδιδάτῳ καὶ πρωτονοταρίῳ τῆς σακέλλης.
>
> Lord, help your servant Basil, spatharokandidatos and protonotarios of the sakelle.[76]

By comparison to their superior little is known about the men who worked for the *sakellion*, but the seals of a small number of *protonotarioi* and *notarioi* have survived. The database which forms the foundation of this study contains eleven seals belonging to *protonotarioi* from this period. Six of these seals belonged to one man, Leo, *spatharokandidatos* and *protonotarios* of the *sakelle*.[77] Like Leo, half of the known *protonotarioi* who lived c. 966–c. 1066 were *spatharokandidatoi* who held just one office. One slightly earlier *protonotarios*, Nikephoros, was an *imperial protospatharios*.[78] However, he was also the judge of the theme of Charsianon, which explains his higher dignity. The final seal from the period is that of Stephen, who chose not to place a title on his seal, and also served as an *asekretis*.[79] The lower ranked *notarioi* are represented by fifteen seals struck by ten men from our period. In terms of their titles the situation is very similar to that observed for the *notarioi* in the other *sekreta*, an early division between *spatharokandidatoi* and *protospatharioi*, skewing more in favour of the latter as the eleventh century progressed. The one exception is a seal belonging to a Theophanes *spatharios* dated to the second quarter of the eleventh century.[80]

3.1.2.2 *The* vestiariou

> Subject to the chartoularios of the vestiarion are ten kinds of titles, namely: imperial notarioi of the sekreton, kentarchos, legatarios, archon of the money, exartistes, chartoularios, kouratores, chosbaitai, protomandator, mandatores.[81]

As with the *sakellion*, with which it probably developed in parallel, the *vestiarion* began life as a sub-department of a larger unit, in this case the *sacrum vestiarium* and the *comitiva sacrarum largitionum* respectively, which, during the seventh or eighth century, became independent and took over many of the functions of its former home, perhaps most notably control of the mint.[82] The *vestiarion* was a treasury and storehouse for precious objects and materials, sometimes coins.[83] Interestingly, the *vestiarion* was also the place where naval supplies were kept.[84] The *chartoularios tou vestiariou* (recordkeeper of the *vestiarion*) was the head of the *sekreton*. Below him were the *imperial notarioi tou sekretou* (clerks of the department); the *kentarchos* (centurion); the *legatarios* (legate); the *archon tes charages* (lit. the *archon* (leader) of the money), the official in charge of minting coins; the *exartistes*, officials involved in the running of the naval facilities in Constantinople; the *chartoularioi* (recordkeeprs); the *kouratores* (curators); the *chosbaitai*, officials responsible for the precious objects stored in the *vestiarion*; the *protomandator*; and the *mandatores*.[85]

3.1.2.2.1 The epi tou vestiariou

> Θεοτόκε βοήθει τῷ σῷ δούλῳ Λέοντι βασιλικῷ πρωτοσπαθαρίῳ ἐπὶ τοῦ Χρυσοτρικλίνου καὶ ἐπὶ τοῦ βεστιαρίου.
>
> Theotokos, help your servant Leo, imperial protospatharios epi tou Chrysotriklinou and epi tou vestiariou.[86]

In the *Escorial Taktikon* the *epi tou vestiariou*, an official recorded as the *chartoularios tou vestiariou* by Philotheos falls four places lower in the hierarchy than his equivalent at the *sakellion*.[87] Like the *epi tou sakelliou*, the number of seals belonging to the *epi tou vestiariou* is small, only fourteen seals recording the work of eleven men. The similarities with the *epi tes sakelles* are limited to the numbers of seals. In terms of status the *epi tou vestiariou* were far behind their counterpart in the latter part of the tenth and early eleventh century. All of the seals dated to this period record the title of *protospatharios*, placing the *epi tou vestiariou* firmly in the middle of the hierarchy with a *roga* of 1 pound of *nomismata*. Starting in the second third of the eleventh century, the *protospatharioi* began to disappear and a new generation of men held the titles of *magistros*, *vestes*, alone and with *patrikios*, and *anthypatos* and *patrikios*. These dignities demonstrate that by c. 1050-60 the *epi tou vestiariou* had moved from the middle of the hierarchy to the top of the middle third or bottom of the upper third of the ladder, a promotion just in excess of what we might expect to compensate for title inflation, putting them slightly ahead of their counterparts at the *sakellion*. In financial terms the change was even more profound with the *roga* for an *anthypatos* of 8 pounds and for a *magistros* of 16 pounds of *nomismata histamenon*. The sigillographic evidence, meagre as it is, would suggest that the position of the *epi tou vestiariou* was becoming more important over time. Rather than standing still like the *epi tes sakelles*, the head of the *vestiarion* was advancing up the imperial hierarchy.

3.1.2.3 The eidikon

> Subject to the epi tou eidikou logou are four kinds of titles, namely: imperial notarioi of the sekreton, archons of the workshops, hebdomarioi, and meizoteroi of the workshops.[88]

The treasury of the *eidikon* likely traces its roots back to the special treasury, the *idike trapeza*, of the praetorian prefecture of the East.[89] It is referred to in the written sources as both the *eidikon* and the *idikon*. These two names were used interchangeably, and would have sounded the same when spoken, but each describes a particular function of the treasury as both special, *idikon*, and dealing with taxes paid in kind, *eidikon*.[90] In its original incarnation the *eidikon* had been the place where payments to the state in kind had been gathered, and it retained this function into the period under consideration here.[91] In its later guise the *eidikon* first appears in the sources in the ninth century, but, like the *genikon*, it had existed as its own department at some point in the seventh or eighth century.[92] It held the money from which the *rogai* of the officials and dignitaries of the empire were paid, and it is possible that the fee which people paid to the state for lower-ranking titles was deposited there.⁹³ As well as money the *eidikon* held goods produced by the imperial workshops and treasures such as gold and silks.⁹⁴ Monies and materials were diverted from the *eidikon* for the outfitting a number of naval expeditions, the surviving documentation for which from this bureau is recorded in *De Ceremoniis*.⁹⁵ The detailed lists of provisions sent on these rather exceptional military expeditions highlight another primary function of the *eidikon*, the production and distribution of military materials to the Byzantine army, both the *tagamata* and the themes.⁹⁶

The staff of the *eidikon* included, the *eidikos*, the controller of the treasury; the imperial *notarioi tou sekretou* (clerks of the department); the *archontes ton ergodosion* (leaders of the workshops), who were in charge of the imperial workshops, which included the *archon tes armamenton* responsible for the production of military equipment and the *archon ton chrysocheion*, overseer of the goldsmiths in imperial employ; the *hebdomarioi*; and the *meizoteroi ton ergodosion*, who had some responsibility over the imperial workshops and the production of silks.

3.1.2.3.1 *The* eidikos

Θεοτόκε βοήθει τῷ σῷ δούλῳ Ἰωάννῃ πρωτοσπαθαρίῳ καὶ ἐπὶ τοῦ εἰδικοῦ τῷ Ῥαδηνῷ.

*Theotokos, help your servant John Radenos, protospatharios and epi tou eidikou.*⁹⁷

The seals and documents which refer to the head of the *eidikon* use variants of his title: *eidikos, epi tou eidikou logou* and *logothetes tou eidikou* are the most frequently observed, with the latter appearing in the eleventh century.⁹⁸ As many of the office-holders referred to as epi tou/tes/ton something in later sources are termed *chartoularioi* in the *Kletorologion of Philotheos*, it is possible that, like the heads of the treasuries of the *sakellion* and the *vestiarion*, the *eidikos* started life as a *chartoularios* (recordkeeper). If so, his promotion to the higher office of *logothetes* (director) in the eleventh century would indicate an overall elevation of his *sekreton*. In the *Escorial Taktikon* the *eidikos* is listed in 151st (total hierarchy) 128th (offices) place, seven rungs lower down that ladder than the *epi tou vestiariou*. The seals struck by the *eidikoi* show a relatively familiar career progression. Few examples survive: only thirty-one seals belonging to twenty-one men. Twenty-six seals belonging to ten men date to either the last third of the tenth century or the first third of the eleventh, and all record the title of *protospatharios* and the single office of *eidikos*. Seals struck in the first half and middle third of the eleventh century display a greater variety of titles: two *protospatharioi*, two *vestes*, one *patrikios* and *hypatos*, who was also a judge of the Hippodrome, and one *vestarches*, with two men choosing to place no dignity on their seals.⁹⁹ This is not a great deal of data on which to rely, and we must remember that in our assessment of seals by third of a century there is considerable overlap between seals dated to the first half of the eleventh century and those dated to the middle third of the century. With that in mind it appears as if the usual title associated with the *eidikos* until c. 1033 was *protospatharios*, and that in the middle third of the eleventh century the position of the office improved considerably, with *vestes* becoming the most common associated dignity.[100] This means that an *eidikos* living in c. 1050 would have held a title that was higher in the ranks than his predecessor of c. 1000, but due to the introduction of more titles by c. 1060 he would have been at the same level as his equivalent from sixty years earlier. In terms of *rogai* this meant an increase from seventy-two *nomismata* in the first third of the century to 864 *nomismata* in the middle third. In terms of status and income the *eidikos* ranked third among the three chiefs of the treasuries.

3.1.2.3.2 The subordinates of the Eidikos

> Κύριε βοήθει τῷ σῷ δούλῳ Θεοδώρῳ πρωτοσπαθαρίῳ καὶ βασιλικῷ νοταρίῳ τοῦ εἰδικοῦ λόγου.
>
> Lord, help your servant Theodore, protospatharios and imperial notarios of the eidikos logos.[101]

There is one broadly dated surviving seal of a *protonotarios* of the *eidikos*, which records that its owner held the rank of *protospatharios*.[102] For the imperial *notarioi* and *notarioi* we are slightly more fortunate: twenty seals survive dated c. 966–c. 1066, which belonged to nineteen people. The *notarioi* living in the tenth century all held the title of *spatharokandidatos*. Those who struck their seals in the first two-thirds of the eleventh century recorded an almost even split 5:4:4 of *protospatharioi*, *spatharokandidatoi* and no title. The sole exception was a lone *patrikios*, c. 1033–c. 1066, who received his title because he was also *praitor* of Constantinople. These seals seem to show a slight elevation of the titles awarded to the *notarioi* at the beginning of the eleventh century, which saw the average *roga* increase from half a pound of *nomismata* to a pound. In terms of their dignities, the *notarioi* of the *eidikon* remained constant for two-thirds of a century while the system changed around them. As with the *eidikos* himself the rest of the staff of the *eidikon* performed worse than their contemporaries in the other treasuries.

3.1.3 Pious foundations, fiscal lands and crown estates

> Κύριε βοήθει τῷ σῷ δούλῳ Ἰωάννῃ προέδρῳ καὶ ἐφόρῳ.
>
> Lord, help your servant John, proedros and ephor.[103]

Discussions of the management of the lands owned by the Byzantine government in the eleventh century quickly became complex to the point where enthusiasts of the word 'byzantine' with a lower-case 'b' will start to nod and smile knowingly. Part of the confusion stems from the three categories of land under consideration. Pious foundations or charitable institutions, *euageis oikoi*, were usually attached to monasteries or churches and drew income from lands attached to them. They could be either imperial or private foundations. Fiscal lands were properties absorbed into the fisc through a number of processes, notably *klasma*, the failure of the owner to pay tax. Crown estates were lands that had usually, though not exclusively, come into imperial possession through conquest. Romanos I Lekapenos began the trend of turning newly acquired territory into crown estates after the conquest of Melitene in 934 and the process continued into the eleventh century.[104] All three categories of property would have generated important revenues and resources for the imperial government.[105] All three classes of land were administered by different bureaus. The organization and relative importance of these changed over time, and it is to this process that we now turn.

3.1.3.1 *The* euageis oikoi

Κύριε βοήθει τῷ σῷ δούλῳ Θεοδώρῳ πρωτοσπαθαρίῳ, οἰκονόμῳ τῶν εὐαγῶν καὶ ἀναγραφεῖ Παφλαγονίας τῷ Καραμάλλῳ.

Lord, help your servant Theodore Karamallos, protospatharios, oikonomos of the pious foundations and anagrapheus of Paphlagonia.[106]

By 1001–19, individual *euageis oikoi* (charitable institutions, usually of a religious nature) were administered by an *oikonomos* (manager), a bureaucrat independent from and perhaps superior to the ecclesiastical or monastic staff of the institution, who reported to the *oikonomos ton euagon oikon*, sometimes termed *megas*.[107] The *megas oikonomos* (great manager) led a department consisting of *chartoularioi* (recordkeepers) and *notarioi* (clerks) who had been in place since at least the ninth century, as well as a deputy, *antiprosopon*, and a *deuteros*.[108] The sigillographic data for most of the officials in the central bureaus are dated to the period that we shall discuss in the next section. The opposite is true, however, for the *megas oikonomos* himself. The earliest seals, dated to the decades on either side of 1033 record the title of *protospatharios*, while those from c. 1050 have more variety: *protospatharios, patrikios, anthypatos* and *patrikios, vestes, anthypatos* and *patrikios*, and *vestarches*.[109] Although the limited amount of evidence (only ten seals owned by seven men) does not allow for firm conclusions, it is fair to say that the *oikonomos* was not adversely effected by title inflation. A *protospatharios* of c. 1033 occupied roughly the same spot in the middle of the hierarchy as a *patrikios* of c. 1050, or an *anthypatos* of c. 1060. The titles of *vestes* and *vestarches* marked a noticeable increase in status in both 1050 and 1060. The income of the *oikonomoi* increased in line with their new titles, from seventy-two *nomismata* for the *protospatharioi* in the first third of the eleventh century, to between 864 and 1,008 for the later *vestai* and *vestarchai*. Through donations many *euageis oikoi* became rich, and those founded by the emperors operated under the same tax status as fiscal lands. Any surplus above operating costs went to the emperor, which meant that these charitable foundations became significant sources of income.[110] The wealth generated by the *euageis oikoi* made them valuable gifts that were given by the emperors to their followers. Constantine IX Monomachos famously gave his chief minister Constantine Leichoudes the property of the Mangana.[111] Later, Isaac I was so determined to bring the income from this gift back to the fisc that he reportedly made its return a condition for the elevation of Leichoudes to the patriarchate.

3.1.3.2 Fiscal lands

Κύριε βοήθει Λέοντι πρωτοσπαθαρίῳ καὶ βασιλικῷ νοταρίῳ τῶν οἰκειακῶν.

Lord, help Leo, protospatharios and imperial notarios ton oikeiakon.[112]

Fiscal land fell under the jurisdiction of the *genikon*, the department responsible for assessing and collecting defaulted-upon land tax. This was certainly the case in 972/3 when the subordinate of the *logothetes*, the *oikeiakos*, was responsible for fiscal lands.[113] By 1032 at the latest, the written material provides evidence for a transformation of the management of fiscal lands with the appearance of the *epi ton oikeiakon* (lit. of the household), sometimes known as the *logothetes ton oikeiakon* with a separate *sekreton* independent of the *genikon*.[114] Both Leo the Deacon and Michael Psellos relate that Basil II (976–1025) implemented a policy of increasing the amount of fiscal lands, and Oikonomides linked the creation of the new *sekreton* to this change.[115]

While Oikonomides's reasoning makes perfect sense, it finds little support in the sigillographic material, not because the seals contradict his hypothesis, but because there are so few seals that can be reliably attributed to the new *sekreton*. The first problem is with the office of *epi ton oikeiakon*, head of the eponymous *sekreton*. Unfortunately, and this is one for the lower-case 'byzantine' enthusiasts, *epi ton oikeiakon* could refer to three things: a member of the imperial household, a class of certain titles (notably *protospatharios*) and the head of the new *sekreton*. Distinguishing between these three on seals is not easy.[116] Obviously, there is a clear difference between someone who was *protospatharios epi ton oikeiakon* and a person who was *protospatharios* and *epi ton oikeiakon*. The inclusion of 'and' splits the term in half, letting us know that we are dealing with two separate statements about the owner of the seal. Unfortunately, this accounts for less than a third of the seals in question. We are still left with two possible identifications, the office or a member of the imperial household. That all-important 'and' is present on seals dated long before the office of the *epi ton oikeiakon* in the sense with which we are concerned existed. Similarly, we find *epi ton oikieakon* listed with other offices, separating it from the dignities on seals dated before the eleventh century, so we cannot use this to differentiate between its possible meanings.[117]

In short, although there are many seals with inscriptions labelling their owner as *epi ton oikeiakon*, exactly what they meant is unclear. It seems slightly cowardly to leave things there and move on. I will instead present the seals most likely to have belonged to holders of the office of *epi ton oikeiakon*, those dating from the eleventh century with a gap between title and office. From the huge total numbers I can identify eighteen seals belonging to nine men, five of whom lived in this period, with a further three spanning this and the following period. Two were *protospatharioi*, one active in 1032.[118] By the second quarter of the eleventh century, Basil Aboudemos held the higher titles of *anthypatos* and *patrikios*, and he was also judge of the Velum, though the order of his offices on the seal suggests that his estate management responsibilities outranked his judicial ones.[119] Likely linked to this period were two other men: one a *patrikios* and *protospatharios*, the other a *vestes*.[120] This brings us to the three men living in the third quarter of the eleventh century: one *vestes*, one *vestarches* and *hypatos* and one *magistros*.¹²¹ From roughly the same period is a seal of the *antiprosopon* of the *epi ton oikeiakon*, Basil Tzirithon *anthypatos* and *patrikios*.¹²² The lowest-level officials in the *sekreton* were the imperial *notarioi*, evidence for five of whom has survived from seals for the period up to c. 1066. Of the five, three were *protospatharioi* and two recorded no titles on their seals.¹²³ It will be noted that the titles held by the *epi ton oikeiakon* almost exactly mirrored those of the *megas oikonomos* discussed earlier, while the imperial *notarioi* held titles equivalent to their counterparts in other *sekreta*.

3.1.3.3 Crown lands

Κύριε βοήθει τῷ σῷ δούλῳ Ἰωάννῃ πρωτοσπαθαρίῳ ἐπὶ τοῦ Χρυσοτρικλίνου καὶ βασιλικῷ νοταρίῳ τῶν ἀποδείξεων τοῦ σεκρέτου τοῦ ἐφόρου τῷ Ἀργυρῷ.

Lord, help your servant John Argyros, protospatharios epi tou Chrysotriklinou and imperial notarios of the receipts of the sekreton of the ephoros.¹²⁴

At some point the *megas kourator* (great curator) was likely placed in charge of the majority of crownlands throughout the empire. The *megas kourator* appeared under Basil I, but the department, in one guise or another, had existed since the sixth century.¹²⁵ He is mentioned in the *Kletorologion of Philotheos* as the head of the *megas kouratorikion* (great department in charge of imperial estates), and he appears in the later *Escorial Taktikon*. On his staff were lesser *kouratores* (curators) and *episkeptitai* (inspectors) who managed imperial properties in the provinces and the capital. However, he was not responsible for all imperial holdings. Individual palaces and monasteries had their own estates from which they drew their resources, and their own *kouratores*, who were sometimes termed *megas*. A number of new departments were set up to manage these palace estates, independent of the *megas kourator*, such as that of the *kouratorikion* of the Mangana which took its final form under Basil I (867–86).¹²⁶ A good example is that of a certain George, owner of a well-known seal in the Dumbarton Oaks collection, which records him as *protospatharios epi tou Chrysotriklinou* and *megas kourator* of the imperial monastery.¹²⁷ George was a *megas kourator*, but not the *megas kourator*. *Kouratores* like George were responsible for lands attached to charitable or religious foundation but were not themselves clerics. While slightly more complex than the situation had been around the time of Philotheos, this is how things sat at the beginning of our period in c. 966. Few seals have survived to provide information about any of the men who supervised imperial estates and worked in Constantinople.¹²⁸

At some point in the early eleventh century the process of managing imperial estates became much more complicated. It is entirely understandable why this should be the case. Between 955 and the death of Basil II in 1025, the Byzantine Empire expanded on virtually every front, and, following in the tradition started by Romanos I in the early tenth century, much of that new land was taken into state ownership. One might expect the increase in the amount of land owned by the crown to have granted the *megas kourator* a certain job security. However, the last time that he appears in the written material is 1012, and he vanishes from the sigillographic record at about the same time.¹²⁹

Figure 3.4 Seal of Theodore *patrikios* and *ephoros*. Dumbarton Oaks, Byzantine Collection, Washington, DC, BZS.1955.1.2143.
Obv. +ΘΚΕ|.ΟΗΘΕΙ|ΤѠCѠΔᕼ|ΛѠ
Rev. ΘΕΟΔ.Ρ,ΠΑΤΡ.Κ,ΣΕΦ.ΡѠ
Θεοτόκε βοήθει τῷ σῷ δούλῳ Θεοδώρῳ πατρικίῳ καὶ ἐφόρῳ.
Theotokos, help your servant Theodore, *patrikios* and *ephoros*.

The eleventh century was one of great change for the management of crown lands. In place of the *megas kourator* the emperors appointed the *ephoros ton basilikon kouratorion* (overseer of the imperial estates).[130] He was certainly in office by 1044, the exact date of creation is unknown, and seals have survived from a variety of offices attached to his *sekreton*, mostly dated to before c. 1066. Seals of six *ephoroi* (overseers) survive from this period, one *patrikios*, a *vestes*, *anthypatos*, and *patrikios*, a *magistros*, one *magistros* and *vestes*, and a *proedros*.[131] This evidence suggests that after a rather humble start, the *ephoroi* were promoted to the level of *magistros* by c. 1040, and largely maintained that dignity to the end of the middle third of the eleventh century. Seals also give us a window into the workings of the department of the *ephoros* and the relative status of his subordinates. The early-eleventh-century *antiprosopon* (deputy) of the *sekreton* of the *ephoros*, Polyeuktos, was a *patrikios*.[132] From the mid-century we know of two *protonotarioi*, a *domestikos* of the *ephoros* and three imperial *notarioi*, all *protospatharioi* except for one of the *notarioi* who was a *spatharokandidatos*.[133] The provincial structure of *kouratoreiai* and *episkepseis* (categories of imperial estates) with which the old *megas kourator* would have been familiar remained intact, they just reported to a new central department. Sadly, we know almost nothing about this department beyond the information from the seals.

3.1.4 Administering an enlarged Byzantium

Sakellarioi, logothetai of the genikon or stratiotikon, those of the sakellion and vestiarion, oikonomoi of the pious foundations, epi ton oikeiakon, and ephors of the imperial kouratorion, eidikoi, gerotrophoi, those of the divine treasury of the Phylax, kouratores of the houses of Eleutherios and Mangana, oikistikoi, and other protonotarioi, logariastai, chartoularioi, imperial notarioi, and notarioi.[134]

The story of the *logothesia*, *sekreta* and treasuries largely seems to set a pattern within which the title inflation and currency debasement of the eleventh century can be seen in operation. Most of the heads of bureaus, the *epi tes sakelles* is a perfect example, were promoted so as to avoid the worst effects of title inflation. It is notable just how often the most important men in each department were promoted progressively throughout the eleventh century to a level that kept them in roughly the same place in the evolving hierarchy. Of course, when we turn to income such promotions greatly increased the *rogai* of many officials. Preserving the status of its employees must have placed an ever-increasing financial burden on the state. However, it is worth noting that all of the offices for which we have evidence of such promotions were held by only one man at a time, and although titles and their *rogai* remained in force after the individual left his position in the bureaucracy, we are not talking about hundreds of men benefitting from higher *rogai* at any one time, more like dozens. We see exactly the same process when we turn to the three new departments set up to manage imperial estates. The *oikonomos* and the *epi ton oikeiakon* began life as *protospatharioi* and moved gradually up the ranks in line with title inflation, perhaps even slightly ahead of it in a few cases. The *ephoros* appears in the sources later, once title inflation was well under way, but jumped into the hierarchy at a level which made him the equivalent of the *oikonomos* and the *epi ton oikeiakon*.

The majority of the offices where more than one man might hold them, such as the lower-clerical positions in the *sekreta*, saw either stagnation or slight promotion revolving around the dignity of *protospatharios*. In financial terms it is impossible to know whether the gradual decrease in the amount of gold paid in the *rogai* to the *protospatharioi* made up for the increased number of men with that title. It is equally beyond our ability to discover how many of these men paid to become *protospatharioi*. In terms of status, it is clear that a title which had been frequently awarded to those in the upper echelons of the Byzantine system was increasingly open to men who had once been relegated to the lower ranks of *spatharokandidatos* and *spatharios*, or who had possessed no title at all. It is not hard to imagine the pressure that this would place as the earlier holders of this formerly elite title demanded to be moved up the ladder away from the newly promoted clerks and bookkeepers. The exceptions to the rule described earlier are the deputies of the *epi ton oikeiakon* and the *ephoros* who held titles above *protospatharios*, namely *anthypatos* and *patrikios* respectively. Although we know frustratingly little about these offices, it is interesting that these deputies held higher titles than their contemporaries in other departments, even the *protonotarios* of the *dromos*, one of the most important second-in-commands in the administration. This might be an indication that although the bureaus created to oversee estate management have left behind little evidence, they were highly valued.

There are a few exceptions to this general picture of slight promotion and treading water, namely the *epi tou vestiariou*, the *eidikos*, the *sakellarios* and the *logothetes tou dromou*. The *epi tou vestiariou* moved up the ranks ahead of inflation, a process which might signal the increasing importance of his treasury in relation to the *sakellion* (stagnant), and *eidikon* (slipping backwards). He was in fact the holder of the highest dignities among all of the treasury chiefs. The *eidikon* meanwhile was one of the few departments to see a decline in the status of everyone who worked there, from the *eidikos* down to the lowest *notarios*. The year 1066 saw them with titles in a lower place in the hierarchy than ever before. Meanwhile the *sakellarios*, who was the second highest ranking bureaucrat in the *Escorial Taktikon*, had seen the titles associated with his position slip from the top of the hierarchy into the lowest third in the course of approximately sixty years. It is possible that the *logothetes ton sekreton*, about which more in the following section, appeared as a general controller of the administration under Constantine IX in the mid-eleventh century before being regularized under Alexios I three decades later.[135] It is possible that the significant drop in the number of seals and the status of the *sakellarios* seen in the sigillographic record supports this conclusion. The *logothetes tou dromou* also bucked all of the trends observed for the other offices in this chapter, but as I said earlier, his was always a unique position, both in terms of its power and the way that the emperors used it to fulfil the role of chief minister. More than any other office in this study, it was shaped by the men who held it, an interesting example of the personal nature of power in Byzantium, and the degree to which an important man, or series of important men, could leave their mark on an office.

3.2 Slipping backwards: The imperial chancery

> *The chartoularios of the inkstand has no subordinates as he serves alone ... Subject to the protoasekretis are thee kinds of ranks, namely: asekretai, imperial notarioi, the dekanos.*[136]

Now we come to a group of officials that have often been grouped together under headings such as the chancery, or the imperial secretariat. This is perhaps misleading for two reasons. Firstly, there is some question over the exact function of a number of these officials, specifically the *mystikos*, *mystographos* and *mystolektes*, and the chancery might not have been their home. Secondly, using a term like chancery gives the impression that the officials worked in a unified department. As seen in the quote from Philotheos with which this section opened this is demonstrably untrue. Leaving aside the reporting structure of the three secretive officials mentioned earlier, we know that the *protoasekretis* was head of a *sekreton*, but that this did not include the *epi ton deeseon* or the *epi tou kanikleiou*, who were independent officials acting alone. What we have here are a number of officials, working in different departments or alone, who were concerned with the production of imperial documents, or other secretarial duties related to the emperor. For now, chancery is a useful catch-all term for these men. One final point needs to be made about the offices we are shortly to investigate; as a whole they constitute the single group with the most regular access to the imperial presence of any that we will discuss in this study. As such there are an interesting case study in the relationship between status and rank and proximity to the emperor. We will turn to these officials in the order in which they appear in the *Escorial Taktikon*, beginning with the *epi tou kanikleiou*, then the *protoasekretis* and his *sekreton*, then the *mystikos*, *mystographos*, *epi ton deeseon* and finally the *mystolektes*.

3.2.1 The *epi tou kanikeliou*

Λέοντι βασιλικῷ πρωτοσπαθαρίῳ καὶ ἐπὶ τοῦ κανικλείου.

Leo, imperial protospatharios and epi tou kanikleiou.[137]

We begin with the *epi tou kanikleiou*, also known as the *kanikleios* or the *chartoularios tou kanikleiou*, the keeper of the Imperial Inkstand.[138] He occupied the 145th (total hierarchy) 122nd (offices) place in the *Escorial Taktikon*.[139] As the name of the office suggests, the *epi tou kanikleiou* was responsible for the imperial stationary, which on the surface does not seem like it would convey great power on its holder.[140] However, many powerful men held the position of *epi tou kanikleiou*, beginning with the first-known holder of the office Theoktistos in the ninth century.[141] Not only did his duties mean that the *epi tou kanikeliou* was present when the emperor signed laws, acts and *chrysobulls*, he had some say over their content and authenticated them with his own signature. He did not run a *sekreton* of his own, as he had no need for one. His power came from his close connection and frequent contact with the emperor.[142] One thing to keep in mind when examining the importance of the men who served as *epi tou kanikleiou* is that the status of an individual could vary greatly depending on imperial favour, and that many imperial favourites held this post. A good example is the tenth-century *epi tou kanikleiou* Nikephoros Ouranos. Near the beginning of his time in the post he held the title of *vestes*. As he grew closer to the emperor Basil II and began to act as a rival and counterweight to the powerful *parakoimomenos* Basil Lekapenos, he was promoted first to *vestes* and later to *magistros*. Which of these three titles most accurately reflects the status of the office? There is a good case that it would be *vestes*, the initial title of Ouranos before his rise to prominence, but there are other arguments which could be made for his later title too. The personal nature of the office coupled with the sparse surviving evidence should make us cautious with our conclusions.

With these warnings in mind, let us turn to the seals. The period c. 966–c. 1066 is represented by eight seals which belonged to five men. This is obviously not much evidence on which to base a reconstruction of the story of the *epi tou kanikleiou*. The earliest seal belonged to a certain Leo and records no title. Of the three men who lived before the end of the first third of the eleventh century two were *protospatharioi* and one held the slightly higher titles of *anthypatos* and *patrikios*. These were not incredibly high titles for the time. *Protospatharios* and *patrikios* were in the process of transitioning from mid-level dignities into titles in the bottom third of the hierarchy, while *anthypatos* was experiencing a similar decline from the upper third to the middle of the rankings. Moreover, there is no way to know in what order these three men filled the post, which is to say that we cannot argue for a progression over time from *protospatharios* to *anthypatos*; for all we know it was the other way around. Having said that, in the mid-eleventh century, the *epi tou kanikleiou* John Libellisios held the titles of *vestes*, *anthypatos* and *patrikios*. By his time *vestes* had replaced *anthypatos* as the lowest title in the top third of the hierarchy, meaning that John had preserved the status of his predecessors.[143] The only *epi tou kanikleiou* whose title we know from texts is the aforementioned and complicated Nikephoros Ouranos. In terms of income a *protospatharios* living c. 966–c. 1033 received a *roga* of seventy-two *nomismata*, while an early-eleventh-century *anthypatos* earned 576. Later, John Libellisios received a *roga* of at least 864 *nomismata*.

If we leave Nikephoros Ouranos to one side or take his initial title as indicative of the status of his office, we can see a situation where the *epi tou kanikleiou* was rather stable in terms of status, but with an income that increased rapidly in the century up to the 1050s. Although we are dealing with individuals, not large groups, perhaps the story of the *epi tou kanikleiou* is indicative of a larger, unsustainable trend in Byzantine government. The status of the office, in terms of the position of the titles granted to its holders, remained largely consistent in the century under consideration; it trod water. However, the income attached to those offices, even with currency devaluation, did not decline apace with the titles themselves. The result was that in preserving the status of the office the emperors had committed to pay out almost twice as much in annual salaries as they had a generation earlier.

3.2.2 The *asekreteion*

> *There is not a man who can say that the torments of hell exceed service in the bureau of the asekretis.*[144]

The *sekreton* of the *asekretai* was home to the elite secretaries who, among other tasks, prepared imperial documents. There were a number of grades of secretaries: at the bottom were the *notarioi*, above them the *asekretai* who were an elite class of *notarioi*, and in charge of the whole was the *protoasekretis* (first secretary), sometimes rendered *protasekretis*.[145]

3.2.2.1 The protoasekretis

> Κύριε βοήθει Λέοντι πρωτασηκρῆτις καὶ χαρτουλαρίῳ τῷ Χρυσοβαλαντίτῃ.
>
> Lord, help Leo Chrysobalantites, protoasekretis and chartoularios.[146]

The *protoasekretis*, or *protasekretis*, the first of the *asekretai* (secretaries), was head of the department that can most accurately be termed the Byzantine chancery.[147] He is first encountered in the *Liber Pontificalis* as the *proto a secreta* (*sic*) in an entry dated to 756 and enters the sigillographic record in the ninth century, although he could have existed earlier than either of these sources suggest.[148] As head of the imperial chancery he met frequently with the emperor. The *protoasekretis* was responsible for making the final version of imperial documents.[149] This included *chrysobulls*, documents signed by the emperor in red ink and secured, as the name suggests, with his golden seal. These were the most prestigious of imperial acts granted to high-ranking Byzantines, important institutions such as monasteries, and foreign rulers. Frequent and close contact with the emperor and his acts made the *protoasekretis* a powerful state official. The similarities to the *epi tou kanikleiou* are obvious, and it is possible to imagine them frequently being in the imperial presence at the same time as the emperor was presented with, then signed, documents. It is not surprising to find famous and powerful individuals in the post of *protoasekretis*, such as the future patriarch Photios and Michael Psellos. The obvious, but possibly semi-official influence of the *protoasekretis* resulted in him having a say over the content of legislation by 959.[150]

From the seals I am aware of eight men who held the office of *protoasekretis* between c. 966 and c. 1066.[151] The seals of five of these eight men, all dated before c. 1033, record the title of *protospathrios*, two, both from the tenth century, in conjunction with that of *patrikios*.[152] The remaining three seals, two of which date close to c. 1033, record no title. That there are no *patrikioi* from later in the eleventh century might hint at a drop in the importance of the *protoasekretis*, but there is far too little evidence to be certain. That the usual dignity attached to the office in the first third of the eleventh century was that of *protospatharios* is borne out by the testimony of the *Peira* which records the existence of Peter, *protospatharios* and *protoasekretis* just before 1025.[153] When we turn to the *roga* for the *protoasekretis* we come to a dismal story of dwindling income. From a high point of 4 pounds of *nomismata* in the first third of the eleventh century the most commonly awarded *roga* of a *protoasekretis* had fallen to 1 pound by the middle third of the century. In both status and income, the *protoasekretis* was slipping backwards by the middle of the eleventh century.

3.2.2.2 The asekretai

δεινῶν με σῴζοις, Παντελεῆμων, Θεοφάνην σὸν οἰκέτην ἀσηκρῆτις.

Panteleimon, may you preserve me from misfortunes, your servant Theophanes the asekretis.[154]

Beneath the *protoasekretis* were the regular *asekretai*, an elite group of *notarioi* involved in the preparation and probably copying of official documents, and the taking of notes at important meetings. The name of the office comes from the Latin *notarii a secretis*.[155] They were the successors to the *referendarii*, acted as imperial secretaries, and had their office in the *kathisma* of the Hippodrome in the Great Palace.[156] Quite when the term appeared is in question, either the fourth, fifth or sixth centuries. The earliest known seals of an *asekretis* have been dated to the fourth/fifth century.[157] As members of the so-called sandaled senate (bureaucrats with titles of *spatharokandidatos* and lower) Philotheos records that they were invited to dine with the emperor at a number of the feasts held during the Twelve Days of Christmas and at Easter.[158] When summoned in order they appear before the *chartoularioi* and imperial *notarioi* of the other *sekreta*, indicating their importance at the time Philotheos was writing.[159]

The titles granted to the *asekretai* were largely consistent over the century under consideration, but that does not mean that there was no change at all. The percentage of men who either did not have a title or chose not to put it on their seals, while remaining well above the halfway mark, dropped steadily throughout the century, from 61.1 to 54.3 per cent. Another drop was in the percentage of low ranks, *strator* and *spatharios*, with a corresponding rise in the figures for the more prestigious titles of *spatharokandidatos* and *protospatharios*. While on the surface this seems like a positive tale of gradual advancement, it is actually one of declining status. While we

Figure 3.5 Seal of Nicholas, *protospatharios* and *asekretis*. Dumbarton Oaks, Byzantine Collection, Washington, DC, BZS.1958.106.3159.

The bilateral inscription on Nicholas' seal begins with a traditional pairing of invocation, name, title, and office on the obverse, but transitions to a more fashionable metrical inscription on the reverse.

Obv. ΚVΡΙ.|ROHΘEIT.|CШΔΟVΛ'Ν.|ΚΟΛΑШΑ͞C.|ΑΘΑΡΙШΚΑΙ|ΑCΙΚ̣Ρ̣,Τ̣,
Rev. Η.ΦΡΑ|Γ'ΑVΤ,ΝΙΚ,|ΛΑΟVΤVΝ|ΧΑΝ·Α͞CΠ·Θ'|ΡΙΟVΤΕΚ'|ΑCΙΚΡ,Τ,
Κύριε βοήθει τῷ σῷ δούλῳ Νικολάῳ πρωτοσπαθαρίῳ καὶ ἀσικρῆτις. ἡ σφραγὶς αὕτη Νικολάου τυγχάνει πρωτοσπαθαρίου τε καὶ ἀσικρῆτις.
Lord, help your servant Nicholas, *protospatharios* and *asekretis*. This happens to be the seal of Nicholas, *protospatharios* and *asekretis*.

Table 3.5 Normalized Seal Data, in Percentages, for the Titles of the *Asekretai* c. 966–c. 1066

Title/Date	Tenth Century Final Third	Eleventh Century First Third	Eleventh Century Middle Third
Anthypatos and *Patrikios*		1.9	0.5
Protospatharios	12.6	12.1	16.5
Spatharokandidatos	22.1	24.9	27.8
Spatharios	2.4	1.7	1
Strator	1.8	0.6	
None	61.1	58.8	54.3

see a higher percentage of *asekretai* with titles in c. 1066 than in c. 966, by that time *protospatharios* occupied the same place in the hierarchy held by *spatharios* a century earlier. Their titles might have been different, but even the highest ranked *asekretai* of 1066 had the same status as the lowest of their predecessors. What about income? The majority of the *asekretai*, those without title, received no additional *roga*, and as we do not know the salary of an *asekretis*, there is nothing more to be said about them. For the remainder where the titles remain consistent throughout the century so too would their *rogai* payments.

These conclusions are built upon as firm a foundation as can be, due to the large amount of evidence upon which it is based, 330 seals belonging to 258 individuals.[160] Furthermore, it is unlikely that the figures displayed above were influenced by the fact that the *asekretai* frequently held other offices, primarily judicial, occasionally notarial. If one examined the different dignities recorded on the seals of the *asekretai* piece by piece, keeping a tally of those who were only an *asekretis* and those who had another job, we would see that for all but one dignity the resulting count would be very nearly even. The exception is the title of *spatharokandidatos*, which is more common on seals of men with multiple offices. As it falls right in the middle of the ranks granted to the *asekretai*, I would suggest that this is further evidence that their title was not influenced by the other offices that they held, but that they held offices at roughly the same level, at least deserving of the same dignity, as *asekretis*.

3.2.2.3 The notarioi

> *Anyone wishing to become a notarios of the asekreteion, if he receives a roga of twenty nomismata, should pay eight pounds.*[161]

Also working under the *protoasekretis* were *notarioi* (clerks).[162] Unfortunately, there is no way of identifying them from their seals. I know of no examples of seals belonging to a *notarios* of the *protoasekretis* or his *sekreton*. There are dozens of seals of *notarioi* which do not record a department, and it has been suggested that these worked in the chancery.[163] While I am inclined to agree that *notarioi* who did not mention a specific jurisdiction on their seals worked in the capital rather than the provinces, I see no reason to presume that they worked in the chancery alone. We know from the ninth- and tenth-century *taktika* that *notarioi* were employed in many departments, and from seals we know of even more. While it would make sense that, due to the nature of the work done there, the chancery would employ many of the *notarioi* who chose not to be specific on their seals, but this does not mean that it employed all of them. The majority of the seals belonging to *chartoularioi* also do not name a specific department to which they were attached, and we know they were not at the chancery. This suggests that the lower-level officials were less likely to place the name of their department on their seals than their higher-ranking colleagues. We will never know quite why. It could have been the fashion for such low-level state employees; it could have been because they were not considered as rigidly attached to a particular *sekreton*, but I do not think that it was because they all worked in the same department. As such, discussing them here would not be appropriate, and in the absence of another department in which to put the generic *notarioi* and *chartoularioi*, I shall discuss them in an appendix following the main chapter.

3.2.3 The *mystikos*

> Ἅγιε Νικόλαε βοήθει τῷ σῷ δούλῳ Νικολάῳ ἀνθυπάτῳ πατρικίῳ βέστῃ καὶ μυστικῷ.
>
> *St Nicholas, help your servant Nicholas, anthypatos, patrikios, vestes, and mystikos.*[164]

Next in the order of precedence presented by the *Escorial Taktikon* was the *mystikos*.[165] The *mystikos* first appears in the sources for the ninth century, in the reign of Basil I (867–86), in the person of Leo Choirosphaktes.[166] However, he does not appear in the

Kletorologion of Philotheos which predates the appearance of the office, making his first appearance in a *taktika* in the later *Taktikon Beneševič* and in the *Escorial Taktikon*.[167] The reason for the absence of the *mystikos* from the otherwise exhaustive work of Philotheos is not readily apparent: Was it a mistake on his part, was the *mystikos* not invited to the kind of functions which his list was intended to facilitate? It seems unlikely that he was of too low a rank to make the grade as Philotheos includes almost everyone then in state service in his document. Unfortunately, like much about the *mystikos*, this remains a mystery. Leo Choirosphaktes was the first in a long line of well-known Byzantines to hold the post, including Nicholas Mystikos, who took his surname from the office which he held before becoming patriarch (for the first time) in 901, Theodore Daphnopates, who served under Romanos I Lekapenos, Constantine VII and Romanos II, the noted jurist Eustathios Romaios, and the chief minister of Constantine IX Monomachos, Constantine Leichoudes. It was clearly a position given to men of ambition and ability, who were rewarded with higher posts or great power by the emperors of the day.

The word literally means secret or private, and it is usually thought that this gives a hint as to the duties of the *mystikos*, that he was in some way connected with the personal or secret aspects of imperial power or of the emperors' lives. That the word itself has an interesting, one might go so far as to say intriguing and perhaps illuminating, meaning is wonderful, as there are no other indications as to the duties of the *mystikos*. Of course, this has not prevented large amounts of ink being spilled on the topic, requiring us to spend even more here. Based largely on the name it has been argued that the *mystikos* was the emperor's private secretary, hence his inclusion in discussions of the imperial chancery.[168] In this role he would have dealt with the private correspondence of the emperors, secret and private indeed. With these duties he was fulfilling some of the duties once the responsibilities of the *protoasekretis*.[169] It has been pointed out that there are no imperial acts drawn up by the *mystikos*, something that distinguishes him from the *protoasekretis*. This conclusion led to the idea that the *mystikos* was not the imperial private secretary, but rather a judicial official and advisor.[170] There is evidence of the *sekreton* of the *mystikos* handling cases, but little of it dates to the tenth or eleventh centuries; it is mostly from the twelfth.[171] It seems that what we have here is the by now familiar case of an official close to the emperor, perhaps with some judicial expertise, being ordered to oversee a dispute, even though he did not currently hold a judicial posting. This would seem to be corroborated by the testimony from *De Ceremoniis* which records a ceremony in which the *koitonitai*, the *katepano* and the *mystikos* all stood together in the throne room of the Chrysotriklinos.[172] As the *koitonitai* and the *katepano* were members of the imperial household, perhaps this is how we should view the *mystikos*. The most recent proposal has been that the *mystikos* organized the gatherings of the emperor's inner circle, the meetings of which were secret and private.[173] This final theory again leads us back to the idea of the *mystikos* as a sort of confidential advisor to the emperor, a man specializing in private activities, which leads us back where we began, to the idea of the office as a sort of private secretary, with responsibilities distinct from those of the more public activities of the *protoasekretis*.[174]

Our period contains records for nine seals belonging to seven men.[175] The earliest four seals, dated between c. 966 and c. 1033 record that their owners held the title of *protospatharios*. At this point there was a transition, with the final two individuals holding more exalted ranks, on the one hand *patrikios*, on the other *vestes*, *anthypatos* and *patrikios*. In this list the *vestes* is the odd man out, holding as he did a title in the top third of the contemporary hierarchy. His fellow *mystikoi* failed to break out of the middle of the scale of honours at best. The sigillographic evidence is supported by the equally scanty written material. Demetrios Polemarchios held the office of *mystikos* before 1025 with the title of *patrikios*. He was followed by Eustathios Romaios, also a *patrikios*. Slightly later, in 1029, the post had fallen to a certain Abramios who was a *protospatharios*.[176] Clearly, it was more usual for the *mystikos* to hold a title in the middle to lower, and increasingly just the lower, end of the hierarchy. However, there is too little evidence to understand how the one *vestes* fit into the overall evolution of the office of *mystikos* or to appreciate how the position responded to the changing hierarchy. Unhelpful in this regard is the career of Constantine Leichoudes, who served as *mystikos* with the dignity of *proedros* c. 1042–55. Not only was he likely *megas oikonomos* of the Tropaiophoros at the same time, he was also the *mesazon* of Constantine IX, an unofficial position which effectively made him prime minister.[177] It is highly likely that his title of *proedros*, the highest then available, was the result of his dominance of the imperial government rather than his possession of the office of *mystikos*.

We know that there was a *protomystikos* by 1057, and that he was in charge of a *sekreton* that could try cases.[178] Who this official was is very much open to question. Solutions have ranged from ignoring the *proto* and accepting him as the *mystikos*, equating him with the *protoasekretis*, and arguing that the *proto* symbolized his ascendency over other officials with the syllables *mysto* in their name, the *mystographos* and the *mystolektes*.[179] None of these solutions is entirely adequate. As noted by Gkoutzioukostas, the theory that the addition of the prefix *proto* to the office of *mystikos* was just a scribal error is disproved by the existence of a seal of Constantine *magistros* and *protomystikos* dated to the third quarter of the eleventh century.[180] It is possible that Laurent was correct in identifying the *protomystikos* with the *protoasekretis*. From the middle decades of the eleventh century, it was certainly not uncommon for the Byzantines to use different names for the same function, *praitor* and *krites* for judge being an obvious example. Furthermore, the titles held by both the *mystikoi* and the *protoasekretai* were largely the same in the century under consideration. However, this could be said for a great many offices in this period, and one of the two known *protomystikoi* also served as *protoasekretis*, and used both terms on his seals, making it unlikely that he was using them as synonyms. That the term designated the head of the *mystoi* is equally unsatisfactory. Everywhere else that we know of a *proto*-something, the prefix is meant to distinguish the head of a group from the rest of the members with the same job title. Hence *protonotarios* for the *notarioi*, *protoasekretis* for the *asekretai*, etc. Such a designation hardly seems necessary to mark the difference between the *mystikos* on the one hand, and the *mystographos* and *mystolektes* on the other, any more than the *eparch* of the city needed to be distinguished from his deputy, the *symponos*, by the addition of a prefix to his office. We are dealing here with entirely different words, and while they all have their first four letters in common, which I admit is unique within a department, I find it hard to believe that any Byzantine who was in a position to need to understand the distinction between the three offices would have needed the help of a prefix.

Where does this leave us? In reality with far too little information to make any conclusions beyond admitting that we simply cannot know why the *protomystikos* appeared when he did, and why he seems to have been a rather rare animal. One of the two known *protomystikoi* who lived in our period held the rank of *proedros*, meant that he was of significantly higher rank than any other *mystikos* before the end of the eleventh century, and this perhaps hints at a special status beyond simply being the *mystikos* or *protoasekretis* by another name. Perhaps the term *proto* was added in this case as a reward to John Xeros, member of an important family with a long association with the Constantinopolitan bureaucracy.[181] In this case, it would be a sign of the malleability of the imperial system when it came to the emperor's will, akin to having the *mystikos* sit in judgement when his office was not of a judicial nature. To me this seems like the most likely option, that what we have is an ad hoc reward for an imperial favourite. Until more information is discovered, however, it remains but a guess.

3.2.4 The *mystographos*

> Κύριε βοήθει τῷ σῷ δούλῳ Κωνσταντίνῳ πρωτοσπαθαρίῳ καὶ μυστογράφῳ τῷ Ἐλεγμίτῃ.
>
> Lord, help your servant Constantine Elegmites, protospatharios and mystographos.[182]

The first appearance of the office of *mystographos* is in an inscription dated to 911/2.[183] It later appeared in the *Escorial Taktikon* in 160th (total hierarchy) 137th (offices) place.[184] That it does so below the *mystikos*, in 149th (total hierarchy) 126th (offices) place, had led to the conclusion that, because of the similarity in the names of the two, the *mystographos* was his subordinate.[185] The duties of the *mystographos* are, like those of the *mystikos*, hinted at only in the name of the office, the writer of secrets. Before the office had come into being, this term was used on occasion as a synonym for *asekretis*.[186] The conclusion is that the *mystographos* acted as secretary during the meetings of the emperor and his closest advisors.[187] It is certainly possible that he was a member of the *sekreton* of the *mystikos*, although there is no evidence either way. Perhaps, whether as a subordinate or not, the *mystographos* acted as a scribe for some of the secret and private activities with which the *mystikos* was involved.[188]

When we turn to the *mystographoi* the surviving seals can be called a large body of evidence; ninety seals belonging to sixty-seven men. It is clear from the inscriptions found on the seals of the *mystographoi* that the most common title associated with the office was *protospatharios*, across the century from c. 966 to c. 1066. While the eleventh century saw some *mystographoi* awarded the higher title of *patrikios*, numbers were never high, and by the middle third of the century the proportion of *protospatharioi* was higher than ever before. Every *mystographos* recorded in documentary material alongside his title was also a *protospatharios*, from Nikephoros, judge of the Hippodrome and *mystographos* in 1029, to Basil, imperial *notarios* of the

Table 3.6 Normalized Seal Data, in Percentages, for the Titles of the *Mystographoi* c. 966–c. 1066

Title/Date	Tenth Century Final Third	Eleventh Century First Third	Eleventh Century Middle Third
Patrikios and *Protospatharios*		1.9	1.3
Patrikios		5.6	
Protospatharios	73.8	75.7	86.6
None	26.2	16.8	12.1

eidikos logothetes, *mystographos*, and judge of the Hippodrome in 1045, and Elpidios Kenchres, *mystographos*, judge of the Velum, *thesmographos*, and *exaktor* in 1053.[189] That the title associated with the office of *mystographos* remained constant meant that although their status gradually slipped, their income did not, remaining constant at seventy-two *nomismata*.

3.2.5 The *epi ton deeseon*

> Κύριε βοήθει τῷ σῷ δούλῳ Γρηγορίῳ πατρικίῳ, πραιποσίτῳ, βεστάρχῃ καὶ ἐπὶ τῶν δεήσεων.
>
> Lord, help your servant Gregory, patrikios, praipositos, vestarches, and epi ton deeseon.[190]

The *epi ton deeseon* (master of petitions), as successor to the late Roman *magister memoriae*, was responsible for receiving, considering and responding to petitions to the emperor.[191] As such he had a remarkable level of control of access to the emperor, although the specific duties that he undertook, and the processes by which petitions were answered are unclear.[192] It has been noted that he was listed by Philotheos as a judicial official, likely as a result of the nature of his work compiling the answers to petitions, answers which would often have taken the form of legal documents.[193] The *epi ton deeseon* was not a palace-bound official but often accompanied the emperor on his travels, whether through the streets of Constantinople or further afield.[194] It is possible that he oversaw regional officials responsible for receiving and forwarding petitions from the provinces.[195] He had once been subject to the *koiaistor*, but by the time that the *Taktikon Uspenskij* was written had become an independent official, answering neither to his old superior nor to the chancery.[196] The office is known on seals from the seventh century, which is, in fact, the earliest mention of the *epi ton deeseon* in any source.[197] Of the bureaucrats listed on the *Taktikon Escorial* he came 21st, 161st (total hierarchy) 138th (offices) overall.[198]

As with many of the other offices that we have examined in this chapter the *epi ton deeseon* shows a remarkable consistency in the titles attached to the post in a period of gradual title inflation. We might assume that frequent contact with the emperor and the control over access to the imperial person that the *epi ton deeson* had would

Table 3.7 Normalized Seal Data, in Percentages, for the Titles of the *Epi ton Deeseon* c. 966–c. 1066

Title/Date	Tenth Century Final Third	Eleventh Century First Third	Eleventh Century Middle Third
Vestarches and *Patrikios*			37
Patrikios			12.6
Protospatharios	70.8	92.1	37.8
Spatharokandidatos	16.6		
None	12.6	7.9	12.6

result in an exalted position in the hierarchy for the office. In fact, no such evidence exists. That there was a general improvement in status during the first third of the eleventh century is shown by the increased number of *protospatharioi* and the disappearance of the lower rank of *spatharokandidatos*. The hierarchy was stable in this period, so this move meant a move up the ladder. This was reflected in the *roga* paid to the *epi ton deeseon*, with the most common value being that for *protospatharios* of 1 pound of *nomismata* up to c. 1033. The middle third of the eleventh century presents a complex picture. Few seals have survived from this period, roughly half the number from either of the previous two periods. Proceeding with the caution due to such small numbers, we can see what could be interpreted as a continuation of the upward trend, with 12.6 per cent attaining the rank of *patrikios*. It must be remembered, however, that by the middle of the century the hierarchy was no longer stable, and that even the title of *patrikios* had slipped from the top of the middle third of the rankings to the middle of the hierarchy by c. 1050, and the top of the bottom third by c. 1060. In terms of status the *epi ton deeseon* had fallen from the middle of the hierarchy in c. 966 to the bottom by c. 1050. At this point there is some evidence from a synodal edict of 1054 which records that the *epi ton deeseon* John held the title of *magistros*, the second-highest title then available, and a lone seal in the Dumbarton Oaks collection of Gregory – *vestarchces*, *patrikios*, and *epi ton deeseon* – hints that things may have been improving for the office.[199] The small number of seals involved skews the figures for average earnings as well. While the most common *roga* remained 1 pound of gold, the presence of Gregory with his high title of *vestarches* pulled the mean average up to 6.9 pounds. Without him it was only 1.75 pounds, still an increase over the figure for the first third of the century, 0.9 pounds.

3.2.6 The *mystolektes*

Θεοτόκε βοήθει Ἰωάννῃ πρωτοσπαθαρίῳ, μυστολέκτῃ, κριτῇ τοῦ βήλου καὶ τῶν Ἀρμενικῶν θεμάτων.

Theotokos, help John, protospatharios, mystolektes, judge of the Velum and of the Armenian themes.[200]

As with the other offices beginning with the syllable *myst*, the only clues as to the duties of the *mystolektes* come from its name. Literally the bearer or revealer of secrets, the

Table 3.8 Normalized Seal Data, in Percentages, for the Titles of the *Mystolektai* c. 966–c. 1066

Title/Date	Tenth Century Final Third	Eleventh Century First Third	Middle Third
Protospatharios	66.6	60.1	70.8
Spatharios	33.3	9.1	
Primikerios		6.1	1.9
None		24.1	27.3

most likely option is that he acted an elite messenger for the emperor.[201] The office does not appear in the *taktika* and is known to us only from the seals of its holders.

The seals of the *mystolektai*, forty-nine from thirty-four men, present a by now familiar picture, but with a twist. The title of *protospatharios* was by far the most common across the century under discussion, although the increase in seals with no title should be noted. As with the office of *mystographos*, by remaining *protospatharioi* across the century from c. 966–c. 1066 the *mystolektai* saw their status and income steadily decline. The twist is the appearance of the title of *primikerios*, a dignity reserved for eunuchs, indicating that a significant number of *mystolektai* were appointed from among the emperor's palatine staff. The inclusion of so many eunuchs, and the fact that there could have been more, as they could also be *protospatharioi*, raises interesting questions about the office of *mystolektes* and whether it was in some way linked to the palace rather than the chancery.

3.2.7 A question of priorities

> *A ray of hope warmed and restored us, and it lightened and kept off the great burden of despair, whereas now the remedy of hope has gone, and misfortune has resulted in a state of confusion, since the ruling sovereign, who in the manner of a river overflows in benefactions and gushes most bounteously to all, lets nary a drop fall on us.*[202]

The picture presented in this chapter is largely one of slipping backwards. The status of a *protoasekretis*, *asekretis*, *mystographos* and *mystolektes* were all lower in c. 1066 than they had been a century earlier, and their income had not increased. There is little evidence for the fortunes of the *mystikoi*, but it looks like they slipped backwards in the early eleventh century, only to pull ahead again in the following decades. The only slightly more numerous sources for the *epi tou kanikleiou* reveal an office standing still in terms of status but increasing its income. The only individual who was consistently better off in both status and income than his earlier counterparts was the *epi ton deeseon*. This was not a case of the more specialized offices receiving preferential treatment. There might have been many *asekretai* and only one *mystographos* or *mystolektes*, but their story was the same. It was also not the case that those officials who had personal contact with the emperor prospered, for the *protoasekretis* suffered just as much as the lesser *asekretai*.

What we have here is an area of government which did not benefit from the supposed generosity of the last of the Macedonians and their associates on the throne. Contrary to the testimony of our more narrative sources, the seals prove that the doors of the senate were not thrown open to the lower orders in the middle of the century, and the majority of those who just qualified for senatorial status through their title of *protospatharios* had little to be grateful for. This is perhaps puzzling as the chancery officials were obviously appreciated for their expertise and skills and were deployed elsewhere in government as a result. A high proportion of the *asekretai*, *mystographoi* and *mystolektai* held other jobs, most commonly as judges, either in Constantinople or in the provinces, and it is likely that the majority of these men began their careers in the chancery. Furthermore, it could be argued that these officials linked to secretarial duties in some way formed an extension of the imperial household. I have already mentioned this in connection with the *mystikos*, but it seems likely for the other officials as well, particularly the *mystolektes*. Generally speaking, only members of the imperial household received customary gifts from individuals obtaining a dignity from the emperor, yet we find the *epi tou kanikleiou* and the *protoasekretis* on this list as well.[203] Frequent contact with the emperor could easily have led to the blurring of the lines between departments until certain of the officials considered in this chapter, and their *sekreta*, were viewed more as extensions of the imperial household than independent units of government. Even so, membership in a group close to the emperor clearly did not automatically bring advancement. It is possible that the imperial government saw no reason to react to the issues of title inflation at this time for these officials. They were doing the jobs that they had done for the last few generations at least, centuries in some cases, and no adjustment was necessary. If we argue that the granting of new, higher titles in this period was the result of a conscious series of policies reflecting changes in government priorities, then we must conclude that the chancery's place in government did not warrant an increase in prestige or income for the men working there.

3.3 Governing the capital

After the address the praipositos gives a command to the master of ceremonies for the curtain to be opened, and he summons the eparch, and when he goes out the praipositos presents him to the citizenry as eparch and father of the City.[204]

As far as the Byzantines were concerned Constantinople had always been special. It was the City, the Royal City, the Megalopolis and a host of other equally imposing epithets. Its citizens also saw themselves as special, an elite group within the imperial population. To a certain extent this elevated view of their capital was not an exaggeration. Even at its lowest point in the eighth century, nothing in the Christian world could rival the great city on the Bosphorus.[205] What was true of Christendom was true for the empire. Constantinople was the empire's city. A number of other towns were impressive for their time, but the capital stood above all. It was not only size that made Constantinople unique. It was home to everything that held the empire together, the imperial court, the patriarchate and, of course, the bureaucracy. The city was also at the ideological core of the empire, and what it meant to be a Byzantine was inextricably linked to the existence of the New Rome and the transference of the imperial ideal from its rapidly decaying mother on the Tiber.[206] Constantinople also stood at the centre of the empire's economy.[207] Taxes flowed into it, salaries streamed out, and the service elite, with their unrivalled purchasing power, made Constantinople one of the largest markets in the known world. As the home of the government and a focus of imperial wealth, Constantinople attracted people from across the empire, seeking their fortune in the service of the emperor. One such man was the aforementioned Michael Attaleiates, who moved to Constantinople, the 'metropolis of culture, the Queen of Cities', and became 'a member of the senate, in spite of my humble and foreign background, and to be enrolled among the elite of the senators (whom the language of old used to call "aristocrats"), and among the most illustrious of the civic [politikon, πολιτικῶν] judges, and to pride myself on public honours'.[208] Constantinople also looked different from the cities in the rest of Europe, with its mixture of medieval buildings set among the surviving open spaces, trophies and monumental architecture of late antiquity. It was the perfect stage for Constantine VII's ceremonies, and there was ample space for the people to join in in the fora, colonnaded streets and the Hippodrome.

The people were one of the reasons that Constantinople was becoming an even more interesting city in our period. For centuries they had been less involved in politics outside of imperially orchestrated events than had been the case in late antiquity. The old chariot racing factions, once the cause of so much trouble, had been reined in, and now performed a set role as the representatives of the people in imperial ceremony.[209] The *demarchs* (heads of the circus factions) even held an official rank, 166th (total hierarchy) 143rd (offices) (Blues) and 167th (total hierarchy) 144th (offices) (Greens) in the *Taktikon Escorial*.[210] There were, however, stirrings that the people were not always going to be compliant. As the tenth century ended there were more of them and they were richer than ever before. And they were becoming involved in politics. A few signs of this had been there for those who were looking in the tenth century. When Romanos I was overthrown by his sons in 944 they were prevented from ousting the true heir, their brother-in-law Constantine VII by the violently expressed will of the people.[211] The same thing happened when Joseph Bringas tried to prevent the successful general Nikephoros Phokas from entering the capital and ascending to the throne in 963.[212] Of course, it is possible to at least partly blame both of these events on the machinations of Basil Lekapenos, and his skills at manipulating the city's populace, but even if we accept this version of events, the 'popular' element to the political theatre of 944 and 963 marks a new beginning of sorts.

The population of Constantinople was quiet, as was almost everyone else, during the reign of Basil II, but it must have continued to grow in size and in wealth, particularly wealth that was to some degree independent of the state, for when the capital's citizens reappear under Basil's successors they had a central place in the political system of the empire.[213] We have already seen how the emperors Constantine IX Monomachos and Constantine X Doukas courted the people of the city, particularly the wealthy merchants and craftsmen of the guilds, and included them in the imperial system.

They are not the only examples: Michael IV and his family rose to power from just such a guild background; Michael V thought that he could rule through the people, dispensing with his adoptive mother the empress Zoe; he was wrong, and paid for his mistake with his eyes. Zoe's younger sister Theodora was torn from her convent by a mob intent on placing her on the throne, and the people of Constantinople were instrumental in the survival of the regime of Constantine IX Monomachos during the revolt of Leo Tornikes, and the later overthrow of Michael VI.[214] This list, which is not exhaustive by any means, is intended to highlight the increased political and financial power of the people of Constantinople. A number of our sources would like us to believe that the cares of the capital, of ruling this huge, complex city, were more than many of the eleventh-century emperors could manage. The rewards for ruling Constantinople well could be great, and failure was fatal.[215] But, of course, they did not rule the city alone. In this most daunting, and potentially life-threatening of tasks, they were aided by the *eparch* and his staff.

3.3.1 The *eparch* of Constantinople

Θεοτόκε βοήθει τῷ σῷ δούλῳ Μιχαὴλ πατρικίῳ καὶ ἐπάρχῳ Κωνσταντινουπόλεως.

Theotokos, help your servant Michael patrikios and eparchos of Constantinople.[216]

The position of *eparch* (prefect) of Constantinople succeeded, and in many ways evolved from the post of *praefectus urbi* established for the capital in 359 by Constantius II. In this role, he was the Father of the City, and second only to the emperor within Constantinople.[217] At the beginning of the tenth century the duties of the *eparch* and his staff with respect to the capital were recorded in the *Book of the Eparch*.[218] He oversaw much of the administration of Constantinople, supervising the food supply of the city, the *demes* (racing factions), the trade guilds, the markets of the capital, including the price of goods, and was in charge of the entertainments of the Hippodrome. He also had authority over visitors from outside of the empire. In the realm of justice, he oversaw his own court, the *eparchikon bema*, with authority over the capital and the surrounding territory, up to one hundred miles from the city, which dealt with civil and criminal cases.[219] The judgements of the *eparchs* of the tenth and early eleventh century could be overruled only by the emperor.[220] He was, in fact, the highest ranking judicial official in the empire until the end of the first third of the eleventh century, and even appeals of the decisions of provincial judges could be brought before him.[221] The *eparch* also commanded the equivalent of a police force in the capital, and controlled Constantinople's prisons.[222] To aid him with his wide-ranging duties, the *eparch* employed a considerable support staff. The *Kletorologion of Philotheos* records fourteen offices under the *eparch*.[223] Of these only two have left behind enough information to be worthy of analysis here, the *symponos* (deputy of the *eparch*) and the *parathalassites* to whom we shall turn in due course. In descending order, the staff of the *eparch* comprised the *symponos*; the *logothetes tou praitoriou*, possibly in charge (director) of the *praitorion* prison; the judges for the regions of Constantinople; the *episkeptitai* (inspectors), who managed imperial properties; the *protokankellarioi*, clerical officials; a *kenturion* (centurion), head of the soldiers or police in the service of the *eparch*; *epoptai* (overseers); *exarchoi*, likely the heads of the guilds; *geitoniarchai*, responsible in some way of districts of Constantinople; *nomikoi*, a law teacher chosen by the guild of notaries; *boullotai*, in charge of affixing seals to the products of the market; *protostatai*; *kankellarioi*, clerical officials; and the *parathalassites*. He was also responsible for monitoring the production of silk through his deputies, the *mitotes*.[224] From a point in the opening decades of the eleventh century, the role of the *eparch* began to contract. A number of his deputies, such as the *parathalassites*, became independent, and his position as the highest legal authority below the emperor was taken over by the *droungarios tes viglas*, who could overrule the legal decisions of the *eparch*.[225] At the same time, his legal jurisdiction in Constantinople itself was limited in ways that we do not fully understand by the newly created *praetor* of Constantinople. The *eparch* remained the head of a tribunal, and was considered a 'great judge', the head of the administration of the city, and continued to supervise the craft and merchant guilds, which he did until at least 1112/13, and probably throughout the twelfth century.[226]

The *eparch* occupied a prominent position among the elite of the empire in the *Taktikon Escorial*, where he was ranked 50th (total hierarchy) 34th (offices) in the hierarchy, making him not only the highest ranked civilian in the list but also the only one to rank above any of the *strategoi*.[227] Few seals of *eparchs* include the qualification 'of Constantinople' in their inscriptions.[228] This is less an issue than it would at first appear, as by our period the label *eparch*, which had once been widespread, was effectively limited to one individual in Constantinople.[229] When it comes to the sigillographic evidence there are eighty-seven seals struck by fifty-six individuals. The seals of the *eparchs* thus more than meet the minimum criteria for normalization, the results of which can be seen in Table 3.9.

In terms of titles the *eparchs* of the end of the tenth and beginning of the eleventh centuries were more likely than not to possess the dignity of *protospatharios*, 48.9 and 65.5 per cent, with the higher ranked among their number as *anthypatoi* and/ or *patrikioi*, and 36.4 and 12.7 per cent respectively. This conclusion is supported by the written evidence. *Eparchs* with the title of *protospatharios* were recorded in

Table 3.9 Normalized Seal Data, in Percentages, for the Titles of *Eparchs* c. 966–c. 1066

Title/Period	Tenth Century Final Third	Eleventh Century	
		First Third	Middle Third
Proedros			6
Magistros and *Vestarches*			17.8
Magistros			17.8
Vestarches			14.9
Vestes, *Anthypatos* and *Patrikios*		3.6	3
Anthypatos and *Patrikios*	19.4		
Patrikios	17	12.7	11.9
Protospatharios	48.9	65.5	6
Spatharios	7.3	5.5	
None	7.3	12.7	22.5

963, 1026 and 1029, and as *patrikioi* in 967, 1025–8, 1033 and 1042.[230] This situation changed rapidly in the middle third of the century. The percentage of *protospatharioi* dropped tenfold, and we see a majority, 56.5 per cent, of the *eparchs* holding the three highest titles then open to individuals not of the imperial family, *proedros*, *magistros* (the most commonly held dignity in this period, 35.6 per cent) and *vestarches*. In the late tenth century, the majority of *eparchs* received a *roga* containing 72 *nomismata*. The highest ranked received 576 *nomismata*, as *anthypatoi*, the lowest as *spatharioi* likely just 12. The average *roga* of an *eparch* at this time was 212 *nomismata*. There was an incease in the range of payments in the first third of the eleventh century; the *rogai* of most of the *eparchs* was seventy-two *nomismata*, while the highest ranked received 864. However, the average payment declined to 132 *nomismata*. From c. 1033, the fortunes of the *eparchs* improved dramatically. While a small percentage remained *protospatharioi*, an equal proportion became *proedroi*, leading to a range of *rogai* between 72 and 2,016 *nomismata*.[231] However, it was the *magistroi* who were the most numerous groups, receiving *rogai* of 1,152 *nomismata*. The average *roga* for this period was 698 *nomisamta*. Moreover, in terms of status the story of the *eparchs* is one of continuous improvement. From the position of *protospatharios*, the qualifying rank for membership of the senate in the tenth and early eleventh centuries, the *eparchs* rose to far higher than this in the middle third of the century, leaving behind the middle of the hierarchy for its upper levels.

The changing titles attached to the office of *eparch* are interesting because they tell a story about the importance of both the civilian arm of government and the city of Constantinople. In the period when the *eparch* was the most highly placed civilian in government, with authority over the life of the capital and the *demes*, the merchant guilds and trade, law and order, and his own court, over half of all *eparchs* held the relatively modest title of *protospatharios*, a figure which jumped to nearly two-thirds in the eleventh century. This placed them firmly in the middle of the contemporary hierarchy of titles. Even those *eparchs* who held the higher title of *patrikios* were still occupying a rung in the middle third of the ladder, and the even smaller number of *anthypatoi* had only just entered the upper levels. As we have seen, the position of the *eparchs* improved in the middle decades of the eleventh century, with *magistros*, the highest- or second-place title available depending on the exact date, becoming the most commonly held dignity. What makes this so interesting is that this was exactly the period when the *eparch* was losing many of his former jurisdictions, including his position as the highest judicial official of the empire and his place as the head of a court of appeal for provincial judicial decisions. As we shall see in the following chapter, it is reasonable to see this as a particularly serious demotion, and the eparch lost his judicial pre-eminence at just the time that the legal profession was becoming elevated within the Byzantine bureaucracy. The traditional view, based on a survey of the documentary evidence which highlights the shrinking portfolio of the *eparchs*, has been to conclude that the office became less important. What then, are we to make of the increasingly important titles that the sigillographic evidence proves were being given to the holders of an office with progressively fewer powers and a substantially reduced remit? A likely answer seems to be that the office of *eparch* was not becoming less important during the eleventh century, quite the opposite. When Empress Theodora took power during the rebellion against Michael V in 1042 in order to seize control over the city, and therefore in Attaleiates' account of the event, the empire, she filled the highest offices, and appointed men to supervise the markets.[232] In this passage we can clearly see the importance of Constantinople at this time, and its synonymous relationship with the empire as a whole, and the importance of the jurisdiction of the *eparch*, the supervisors of the markets, his subordinates, being the only specifically mentioned functionaries.[233] This passage from Attaleiates underlines what I would suggest is the key to understanding the developments seen in the seals of the office of the *eparch*, the growing size, wealth and population of Constantinople in this period, and the central place that the capital and its citizens had in the political system of the empire. Supplying the capital, organizing shipping, harbours, taxation of goods, storage of food, keeping track of visitors, must have been an ever-expanding burden, and those were just the duties of the *eparch* concerned with goods and people coming to the city. Inside Constantinople he had to manage the guilds, the markets, law and order, and almost every aspect of daily life, not to mention the fact that his remit extended one hundred miles from the city. When we add in the greater role that the courts had in the government of the eleventh century, the responsibilities of the *eparch* begin to look overwhelming. There was simply more for bureaucrats to do than ever before, and nowhere was that truer than in the capital. In such circumstances, it would be logical to focus the responsibilities of the *eparch*, in this case on the administration of Constantinople, assigning other duties to different officials or to newly elevated subordinates. The inscriptions on their seals prove that the changes to the responsibilities of the *eparchs* was not a demotion, but a restructuring, after which they were more important than ever, allowing the Father of the City to focus on the smooth operation of Constantinople.

3.3.2 The *symponos*

> Ὁρῶν σφραγῖδα συμπόνου νοσοκόμου ὅρον φύλαττε τρυτάνην καὶ stathmia …
>
> As you look at the seal of the symponos and nosokomos observe the specified unit of measure in the scale and weights.[234]

The *symponos* functioned as the *eparch*'s deputy particularly in matters related to trade and the regulation of merchants and the guilds. As the seal, possibly belonging to an Eustathios *symponos*, quoted earlier notes, he was responsible for the measures, scales and the weights used in monitoring and conducting transactions in the markets of Constantinople. The *Book of the Eparch* makes it clear that the guilds of the city received their measures, weights and scales, authenticated by the seal of the *eparch*, from his office.[235] Furthermore, the *eparch*'s staff regularly inspected the guild premises to ensure that the officially sanctioned equipment was being used, a duty which fell to the *boullotai*, junior officials, literally the inspectors of the seals, and, as the case of our anonymous seal owner shows, to the *symponos*.[236] It is possible that he also functioned as the *eparch*'s deputy in judicial matters as well.[237] He appears in the *Kletorologion of Philotheos* as the senior member of the *eparch*'s staff.[238] Furthermore, although there

Figure 3.6 Seal of Nicholas *hypatos*, judge of the Hippodrome and *symponos*. Harvard Art Museums/Arthur M. Sackler Museum, Bequest of Thomas Whittemore, 1951.31.5.1348.
The obverse of this elaborate seal of Nicholas depicts the Mother of God standing with a medallion of Christ flanked by saints Theodore and Nicholas.
Rev. Rev. +KER,Θ,|NIKOΛAω|VΠATωKPI|THEΠITOV|IΠOΔPOM,|SCVMΠO|Nω
Κύριε βοήθει Νικολάῳ ὑπάτῳ κριτῇ ἐπὶ τοῦ Ἱπποδρόμου καὶ συμπόνῳ.
Lord, help Nicholas, *hypatos*, judge of the Hippodrome and *symponos*.

Table 3.10 Normalized Seal Data, in Percentages, for the Titles of *Symponoi* c. 966–c. 1066

Title/Period	Tenth Century Final Third	Eleventh First Third	Eleventh Middle Third
Magistros			1.7
Protovestarches			1.7
Vestarches			6.7
Patrikios			15.1
Hypatos		2.6	2.5
Protospatharios	46.2	38.5	20.3
Spatharokandidatos	30.8	21.1	5.1
Spatharios	11.5	5.3	2.5
None	11.5	32.5	44.3

has been debate over the number of *symponoi*, due to a particular interpretation of a sentence in the *Book of the Eparch*, there was usually only a single *symponos*.[239]

The *symponos* does not appear in the *Taktikon Escorial* or the *Taktikon Beneševič* (934–44), and we must turn to the *Kletorologion of Philotheos* before we find him in a list of precedence, where he is ranked among the lowly *spatharioi*. With no documentary record for the position of the *symponoi* in the hierarchy at the beginning of our period we must turn to the seals. There are ninety-five surviving seals struck by sixty-three sigilants. The data from these seals is shown in a normalized form in Table 3.10.

The titles attached to the office of *sympanos* followed a trajectory that was similar to that of its superior the *eparch*, although starting at a lower base. The final third of the tenth century saw fewer than half of the *symponoi* qualifying for membership of the senate, a status maintained into the first third of the eleventh century. It was at this point that the status of a significant number of *symponoi* increased with a large drop in the percentage of *spatharioi*, *spatharokandidatoi* and *protospatharioi*, and an increase in other ranks, particularly *patrikioi* and *vestarchai*, but with a lucky few attaining the title of *magistros*. Analysing the seals of the *symponoi* in terms of *roga* inflation and average stipends is tricky because of the large proportion of sigilants who chose not to record their titles on their seals. I will discuss this phenomenon later, and do not want to preempt myself here, except to say that in the specific case of the *symponoi* I believe that we may see a fashion that developed out of devaluation to not record titles from the lower end of the hierarchy which could explain the 32.5 and 44.3 per cent of seals from the first two parts of the eleventh century. From the little evidence that we do have, the *symponoi* seem to have shared in their superior's good fortune, though to a lesser extent, perhaps a further indication of the status which being a part of the government of Constantinople could bring.

3.3.3 The *parathalassites*

> *In the past the streams of the sea used to be salty;*
> *now they are sweet. But do not be surprised;*
> *for the sea boasts a judge who removes all bitterness,*
> *with the mellifluous name, the sweet Melias.*[240]

The office of *parathalassites* appears only in the *Kletorologion of Philotheos*, and even then is not mentioned in the list of precedence itself, but rather in the descriptions of the officials within each department, where it is listed last among the subordinates of the *eparch*.[241] The *parathalassites* (literally 'by the sea') controlled the port of Constantinople, and was responsible for the import taxes on good being brought into the city.[242] The *Peira* claims that 'those who sail the seas' fell under his jurisdiction.[243] Furthermore, he was known to act as a judge on occasion.[244] The *parathalassites* is not much in evidence in the sigillographic record. The office is represented by only two men, Theodosios, possibly Monomachos, and John, up to c. 1066.[245] In the first half of the eleventh century Theodosios held the title *protospatharios*, John those of *vestes*, *anthypatos* and *patrikios*. I suspect that these two men represent two very different stages in the evolution of the office of *parathalassites*. Theodosios the *protospatharios* was likely a typical *parathalassites* as subordinate to the *eparch*, holding a title that was beginning to become devalued, existing in a mid-level position among those responsible for the smooth operation of life in the capital. John, the *vestes*, belonged to the early stages of a new order. Although not far removed in time from Theodosios, John's title was seven ranks higher than that borne by his predecessor and, depending when exactly he lived, possibly only three rungs from the top of the *cursus honorum*. This was an above inflation promotion, and although conclusions based on so few individuals are tentative at best, likely coincided with the elevation of the office of *parathalassites* from a position subordinate to the *eparch* to the head of its own department, which was accompanied by a widening of the office's territorial jurisdiction beyond the capital.[246]

3.3.4 The *praitor* of Constantinople

Θεοτόκε βοήθει Στεφάνῳ πατρικίῳ καὶ πραίτωρι Κωνσταντινουπόλεως.

Theotokos, help Stephen patrikios and praitor of Constantinople.[247]

The final official that we will discuss here is the *praitor* of Constantinople.[248] There has been a certain amount of confusion over the identity of this office. The question is whether the *praitor* of Constantinople can be equated with the *logothetes tou praitoriou*. The first mention of the office of *praitor* is in the history of Leo the Deacon, which records him arresting two women for attacking Emperor Nikephoros II Phokas in 967–8.[249] Ahrweiler believed that this official was the *praitor* of Constantinople, and that Nikephoros II had created the position sometime after his coronation in 963.[250] Oikonomides, however, concluded that the term *praitor* was probably an alternate way of describing the *logothetes tou praitoriou*, who served on the staff of the *eparch*.[251] Later, McGeer, Nesbitt and Oikonomides accepted that the official operating under Nikephoros II was likely the *praitor* of Constantinople, but that the origins of this office remained unclear. The *logothetes tou praitoriou* is listed second in the rankings of the *eparch*'s staff, behind the *symponos*. His area of authority included the *praitorion*, the *eparch*'s headquarters, and the prisons housed there. His policing duties certainly seem appropriate for an official who arrested those who assaulted the emperor.[252] Neither office is mentioned in the *Taktikon Escorial*, but, as we saw with the *symponos*, nor were any of the other deputies of the *eparch*. The most convincing case for the identity of the *praitores* of Constantinople was made by Andreas Gkoutzioukostas. He argued that the *praitor* of Constantinople was a completely different office from the *logothetes tou praitoriou*. Both clearly existed in the eleventh century, but the usual dignity recorded in the scant sources regarding the *logothetes* was *spatharokandidatos*, whereas for the *praitores* we see *magistros*, *vestes* and *patrikios*.[253] Gkoutzioukostas concludes that the office of *praitor* of Constantinople came into existence in the eleventh century and that its creation was related to the evolution of the role of the *eparch* of the city. Perhaps the *praitor* took over some of the judicial duties of the *eparch*.[254]

The office came into existence too late to feature in the *Taktikon Escorial*, and has left no record in the sigillographic evidence that is firmly dated to either the last third of the tenth or the first half of the eleventh centuries, with the exception of one seal in the Dumbarton Oaks collection, dated broadly to the eleventh century, which preserves neither the name nor the title of its owner.[255] The sudden appearance of the *praitores* of Constantinople in the sigillographic record around c. 1050 supports the idea that the office was created either in concert with, or as a result of, the readjustment of the functions of the *eparch*. Only seven individuals are known from seven seals, and one of these, dated to the second half of the eleventh century, is open to debate, as it simply identifies its owner as *praitor*, without any particular jurisdiction.[256] All of the seals under consideration fit equally into this and the following chapter, so I will discuss them here and reference them there. It is likely that the earliest of the seals of the *praitores* belonged to Theodore, *patrikios* and imperial *notarios* of the *eidikon* and *praitor* of Constantinople.[257] Of the remaining seals, all dated to the second half of the eleventh century, there is one further *patrikios*, Stephen, an *anthypatos* and *patrikios*,

Niketas, who was also an imperial *notarios* of the *eidikon*, Niketas Argyros, *magistros*, and Leo, *magistros*, *vestarches*, judge of the Velum, and *praitor* of Constantinople.[258] The dignities which they were awarded suggest that the *praitores* of c. 1050 onwards were operating at a similar, or occasionally slightly lower, level to contemporary *eparchs*. As a result, it is possible to tentatively conclude that the *praitores* were not subordinate to the *eparchs*. Exactly what the *praitores* did is unclear. It has been suggested that the name for the new post, *praitor*, was inspired by the use of the term slightly earlier for the theme judges. Gkoutzioukostas, hypothesized that the *praitor* was created to carry out some of the judicial duties which were being pulled from the *eparch*, namely his role as the chief judge within Constantinople itself. It is not hard to imagine, though impossible to prove, a situation where the *eparch* remained a 'great' judge, but relinquished control over the regional judges of the capital to the *praitor*. However, the theme judges were misleadingly named, and there is ample evidence that they were not jurists, but administrators with judicial duties attached.[259] If the *praitores* of Constantinople are etymologically linked, it is equally, in fact more, likely that they were involved in some aspect of the administration of the capital, not its courts.

3.3.5 At the center of empire

> *But, if you ever desire to go and do obeisance to the imperial power, partly to do obeisance in the holy churches, partly to see the fine organisation of the Palace, and of the City, do this once; only, from then on, (if you do this again), you are a slave, and not a friend.*[260]

The evidence that I have presented here of seals struck by those involved in the government of Constantinople is reasonably extensive. In total, we have examined four offices and 129 people. In their own way, and to varying degrees, the offices of *eparch*, *symponos* and *parathalassites* grew in importance in the first two-thirds of the eleventh century. In particular the *eparchs* and *parathalassitai* experienced above inflation promotions in terms of title and income. While we might not find this surprising for the newly independent *parathalassites*, who it could be argued was only being promoted to a level consummate with his new responsibilities, this was clearly not the case with the *eparch*, whose jurisdiction was narrowing at the same time that his status was increasing. The obvious answer is that the reason for the growing importance of these officials can be found in their territorial jurisdiction not their specific remits: they ran Constantinople. The new position of *praitor* was granted an exalted rank from its creation, a fitting reward for the man who was probably in charge of the courts of an expanding, and ever more important city. The written sources hint at the transformation of the government of the capital, but their evidence is too easy to ignore. The emperors of the early eleventh century made a special effort to win over the people of Constantinople, and once won, to keep their affections. Michael V thought that he could rule through the merchants and artisans of the capital rather than the elite, if we are to believe Psellos, and courted them accordingly, testing their loyalty before removing the empress Zoe from power by staging a lavish Easter procession through the streets of the capital.[261] Constantine IX took personal command of all attacks on Constantinople itself, such as the Russian attack of 1043 and the revolt of Tornikios in 1047, and was sure to be seen doing so by the citizens of the city.[262] When Tornikios besieged Constantinople, Constantine promised the people entertainments if they would help with the siege, and later in life while suffering from numerous maladies and in great pain Monomachos nonetheless performed his public ceremonial role for the sake of the people of Constantinople.[263] In a similar situation in 1057 Michael VI lavished gifts on the people of Constantinople in the hope that their support would be enough to preserve his throne from the rebellion underway in Anatolia.[264] The successful leader of that rebellion, Isaac I Komnenos, removed his troops from the city in part to please the people, and himself lost a great deal of their goodwill when he arrested the patriarch Keroularios.[265]

Often portrayed as pandering to the mob or selling titles to the upwardly mobile and urban newly wealthy, by contemporary Byzantines and modern scholars alike, these actions are seen as those of weak men trying to buy the support of the capital. The sigillographic evidence adds a little nuance to this view, and by starting with them and viewing the actions of the emperors through the lens they provide we can see the edges of a subtler imperial policy. The emperors were responding to developments in the nature, size and wealth of the city and its population that made Constantinople's governance much more important than ever before. This might well be why so few of the emperors left Constantinople, a characteristic that this period shares with the last time that the city was as capable of political involvement, the fifth and sixth centuries. It is obvious that this policy created resentment in some circles, from the provincial Kekaumenos for whom everything would have been better if only the emperors had left Constantinople more, to Psellos who resented the inclusion of the ill-educated masses in the imperial system. However, when we cut out the biases of our written sources and return to the question of how the functions of imperial government helped an emperor maintain his position, the reasoning behind a robust policy for administering the capital is readily apparent. After all, the only emperors to lose the throne up to c. 1066, Michael V, Michael VI Bringas and Isaac I Komnenos, lost the capital, not the empire.[266] It should also not be forgotten that most of the emperors of this period were Constantinopolitan: Romanos III Argyros, despite being from a provincial family, had lived in Constantinople for much of his life and served as *eparch* before being crowned, Michael IV was a moneychanger (*argyramoibos*), his nephew was the son of a caulker (*kalaphates*), and the Monomachoi were a Constantinopolitan family, as were the Bringas. Constantinople had moved from being a stage for, and home to, imperial government, to be a virtual empire in its own right. And imperial policy and the bureaucracy had adapted to meet the challenges that this new reality presented.

3.4 A new bureaucratic elite: The judiciary

And what concern, what manner of work or endeavor, is more fitting to His Majesty than concern for the laws? For the honor of an emperor is, according to the saying, to love judgement.

Constantine IX Monomachos, *Novella constitutio*, 1047[267]

Our exploration of the Byzantine judicial system, starting in c. 966, begins at a time where the laws of Byzantium, and their impact on good government and the relationship between powerful and poor, government and governed, had been hot topics in elite circles for almost a century.[268] Basil I, the founder of the Macedonian dynasty, produced the *Procheiros Nomos*, more commonly known as the *Prochiron* in the 870s as a handbook of imperial law.[269] It contained a selection of the most frequently used laws, and aimed to improve and widen access to the law, and improve instruction therein.[270] The next piece of Macedonian legal codification was the *Eisagoge tou nomou*, dated between 880 and 888, which owed a great deal to Photios, Patriarch of Constantinople.[271] By far the most ambitious of the early Macedonian legal works was published by Leo VI in 888 and was known to the Byzantines of the eleventh century as the *Basilika*.[272] The *Basilika* was a completely updated and mostly translated version of Justinian's sixth-century *Corpus Iuris Civilis*. To the Byzantines of the early Macedonian dynasty, and those living in our period, the law was important both for the benefits it brought to society and because of its innate Romanness. From the early historians of the Republic looking on the Twelve Tables, through the early empire, Theodosius, Justinian, the Iconoclast emperors and to Basil I, the Romans viewed their legal tradition with pride and as a part of what defined them as Romans. It has been argued that one reason Basil I implemented the great codification of Roman law completed by his son Leo VI was to reclaim the mantle of Rome from usurping Carolingians in the West.[273] Leo VI explicitly linked his own legal revisions with the work of the Great Justinian in the sixth century.[274] It is undeniable that a large degree of the work that the early Macedonians, Basil I and Leo VI, put into codifying the empire's laws, was a case of antiquarian image-building as much if not more so than a genuine attempt to reform the legal code.

Having said that, it should be noted that the early Macedonians were not solely concerned with the laws of late antiquity: they also issued new legislation. Leo VI promulgated a series of new laws, collectively known as the *Novels of Leo VI*. As the most recent work on the topic has noted, 'This flurry of legislative activity was the most extensive of any emperor after Justinian.'[275] Leo's *Novels* largely represent an attempt by the emperor to update late antique law to medieval situations.[276] As such they show that the second Macedonian was concerned to some degree with improving the quality of legislation, and thus his subjects' access to justice. Leo's heirs followed in his footsteps and issued a series of quite famous laws, collectively known as the Macedonian Land Legislation. These laws fall into two categories, those with the stated aim of protecting the poor against the powerful (*dynatoi*), and those that protected the lands which were supposed to support military duty.[277] Whether we view the first category as a genuine attempt to place the most vulnerable in the empire under imperial protection through the law, or as a tool with which the emperors could attack those who threatened them, the idea that the ruler could legislate away the empire's problems seems to stem from the general dynastic interest in law as legitimizing both the Romanness of the empire and imperial power.[278]

It was important for emperors to be seen to be champions of the law and justice, and not just because of link between the legislative tradition and the glory of Rome. The law was also a gift from the divine, as Basil I clearly stated at the beginning of the *Prochiron*, a sentiment repeated elsewhere in the codifying works of the early Macedonians and in the land legislation of their successors.²⁷⁹ As the law was a blessing from God, so justice through that law was a gift from the ruler to his subjects.²⁸⁰ Psellos has great fun with this imperial topos in the *Chronographia*. Romanos III Argyros, for all that he was previously a judge of the Hippodrome and *eparch* of Constantinople, was portrayed as ignorant of the law; Michael IV was equally inexperienced, but at least he was intelligent; and Constantine IX Monomachos might have been useless and lazy, but at least he had Psellos and his friends to advise him. When Psellos wanted to heap praise on an emperor, his grasp of the laws was a favourite trope.²⁸¹ Although Psellos is the most humorous of the authors to make this connection, he was not alone. Attaleiates praised Michael V for desiring to restore lawful government and Kekaumenos had much to say about the place of justice in the actions of a good ruler. Of course, we should perhaps not be surprised that Psellos the scholar and Attaleiates the judge would use knowledge and understanding of the law as a way to assess emperors. However, their works do show that the imperial topos of the law-giving emperor was taken seriously by at least some areas of Byzantine society.

That a widening circle of Byzantines was interested in the law and its application is suggested by the collections of non-imperial legal texts that abounded in the eleventh century.²⁸² For instance, the *Basilika* was the subject of commentaries and scholia which together number over two million words.²⁸³ For the purposes of this study, which is after all concerned with the mechanisms of the state rather than the law itself, the most interesting is the *Table of contents of the book called a record of experience by some, a teaching manual by others, drawn from the acts of the distinguished lord Eustathios Romaios*, more commonly known as the *Peira* (experience). This was a collection of the decisions and verdicts of Eustathios Romaios collected and edited by an anonymous assistant, pupil or colleague.²⁸⁴ It was written in the late 1030s or 1040s and contains seventy-five numbered chapters, each using the cases tried by Eustathios Romaios to tackle a different theme.²⁸⁵ The *Peira* is a valuable source for the procedures behind the verdicts of the courts: which judges were involved in what type of cases, how did appeals work, and who could be overruled and by whom? We will turn to the *Peira* frequently in the coming pages as we attempt to recreate the changing judicial structure in the eleventh century.

There has been much discussion of the nature of several offices traditionally considered to have dealt with matters of justice and whether they can legitimately be called judicial. The controversy arises because of the fluidity of the imperial system: anyone so directed by the emperor was a judge no matter what office he held, and because department chiefs had judicial jurisdiction over the men serving in their *sekreta*.²⁸⁶ The confusion that these two factors bring to any assessment of the Byzantine judiciary means that when an office holder is recorded as sitting in judgement, it is hard to know whether he was a judicial official, or someone with a particular or temporary jurisdiction. The simple fact is that without more evidence we can never be sure whether many of the offices traditionally seen as judicial were so in reality. Arguments relying on the name of an office to indicate its area of responsibility are flawed due, among other things, to the Byzantines' frequent recycling of ancient titles, thus the *kensor* had nothing in common with the ancient *censor*, and, contrary to one early theory, the judges of the Hippodrome were not concerned with chariot racing, an understandable assumption that was nonetheless incorrect. Similarly, looking for instances in the written material where a man was active as a judge, and then assigning judicial duties to his office is problematic because of the reasons outlined earlier. As a result, we will here deal with those offices for which a firm case can be made that their primary duties were judicial, the *droungarios tes viglas*, the *epi ton kriseon*, the *koiaistor*, the *antigrapheus* and the 'city judges' – the judges of the Hippodrome and the judges of the Velum. While these are not the only judicial offices active in the eleventh century, they are those firmly in the judicial camp for which there is enough evidence for a meaningful discussion of their evolving role within the Byzantine state.

All of which leads us to our discussion of the Byzantine judicial system. Renewing laws and wanting to be seen as Roman was all well and good, as was trying to legislate the empire into a desired state, but the emperors of the late tenth and eleventh centuries did far more than that: they reformed the judicial system as well. These changes went far beyond the imperial image or antiquarianism, by fundamentally changing the nature of government. The application of the law was as important a focus as the law itself. As we examine each judicial office we will see four trends emerging from the sigillographic evidence: the elevation of the place of the law itself in the imperial system, a rise in the status of some of the judiciary, the increase in the complexity and sophistication of the empire's legal apparatus, and a move towards the centralization of legal power in Constantinople.

3.4.1 The *koiaistor*

> Θεοτόκε βοήθει τῷ σῷ δούλῳ Θεοδώρῳ βασιλικῷ πρωτοσπαθαρίῳ ἐπὶ τοῦ Χρυσοτρικλίνου καὶ κοιαίστωρι τῷ Δεκαπολίτῃ.
>
> Theotokos, help your servant Theodore Dekapolites, imperial protospatharios epi tou Chrysotriklinou and koiaistor.[287]

Before turning to a judicial system undergoing monumental changes, we will consider an office that had its roots in late antiquity and was a model of stability. The office of *koiaistor* (Latin quaestor) displayed a remarkable consistency in rank and duties throughout the ninth to eleventh centuries. In the *Kletorologion of Philotheos* the *koiaistor* falls thirty-fifth in the list of *axiai dia logou*, in the *Taktikon Beneševič* its ranking was fortieth and in the *Taktikon Escorial*, one hundred and twenty-sixth.[288] On the surface these rankings do not seem to represent consistency. However, the diminished position was due to the creation of new provincial military commands between 899 and 934–44, and even more new posts in the army, both in the *themes* and in the *tagmata*, between 934–44 and 971–5. In all three *taktika* the *koiasitor* was the fourth highest ranked bureaucrat and came second only to the *eparch* when it came to judicial officials. The office of *koiaistor* had its origins in two earlier positions, the late Roman *quaestor sacri palatii*, created by Constantine I, who acted as a legal advisor to the emperor, drafted laws and dealt with petitions sent to the imperial court, and the *quaesitor*, a Constantinopolitan judicial position created by Justinian in 539. In terms of function, the duties of the *koiaistor* blended those of the Constantinian and Justinianic creations. The *koiaistor* chaired a tribunal, one of the four permanent courts of the capital, with jurisdiction over cases involving wills, family law, forged documents and disputes between landlords and their tenants, and even criminal cases.[289] He also aided in the creation of imperial laws, and had some responsibility over foreign visitors to the capital and beggars in Constantinople.[290] The tendency towards consistency with the office of *koiaistor* extended to its duties, which remained constant throughout the eleventh century.[291]

When we turn to the seals belonging to the *koiaistores* this study incorporates fifty seals belonging to thirty individuals, plus evidence of a further seven men from written records. This is a respectable number considering that the position was occupied by only one person at a time. The normalized data gleaned from the seals can be seen in Table 3.11.

While the number of both seals and represented individuals is not as large as we would like, these figures do allow us to draw some tentative conclusions. At the time of the *Escorial Taktikon* an individual with the position of *koiaistor* would likely be awarded the dignity of *protospatharios*. A smaller number of individuals would find themselves with dignities lower, *spatharios*, and much higher, *magistros*, but clearly the title most frequently associated with a *koiaistor* was *protospatharios*. This was still the case in the first third of the eleventh century. It was in the middle of the century that the situation changed, with the percentage of *koiaistores* with the rank of *protospatharios* dropping by half. The difference was made up by higher ranks, including *protoproedros*, one of the highest ranks at that time, which had itself only just been created. The elevation of the *koiaistores* was accompanied by substantial increases in the value of the *rogai* distributed to these men. Discounting those for whom we have no recorded title, the average *roga* paid out to the *koiaistor* was 1.95 pounds of gold in the final third of the tenth century, 1.57 pounds and 10.37 pounds of gold in the first and middle thirds of the eleventh century respectively. It is clear that their income remained largely steady c. 966–1033, before increasing nearly sixfold for almost half of them in the middle third of the eleventh century. This pattern is somewhat supported in the patchy documentary evidence. There are seven mentions of a *koiaistor* dated to the first third of the eleventh century, which record individuals holding the ranks of *protospatharios*, *anthypatos* and *patrikios*, and *vestes*, *athypatos*,

Table 3.11 Normalized Seal Data, in Percentages, for the Titles of *Koiaistores* c. 966–c. 1066

Title/Period	Tenth Century Final Third	Eleventh Century First Third	Eleventh Century Middle Third
Protoproedros			11.8
Proedros			11.8
Magistros	5.9		
Vestes			11.8
Patrikios and *Protospatharios*		19	11.8
Protospatharios	76.5	81	41.2
Spatharios	5.9		
None	11.8		11.8

and *patrikios*.²⁹² From this evidence, we can discern a clear development in the status of the office which became increasingly elevated for a significant proportion of *koiaistores* during the middle third of the eleventh century, advancing above the rate of inflation for titles.

3.4.2 The *antigrapheus*

> Κύριε βοήθει Λέοντι σπαθαροκανδιδάτῳ καὶ ἀντιγραφεί.
>
> Lord, help Leo spatharokandidatos and antigrapheus.²⁹³

The *antigrapheus*, a deputy of the *koiaistor*, is not much in evidence in either the sigillographic or documentary record. We know of only fourteen individuals from just twenty-one seals.²⁹⁴ As such it is difficult to make meaningful conclusions and the data cannot be adequately normalized. There was a general inflation of the titles awarded to the *antigrapheis*, from roughly two-thirds being *spatharioi*, at the bottom of the hierarchy, with the remainder an equal split of *spatharokandidatoi* and *protospatharioi*, both in the middle of the hierarchy, in the final third of the tenth century, to 50 per cent *spatharioi* in the first third of the eleventh century, with the remaining half divided evenly between *spatharokandidatos* and *protospatharios*. This trend continued into the middle third of the eleventh century, with the majority of *antigrapheis* holding the rank of *spatharokandidatos*; eleventh place out of twelve. The evidence for the *antigrapheis*, although never plentiful, drops noticeably in the final third of the eleventh century. The transition from majority *spatharioi* to largely *spatharokandidatoi* probably reflects the fact that the dignity of *spatharios* was dropping out of use at this time. Both titles occupied the lowest rung in the hierarchy at the time that they were given to the *antigrapheis*. What seems certain is that while the *koiaistor* was being promoted well above inflation, his deputy was slowly slipping in both the hierarchy and in terms of his income as the eleventh century progressed.

3.4.3 The *droungarios tes viglas*

> Κύριε βοήθει τῷ σῷ δούλῳ Εὐσταθίῳ μαγίστρῳ καὶ δρουγγαρίῳ τῆς βίγλας.
>
> Lord, help your servant Eustathios, magistros and droungarios tes viglas.²⁹⁵

The four trends in the development of the judiciary outlined in the introduction to this section are nowhere more apparent than in the history of the office of *droungarios tes viglas* (Commander of the Watch). The office of *droungarios tes viglas* was not as old as that of *koiaistor*, but was still verging on venerable, and unlike its older cousin has an interesting, and in fact unique, story of changing responsibilities and status in the eleventh century. The *Vigla* (Watch) was one of the *tagmata*, the mobile army of the Byzantine Empire dating from the eighth century, and the *droungarios* was its commander.²⁹⁶ The responsibilities of the *Vigla* in Constantinople included the security of the Great Palace and guarding the Covered Hippodrome, home to many of the law courts of the empire, duties which brought the *droungarios* into frequent

Figure 3.7 Seal of Eustathios *magistros* and *droungarios tes viglas*. Dumbarton Oaks, Byzantine Collection, Washington, DC, BZS.1958.106.5598.
This seal likely belonged to the well-known jurist Eustathios Romaios, who helped establish the *droungarios tes viglas* as the preeminent legal authority in the empire.
Obv. ...ΗΘΕΙΤШCШΔΟVΛШ
Rev. ΕVCΤΑΘ,|ΜΑΓΗCΤ.|CΔΡ8Γ..|P,ΤΗCRI|ΓΛΑ
Κύριε/Θεοτόκε βοήθει τῷ σῷ δούλῳ Εὐσταθίῳ μαγήστρῳ καὶ δρουγγαρίῳ τῆς Βίγλας.
Lord/Theotokos, help your servant Eustathios, *magistros* and *droungarios tes viglas*.

contact with, and increasing participation in, the judicial process. In the *Taktikon Escorial* the *droungarios* of the *Vigla* was placed 128th (total hierarchy) 106th (offices) in the rankings.[297] However, from c. 1030 the function of the *droungarios* evolved from a military command into a judicial posting.[298] The *droungarios* of the *Vigla* came to chair one of the four permanent courts of Constantinople. Exactly which court, and in which period, is unclear. Did the *droungarios* chair the Court of the Hippodrome or his own tribunal which happened to meet in the Covered Hippodrome? Could he have done both?[299] No matter the exact arrangements, it is clear that the tribunal chaired by the *droungarios* had wide-reaching powers, a precedent set by one of the first, possibly the second, *droungarios* with a solely judicial role, Eustathios Romaios. Many of the verdicts and decisions recorded in the *Peira* date to Eustathios' tenure as *droungarios tes viglas*, and they record the remit of his court. The *droungarios* of the *Vigla* clearly had jurisdiction over both civil cases, property disputes, contested dowries and issues of inheritance, which are well represented in the *Peira*, and criminal cases including torture, rape and murder.[300] Plaintiffs could appeal to the court of the *droungarios* concerning the decisions of the other courts of the empire, both those in Constantinople and the provinces.[301] As *droungarios* Eustathios Romaios overruled the *eparch* and the *koiaistor*, two officials previously only answerable to the emperor, as well as city judges from Constantinople and theme judges. There are also cases from the provinces which almost certainly went straight to the *droungarios* for his consideration with no mention of the provincial judicial authorities.[302]

The cases adjudicated by Eustathios concerned powerful *dynatoi* and poor peasants, monks, bishops, villagers and townsmen, free men and slaves.[303] The authority over justice empire-wide that this broad remit implies, and the fact that the *droungarios*'s court also promulgated laws led Nicolas Oikonomides to consider the *droungarios tes viglas* more of a 'Minister of Justice' than a judge.[304] This position is supported by the sheer number of cases referred to the *droungarios* and his tribunal directly by the emperor. In these cases, the *droungarios tes viglas* was acting as the emperor's proxy in an obvious way. It could be argued that the *Peira* represents the work of one particular *droungarios*, and that there is no guarantee that later holders of the office had the same powers that he held. That this was not the case is hinted at by the addition of *megas* to the name of the office and by a document issued by Constantine IX Monomachos in 1045 for his Nea Mone on Chios where the *droungarios tes viglas* is listed before the other judges in a place of precedence. The impression given by these two widely separated pieces of evidence for a continuity of high status for the *droungarioi* after Eustathios Romaios is reinforced by the testimony of the lead seals.

As we might expect from a high-ranking post filed by one individual at a time, there are not many surviving seals that belonged to the *droungarioi*. For the period from the late tenth to early twelfth century there are thirty-two seals, struck by fifteen men.[305] To this can be added four individuals recorded in the written sources where both office and title were mentioned.[306] From the available evidence, it seems that the *droungarioi* serving in the final third of the tenth century (involving two of our fifteen individuals, Damian and Theodore) held titles in the upper-middle and lower top range of the hierarchy as it existed at that time, *patrikios* and *protospatharios*, and *anthypatos* and *patrikios*, respectively.[307] The known *droungarioi* remained at about this position into the eleventh century, and most of the seals record the dignity of *patrikios*, either alone (Kyriakos) or alongside *anthypatos* (Theodore) or in combination with *anthypatos* and *protospatharios* (Theophylaktos).[308] The exceptions are two seals belonging to a certain Eustathios, who may be identified with the famous jurist and subject of the *Peira* Eustathios Romaios.[309] The difficulty with this identification is that the seal does not provide a family name. However, we know that Eustathios Romaios served as *droungarios* at about the time that these seals were struck, and that before being given this office, between 1031 and 1034, he held the titles of *vestes*, *anthypatos* and *patrikios*, and he was promoted to *magistros* before 1034.[310] The two seals belonging to an Eustathios record the same titles that Romaios bore in the two phases of his career as *droungarios*. This makes it likely that the seals belonged to Eustathios Romaios. Furthermore, as a *magistros* Eustathios held the highest title then available. A later, anonymous, holder of the office also held the title of *magistros*, paired with *vestarches*, both firmly in the top third of the hierarchy.[311] In terms of both status and compensation the *droungarioi* saw an improvement in their circumstances over the course of the eleventh century. Until Eustathios's time the *droungarioi* were either *patrikioi*, with *rogai* of 288 *nomismata*, or *anthypatoi*, 576 *nomismata*. As a *vestes* Eustathios was entitled to 864 *nomismata*, rising to 1,152 following his promotion to *magistros*.

These figures are quite revealing. From a relatively high position at the end of the tenth century, the income, and presumably the prestige, of the office of *droungarios tes viglas* dropped in the opening decades of the eleventh century, before noticeably rising when occupied by Eusathios Romaios. The *droungarios* remained a very high-ranking individual throughout the second third of the eleventh century, proof that Eustathios himself was not an anomaly. The significant increase in the status of the *droungarioi* occurred at precisely point of transition from a military to a judicial office. As Oikonomides pointed out, the change in the nature of the office of *droungarios tes viglas* must have occurred in the reign of Romanos III Argyros, and was a major addition to the judicial structure of the empire.[312] This is a rare piece of evidence where we can see a position within the Byzantine army transform into a civilian judicial office, with the latter being accorded significantly more prestige than it had been given during its military incarnation. It is telling that when she seized power following the death of Constantine IX Monomachos, Empress Theodora promoted her most trusted followers to high office as a means of securing her power. Only three offices were specifically listed by Skylitzes who recorded these events, Theodore was made *domestikos ton scholon*, effectively head of the army, Niketas Xylinites was given the post of *logothetes tou dromou*, and Manuel was made *droungarios tes viglas*.[313] Theodora took power through control of the army, internal communications and justice. The transformation of the office of *droungarios* from second-rate military post to one of the three most important posts for controlling the throne in just over twenty years is quite a remarkable one, both for the office and for its impact on the government of the empire. His tribunal interpreted the meaning of the law, debated legal procedures and applied their rulings to the other courts of the capital and those in the provinces. This was a new approach to the use of the law in government, and an enhancement of the role of the Constantinopolitan judiciary's place in that process.

3.4.4 The *politikoi dikastai*: The 'city judges'

Do not feel compassion for anyone in judgment because of philanthropia, but if someone is a dear friend of yours and he is about to be judged, beg leave of judging such a case so that you do not judge unjustly. Far be it for you that you disgrace yourself, and your friend will be judged by the city judges.[314]

Although often referred to in the written sources as the *politikoi dikastai*, the city judges, this term does not appear on seals. Instead we see a term for two categories of city judges, the judge of the Velum, and the judge of the Hippodrome both of which can be found appearing frequently in the documentary material as well.[315] As offices with multiple holders the judges of the Hippodrome and the judges of the Velum have left behind a large number of seals. However, before turning to the sigillographic material we shall discuss some of the questions surrounding the city judges: What was their function, did they form a single or multiple tribunals, how many of them were there, and what, if any, were the differences between the judges of the Hippodrome and the judges of the Velum? We shall then turn the seals to see where they can add to the attempt to answer these questions.

The answer to the question of numbers could provide clues to the number and function of tribunals, so we shall begin our quest there. With the judges of the Hippodrome and the judges of the Velum we come to a different class of official from those that we have discussed earlier. The offices discussed earlier were held by one man at a time, however there were many judges. Exactly how many is open to question. Balsamon, possibly, says that there were twelve judges of the Velum, as, again possibly, does the *Ecloga Basilicorum*.[316] However, it is unclear whether the text means twelve judges in total, and exactly which judges these were.[317] Furthermore, this evidence comes from almost two centuries (1142) after the first appearance of the judges of the Hippodrome and the judges of the Velum in the *Escorial Taktikon*. How accurately this twelfth-century picture represents the tenth- and eleventh-century judiciary is very much open to question.[318] That this evidence is an unreliable source for the eleventh-century judicial structure becomes clear when one remembers that the two types of judges, Velum and Hippodrome, likely merged at the end of the eleventh century, about which more below.[319] Using mid-twelfth-century evidence created in a Byzantium that had undergone profound changes of government to tackle tenth- and eleventh-century questions seems like a flawed approach borne of an unwillingness to leave a question unanswered. Exactly how many judges there were at any one time, and what relationship this had to the number of judges assessing each case must remain a mystery.

So far, I have spoken about the judges of the Hippodrome and the judges of the Velum together, but were they the same thing? Again, modern opinion has been divided between those who see them as basically the same thing and those who see the judges of the Velum as superior to judges of the Hippodrome, perhaps even an elite group of judges existing within the greater whole.[320] The career of Elpidios Kenchres, who started his career as judge of the Hippodrome before becoming a judge of the Velum supports this view of the judicial hierarchy. However, there is no way to know whether his career was typical, nor whether what we are witnessing was a promotion or the accumulation of another office. Whether the two types of judges were separated by more than their name informs many of the arguments about their operation and function.

This brings us to the question of the tribunals themselves. Exactly how the two groups of city judges, Velum and Hippodrome, operated has almost as many possible answers as there are historians who have considered the issue.[321] Did they sit together or were there separate tribunals, a Court of the Hippodrome and a Court of the Velum?[322] Did they have their own tribunals, or did they make up the panel in the courts of the higher judges, the *eparch*, *koiaistor* and *droungarios tes viglas*? We know that there was a court in the Covered Hippodrome, first recorded in the reign of Michael I Rangabe (811–13) by Theophanes.[323] No mention was made at this time of judges of the Hippodrome, who are not recorded until the end of the tenth century, but presumably took their name from the location of the court.[324] Oikonomides was of the opinion that the term 'judge of the Hippodrome' became necessary only with the creation of judge of the Velum as a way to distinguish the two groups.[325] It is important to note that Theophanes does not mention a specific tribunal, a Court of the Hippodrome, which does not appear in the sources until the mid-eleventh century.[326] What about a court of the Velum? No such court is ever mentioned in the sources.[327] However, it has been argued that the eponymous curtain could be the clue to an answer. The exact nature and function of the velum/curtain has been much debated. Curtains were important in Byzantium as a way of separating people; they appear frequently in imperial ceremonies dividing the emperor from everyone else. The question of how this related to the judges of the Velum has been a cause of speculation: Was the tribunal set behind a curtain, and if so was it a permanent fixture, or was it retracted? Could it have separated the judges of the Velum from the lesser judges of the Hippodrome, or did the emperor sit behind a curtain on those occasions when he joined the tribunal?[328] Depending on which of these answers the scholar finds convincing, it is possible to argue that the curtain meant that the judges of the Velum must have had their own tribunal or that they shared their bench with their colleagues of the Hippodrome. The only constant is a prominent piece of drapery. The simple fact is that the only thing we know about this particular curtain is that it gave its name to the judges of the Velum; the rest is pure guesswork.[329] The *Peira* does not even mention the judges of the Velum.[330] It has been suggested that the judges of the Velum formed the elite within the city judges, and that from the 1030s they sat alongside the *droungarios*, forming his supreme tribunal.[331] There is ample evidence of other judges sitting alongside the 'great' judges in the capital, particularly the *droungarios*. Oikonomides believed that the judges of the Velum, as the senior city judges, were the ones who sat alongside the *droungarios* once he had become the empire's chief jurist.[332] The *Peira* rarely specifies which type of judge sat on which bench, mostly they are referred to as so-and-so the judge. However, there are instances where the individual mentioned in the *Peira* can be connected to another source which recorded more information. For example, the Ophrydas mentioned in *Peira* 16.9, 19.5 and 51.16 was probably Michael Ophrydas, recorded on his seal as *vestes*, judge of the Velum and imperial *notarios* of the *ephoros*, and (Leo) Thylakas, *Peira* 16.9, a well-known judge of the Hippodrome.[333] With respect to the tribunals there is enough evidence to provide tantalizing hints, but far too little for concrete conclusions. At best, we can say that the judges of the Hippodrome and judges of the Velum sat in a number of tribunals chaired by different officials, although because our main source concerns Eustathios Romaios we have most evidence for the court of the *droungarios*. We also know that they sometimes sat with others of their own order, and also came to decisions alone on occasion. In short, it seems likely that they were everywhere.

The status and function of the city judges are inextricably linked. Much has been made of the distinction between the 'great' judges or *archontes*, such as the *droungarios tes viglas*, and the 'small' judges, the judges of the Hippodrome and of the Velum.[334] The important difference here is that, the 'great' judges chaired tribunals and had the power to pass judgements in a greater variety of cases than the 'small' judges who acted as their assistants or tribunal members, or gave verdicts on lesser cases. How we understand the relationship between different classes of judges will shape our understanding of the entire judicial system. The problem with the argument about great and small judges for our period is that the source on which it is based, the *Ecloga Basilicorum*, was written in 1142 and describes a legal landscape that was in all likelihood different from that of the late tenth and eleventh centuries.[335] This text presents a judicial world in which the city judges played second fiddle to more powerful magistrates, including the theme judges of the provinces, who were numbered among the 'great' judges. In the eleventh century, there is evidence that this was not always the case. Furthermore, in 1045, in a clearly hierarchical list of judges, the city judges were listed immediately following the *droungarios*, but before, and thus presumably ranked higher than, the theme judges.[336] The officers whom the *Ecloga Basilicorum* designates as great were always of a higher importance as magistrates than the city judges. However, as judges, there is ample evidence that the theme judges were far less highly valued.[337] The key to understanding this distinction lies in the opinion that the city judges were legal experts, professional judges, in a way in which the theme judges were not. An interesting element of this difference has been recently explored by Zachary Chitwood with respect to the legal fees, *ektagiatika* or *sportulae*, paid to judges by litigants.[338] In his two novels on legal fees, Constantine VII stated that theme judges were allowed to charge legal fees, while city judges were not.[339] As the emperor put it, 'None of the city judges [is allowed] to receive anything for any sort of reason, but they [must] instead have clean hands and disdain all money.'[340] As Chitwood states, this situation likely came about because the lower provincial courts were not as highly regarded as the central Constantinopolitan tribunals, which acted as courts of appeal for decisions made in the themes.[341] Fear of review by the city judges certainly influenced the advice written down by Kekaumenos to theme judges with which we opened this section. It would be an unusual judicial system that made 'great' judges subject to review by 'small' judges, further reinforcing the notion that either the testimony of the *Ecolga Basilicorum* does not apply to the eleventh century or that in this case it does not reference judicial powers.

This brings us to the duties of the city judges. Modern scholars often liken the judges of the Velum and the judges of the Hippodrome to modern supreme court justices.[342] It is clear from the descriptions of cases in the *Peira* that they were part of the review and appeals process by which the actions of other judges were assessed. Much of the evidence for the operations of the tribunals of the capital comes from the decisions and verdicts of Eustathios Romaios as recorded in the *Peira*. In fact, this text covers his judgements throughout his career from his time as judge of the Hippodrome to *droungarios tes viglas*. Even as *droungarios* Eustathios was serving on a tribunal with judges of the Hippodrome and the Velum, and all of the types of cases considered by him were subject to their judgement as well. At various times city judges, whether of the Court of the Hippodrome or other tribunals, permanent or ad hoc, are recorded sitting under the chairmanship of variously the *eparch*, the *koiaistor*, one of their own number, and increasingly as the eleventh century progressed the *droungarios tes viglas*. From the time when the *droungarios* rose to prominence as the highest judicial authority in the empire, he regularly chaired a tribunal made up of city judges, some of whom are known to have been judges of the Hippodrome or the Velum, possibly in the Covered Hippodrome.[343] As demonstrated by Oikonomides, the court of the *droungarios* operated in a very modern fashion. The *droungarios* himself was but one judge, and a majority of the judges had to agree before a verdict was passed.[344] As well as the written verdict of the majority, litigants would receive a written record of the minority view as well, in case of appeal.[345] Thus while it might be correct to view the city judges as assistants to the greater judges, the *droungarios*, *eparch* and *koiaistor*, at least in the court of the *droungarios* they operated almost as equals.[346] While these conclusions might seem a little vague, to try to do more with the available evidence would be to stretch it past breaking point. What can be said for sure is that as the tenth century became the eleventh century there was an active and increasingly vocal group of jurists working in the Covered Hippodrome and elsewhere in various tribunals chaired by assorted officials, particularly the *droungarios tes viglas*, and they were at the very center of the interpretation and application of the law in Byzantium.

Aside from their work in the capital, judges of the Hippodrome and judges of the Velum also undertook tasks outside of Constantinople. In the *Peira* Eustathios Romaios is recorded as travelling through the towns close to Constantinople to hear cases, and also as spending a time as an *anagrapheus*.[347] Such provincial assignments were not uncommon. A recent study has used the archives of the monasteries on Mount Athos to examine the role of the judges from Constantinople as provincial judges in the theme of Boleron, Strymon and Thessaloniki.[348] Now we must explore the sigillographic evidence, to see what the seals can add to our understanding of the city judges.

3.4.4.1 The judges of the Velum

Θεοτόκε βοήΘει Θεοδώρῳ πατρικίῳ καὶ κριτῇ τοῦ βήλου τῷ Πρωτευοντι.

Theotokos, help Theodore Proteuon, patrikios and judge of the Velum.[349]

The judges of the Velum make their appearance in the Byzantine sources in the *Taktikon Escorial*. At this point they were not particularly important, they ranked 182nd out of a total of 198 positions (total hierarchy) and 159th out of a total of 175 (offices).[350] They were the second-lowest ranked official attached to the dignity of *protospatharios*, itself only in the middle of the hierarchy, and the fourth lowest-ranked bureaucrats in the whole *Taktikon*. The sigillographic evidence, from 329 seals belonging to 182 individuals, shows that their fortunes changed for the better during the eleventh century. As we can see from Table 3.12, 85 per cent of the judges of the Velum were *protospatharioi* in the final third of the tenth century, a figure consistent with the

Table 3.12 Normalized Seal Data, in Percentages, for the Titles of Judges of the Velum c. 966–c. 1066

Title/Period	Tenth Century Final Third	Eleventh Century	
		First Third	Middle Third
Proedros			1.6
Magistros and Vestarches			1.6
Magistros and Vestes		5	4.7
Magistros		2	9.9
Protovestarches			0.6
Vestarches and Patrikios			0.3
Vestarches and Hypatos			1.3
Vestarches			10.6
Vestes, Anthypatos and Patrikios			1.9
Vestes and Patrikios			0.9
Vestes		7.3	9.2
Anthypatos, Patrikios and Hypatos		1.8	0.9
Anthypatos and Patrikios		2.7	4.4
Patrikios and Hypatos	14.3	5	6.2
Patrikios		11.9	12.4
Protospatharios and Dishypatos			0.9
Dishypatos		0.9	0.3
Hypatos and Protospatharios		2.7	2.5
Hypatos		0.9	1.2
Protospatharios	85.7	49.3	23
Spatharokandidatos		1.8	0.3
None		6.4	5.3

Figure 3.8 Seal of Constantine *vestarches*, judge of the Velum and *megas kourator* of the *sekreton* of the Mangana. Dumbarton Oaks, Byzantine Collection, Washington, DC, BZS.1958.106.5709.
The obverse shows a medallion of Christ flanked by the standing figures of Sts. Nicholas and Menas Kallikelados. This unusual iconography was associated with the family or followers of Patriarch Michael Keroularios, Constantine was his nephew who would later become *sebastos* and *droungarios tes viglas*.
Obv. KE|RO|HΘEI|TωCω|ΔΥΛω
Rev. +KῶNRE|CTAPX,KPIT,|TΥRHΛΥSM̃|KΥPATOP,TΥ|CEKPETΥT|MAΓΓAN,
Κύριε βοήθει τῷ σῷ δούλῳ Κωνσταντίνῳ βεστάρχῃ, κριτῇ τοῦ βήλου, καὶ μεγάλῳ κουράτορι τοῦ σεκρέτου τῶν Μαγγάνων.
Lord, help your servant Constantine *vestarches*, judge of the Velum, and grand *kourator* of the *sekreton* of the Mangana

evidence from the *Taktikon Escorial*. The percentage of *protospatharioi* dropped by over 40 per cent in the opening decades of the eleventh century, and subsequently more than halved by c. 1066. This was the result of a gently increasing number of judges holding higher titles, most frequently *patrikios*. The cautious movement up the hierarchy continued into the middle third of the century. The groupings around *patrikios*, by this point a rather lowly title and *anthypatos*, an upper-middle rank, remained of approximately the same size. Most significant in this period are the high numbers of judges holding high-ranking dignities – *vestarches*, *magistros* and *proedros* – accounting for almost a third of the total, far more than were still *protospatharioi*. The move up the hierarchy which had started as a crawl at the beginning of the eleventh century had progressed to a gentle stroll. Documentary evidence provides us with evidence for specific moments in this process. We know of judges of the Velum with the titles of *protospatharios* in 1029 and 1045, *vestes*, *anthypatos* and *patrikios* in 1045, *hypatos* in 1056 and 1062, *anythypatos* and *patrikios* in 1059, *dishypatos* in 1060.[351]

The wide range of titles held by the judges of the Velum after c. 1000 makes it more difficult to assess their *rogai* than for almost every other office. As such examining the mean, range and most common payment is especially crucial. In all three time periods the largest single group of the judges were *protospatharioi*. As such the most common value for the *roga* was 1 pound of *nomismata*. However, the percentage of judges receiving the most common stipend decreased over time, until by the middle third of the eleventh century three quarters of the judges of the Velum were receiving more than that. This is where the average payment comes in. The figures in all three periods are 1.43, 2.52 and 6.71 pounds of *nomismata* respectively. Although the payment which accounted for the largest single group of judges remained that of the *protospatharios*, it is clear from these figures that as a group they were becoming wealthier as a result of their gradual increase in status.[352]

Based on our experience so far, it is right to question whether the spread of the judges of the Velum across the hierarchy might be the result of the offices that they held. Of the 182 men assessed for this study, only twenty-six are recorded as just a judge of the Velum on their seals, the rest held at least one other office concurrently with that of judge. Although they fall below the stated minimum in terms of numbers, a quick experiment with normalization is illuminating. When the data from these 'exclusive judges' is normalized and then compared to our multitasking magistrates, the spread of titles is almost the same for each period, including for the final third of the eleventh century, to which we shall turn in the next chapter. The exception is that there are no men represented by the seals who were just judges of the Velum with the lowest titles recorded, *spatharios* and *spatharokandidatos*. If the figures for the two groups (exculsive and multitasking judges) are placed side-by-side of the twenty-four titles and groups of titles which they held, only four, which happen to be the largest single groups, show a difference of more than three per cent. Clearly, multiple offices did not necessarily impact upon the titles an individual held in any significant way. It seems likely that when a Byzantine was given multiple posts, including that of judge of the Velum, that all of his offices were at roughly the same level at the time of appointment.

3.4.4.2 *The judges of the Hippodrome*

Κύριε βοήθει τῷ σῷ δούλῳ Χριστοφόρο βασιλικῷ πρωτοσπαθαρίῳ καὶ ἐπὶ τοῦ Χρυ σοτρικλίνου καὶ κριτῇ τοῦ Ὑπποδρόμου.

Lord, help your servant Christopher, imperial protospatharios and epi tou Chrysotriklinou and judge of the Hippodrome.[353]

With the judges of the Hippodrome we come to another truly large group of judicial seals, 376 to be exact, struck by approximately 232 individuals. The normalized data from these seals can be seen in Table 3.13.

The earliest reference to the judges of the Hippodrome is found in the *Taktikon Escorial*, where they occupied the 186th (total hierarchy) 163rd (offices) position in the hierarchy.[354] They fell behind such luminaries as the *minsourator*, who oversaw the emperor's tent on campaigns and the *protospatharioi* attached to the households of retired *strategoi*. They, in fact, occupied a spot only twelve places above the very bottom of the list, and only two bureaucrats ranked lower than them. From c. 966 to c. 1066 the majority of judges of the Hippodrome were also *protospatharioi*, with *spatharokandidatos* as the second most common dignity c. 966–c. 1033. Nevertheless, times were changing. In the first third of the eleventh century a small number of judges gained access to titles above that of *protospatharios* for the first time, and as the hierarchy was largely static at this time, we must view these as an overall increase in status, even if a modest one from *protospatharios* to *patrikios*. This gradual progression

Table 3.13 Normalized Seal Data, in Percentages, for the Titles of Judges of the Hippodrome c. 966–c. 1066

Title/Period	Tenth Century Final Third	Eleventh Century First Third	Eleventh Century Middle Third
Proedros			0.6
Magistros		0.5	0.7
Vestarches			1.5
Protovestes			0.9
Vestes, Anthypatos and *Patrikios*			1.4
Vestes and *Hypatos*			0.9
Vestes			1.8
Anthypatos and *Patrikios*			2
Anthypatos			0.9
Illoustrios			0.4
Patrikios and *Hypatos*			3.2
Patrikios		1.5	5.3
Hypatos and *Protospatharios*		1.2	1.6
Hypatos		2	4.1
Protosptharios	89.6	81.9	64.1
Spatharokandidatos	5.5	10	3.8
Spatharios	3.1	0.7	
None	1.8	2.2	7.1

continued into the middle decades of the century. Although the numbers with no title rose, this does not cover the drop in the percentage of those holding the lowest titles, which is explained by an increase in the range of dignities held by the judges. This change saw just over one quarter of the judges of the Hippodrome with titles above that of *protospatharios*, with the largest single groups belonging to the next titles up the ladder, *hypatos*, 5.7 per cent, and *patrikios*, 8.5 per cent. In terms of status the judges of the Hippodrome were slipping backwards. Even as a *patrikios* a judge of c. 1060 was in the bottom third of the hierarchy, whereas a *protospatharios* of sixty years earlier had been in the middle.[355] The scant documentary evidence provides a complimentary picture for the first two-thirds of the eleventh century. Two-thirds of the judges of the Hippodrome who are recorded with their titles were *protospatharioi*, the remainder were *hypatoi* with two exceptions (one *anthypatos* and *patrikios*, and one *illoustrios*).[356] As with the judges of the Velum, we might look for an explanation for the variety of titles given to the judges of the Hippodrome in the variety of offices that they held. As with their colleagues this avenue of investigation is a dead end. A clear majority of the judges of the Hippodrome who held the highest titles recorded in the middle third of the eleventh century held no other office or held a minor clerical post that does not explain their title.

In terms of income the majority of the judges of the Hippodrome received the seventy-two *nomismata* granted to *protospatharioi* for the entire period. Although the upper limit of the range of payments increased up to 2,016 *nomismata* this is more of an indication of the vast difference between the payments made to someone at the bottom of the hierarchy by comparison to someone higher up than it is a sign of the increasing fortunes of the office and its holders in general.

The fate of the judges of the Hippodrome c. 960–c. 1066 can be neatly summed up by comparing the careers of two well-known judges: Eustathios Romaios and Elpidios Kenchres. Eustathios was born in the 950s or 960s and served as judge of the Hippodrome for most of his career, initially with the title of *protospatharios*.[357] He gradually rose through the court hierarchy, attaining the rank of *patrikios* by 1025.[358] Sometime later, c. 1028, he rose to the office of *mystikos*, and may have received the new title of *vestes* at this time, and later became *exaktor*.[359] At the same time, he continued to amass titles, and by October 1029 he was *vestes*, *anthypatos* and *patrikios*, as well as *logothetes* of the *dromos*. Later still Eustathios became *koiaistor*, then finally *droungarios tes viglas* with the title *magistros*, at some point between 1030 and 1034.[360] While a judge of the Hippodrome, Eustathios became a well-respected legal authority, the inspiration behind the *Peira* legal handbook discussed earlier. Eustathios was in his fifties before reaching high rank, and before accumulating other offices apart from judge of the Hippodrome.

We first encounter Elpidios Kenchres in August 1056, involved in a legal dispute with Michael Psellos, the adoptive father of his fiancée Euphemia.[361] Due, we are told, to the influence of his future father-in-law, Elpidios advanced quickly through a career that had taken Eustathios decades to complete. Elpidios was engaged to Euphemia for under three years, roughly between the ages of eighteen and twenty-two. During that time he was made a judge of the Hippodrome, judge of the Velum, *thesmographos*, *mystographos* and *exaktor*, all before the age of twenty-two.[362] Promotion, of course, could be the result of many factors, with not every option being open to everyone, and higher jobs were limited to either the most talented individuals or those who could take advantage of family connections and friends to advance their careers. For all his talents Eustathios Romaios had to wait until his friend and fellow judge Romanos Argyros was in a position to promote his career, and for all his apparent lack of talent Elpidios Kenchres advanced rapidly because he had a highly placed patron. The difference between the stories of the two men is noteworthy, however, not because of the unremarkable observation of the importance of patronage in career progression. Eustathios and Elpidios clearly viewed the position of judge of the Hippodrome differently, and I would suggest that the sigillographic evidence suggests that this was a phenomenon not limited to two men, but perhaps symptomatic of the outlook of their respective generations, and of those shaping the imperial system. Eustathios used his position as judge to rise slowly through the ranks and to make a lasting contribution to the scholarship of legal interpretation and jurisprudence.[363] Elpidios Kenchres, judge of the Hippodrome at the age of eighteeen, used the position as a stepping stone to higher offices; it was not an end in itself.

When we place the lives of Eustathios Romaios and Elpidios Kenchres alongside our sigillographic evidence we can see that Eustathios's life coincided with the high point for the judges of the Hippodrome in terms of status and income, that of Elpidios with the beginning of the decline. The creation of a tribunal of judges of the Hippodrome at some point between 934 and 971 would seem to reflect the generally increased importance of the legal profession and of the place of the law and its practitioners in the operation of the Byzantine Empire that is visible throughout the late tenth and eleventh century. However, whereas the higher officials, such as the *droungarios tes viglas* and the *koiaistor*, reached the heights of the *cursus honorum*, and the judges of the Velum saw gradual advancement right up to c. 1066, the judges of the Hippodrome hit their peak earlier, in the first third of the eleventh century. For the next thirty years, but for a few of their number, their position and income stagnated at best, more likely it declined. The majority of the judges did not receive promotions in compensation for title inflation and currency debasement, which was beginning to have an effect by c. 1050 at the latest. Modern scholarship might well regard a judge of the Hippodrome as a Byzantine version of a contemporary supreme court justice, but in terms of their place within the imperial system they were anything but supreme.

3.4.4.3 *The city judges*

Returning to the four questions with which we began this survey – how many judges there were, what the differences between the two types of judges were, how many tribunals there were and what the function of the judges was – we see that the seals are rather more useful in attempting to answer some questions than others. When it comes to numbers, the seals are not very revealing. There are roughly fifty more seals of the Hippodrome than that of the Velum, representing a similarly higher number of individual judges. Does this mean that there were more judges of the Hippodrome than of the Velum? Possibly the disparity in the figures could result from the chance survival of more seals that were once owned by the judges of the Hippodrome, but when we consider the numbers involved, it is equally likely that there were more judges of the Hippodrome than judges of the Velum. Sadly, this does not get us any closer to absolute numbers. Nor can we advance the conclusion made earlier that the city judges were probably everywhere; the seals certainly have nothing to add to the question about the existence of a court of the velum. When it comes to the difference between the judges and their function the seals have more to say. It is clear that from at least the end of the first third of the eleventh century the judges of the Velum outranked the judges of the Hippodrome. Not only did the judges of the Velum receive higher titles, and thus greater salaries, than the judges of the Hippodrome, but the gap widened over time. There was a difference in status and income, and presumably a difference in function. If we are searching for the city judges most likely to have sat alongside Eustathios Romaios and his successors on the empire's highest court, then the judges of the Velum are the obvious candidates, particularly as their status increased at the same time that Romanos III was reforming the position of *droungarios tes viglas*. As a result of the disparity in rank it is likely that the judges of the Hippodrome and Velum performed different tasks or sat, at least sometimes, on different tribunals. The distinction between the two is demonstrated by the seals of twenty-two judges of the Velum who were also judges of the Hippodrome. Even if one outranked the other, the fact that a man could be both at once demonstrates that one did not supersede the other, and that he could continue to perform both functions, which must have been distinct.

Before moving on we must address one final question: What can their participation in the administration of the themes tell us about the city judges? Out of the 184 judges of the Velum for whom seals survive, 74 also held a provincial office, for the judges of the Hippodrome the figure is 113 out of 235 known men. While some very few served as *anagrapheis* and *kouratores*, and there were even two *strategoi*, the overwhelming majority were theme judges.

Table 3.14 Percentage of Judges of the Velum and Judges of the Hippodrome Who Served as Theme Judges c. 966–c. 1066

Judges/Period	Tenth Century Final Third	Eleventh Century First Third	Eleventh Century Middle Third	Eleventh Century Final Third
Judges of the Velum	30	31	38.9	30.3
Judges of the Hippodrome	41.5	44	45.3	35.8

As can be seen from Table 3.14, a higher percentage of known judges of the Hippodrome served as theme judges than judges of the Velum.[364] Although both sets of judges sent some of their number to the provinces the judges of the Hippodrome were always more likely to undertake service outside of the capital. Perhaps leaving the comforts of the capital for the uncertainties of provincial life was a young man's game? Maybe the judges of the Velum were more valuable on hand in the capital, and so went less frequently to the themes? What can be inferred is that the presumably more expert judges were not the ones most frequently performing judicial duties in the themes, a further indication that the twelfth-century distinction between 'great' and 'small' judges might not be easily applicable to the preceding period.

3.4.5 The *epi ton kriseon*

Κύριε βοήθει τῷ σῷ δούλῳ Μιχαὴλ μαγίστρῳ βέστῃ καὶ ἐπὶ τῶν κρίσεων.

Lord, help your servant Michael, magistros, vestes, and epi ton kriseon.[365]

Having discussed old offices with consistent duties and those with evolving jurisdictions, as well as recent positions with changing responsibilities, we arrive at our first eleventh-century innovation, the *epi ton kriseon*. The position of *epi ton kriseon* is a frustrating one to analyse. On the surface, there is a rather clear story of government reform, but once we delve deeper using the seals, the waters become murky. Emperor Constantine IX Monomachos created the office of *epi ton kriseon* (literally 'of the legal decisions') between 1043 and 1047 and placed him at the head of a new bureau, the *sekreton ton dikon* (bureau of case rulings). To what purpose has caused some debate. One view is that the *epi ton kriseon* oversaw a new court charged with hearing civil cases, and thus became one of the chief judges of the empire.[366] However, in most interpretations, the *epi ton kriseon* was charged with increasing central control and standardization of an element of provincial administration, although possibly still acting as a judge. Exactly which area of the government of the *themata* has been disputed.[367] Possibilities advanced include the judicial – reviewing and overseeing the legal decisions of theme judges (who often lacked specialist legal education), collecting and storing provincial judicial decisions with the aim of preventing corruption – and the administrative, the handling of provincial administrative issues (the term *sekreton* is a key feature of this argument), and an agency to control and coordinate provincial administration.[368] That this move by Monomachos was seen as something new and innovative by contemporaries can be seen in the description of the reform by

Attaleiates.³⁶⁹ In fact, it is one of the few domestic policies recorded by Attaleiates for the whole of Constantine IX's reign. His description of the event can shed light on the functions of the *epi ton kriseon*. Attaleiates says that, 'He [Monomachos] also founded a bureau for private legal cases, calling its overseer *epi ton kriseon*. Provincial judges were to set their verdicts down in writing and deposit copies of them with this bureau, in order to be free of all suspicion.' Attaleiates records the creation of the *sekreton ton dikon* and the *epi ton kriseon* immediately after describing Monomachos's new law school, which we know aimed to standardize legal education in the capital. As a high-ranking judge Michael Attaleiates was probably well aware of the duties of the *epi ton kriseon*, and his grouping of the two events, the creation of the law school and of the new *sekreton* was likely no accident. His description of the purpose of the *epi ton kriseon* most strongly aligns with an interpretation of the office as one with judicial as opposed to administrative responsibilities. That it was established to allow theme judges to be 'free of all suspicion' suggests that the *sekreton ton dikon* acted (as its name implies) as a central repository for their paperwork in case of charges of corruption. The remaining question is whether the *epi ton kriseon* had oversight powers with respect to the theme judges, and if so what these were. Put another way, did the *epi ton kriseon* and his department collect and preserve the documents of theme judges, or did they review and if necessary correct them? Attaleiates's comment clearly describes the first of these possibilities, and is certainly broad enough to encompass the second, but we cannot be completely sure without more evidence. Considering the appellate nature of the tribunal of the *doungarios tes viglas* at the time that the *epi ton kriseon* came into being, it is possible that the new department was intended to facilitate and perhaps supplement the work of the *droungarios* in overseeing provincial judicial decisions. In this interpretation, the *epi ton kriseon* would be a judicial official and a legal expert, but not primarily a judge as such, except in as much as any official could act as a judge in areas under their purview.

Beyond Attaleiates the activities of the *epi ton kriseon* are described in only four documents from our period. In 1056, the *epi ton kriseon* was one of the men ordered by Empress Theodora to hear the case of Psellos versus Elpidios Kenchres.³⁷⁰ This is a problematic example as, firstly, it has nothing to do with the *themata*, and, secondly, it records the creation of an ad hoc court created at the whim of the empress. As such it is only useful in as much as it proves that the *epi ton kriseon* was a competent official with enough legal training to be considered fit to judge a case, which is not surprising, but not necessarily indicative of his regular duties. The other three examples, dated to 1062, 1087 and 1093/1112 do concern legal matters in the provinces but are equally troublesome. In 1062, the *epi ton kriseon*, alongside important judges from Constantinople, was a signatory on a document concerning a review of the property of the Iviron monastery on Mount Athos.³⁷¹ What is not clear is the function of the *epi ton kriseon* in this case; he could have been a judge like the other signatories; he could have been acting as the keeper of, and expert on, provincial judicial decisions, or both. In 1087, he adjudicated a dispute over property on the island of Leros at the behest of the emperor Alexios I.³⁷² Here the *epi ton kriseon* was clearly acting as a judge, but again, at the express order of the emperor who was involved personally in the dispute, which raises questions about function though certainly not competence. Finally, in 1112, the *epi ton kriseon* George Nikaeus certified the copy of a document granting the widow Kale authority to act as her late husband's executor, which he had originally witnessed nineteen years earlier as *koiaistor*.³⁷³ He signed and sealed the document with his new office and titles, but there is nothing in this case to prove that he acted as he did because he was *epi ton kriseon*. In fact, this case tells us more about his tenure as *koiaistor* than as *epi ton kriseon*.³⁷⁴ One final piece of evidence in support of this stance is that every other time that an official is known as an *epi ton/tes/tou* something (e.g. the *epi tou kanikleiou*), they were originally known as *chartoularios epi ton/tes/tou*; they were record keepers. Perhaps Constantine IX, in creating his new *sekreton* was adhering to this tradition.

The creation of the *epi ton kriseon* and the *sekreton ton dikon* was a rather monumental move by the emperor. In some ways, it could be seen as having the potential to dramatically reduce the judicial powers of the theme judges, both with respect to the provincials themselves and the central government. As with his law school Monomachos was aiming for a professionalization and standardization of the application of the law. Although technically all imperial subjects could appeal judicial cases to the emperor himself, and at least at the end of the ninth century to the *eparch* or *koiaistor*, this was the first time that a process had been created to facilitate this through an expansion of central government.³⁷⁵ Monomachos's decision to create the post of *epi ton kriseon* speaks to both that emperor's high regard for the law as an instrument of imperial authority, and his desire to see a regular and consistent application of both. That the route to achieving this aim was to centralize the exercise of authority in the capital is also illuminating.

Turning to the seals we would hope to see a glimpse of the *epi ton kriseon* in action, unfortunately the picture is not so clear-cut. In the database used for the present study

Figure 3.9 Seal of Niketas *proedros* and *epi ton kriseon*. Harvard Art Museums/Arthur M. Sackler Museum, Bequest of Thomas Whittemore, 1951.31.5.340.
The obverse shows a standing Mother of God Nikopoios. Niketas is one of a very small number of men who can be firmly identified as having held the office of *epi ton kriseon*.
Rev. +ΘK̅E̅|ROHΘEI|NIKHTA|ΠPOEΔPW|SEΠITWN|KPICEW|-N-
Θεοτόκε βοήθει Νικήτᾳ προέδρῳ καὶ ἐπὶ τῶν κρίσεων.
Theotokos, help Niketas *proedros* and *epi ton kriseon*.

the position of *epi ton kriseon* is represented by four seals, belonging to only two men.[376] One of these men (Michael) held this position in the middle third of the eleventh century, the other (Niketas) in the second half of the century. Michael held the titles of *magistros* and *vestes*, Niketas was a *proedros*.[377] In the contemporary hierarchy of dignities they fell squarely in the top third. In the middle of the eleventh century, Michael would have received a *roga* containing 16 pounds of *nomismata* as a *magistros*. Meanwhile, Niketas received between 28 pounds *nomismata* from the *roga* attached to his higher title of *proedros*. An anonymous holder of the office is recorded in the archives of the Iviron monastery from a document dated to 1062; he was also a *proedros*.[378] Niketas lived after Michael and had a higher rank, which also happened to be the same as the anonymous *epi ton kriseon* from 1062. All held only the office of *epi ton kriseon*, so their status was based purely on that function. The status of the three men was roughly equivalent, considering the title inflation of the decades that separated them.

That the data is so limited is in itself quite shocking. However, we must remember that the office of *epi ton kriseon* was held by one man at a time, and was created no earlier than 1043, and thus existed for only twenty of the years covered by this chapter. We can say with some certainty that the *epi ton kriseon* was an important person. Michael must have been one of the earliest, if not the first, *epi ton kriseon*, and as a *magistros* he held the highest title open to non-imperial men at that time. Constantine clearly intended his new overseer of provincial judicial decisions to be ranked among the major offices of state. With the title of *magistros* Michael held a rank comparable to that of a contemporary *droungarios tes viglas*, who was at that point transitioning into the most important judicial official in the empire, and the *eparch* of Constantinople, to name but two other offices.

3.4.6 The *thesmographos, thesmophylax, exactor* and *kensor*

Θεοτόκε βοήθει Μιχαὴλ κένσωρα καὶ κριτὴν Παφλαγονίας τὸν Ἐξαμιλίτην.

Theotokos, help Michael Hexamilites, kensor and judge of Paphlagonia.[379]

Before leaving the question of the judiciary we must turn to the question of a number of other offices which might have been judicial in nature: the *thesmographos, thesmophylax, exaktor* and the *kensor*. Three unsatisfactory methods have been used to determine the nature of these jobs, firstly looking for a better documented late antique incarnation of the office, then projecting its duties forward to the tenth and eleventh century; secondly, by examining the seals belonging to these officials and assessing them based on the other offices that they held, the idea being that men would specialize in certain areas, financial or judicial for instance; thirdly, an alternate approach has been to assign jurisdictions to these offices based on their appearances in the written material. Unfortunately, as we shall see, these approaches are all problematic.

Even when there is evidence that a tenth-/eleventh-century office shared its name with a position from earlier in Byzantine history, as did that of *exaktor* for instance, there is usually a period of centuries where that office vanishes from the sigillographic and written record. The case for direct continuity is, thus, tenuous. This leaves us with the possibility that the office was resurrected under the same name, to fulfil the same function, after a gap of hundreds of years. We have seen examples of the Byzantines looking into their administrative history when searching for names for new offices and titles, however moving from antiquarian label selection to recreating the exact function of a position is a rather large leap. At best, we might be safe in assuming that the Byzantines knew enough of their own history to choose a name that was in the same general area. For example, when the late antique office of *doux* was brought back at the end of the tenth century it remained a military office, but with a different function from its earlier incarnation. Appearances in the written material can be equally misleading, as they often tell us more about the man involved than his office. Furthermore, they are skewed by the types of sources that we possess. The predominance of the *Peira* in discussions of the life of early-eleventh-century Constantinople can make everyone look like a jurist, but the work is a collection of legal decisions. How different would our outlook be if a complimentary work on the treasuries had survived? Equally unsatisfactory, but the best indicator that we have of the function of an office, is the other positons recorded alongside it on seals. The obvious problem is that many Byzantines worked in a variety of areas at any one time; financial officials were often judges for instance. With no other data to work with I shall include a discussion of the various offices recorded on seals, if only to provide the information for those who might wish to tackle this issue further.

The *thesmophylax* is known from thirteen seals belonging to eight men and two appearances in written sources.[380] The earliest mention of the *thesmophylax* is in the *Escorial Taktikon* where the office occupied the 163rd (total hierarchy) 140th (offices) place.[381] The exact duties of the *thesmophylax* are open to question because of the paucity of the sources. *Thesmophylax* means guardian of the law, and as a term had been used by Philo of Alexandria to describe Moses, and was the title of magistracies in the Greek and Hellenistic world.[382] That he was in some way a judicial official is generally accepted, but the specifics are where there is division. Suggestions include a policeman, a court record keeper and an underling of the *droungarios tes viglas*.[383] The evidence for all three positions is minimal. However, *Peira* 61.6 shows Eustathios Romaios, as *droungarios*, ordering an anonymous *thesmophylax* to investigate a disturbance in the Hippodrome between an unnamed *protospatharios* and a *kandidatos*, and to take statements. This certainly suggests that the *droungarios* could command the *thesmophylax*, but with just one occurrence and little context we have no idea of whether this situation was in any way normal. Similarly, we have three examples of the same seal with an interesting inscription, Κύριε βοήθει Γεωργίῳ πατρικίῳ κριτῇ τοῦ βήλου θεσμοφύλακι τῶν κρίσεων καὶ συμπόνῳ, Lord help George, *patrikios*, judge of the Velum, *thesmophylax* of the *kriseis*, and *symponos*.[384] This inscription states that George was the *thesmophylax* of the judgements, implying that he in some way guarded the judgements of the court, perhaps he was in charge of the court records.[385] The minimal evidence suggests that the *thesmophylax* was a judicial official, not necessarily a judge, but linked to the court. One final piece of evidence, tenuous as it seems, is that of the eight *thesmophylakes* known from seals, five were also judges, one was a *tribunos* and two held the no other office.[386] While I am not completely convinced that we can always extrapolate the duties of an office from those jobs with which is it associated, the high proportion of overlap involved in this case, five out of six judges with more than one job, is certainly suggestive. The *thesmophylax* appears in the *Escorial Taktikon* at exactly the same time as the judges of the Hippodrome and judges of the Velum, and it is not unreasonable to view them all as part of the same expansion of the judicial apparatus.

In terms of status, the sigillographic evidence is remarkably consistent. All of the seals are dated to the period under consideration here, c. 966–c. 1066, with two dated to the end of the tenth/early eleventh, three to the mid-eleventh, and two more broadly to the first two-thirds of the eleventh. With the exception of one of the mid-eleventh-century seal, belonging to a *patrikios*, all belonged to *protospatharioi*. This title would have placed the early *thesmophylakes* at roughly the same level as the judges of the Velum and judges of the Hippodrome, even though they came nineteen and twenty-three (in both the total hierarchy and that limited to offices only) places ahead of them in the *Escorial Taktikon* respectively. During the developments of the eleventh century the *thesmophylakes* shared more in common with the judges of the Hippodrome than the judges of the Velum, staying put as *protospatharioi*, while the hierarchy changed around them, and their status declined.

Linked, and possibly subservient to, the *thesmophylax* was the *thesmographos*, the writer of the laws.[387] The *thesmographos* does not appear in the *Escorial Taktikon*, meaning that either he was of too low a rank to make the list or the position was created after c. 975. The latter conclusion is supported by the sigillographic material. A total of ten seals belonging to eight men survive, all dated to the eleventh century. All eight men were *protospatharioi*. They fell into the same unenviable position as the *thesmophylakes* and the judges of the Hippodrome, steadily drifting down the imperial hierarchy of dignities.[388] Although the number of seals is low for both offices, the fact that almost all of the *thesmophylakes* and all of the *thesmographoi* were *protospatharioi* makes it difficult to tell who was the supervisor, who the subordinate, or even whether the two offices worked together at all.[389] Based on the name of the office it is possible that the *thesmographos* was responsible for writing judgements, or perhaps for documents once written.[390] The judicial nature of the position is perhaps revealed on the seals, where half of the *thesmographoi* are shown to have also been judges of one type or another.[391] The court case between Psellos and his son-in-law-to-be Elpidios Kenchres suggests that there were multiple *thesmographoi* at any one time. Elpidios Kenchres himself was a *thesmographos*, as were two of Psellos's witnesses, Michael and Gabriael Xerites.[392] As with the *thesmophylax* the most that we can conclude is that the *thesmographoi* were officials concerned with the law, possibly attached to the courts.

The office of *exaktor* is the most difficult of those considered so far to place. Were the *exaktores* fiscal officials who occasionally took part in tribunals when their expertise was relevant, were they fiscal judges, or were they high-ranking jurists?[393] Unsurprisingly considering the range of modern interpretations, the evidence is contradictory. The late antique *exaktores* were fiscal officials, tax collectors, and while there is ample evidence that there was no continuity between this office and that which reappeared in the *Escorial Taktikon* after a gap of centuries, a twelfth-century text muddies the waters somewhat.[394] John Tzetzes describes contemporary *exaktores* as fulfilling the same role as their late antique counterparts.[395] Do we believe Tzetzes's testimony, or, like Oikonomides, do we consider him to be intentionally archaicizing?[396] Was Tzetzes referencing the first incarnation of the office, or perhaps simplifying the duties of a fiscal judge? Magdalino presents a case in the *Peira* where the *exaktor* is clearly linked to the fisc in support of the conclusion that the office had the duties of a fiscal judge.[397] In a dispute between a poor man and a *patrikios* over a property, the *exaktor* said, 'We were forbidden to judge concerning ownership, for it was not in order for the fisc to give judgement. But we allowed the poor man to bring an action against the estate of the *patrikios*, in order that he might, if at all possible, obtain some substance.'[398] This particular case does make the *exaktor* sound like a fiscal judge, but this was not the only case he adjudicated as recorded in the *Peira*, not all of which are so obviously related to a financial bureau.[399] A problem that we face is that the *Peira* likely records only the cases tried by Eustathios Romaios as *exaktor*, and it could be that he was a special case. Moreover, if the *exaktor* was a fiscal official, it would be in keeping with Byzantine practice to have him sit in judgement over fiscal cases, without this making him a judicial official.

It is possible that the seals might help us discover the function of the *exaktores*. It has been pointed out that the seals belonging to *exaktores* include a large number of fiscal offices.[400] Of the forty individuals who held the office of *exaktor* c. 966–c. 1100 six were only *exaktores*, eighteen were judges of the Hippodrome or Velum, eleven were provincial judges, nine worked as a *notarios*, *asekretis*, or *chartoularios*, two were *kommerkiarioi*, three were *kouratores*, two were *symponoi* and two were *anagrapheis*. Breaking this down, eighteen were judicial officials, eleven worked in the provincial administration, but exercised some judicial duties – nine in the central bureaucracy and two in the government of Constantinople – three managed imperial estates, and four were concerned with the collection of various taxes. On balance, it does not look like we can declare that the *exaktores* were fiscal officials brought in to oversee trials relevant to their area of expertise. We could tentatively claim that they were judicial officials. Just under half their number were also judges of another kind in Constantinople, a figure which rises to two-thirds if we consider the theme judges to have been at least partly judicial officials. Of course, this means that between a half and a third of the men concerned did not hold judicial office at the same time that they were an *exaktor*. A final consideration, though perhaps anecdotal, is that two of the best known men to be *exaktores* were Eustathios Romaios and John Xiphilinos, two of the most important jurists in Byzantine history. Not only that, it was as *exaktores* that they were chosen to become *droungarios tes viglas* and *nomophylax* respectively. Based on so little evidence all conclusions must be guarded, but we hesitantly conclude that the *exaktores* were judicial officials, and so can include them in the current section.

Thirty-nine individuals represented by fifty-one seals were *exaktores* during the period c. 966–c. 1066. The data from their seals is presented in Table 3.15.

It is immediately clear that *protospatharios* was the dominant title held by the *exaktores* in all three time periods. As we have seen with other judicial officials, the range of titles became increasingly more diverse in the eleventh century. They are perhaps most comparable to the judges of the Hippodrome, who also saw a diversification of title, taking a small minority of their number to the lower-middle ranks in the first third of the eleventh century, a phenomenon that continued in the middle of the century. The comparison is strengthened when we observe that the *exaktores* who were

Table 3.15 Normalized Seal Data, in Percentages, for the Titles of *Exaktores* c. 966–c. 1066

Title/Period	Tenth Century Final Third	Eleventh Century	
		First Third	Middle Third
Vestes			2
Anthypatos and *Patrikios*		3.8	8
Illoustrios			2
Patrikios		3.8	2
Protospatharios	83.3	63.5	58.9
Spatharokandidatos			6
Spatharios		11.5	
None	16.7	17.3	21.1

anthypatoi, the highest rank reached with the exception of one individual, were also judges of the Hippodrome. The earnings of 63.5 per cent of *exaktores* held steady at 1 pound of *nomismata* between the last decades of the tenth century and the early years of the eleventh century. While some lucky few received more, up to 8 pounds for the *anthypatoi*, 12 per cent held the rank of *spatharios*, who earned a *roga* lower than that of the *spatharokandidatoi* at 0.5 pounds of gold. The story continued in this vein in the middle of the eleventh century. While the proportion of higher-ranking *exaktores* increased slightly, the vast majority remained *protospatharioi*, with *rogai* of 1 pound of *nomismata*. The mean average for each period is 1 pound of *nomismata* for the final third of the tenth century, 1.34 pounds for the first third of the eleventh century, and 2.15 pounds for the middle third of the century. Here again the appropriate comparison is with the judges of the Hippodrome. Both offices were created in the tenth century, occupants of both overwhelmingly held a reasonably important title in the middle of the hierarchy, *protospatharios*, and both saw their position decline gradually in terms of income, and slightly faster in terms of status by c. 1066. The many parallels between the *exaktores* and the judges of the Hippodrome might seem surprising considering that when both offices first appeared in the *Escorial Taktikon* they occupied the 148th (total hierarchy) 125th (offices) and 186th (total hierarchy) 163rd (offices) positions respectively. Based on these two offices, it is possible that there was not as much difference in the dignities awarded to the offices in the final third of the *Escorial Taktikon* as their positions on the list would indicate. Furthermore, although the *exaktores* outranked the judges of the Velum 182nd (total hierarchy) 159th (offices) at the time that the *Escorial Taktikon* was written, they clearly slipped below them in the hierarchy after c. 1030. One area where the *exaktores* are not comparable to the judges of the Hippodrome is the high percentage of their seals which record no title. For no other office have we seen such a consistent, and high, proportion of seals with no title. It is possible that these men held titles which they considered too humble to be worth recording; the 11.5 per cent of *exaktores* who were *spatharioi* must have been almost in this category.

The final office which we will consider before leaving the judiciary behind is that of the *kensor*. The *kensor* first appears in the *Escorial Taktikon* where it occupied the relatively high position of 143rd (total hierarchy) 120th (offices) in the hierarchy, making

Table 3.16 Normalized Seal Data, in Percentages, for the Titles of *Kensores* c. 966–c. 1066

Title/Period	Tenth Century Final Third	Eleventh Century First Third	Eleventh Century Middle Third
Vestarches			9.5
Vestes, *Anthypatos* and *Patrikios*		17.7	4.7
Illoustrios			6.4
Protospatharios	50	29.5	22.1
None	50	52.8	57.3

it the eleventh-highest place held by a bureaucrat.[401] When it comes to determining the function of the *kensor* we are in a similar situation to that observed for the *exaktor*: far too little evidence to ever be sure. The *kensor* appears in a judicial context in one case in the *Peira*.[402] Beyond that there is no documentary evidence to prove that he was a judicial official. We are also in a worse position when it comes to the sigillographic material, only thirty-six seals belonging to twenty-four men survive dated c. 966–c. 1133. Of these men, four were only *kensores*, one was *parathalassites*, two were administrators, three worked in the central or provincial financial administration or tax collection, four managed imperial estates, seven were theme judges, and eight were judges in Constantinople. There is not enough evidence here to draw firm conclusions as to the function of the *kensores*, but the largest single grouping is of judicial officials, or perhaps administrators if we combine the relevant groups into one.[403] Rare mentions of a *protokensor* suggest that there were multiple *kensores* under his leadership.[404] As such I shall consider the *kensor* here with the judicial officials, but with the admission that his inclusion here is by no means secure.[405]

The figures for the *kensores* draw immediate comparison with those for the *exaktores*. Both were more likely than not *protospatharioi* in all three periods under consideration, and both have a high percentage of seals without titles. This latter phenomenon is even more pronounced on the seals of the *kensores* than those of the *exaktores*. Trying to explain the few higher titles by looking at their other offices at first seems illuminating: the *vestarches* was also judge of Cappadocia, but the *vestes* and the *illoustrios* were only *kensores*.[406] Of course, with such a small sample group factors related to the individual in question have a greater chance of influencing the whole. It is perhaps no accident that the *vestes* was a member of the still prestigious, though declining, Phokas family, and that the *vestarches* was the well-known Symeon Ouranos. It is safest to conclude that the majority of the *kensores* were always of the rank of *protospatharios* or lower, with all of the repercussions that this had in terms of declining status that we discussed in the preceding pages.

Before leaving the law behind we will consider eight more seals, which, although they probably did not belong to an office holder, or at least his office is not what makes them interesting, they do speak to the importance of the legal profession in the eleventh century, and have something to say about the relationship between the state and the guilds of Constantinople. Between 1040–90 Nicholas Katechanas struck two similar seal designs, one with the inscription + Κ(ύρι)ε βοήθει τῷ σῷ δούλῳ Νικολάῳ (πρωτο)σπαθαρίῳ | (καὶ) πριμικηρίῳ τῶν συνηγόρων τῷ Κατιχανᾷ (Lord help, Nicholas Katechanas, *protospatharios* and *primikerios* of the advocates) and the second with the inscription Κ(ύρι)ε β(οή)θ(ει) Νικολά(ῳ) (πρωτο)σπαθ(α)ρ(ίῳ) θεσμογράφ(ῳ) | καὶ π ρ(ι)μικηρί(ῳ) τῶ(ν) συνη[γό]ρω(ν) τῷ Κατηχα(νᾷ) (Lord help, Nicholas Katechanas, *protospatharios*, *thesmographos* and *primikerios* of the advocates).[407] The interesting element of these inscriptions is the term *primikerios* of the advocates. *Primikerios* was a designation meaning first or senior, perhaps leader. As such there are a few possibilities for what this seal might show. We know that the advocates had their own guild, as it is mentioned in the tenth-century *Book of the Eparch* and also in Constantine IX's *Novella constitutio*. *Primikerioi* are traditionally associated with state service, so it is possible, although in my view unlikely, that Nicholas Katechanas was a government official with some power over the guild of advocates. No such cooption of the guild by the state is mentioned in the sources, and Nicholas is the only known holder of the position. More likely in my opinion is that Nicholas was president of the guild of advocates, and that what these seals demonstrate is the opening up of the senate, and the imperial hierarchy in general, to the guilds under Constantine IX Monomachos, a process extended by Constantine X Doukas. Although Nicholas occupied the office of *thesmographos* on the second type of seal, before that he was a *protospatharios* without being a state servant. This in itself was not unheard of, as there are many seals and documentary records of individuals who must have bought or been given the titles because of their importance to local communities for instance. This is probably what happened with Nicholas: his position as the leader of a particularly important guild, one that was instrumental to the functioning of the state even if not officially a part of the government, saw him raised to the rank of *protospatharios*. His seals, though lone examples, are indicative of the importance of the legal profession to the empire in the eleventh century, particularly that of the capital.

3.4.7 The law school

> *Therefore it shall be as it has already been stated, a place set aside there for lovers of legal learning, which Our Power has granted to them, in which [Our Power] also established a didactic chair, and this glorious building shall be called the school of law, and the teacher the nomophylax didaskalos.*[408]

No discussion of the eleventh-century judiciary would be complete without mentioning the law school established by Constantine IX Monomachos between 1043 and 1047.[409] The law school, *Didaskaleion ton nomon*, was announced in the *Novella constitutio*, a draft of an imperial novel authored by John Mauropous, which has been the subject of a recent study and translation by Chitwood.[410] The same document also announced the creation of a new office, that of the *nomophylax didaskalos*, who acted as head of the law school, and possibly overseer of legal education elsewhere in the city.[411] The first, and perhaps only, known holder of the position as originally created was John Xiphilinos. Seals belonging to a *nomophylax* are incredibly rare, and the majority, dating to the twelfth century, were probably owned by holders of a similarly named ecclesiastical office, not a judicial official, and not linked to legal education. In fact, the law school itself soon collapsed, and likely did not outlive the emperor who founded it. John Xiphilinos, along with his friends Constantine Leichoudes, John Mauropous and Michael Psellos, all fell from grace and were forced to enter self-imposed exile in the church. Xiphilinos supposedly was attacked by the old guard of jurists who disliked his new law school and everything that it represented. Exactly what this was is hard to decipher, as our main source for the dispute is the funeral oration which Psellos delivered following the death of his one-time friend. Picking apart the cause of the anger directed towards Xiphilinos from the often self-serving recollections of Psellos is tricky, to say the least. Psellos presented Constantinople as bereft of suitable legal education, where the existing class of jurists cared neither for the law itself nor for any form of ordered instruction therein.[412] Into this educational wasteland stepped John Xiphilinos, who taught the law in a new scientific manner, something which his predecessors had never done. The *Novella constitutio* hints that Psellos was to some degree repeating the official line. In it Constantine IX, after heaping much praise on his predecessors for their work revising the laws notes that they 'left the divine education like a ship without a helmsman in the middle of the sea of life'.[413] The educational revolution proclaimed in the *Novella constitutio* and by Psellos is not much in evidence in the description of methods evident in surviving documents.[414] However, as a state-sponsored institution, with what must have been to some degree state-authorized qualifications, the idea of the school was revolutionary.[415] It was entirely in keeping with Constantine IX Monomachos's creation of the *sekreton ton dikon* and the *epi ton kriseon*, that one of the stated aims of the new school was to standardize and raise the level of legal education. We see in the policies of Monomachos a desire to provide consistent and clear access to the law across his empire, a move which he hoped his

Figure 3.10 Constantine IX Monomachos (1042–55) Miliaresion, 1042–55, Constantinople. Harvard Art Museums/Arthur M. Sackler Museum, Bequest of Thomas Whittemore, 1951.31.4.1581.
This coin of Constantine IX depicts the Mother of God on the obverse and the emperor in military attire on the reverse. The inscription takes the form of a prayer to the Virgin, asking for her protection for the frequently threatened Monomachos.
Obv. ΔЄCΠΟΙΝΑCѠZΟΙC
Rev. ЄVCЄBHMONOMAXON
Δέσποινα σῴξοις εὐσεβῆ Μονομάχον.
O Lady, preserve the pious Monomachos.

successors would continue, as he put it, 'May the sun never look down on such an outrage …' as there being no *nomophylax*.[416]

Constantine IX not only founded a school of law; he created a new state-funded position to oversee its activities. The *nomophylax* was envisioned as much more than a teacher, as the guardian of the laws he was to be the supreme legal expert in the empire.[417] He was to shape the legal minds of tomorrow; his words were literally the law. The *Novella* (chapter 8) also makes it clear that the *nomophylax* was, as his name suggests, the man who was supposed to prevent error from creeping into the interpretation of the law. This is why Psellos described him as 'the president of the court', 'commander of the judges' and 'leader of the laws'.[418] These rather impressive descriptions of the new office are at odds with the text of the *Novella constitutio*, which says that the *nomophylax* should be ranked among the *senators*, but after the *epi ton kriseon*, a position which would hardly leave him as chief of the judges.[419] Furthermore, Xiphilinos was given the title of *illoustrios*, as opposed to the much higher title of *magistros* which was usual at this point for the actual chief judge, the *droungarios* of the Vigla. One suspects that Xiphilinos received a middling title for a middling office and that Psellos's descriptions of his friend belong in the realm of rhetorical flourishes rather than reality. The new *nomophyax* was subject to attacks from the established judiciary. Pellos wrote a passionate defence of his friend and of the office of *nomophylax*.[420] In this defence he mentions an attack on Xiphilinos by Ophrydas, a colleague of Eustathios Romaios who appeared a number of times in the *Peira*.[421] Ophrydas was dead by the time that Psellos replied, but his pamphlet had already circulated widely and created enough controversy that a retort was required. Psellos makes it clear, in quite insulting terms, that Ophrydas was the front man, not the real instigator of the attacks on Xiphilinos.[422] The real culprit was an educated public official who knew Xiphilinos well. The *nomophylax* was accused of being too young to occupy such an exalted position, and of being a mere self-taught judge. Psellos pointed out that the judges and educated elite in Constantinople all agreed that Xiphilinos was the best candidate for the position at the time of his appointment.[423] At the same time Xiphilinos himself had to testify before a panel of judges and defend his position.

What was the cause of the attacks on Xiphilinos? As we have said his teaching was not terribly revolutionary, perhaps it was the monopoly that the *nomophylax* had over granting the credentials of newly qualified jurists. Or was it the wide-reaching responsibilities of the *nomophylax* as the 'commander of the judges' that the 'old guard' in the person of the judge Ophrydas rebelled against? It is possible to see that the responsibilities of the *nomophylax* could have overlapped considerably, and thus presumably superseded, those of the *droungarios tes viglas*. Was there, perhaps, a battle behind the scenes at the imperial court, not over the *nomophylax*'s authority over legal education, but over who would be the empire's chief judge and have the final say (not counting the emperor) when interpreting the law? If so, it is clear who won. In large part due to the actions of his enemies at court, the law school was gone by 1054 at the latest, the position of *nomophylax* neutered, with John Xiphilinos forced into monastic exile, while the tribunal of the *droungarios* continued to sit, and was soon elevated to *megas droungarios*. Whatever the origin of the dispute, in administrative terms

Constantine IX had failed to create a new centralized legal educational system and failed to establish the *nomophylax* as a legal authority and arbiter.

3.4.8 The rule of law c. 966–c. 1066

> Both righteousness and discernment are the foundation of this throne. These are entirely impossible to accrue to an emperor, except from and through the law. It is through it that emperors rule.[424]

The most eye-catching and oft discussed legal reforms of the Macedonian period are the codifications of Roman law with which the dynasty's founder Basil I, continued by his son Leo VI, sought legitimacy for himself and to some extent the mantle of ancient Rome for his people, and the law school founded Constantine IX Monomachos, husband of Zoe, Basil's great-great-great-granddaughter. It has recently been argued that the law school was the final stage in the Macedonian legal revival, which represented both the importance of the Roman legal tradition to the emperors and the power and influence of Constantinopolitan jurists. Both of these statements are undeniably true, the foundation of the law school was a triumph for the legal profession and a symbol of its position at the heart of the Constantinopolitan establishment. It was also a sign, and a symptom, of the complete transformation of some of the most important elements of imperial government by Constantine IX's predecessors. The Macedonians, over a period of about a century, reformed the legal apparatus of the empire and gave great power to jurists. The law school was the last part of this process, and in some ways the least important, and not just because we know it failed. It was a demonstration of the power of the judiciary and of the legal profession in general, but it changed little in terms of the status or position of the judicial bureaucracy. It is fair to say that to be in a position to be exalted as the judiciary was by Constantine IX in 1047, one must already be important. The real story is not that the *Novella constitutio* exalted the legal profession, but that the judiciary already had power and status before Constantine came along. Evidence that changes were afoot, changes that were structural, and not linked to some quest for ancient legitimacy or intellectual prestige, date to the composition of the *Escorial Taktikon*, seventy years before Constantine IX. A whole raft of new judicial positions appeared for the first time in this text, from the *thesmophylax* to the *exaktor*, and someone took the decision to formally constitute two groups of city judges into the judges of the Velum and the judges of the Hippodrome. New positions presumably meant new work. Simply put, there was more demand for legal professionals by 975 than there had been when the *Taktikon Beneševič* was written forty years earlier. Considering that the empire was larger, its population was growing, and its capital more developed, and that these changes were if anything accelerating, that there was more for bureaucrats to do should not come as a surprise. This was change that no one advertised; it was not done in a way that served the propagandistic desires of the emperor, but it did mark the beginning of a new way of running the empire.[425]

With new positions for jurists came more power and increased status. The new judicial officials might have been close to the bottom of the hierarchy recorded in the

Escorial Taktikon, but they made the list; many did not. Although promotion to higher ranks came only for a select few of the judges of the Hippodrome – *thesmophlakes*, *exaktores* and *kensores* – the judges of the Velum saw their status increase more generally, particularly after c. 1033, and there is evidence of their increased role in the empire. Although the generation of legal bureaucrats serving around 975 have left little evidence of their place in the imperial administration beyond scattered seals and a few lines in the *Escorial Taktikon*, they laid the foundations which saw the next generation, that of Eustathios Romaios and Romanos Argyros, oversee the transformation of the Byzantine legal system, leading to jurists taking their place at the heart of imperial government. The power of Eustathios and his colleagues' legal training is amply demonstrated by their formulation of the attacks of Patriarch Alexios Stoudites on the members of the Church of the East in suitably legal vocabulary, and in the *Peira*, both in terms of the stories that it recounts, and the fact that the book exists in the first place.[426]

The transformation of the Byzantine judiciary from a group on the fringes of imperial government to a major power in the realm is apparent in the glowing words with which the judiciary and legal education were described in the *Novella constitutio*. Directly addressing the new generation of men about to be trained by John Xiphilinos, Monomachos said, 'For it is clear that Our Majesty, as well as those always reigning after us for the rest of time, shall prize you, who acquired a glorious name and reputation by your legal education, before others in the distribution of offices. We shall render a fitting recompense for [your] good decision.'[427] As a grand imperial proclamation full of rhetorical flourishes, it is both an incredibly important document, proclaiming the exalted status of the judiciary, and virtually meaningless. We know from the inscriptions commissioned by the legal professionals of the empire for their seals that not all of those with legal education were at the front of the line when the rewards of state service were handed out. Constantine did not choose to reward all jurists; he did not elevate all judicial positions, even those of relative importance such as the judges of the Hippodrome, and he did nothing to halt the steady decline in the financial situation of those same judges and those like them. His own fiscal policies, in fact, made their position worse. The seals reveal that in reality the promotion of the judiciary, which started before Constantine and continued under him and his immediate successors, was much more thoughtful than implied by the *Novella constitutio*. It was a more selective process, targeted at specific offices, and had the flavour of reform with the aim of improving government, rather than promotion because of some abstract concept of the value of the law. The movement of which the *Novella constitutio* was a part was all about the growth of a particular form of government, with the rule of law at its heart, a law embodied by a powerful group of Constantinopolitan jurists. From the mid-tenth century, this group had an increasing say in how the empire was run. It also speaks to the centralizing tendencies of the Macedonians, something which can be seen in the actions of many of the emperors between Basil I and Constantine IX. By Constantine's reign Constantinopolitan jurists received cases from the provinces, overruled other judges, interpreted the law for all of the emperors' subjects, and were sent out as provincial administrators to bring their knowledge to the themes.

The unnamed emperor or emperors whose efforts are reflected in the *Escorial Taktikon* and the earliest seals deserve a lot of the credit for starting the process of reform, but so too does Romanos III Argyros. Transforming the *droungarios tes viglas* from a second-rate-military post into the minister of justice, with sweeping authority over the implementation and interpretation of the law, and the knock-on effect that this had on the position of the judges of the Velum, was probably the most radical government reform of the eleventh century. The much better-known reforms of Constantine IX, the ephemeral law school and the *sekreton ton dikon* and the *epi ton kriseon*, were in some senses simply gilding the lily, setting up support mechanisms for the larger preceding transformation.

Only a few specific emperors are visible in this process: Constantine IX because of the *Novella constitutio* and the writings of men who witnessed his reign, Romanos III because of the *Peira* and the surviving seals. Both have been heavily criticized as weak emperors living in a sixty-five-year period with no strong ruler in Byzantium. As Anthony Kaldellis has recently shown, this is an unfair categorization of emperors who were by and large no worse than any others to sit on the throne. Furthermore, it is clear from the *Escorial Taktikon* that the legal reforms which we have discussed in this chapter began as early as the reign of Romanos I Lekapenos, and that some of the major features of the new system had taken shape by the end of the reign of John I Tzimiskes. No one has ever accused these men, or the emperors between them of being weak. The sigillographic evidence shows that the system continued and grew under Basil II, the very model of a strong autocrat. We cannot say that the judiciary rose to prominence because of a period of insecure or feeble emperors; after all, it was during a period of strong imperial rule, under Basil II, that they became important enough to become authorities on how the empire should function, and for one of their number to rise to the throne and be accepted as emperor by his people. Imperial weakness does not explain the rise of the judiciary; in fact, it contradicts what we have seen: strong, involved government and expanding central power over the way that the empire was run. The most likely explanation is that the evolution of the judiciary into a true power within the government was that the empire needed them. They were the solution to a part of the problem of running an empire which was growing rapidly in almost every way possible, throwing up new challenges for those on the throne. Whatever the impetus behind the works of Basil I and Leo VI the later Macedonians were at least partly, and I would say largely, concerned with the requirements of governing their increasingly large, complex, wealthy and densely populated empire. The reforms visible in the *Escorial Taktikon*, and the works of Romanos III and Constantine IX, were born of necessity, whatever their value as part of the imperial image.

4

The collapse of civilian government, c. 1066–c. 1133

More than anything else the emperor desired to increase the public funds and to supervise private trials, even if it meant devoting the greater part of his reign to these efforts. ... As a result, Roman society was shaken by sycophantic accusations, sophistic tricks, a swarm of judicial technicalities, and the complexity of bureaucratic procedures.[1]

The inspiration behind the opening quote of this chapter from Attaleiates's *History* is the fact that I think it encapsulates most modern views of the eleventh century, as a period of general mismanagement which gradually undermined the empire from within at the same time that it was being threatened from without. As noted in the last section, the sigillographic material for the earlier parts of the eleventh century presents almost no evidence for wanton mismanagement, and rather more for a careful restructuring of the Byzantine government to fit the needs of the eleventh-century empire. While there is some evidence for maladministration of the type described by Michael Attaleiates and Michael Psellos in the period covered by this chapter, especially during the reigns of Michael VII and Nikephoros III, the seals present a more nuanced picture. There is no evidence for indiscriminate promotion, and little for the leaps up the hierarchy described by Attaleiates.

The last decades of the eleventh century saw changes to the nature of office-and title-holding that have an impact on our means of analysing the imperial government. Firstly, during the reign of Nikephoros III Botaneiates the empire became so short of money that he had to stop paying *rogai*. As we have seen, many Byzantine bureaucrats derived considerable income from their titles, so the impact of this change must have been devastating, especially after years of currency debasement. For us this presents a problem because we can no longer use income as a method of determining the relative importance of various offices after c. 1080. I will still include these calculations where I think they are illuminating, but they are only valid for the first decade and a half of the period covered by this chapter. Secondly, during the 1080s Emperor Alexios I Komnenos began an overhaul of the titles of the empire, creating a new system which placed his family and allies over everyone else. It took decades for this new system to reach maturity, but the essentials were put in place during the 1080s, and we can see the changes it wrought almost immediately in the sigillographic record. To some degree the old system continued to exist into the twelfth century, but as a second-class set of dignities for those without imperial connections. We can account for this when assessing status, but it must be borne in mind that the hierarchy under the Komnenoi was completely different from that under their predecessors, and that direct comparisons might be misleading.

The aim of this chapter is to address three questions: What evidence is there for the sort of mismanagement recorded in the histories of the period? What was the condition of the bureaucracy on the eve of the Komnenian age? And how did the bureaucracy and the place of bureaucrats in the imperial system change during the reign of Alexios I Komnenos?

4.1 Reform and consolidation: The *logothesia* and treasuries

> *And against the emperor himself too, who was not managing affairs in a truly imperial manner, but rather tyrannically and illegitimately and, by administering affairs in an improvident way, was leading the Ausonians over a sheer cliff.*[2]

In the previous section, to build a picture of the various departments of the Byzantine government we relied heavily on the seals belonging to the heads of the bureaus, but the seals of their subordinates contributed greatly as well. In the last third of the century the amount of evidence for everyone below the chief of the department shrinks noticeably, and we are unfortunately more reliant on their careers to tell the story of government than ever before. We will mostly be encountering *sekreta* and offices discussed in the previous section, however Alexios I created three new positions in the first two decades of his reign, and we shall incorporate them in the appropriate place.

4.1.1 The *logothetes ton sekreton*

> Τοῦ σεβαστοῦ καὶ λογοθέτου κῦρ Μιχαήλ.
>
> The sebastos and logothetes lord Michael.[3]

The first official whom we must consider takes us to into the Komnenian period. The *logothetes ton sekreton* (director of the departments) makes his appearance in the text of a lost *chrysobull* of 1081, fortunately recorded by Anna Komnene, in which Alexios I granted complete control over the administration to his mother Anna Dalessene.[4] This was a new position, not simply a reworking of the office of *sakellarios*. The *logothetes* had much more authority than oversight of the finances of the *sekreta*, all of the other *logothetes* and department chiefs reported to him, and he reported to Anna Dalessene, and later to the emperor. That the new *logothetes* was an important man is reflected in the dignities held by the occupants of the office. The earliest known *logothetes*, Sergios Hexamilites in 1082, held the title of *protoproedros*, his successor in 1089 was *protonobelissimos* and *megalepiphanestatos*.⁵ At the Blachernai Synod in 1094, Michael *logothetes ton sekreton* held the exalted dignity of *sebastos*, and he still held both office and title in 1108.⁶ Gregory Kamateros served as *logothetes ton sekreton* in 1118, probably with the title of *nobelissimos*.⁷ Although few men held the office in our period it is clear that the *logothetes ton sekreton* was always intended to be one with a prestigious position within the Komnenian hierarchy. The lowest title, *nobelissimos*, was in the bottom third of the hierarchy when Gregory held it, but it was in the hierarchy even though by 1118 there were very few titles left. Meanwhile Michael was a *sebastos*, a title which he shared with imperial princes. Moreover, Sergios, Michael and Gregory belonged to families that were significant at the time they held office. We have encountered the Hexamilitai throughout this study. Gregory Kamateros married into the imperial family, as did Michael, who was the son of Constantine, nephew of patriarch Michael Keroularios.⁸ Through both their titles and connection to the reigning dynasty, the *logothetai ton sekreton* were a part of a different level of society from their subordinate bureaucrats, as we shall see in the following pages. The creation of the *logothetes ton sekreton* placed a layer between the emperor and the other *sekretikoi*. While perhaps not intentional, this must have lessened the prestige of their offices by decreasing the contact that they had with the emperors. More than that, it must have made it harder for everyone else to gain access to the imperial presence, with all of the possibilities for career progression that this provided.⁹

4.1.2 The *Sakellarios*

Θεοτόκε βοήθει Μιχαὴλ μαγίστρῳ καὶ βασιλικῷ πρωτονοταρίῳ τοῦ μεγάλου σακελ λαρίου τῷ 'Αγαλλιανῷ.

*Theotokos, help Michael Agallianos, magistros and imperial protonotarios of the megas sakellarios.*¹⁰

It is not stated anywhere in the Byzantine sources that the *sakellarios* ceased acting as the controller and coordinator of the empire's fiscal apparatus. However, as we saw in the last section the sigillographic evidence for the *sakellarioi* does not point to them holding a very elevated position from the mid-eleventh century, and this continued to be the case in the following decades. Assuming that seals are, to some degree, evidence of contact between individuals or their departments, the *sakellarios* must have been

Table 4.1 Normalized Seal Data, in Percentages, for the Titles of *Sakellarioi* c. 1066–c. 1133

Title/Date	Eleventh Century		Twelfth Century
	Middle Third	Final Third	First Third
Magistros		60	100
Protospatharios	100	40	

comparatively uncommunicative. There is so little evidence that individuals can distort the overall picture. It seems likely that the *sakellarios* was fading by the middle of the eleventh century, and one wonders whether the position still had its wide-ranging responsibilities when it was awarded to Constantine the nephew of the patriarch in either 1057 or c. 1065.[11] At this point he was in his early twenties, and oversight of all of the empire's finances seems an unlikely set of responsibilities to award to a relatively inexperienced young man no matter how much the emperor of the day wanted to ingratiate himself with the supporters of Keroularios.[12]

There are two pieces of evidence for the continued importance of the office of *sakellarios* in the later eleventh century: the addition of the epithet *megas* and the career of Michael of Neokaisarea. From 1079, we see the occasional appearance of the *megas sakellarios* in written sources.[13] It would be unusual to add to the name of the office in such a way if it had experienced a serious decline in fortunes.[14] A recap of the career of Michael of Neokaisarea might help untangle this issue. Michael was appointed *sakellarios* in 1071 and held the office throughout the reign of Michael VII Doukas (1071–8). He became notorious for confiscating the *skalai*, the landing stages and piers, of the docks of Constantinople from their rightful owners as a way of increasing the state revenues. Attaleiates records both this action, and how they were restored by the dedicatee of his work, Nikephoros III.[15] Oikonomides suggested that this passage in Attaleiates defined the entire remit of the *sakellarios* in this period.[16] While I disagree with Oikonomides, that the *sakellarios* was in charge of implementing a particular imperial fiscal policy in no way guarantees that the specific policy defined his entire jurisdiction, I do think that the story of Michael of Neokaisarea might provide a clue as to what had happened to the office of *sakellarios*.[17] Up until his tenure there is clear evidence of an office in decline. Michael himself was so hated that when he died in exile in the Balkans his corpse was stoned by the crowd – this implies a great degree of notoriety for the controller of the landing stages of the capital. I would suggest that the office experienced a revival under Michael after decades of decline, perhaps not as a general controller of finances, but as an agent of imperial fiscal policy. This line of reasoning tallies with the first-known appearance of the *megas sakellarios* in 1079 when he was forced by the collapse of the *eidikon* to supervise the payment of that year's *rogai*.[18] A subordinate, Michael Agallianos, *magistros* and imperial *protonotarios* of the *megas sakellarios*, has left seals dated to the end of the eleventh/beginning of the twelfth century.[19]

4.1.3 The *megas logariastes ton sekreton*

One piece of evidence strongly hinting at a narrowing of the role of the *sakellarios* by the end of the eleventh century is the creation of a new financial controller for the *sekreta* in the 1090s by Alexios I Komnenos, the *megas logariastes ton sekreton* (great accountant of the departments).[20] The exact date at which the emperor implemented this reform is unknown, but the office appears in the written sources in 1094.[21] His duties, management of the financial affairs of the *sekreta*, and documentation of all financial acts, are almost identical to those assigned to the *sakellarios* in earlier times. Little is known about the *megas logariastes ton sekreton*'s place in the hierarchy under Alexios for two reasons. Firstly, there are few mentions of the office in any medium, and secondly the *megas logariastes* is hard to identify even when he does appear in the sources because his jurisdiction is not specified, and we know of another *megas logariastes* in charge of government properties. Frustratingly, one of the most significant bureaucratic reforms of the 1090s has left behind little indication of where the men involved sat in the hierarchy.

4.1.4 The *sekreton tou genikou*

Θεοτόκε βοήθει τῷ σῷ δούλῳ Βασιλείῳ προέδρῳ καὶ γενικῷ λογοθέτῃ τῷ Ξηρῷ.

Theotokos, help your servant Basil Xeros, proedros and genikos logothetes.[22]

It has long been argued that the department of the *genikon* went into decline in the mid-eleventh century. The impetus behind this was the creation of the *sekreton* of the *epi ton oikeiakon*, which removed fiscal lands from the control of the *genikon* at just the time when these lands were becoming increasingly important.[23] At about the same time, the *oikistikos* became an independent official, removing further responsibilities from the *genikon*.[24] In spite of these reversals, the *genikon* remained the main *sekreton* for the assessment and collection of the property tax throughout the eleventh century, until losing even this function to the *sekreton* of the *epi ton oikeiakon* in the twelfth.[25]

The sigillographic evidence does not support the idea of a mid-eleventh century decline for the *sekreton tou genikou*, if we take the *logothetes* to be representative of his department. We saw in the last section how the *logothetai* had experienced at best a stagnation in their status. This process was reversed in the final third of the eleventh century, when we see modest promotion. In seals dated right up to 1100 the most common title held by the *logothetai tou genikou* was *proedros*, followed by *vestarches*, a big jump from *protospatharios* and *patrikios* in the

Table 4.2 Normalized Seal Data, in Percentages, for the Titles of *Logothetai tou Genikou* c. 1066–c. 1133

Title/Date	Eleventh Century		Twelfth Century
	Middle Third	Final Third	First Third
Proedros	16.4	42.9	25
Vestarches and Patrikios	5.5	11.4	
Vestarches	8	8.6	
Vestes	10.9	5.5	
Anthypatos and Patrikios	10.8	5.8	
Patrikios	21.4	5.8	
Protospatharios	21.5		
None	5.5	20	75

previous time period.[26] This moved them from the bottom to the top third of the hierarchy. Assuming that these men were *proedroi* before Nikephoros III was forced to suspend payment of *rogai*, they would have received 28 pounds of *nomismata*. During the 1090s *proedros* became a less prestigious title, but was still awarded to important officials, unlike the titles that had once been below it in the hierarchy which dropped out of use. Although there is ample evidence for a loss of prestige for the *genikon* at the very end of the eleventh century, and certainly in the twelfth, the data from the seals suggest that up until this point it remained relatively important. A possible explanation that reconciles Oikonomides's arguments with the seals is that the *genikon* provides us with our first glimpse of the result of the generous promotions granted out after the reign of Isaac I, but particularly under Nikephoros III. If, as Attaleiates says, Nikephoros promoted people to titles four places higher than their current rank, that would have carried a *patrikios* half way to *proedros*, so even greater generosity is implied here.

When we turn to the subordinates of the *logothetes*, stagnation remained the order of the day. We should discount the *vestarchai* and *vestai* as they all held another office that more readily explains their title, such as theme *krites* or *kourator*. For the majority of men who were *protospatharioi* the final decades of the eleventh century was a time of declining status and income. With one exception, the evidence from the seals is supported by that from written sources. From 1087 to 1088 we know of one *megas chartoularios* with no title, one *dishypatos*, a *vestarches* and two *magistroi*, the latter three were also judges of the Velum which likely explains their titles.[27] The exception is a lone *protoproedros* who recorded only his position as *megas chartoularios*. The story is similar further down the rankings with the *chartoularioi*. The only positive note is the disappearance of the *spatharokandidatoi*, who moved up one level.

The *genikon* as a department was hardly flourishing in the later eleventh century. The majority of its employees were awarded the title of *protospatharios*, an increasingly worthless rank. Meanwhile the *logothetai* experienced a considerable promotion after a period of stagnation, but even then they were among the lowest ranking of the chiefs of the *sekreta*.

Table 4.3 Normalized Seal Data, in Percentages, for the Titles of the *Megaloi Chartoularioi tou Genikou* c. 1066–c. 1133

Title/Date	Eleventh Century	
	Middle Third	Final Third
Vestarches	4.8	10.8
Vestes	9.5	22.2
Hypatos and Protospatharios	7.1	
Protospatharios	66.7	67
Spatharokandidatos	7.1	
None	4.8	

4.1.5 The *sekreton tou stratiotikou*

Θεοτόκε βοήθει Νικηφόρῳ πατρικίῳ, ὑπάτῳ καὶ βασιλικῷ χαρτουλαρίῳ τοῦ στρατιωτικοῦ τῷ Ἀδραμυτηνῷ.

Theotokos, help Nikephoros Adramytenos, patrikios, hypatos, and imperial chartoularios of the stratiotikon.[28]

The fortunes of the *stratiotikon* are difficult to trace. It last appears in the written sources in 1088, but the exact date of its dissolution remains unknown.[29] Evidence for the *logothetes tou stratiotikou* becomes incredibly rare in the second half of the eleventh century. However, such evidence as we have paints a consistent picture of an office regarded far below its fellow *logothetai*. From their seals we know of Michael Radenos – *magistros* and *vestarches* – and Michael – *vestarches*, *vestes*, *anthypatos* and *patrikios*.[30] The *logothetes* known from texts in this period also happens to be the last recorded holder of the office, Niketas, *magistros*.[31] By 1088, *magistros* was slipping towards the middle of the hierarchy, and our evidence hints at a consistent rank across the decades, which would have resulted in a sharp drop in income. Why the *stratiotikon* should vanish is an interesting question. Oikonomides linked its decline to the changing methods of military recruitment and the disappearance of the theme armies in the eleventh century.[32] Whatever the reason behind his disappearance it is clear that the *logothetes tou stratiotikou* had been declining for some time. He was never as highly ranked as his counterpart in the *genikon* for instance, and his lower mid-century rank reflected this. He continued to be comparatively lowly rewarded for the head of a *sekreton* into the 1070s and 1080s, which leaves open to question just how indiscriminate and widespread the promotions doled out by the last emperors of the eleventh century were.

In an interesting contrast to the subordinates of the *logothetes tou genikou* who mostly languished at the level of *protospatharios*, those of the *logothetes tou stratiotikou* were promoted to dignities that gave them a position in the middle of the hierarchy, in some cases falling close behind or equal to their superior. Of the known *megaloi chartoularioi* John Beriotes was *vestes* judge of the Velum and imperial *notarios* of the *sakellion*, and John Chrysoberges held the title of *vestarches* in 1088.[33] In the third quarter of the eleventh century, Nikephoros Adramytenos was *patrikios* and *hypatos*, and later in 1088 Anastasios Matzoukes held the title of *protovestes*.[34] Here we are presented with a contradiction, a *logothetes* refused promotion, but his subordinates promoted above the level of their contemporaries in the other *sekreta*.

Table 4.4 Normalized Seal Data, in Percentages, for the Titles of the *Chartoularioi tou Genikou* c. 1066–c. 1133

Title/Date	Eleventh Century	
	Middle Third	Final Third
Anthypatos and Patrikios	4.7	
Patrikios and Protospatharios	13.8	
Patrikios	6.9	18.8
Protospatharios	37.5	81.2
Spatharokandidatos	37.1	

4.1.6 The *sekreton tou dromou*

Τὸν Ἀριστηνὸν νῦν λογοθέτην δρόμου τὸν Μιχαὴλ δείκνυσι σφραγίδος τύπος

The impress of the seal shows that Michael Aristenos is now logothetes of the dromos.[35]

As far as we can tell the operation of the *sekreton tou dromou* and its officers in the later eleventh century was much the same as it had been before. The big change in function is first recorded in the middle of the twelfth century when the *logothetes*, or in his absence the *protonotarios*, acted as a sort of chancellor for the emperors.[36] When did this situation arise? Oikonomides has suggested that it could have happened as early as the last years of Alexios I.[37] Of the three *logothetai* discussed here the *logothetes tou dromou* had by far the best fortune in the last third of the eleventh century. Niketas Xylinites's dignity of *proedros* became the norm for the *logothetai tou dromou* into the 1070s.[38] As so often happened with the office of *logothetes tou dromou* it was awarded to an important individual with an inflated title, in this case Nikephoritzes, the mastermind of many unpopular policies during the reign of Michael VII Doukas. With this office and the extraordinary title of *hypersebastos*, Nikephoritzes, like so many *logothetai tou dromou* before him, acted as chief minister to the emperor.[39] There is no indication of a change in duties for the *logothetes* in the documents of the period. In 1086, John *protoproedros* served as *logothetes*, and later, in 1094, the office was filled by Andronikos Skleros *protonobelissimos*.[40] The last two examples show us how the *logothetes tou dromou* was absorbed into the upper echelons of the Komnenian bureaucracy, although it should be noted that its holders still occupied titles from the lower end of the hierarchy, although as a *protonobelissimos* Andronikos Skleros was a member of the elite among bureaucrats. There is little evidence for the *protonotarios*, but considering the importance attached to the position it is worth exploring. At some point after c. 1066 George Kibyrraiotes held the title of *proedros*.[41] Psellos addressed a letter to Eustratios Choirosphaktes *magistros* and *protonotarios tou dromou* in 1068, and later, in 1082, a member of the same family, Constantine Choirosphaktes *protoproedros*, was present at the trial of John Italos.[42] The impression given is one of slow advancement over two decades, although it is impossible to know whether Constantine received his title as a part of the early Komnenian reforms, or before Alexios came to the throne.[43]

4.1.7 The treasuries of the *sakellion*, *vestiarion*, and *eidikon*

Λέοντι μαγίστρῳ καὶ ἐπὶ τοῦ βεστιαρίου τῷ Σκληρῷ.

Leo Skleros, *magistros* and *epi tou vestiariou*.[44]

The three public treasuries – the *sakellion*, *vestiarion* and *eidikon* – have interesting and intertwined histories in the literature on the period. As there is also a noticeable decrease in the evidence for the officials who worked within them in the late eleventh century, it makes sense to discuss them together. We shall first discuss the heads of the three treasuries before turning to their subordinates. The *sakellion* had long been the primary

Figure 4.1 Seal of John Beriotes, *vestes*, judge of the Velum, *megas chartoularios* of the *stratiotikon logothesion*, imperial *protonotarios* of the *sekreton* of the *sakelle*. Harvard Art Museums/Arthur M. Sackler Museum, Bequest of Thomas Whittemore, 1951.31.5.1267. John, member of a family from the Balkans, is an example of the diverse funtions that one individual might perform in the Byzantine bureaucracy, in his case judicial, administrative, and financial.

Obv. + ΘKER,Θ,|TѠCѠΔႬΛѠ|IѠRECT,KPIT,|TႬRHΛ,M̄XTႬ|ΛAP,TႬCTPA|TIѠTIKႬ
Rev. ΛΟΓΟΘEC,|SR̄ĀNOTA|PI,TႬCEKPE|TႬHCCAKE|ΛΛHCTѠRH|PIѠTH
Θεοτόκε βοήθει τῷ σῷ δούλῳ Ἰωάννῃ βέστῃ κριτῇ τοῦ βήλου μεγάλῳ χαρτουλαρίῳ τοῦ στρατιωτικοῦ λογοθεσίου καὶ βασιλικῷ νοταίῳ τοῦ σεκρέτου τῆς σακέλλης τῷ Βηριώτῃ.
Theotokos, help your servant John Beriotes, *vestes*, judge of the Velum, *megas chartoularios* of the *stratiotikon logothesion* and imperial *notarios* of the *sekreton* of the *sakellion*.

repository for imperial wealth in the form of coinage, with most of the revenue of the state ending up in its coffers. In the written sources, the *sakellion* appears less and less frequently from the late eleventh century, eventually vanishing in 1145.[45] The *vestiarion* became the main treasury in the twelfth century replacing the *sakellion*.[46] Meanwhile, the *eidikon* vanishes from the written sources after a last appearance in 1088.[47] None of these processes are apparent in the sigillographic evidence. However, seals do complement the written evidence, which is not only rather opaque, but clustered at the beginning and end of the period under discussion; seals help fill in the gap.

The *eidikon* has the most dramatic story. Its decline is traced to 1079 when the *eidikon* could no longer pay the *roga* to office and title holders. When individuals purchased titles, their payment went to the *eidikon*, and it was from here that *rogai* were drawn. However, Nikephoros III gave away so many titles for free that there was not enough money in the *eidikon* to make the required payments – hence the need for the *sakellarios* to step in.[48] The three *eidikoi* known from seals all date to both before and after the bankrupting of their department, and there is no hint at a decline in their fortunes. All three were named Constantine: one Mytilenaios, one Blachernitees and one without a family name.[49] All three were *proedroi*, which marked a slight increase in their status over the mid-eleventh century.[50] Although not spectacular, the dignity of *proedros* placed them ahead of contemporary *logothetai tou genikou* or even the *sakellarios*. There is nothing in the seals to explain the end of the treasury.

For the *sakellion* and the *vestiarion* there is no evidence that the twelfth-century collapse of the former and the elevation of the latter was foreshadowed in the eleventh century. The six known *epi tes sakelles* held the titles of *vestarches*, *magistros*, *proedros* and *protoproedros*, while their counterparts at the *vestiarion*, of whom we know two, were a *vestes* and a *magistros*.⁵¹ The *epi tes sakelles* were consistently awarded higher dignities than the *epi tou vestiariou*, the opposite of what we have been led to expect from the written material from the twelfth century. While *vestarches* and *magistros* were on the lower end of hierarchy, the presence of a *protoproedros* might suggest that for a while at least the *epi tes sakelles* was incorporated into the lower end of the Komnenian elite. The most consistently high-ranked office, the only one where all known holders featured in the upper tier of the hierarchy, was the *eidikos*, the head of the treasury which vanished in 1088.

The subordinate staff of the three treasuries present a similarly contradictory image. There is almost no evidence for the subordinates of the *epi tou vestiariou* beyond singular mentions of individual office-holders. We know that they existed, but there is not enough information to chart their importance, or even to tell if their positions remained permanently filled over the decades. Meanwhile, two *protonotarioi* of the *sakellion* with the title of *magistros* or *vestes* have left seals. A direct comparison is possible one step down on the hierarchy at the level of imperial *notarios*. Two of these are known from the *sakellion* with the title of *hypatos* or *vestes*, and three from the *eidikon*: one *protospatharios* and two *anthypatoi* and *patrikioi*.⁵² This broad spread of titles for subordinate officials is the opposite of the flattening of the hierarchy observed in the previous section. Anyone in an office which had been filled by *protospatharioi* c. 1050 who was an *anthypatos* or a *vestes* in c. 1080 had been promoted above the rate of title inflation, moving from the bottom third to the middle of the hierarchy. Their *rogai* had also increased, and in some cases quite dramatically; up to 8 pounds for the *anthypatoi* and 12 for the *vestai*. There is no evidence of decline here, though there is perhaps of mismanagement. There is no other reason that I can see for these particular *notarioi* to be promoted so far above inflation when their contemporaries from other *sekreta* remained *protospatharioi* at best.⁵³

Oikonomides put the end of the *sakellion* down to the comparative demonetization of the state under the Komnenoi.⁵⁴ While this may be so, there had been no negative impact on the *sakellion* by the end of the eleventh century. It is possible to imagine certain of the functions of the *sakellion* moving to other departments, such as the responsibility for charitable institutions, but even this did not stop the highest-ranked individual treasurer of whom we know from being an *epi tes sakalles*, and for his subordinate the *protonotarios* from holding a title equivalent to the *epi tou vestiariou*. Similarly, it is easy to understand the rapid fluctuations in the fortunes of the *eidikon* without having to resort to the bankruptcy of 1079. One of the primary functions of the *eidikon* was to pay the *rogai* of officials and titleholders. It is conceivable that this duty made the *eidikos* particularly important among the treasury chiefs, and that once these payments ceased it was only a matter of time before the *eidikon* was absorbed into another treasury. In fact, the *vestiarion* likely survived because of all the treasuries it was the one which managed to maintain control over its diverse functions into the middle of the twelfth century.⁵⁵

4.1.8 Pious foundations, fiscal lands and crown estates

> Registered at the sekreton of the megas logariates of the euagon sekreton in the month of August, indiktion 7.⁵⁶

4.1.8.1 Fiscal lands

Θεοτόκε βοήθει ᾿Ιωάννῃ πρωτοπροέδρῳ καὶ ἐπὶ τῶν οἰκειακῶν τῷ Βηριώτῃ.

Theotokos, help John Beriotes, protoproedros and epi ton oikeiakon.[57]

We know little about the operation of the office of the *epi ton oikeiakon* in the later eleventh century. The assumption is that it was business as usual. There are a handful of seals, notably two belonging to John Beriotes, *protoproedros* and *epi ton oikeiakon*, dated to the late eleventh century.[58] Based on the evidence from other offices it is reasonable to conclude that John was in position during the first decades of the reign of Alexios I. This conclusion is supported by the elevated dignities held by Theoktistos Eulampes *dienergon* of the *sekreton* who was *protovestarches* in 1087 and 1088.[59] Also, in 1088, Basil Gorgonites was *protovestarches*, and *megas chartoularios* of the *sekreton* of the *oikeiaka*.[60] Fifteen imperial *notarioi* are known from a limited number of sources in this period. Eight of the fifteen did not record a title, five were *vestai*, and a *dishypatos*, and one a *protovestarches*.[61] This is quite an array of dignities limited to a short span of time, 1079 to 1092, with all but two of the *vestai* dated to 1087–8. As *vestai* they preserved the status of their *protospatharios* predecessors, while greatly increasing their income.[62] Why did these imperial *notarioi* so outperform the majority of their contemporaries? I can see two options, firstly, that their dignities reflect the importance increasingly placed on this *sekreton* and its central role in the finances of the state, or secondly, that the importance of the *sekreton* left them in a position to request and receive higher titles. This is a subtle difference, and either conclusion immediately runs into trouble when we remember that the *epi ton oikeiakon* himself was not promoted to anywhere near the degree that his underlings were. We do know that the fortunes of the *sekreton* continued to improve and that later in the twelfth century it became the main office for the collection of provincial taxes.[63] With this step it finally usurped the main responsibility of the *genikon*, the department to which it had once belonged.

4.1.8.2 Crown lands and *euageis oikoi*

Θεοτόκε βοήθει Θωμᾷ ὑπάτῳ πατρικίῳ ἀντιπροσωποῦντι τῷ οἰκονόμῳ τῶν εὐαγῶν οἴκων τῷ Ξηρῷ.

Theotokos, help Thomas Xeros, hypatos, patrikios, antiprosopon of the oikonomos of the charitable foundations.[64]

Both the *ephoros* and the *megas oikonomos ton euagon oikon* do not feature much in the sources for the later eleventh century, and the assumption is that they continued to operate as best they could. This must have been particularly difficult for the *ephoros*. Many of the lands under his control were in parts of the empire that were being lost to the Seljuks after 1071 or under threat from the Normans and Pechenegs in the 1080s. We know from the sole seal from this period that the *ephoros* maintained his dignity as *magistros* and *vestes* up to c. 1080, which of course meant a decline in terms of income, but a roughly level status when compared to earlier *ephoroi*.[65] The lone seal of a subordinate records the imperial *notarios* Michael Ophrydas, judge of the Velum and *vestes*.[66] Meanwhile the properties under the authority of the *megas oikonomos* continued to be profitable and were frequently given out as gifts by the emperors.[67] By the 1070s, different officials were appointed to run charitable properties in the eastern and western halves of the empire.[68] It is from this period that the majority of the sigillographic evidence for the subordinates of the *megas oikonomos* comes. We know of an *antiprosopon*, Thomas Xeros *patrikios* and *hypatos*; George *vestarches*, *hypatos* and judge of the Velum and *deuteros* of the charitable foundations; Michael *patrikios* judge of the Hippodrome and *chartoularios*; and two imperial *notarioi*, Gregory Kamateros *protospatharios*, *mystographos* and judge of the Hippodrome; and Nicholas Matzoukes who was also *exactor*.[69] There are no seals of the *oikonomos* himself, but the titles of his deputy, the *antiprosopon*, suggest that he was of roughly the same level as the *logothetes tou genikou* or higher. His subordinates were outperforming many of their contemporaries in equivalent positons. Considering the success of the *megas oikonomos* it is perhaps surprising to find both him and the *ephoros* vanishing from the sources in 1088, along with the *kouratorikion* of the *Mangana*.[70] In their place we find the *euage sekreta* under the control of the *megas logariastes ton euagon sekreton*, who first appeared in 1099.[71] The name of the new department, which merged *euageis oikoi* and crownlands, demonstrates the degree to which the former had become dominant by the last decade of the eleventh century.[72]

4.2 The chancery: A part of the imperial household?

> *John was a nobleman who from his early childhood had been under the emperor's protection and for a long time served him as hypogrammateus. He was a man of active mind, with a sound knowledge of Roman law, prepared to extol the emperor's ordinances as long as they were written in language worthy of his Imperial Majesty.*[73]

4.2.1 The *epi tou kanikleiou*

> Τοῦ κανικλείου ἡ σφραγὶς Εὐσταθίου ἄρχοντος ἐθνῶν καὶ στόλου χελανδίων.
>
> *The seal of Eustathios, epi tou kanikleiou, commander of foreign mercenaries and a fleet of warships.*[74]

In terms of duties nothing changed for the *epi to kanikleiou* at the end of the eleventh century.[75] We left this office in the hands of John Libellisios in the mid-eleventh century with the titles of *vestes*, *anthypatos* and *patrikios*. I know of two individuals from seals who held this office between John and the end of our period: Gregory – *proedros*, judge of the Velum and *epi tou kanikeliou* – and Eustathios Kymineianos, who, as well as being *epi tou kanikleiou*, held the position of *ethnarch* in the Byzantine

Figure 4.2 Seal of Eustathios *epi tou kanikleiou*, *ethnarches* and grand *droungarios* of the fleet. Dumbarton Oaks, Byzantine Collection, Washington, DC, BZS.1955.1.4060.
The obverse shows the Mother of God seated on a backless throne, the reverse St. Michael standing, holding a labarum and a globus cruciger, both surrounded by circular metrical inscriptions proclaiming Eustathios' unusual combination of offices.
Obv. +TႯKANIKΛEIႯHCΦPAΓICEVϤAΘIႯ
Rev. APXONTOCEΘNШNSϤOΛႯXEΛANΔIШN
Τοῦ κανικλείου ἡ σφραγὶς Εὐσταθίου ἄρχοντος ἐθνῶν καὶ στόλου χελανδίων.
The seal of Eustathios, *epi tou kanikleiou*, commander of foreign mercenaries and a fleet of warships.

army and *megas droungarios* of the Byzantine fleet.[76] Three more are known from written sources: Basil, who was a *vestarches* known from a letter of Michael Psellos dated to 1068, an anonymous *protoproedros* from monastic records from Patmos dated 1087, and Manuel Philokales, *protonobelissimos* who attended the synod of 1094.[77] When we put these men in order and consider their titles, the order is as follows: *vestes*, *anthypatos* and *patrikios*, followed by *vestarches*, then *proedros*, with *protoproedros* next, and *protonobelissimos*, with Kymineianos's title a mystery. This looks like a clear progression up the hierarchy from John Libellisios in the mid-eleventh century to 1094 and Manuel Philokales, with a step or two up the ladder every decade or so.

How did these promotions play out against a backdrop of title inflation, hierarchy redesign and currency devaluation? John Libellisios's highest title fell squarely in the middle of the pack. Gregory and Basil, as *proedros* and *vestarches* respectively, held titles that fell to either side of the line dividing the top and middle thirds of the hierarchy. The anonymous *protoproedros* and Manuel Philokales's titles put them in the bottom of the top third of the contemporary hierarchy, but this would have meant that, in the new Komnenian system, they held exalted titles for men not of the imperial family. Unlike many of his contemporary holders of a bureaucratic office Philokales held a title that was carried over into Alexios I's new system. There is more than a hint of the trend noted in the previous section where the *epi tou kanikleiou* was transitioning, if it had not already become, a part of the imperial household. Manuel Philokales was close to the emperor and accompanied Alexios I on campaign, and Eustathios Kymineianos was a palace eunuch.

4.2.2 The *asekreteion*

One might well say that the recompense brings joy, but fie on that – don't say it, don't even utter it, don't remind me of the issue of Job nor of the dead in Hades, since the reminders alone are enough to make me choke.[78]

4.2.2.1 *The* protoasekretis

Θεοτόκε βοήθει Ἰωάννῃ πρωτοασηκρήτῃ τῷ Σολομῶντι.

Theotokos, help John Solomon, protoasekretis.[79]

The story of the *protoasekretis* is much like that of the *epi tou kanikleiou* in that his duties remained unchanged in the latter part of the eleventh century, although in 1106 the office moved from the *asekreteion* to become a judge.[80] The two offices were also alike in the gradual progression of their titles up the hierarchy. We left the *protoasekretis* more often than not bobbing around the level of *protospatharios*, but with a late glimmer of something better to come in the person of Epiphanios Philaretos, *magistros*. This jump came rather suddenly in the early second half of the eleventh century, and once made the *protoasekretai* never looked back. Our evidence is scanty, as with almost all offices with but one occupant, but consistent. The one firmly dated seal to provide a title (there are more without this information) was owned by John Xeros, *magistros* and *vestes*.[81] This was probably created a little later than a letter from Psellos, written in 1068, which records the existence of Aristenos, *vestarches* and *protoasekretis*.[82] Three years later Eustratios Choirosphaktes held the post with the title of *magistros*, and eleven years later in 1082 documents preserved in the archives of the Vatopedi monastery on Mount Athos mention a John, *protoproedros*.[83] Jumping ahead nearly two decades to 1100 Gregory Kamateros was *protoasekretis* with the dignity of *nobelissimos*.[84]

Seeing the progression up the hierarchy for the *protoasekretai* is easy, but dating it with so few pieces of evidence so widely spaced throughout the period is more challenging. The move from *vestarches* to *magistros* seems to have happened in the late 1060s and very early 1070s. How long they occupied this level, the top of the middle of the hierarchy, is a mystery because of the eleven-year gap in our evidence. One year into the reign of Alexios I we have a *protoproedros*, but the unanswerable question is, does John's rank reflect the position of the *protoasekretis* under the system that Alexios was changing at that very moment, or its place in the new Komnenian hierarchy? Gregory Kamateros certainly represents the position at a point where the system was more settled, but with him we have the added complication that he had married into the extended imperial family when he wed Eirene Doukaina, and his title could just as easily reflect this fact as the importance of his office. That Gregory's rank is indicative of the importance attached to his job is suggested by the fact that his titles changed with each job he held, from *protokouropalates* as *praitor* of Peloponnese and Hellas, to *pansebastos sebastos* later in his career as *megas logothetes*.[85] While we cannot know whether there was a period of advancement in the later 1070s for the *protoasekretai*, we can conclude that the office was highly regarded under Alexios I, achieving a position

4.2.2.2 The Asekretai

Βουλὰς βεβαιῶ καὶ λόγους Κωνσταντίνου Φιλοκάλωνος Σέτη τοῦ ἀσηκρῆτις.

I certify the decisions and correspondence of the asekretis Constantine Philokales Setes.[86]

The data gleaned from the seals for the *asekretai* is presented in the Table 4.5. It should be noted that while there is ample evidence from the eleventh century, only two seals make up the figures for the twelfth century, a lack of evidence hinted at by the very round numbers recorded in that column. This is certainly not enough data with which to make conclusions, and I include it here only for the sake of completeness and transparency.

Similarly limited is the written material for this period. Two *asekretai* are known from 1104, Constantine and John.[87] Both held the second office of *anagrapheus*, and both, we can only assume as a result of this latter position, were *kouropalatai*. This assumption stems from the sigillographic material for the decades leading up to 1104, which does not record a title even close to that of *kouropalates*.[88] Instead we see a steady decline, with fewer *protospatharioi* and *spatharokandidatoi*, and more seals of *asekretai* recording no title at all. While this does not have to mean that they in fact held no title, considering the downward trend observed in the last section this seems to be the most likely conclusion. In the early twelfth century the *asekretai* effectively disappeared. While such a transition might seem to have more to do with vocabulary than function, it is clear that the *asekretai* had never been particularly highly valued, being elite only among the *notarioi* of the *asekreteion*, and must have found the closing decades of the eleventh century increasingly hard as ever scarcer imperial resources were routed elsewhere. This is reflected in the *roga* given to the most elevated of their number, the *protospatharioi* of just 1 pound of *nomismata*.

Table 4.5 Normalized Seal Data, in Percentages, for the Titles of the *Asekretai* c. 1066–c. 1133

| Title/Date | Eleventh Century | | Twelfth Century |
	Middle Third	Final Third	First Third
Anthypatos and Patrikios	0.5		
Protospatharios	16.5	10.9	
Spatharokandidatos	27.8	10.2	60
Spatharios	1	1.4	
None	54.3	77.6	40

4.2.3 The *mystikos*

Κύριε βοήθει Μιχαὴλ προέδρῳ καὶ μυστικῷ τῷ Φιλοκάλῃ.

Lord, help Michael Philokales, proedros and mystikos.[89]

The duties of the office of *mystikos* remain somewhat of a mystery in this period too. Paul Magdalino suggested that during the reign of Alexios I Komnenos the *mystikos* became a financial coordinator. However, as the evidence for the expanded role and importance of the *mystikos* dates to the reign of Alexios's grandson Manuel I, which just happens to coincide with the disappearance of the treasury of the *sakellion* in 1145; it is possible that the transition was much later.[90] In terms of status we have little evidence. Although seals of four men from this period are known, only one, Michael Philokales, recorded his title, *proedros*.[91] While this is the same dignity held by Constantine Leichoudes two-and-a-half decades earlier, we have already discussed the special nature of his appointment, and a comparison with the titles in the middle to lower end of the hierarchy held by most *mystikoi* is more valid. With this in mind we can argue for a rather significant jump in the status of the *mystikos* between the mid-eleventh century and the 1070s, up to the bottom of the top third of the hierarchy. I concluded the earlier discussion of the *mystikoi* by noting the frequency with which the office was held by members of the imperial household. None of the seals from this period present similar evidence. With the exception of those of Michael Philokales, none record anything more than their owners' names and the single office of *mystikos*. However, the *Diataxis* of Michael Attaleiates does record a John, *mystikos praipositos epi tou koitonos*, which made him a member of the imperial household and likely a eunuch. The connection between the *mystikoi* and the imperial household was obviously not completely broken in the second half of the eleventh century.

4.2.4 The *mystographos*

Κύριε βοήθει τῷ σῷ δούλῳ Κωνσταντίνῳ πρωτοσπαθαρίῳ καὶ μυστογράφῳ τῷ Ἐλεγμίτῃ.

Lord, help your servant Constantine Elegmites, protospatharios and mystographos.[92]

The story of the *mystographoi* continued to be one of steadily slipping behind in the last third of the eleventh century. Although *protospatharios* remained the penultimate title

Table 4.6 Normalized Seal Data, in Percentages, for the Titles of the *Mystographoi* c. 1066–c. 1133

	Eleventh Century		Twelfth Century
Title/Date	Middle Third	Final Third	First Third
Patrikios and Protospatharios	1.3	2.2	
Protospatharios	86.6	74.6	
None	12.1	22.9	100

on the ladder, there were just so many more dignities in the hierarchy by the last third of the eleventh century that in terms of status the *mystographoi* were worse off than ever. As with the *asekretai*, I suspect that their increasing loss of status was the reason that a higher proportion of the seals than ever before make no mention of the title. The sole *mystographos* recorded in a documentary source from this period alongside his title was a *dishypatos*, putting him between the majority *protospatharioi* and the tiny minority of *patrikioi*.[93] A small number of seals have been dated to the eleventh/twelfth century, and none mention a title. It is likely that these seals represent the last of the *mystographoi*, as their final appearance in the written sources was in 1100.

4.2.5 The *epi ton deeseon*

Θεοτόκε βοήθει Ἰωάννῃ πρωτοπροέδρῳ καὶ ἐπὶ τῶν δεήσεων τῷ Σολομῶντι.

Theotokos, help your servant John Solomon, protoproedros and epi ton deeseon.[94]

The *epi ton deeseon* is a tricky office to place in the administrative structure. Over time he has been included by modern scholars in discussions of both the chancery and the judiciary, concerned as he was with petitions to the emperor. Furthermore, by the mid-twelfth century the *epi ton deeseon* was one of the most important judges in the empire. With the hindsight that this knowledge brings, it is tempting to assign the *epi ton deeseon* to the judiciary, and then argue that he fits with the pattern discernible in that area of a surge of importance in the mid-1000s which continued into the latter third of the eleventh century. I have argued previously that mid-twelfth-century texts should not dictate our interpretation of eleventh-century sources; however, the *epi ton deeseon* was almost unique among the members of the chancery, as we can see from the sigillographic data.

The transformation in the importance of the post of *epi ton deeseon* which occurred in the mid-eleventh century continued in the subsequent decades. While the percentage of seals recording no title and those owned by *patrikioi* remained steady, there were no longer any *protospatharioi* or *vestarchai*, and every other *epi ton deeseon* known from his seals held a title from *magistros* upwards, putting them in the upper third of the hierarchy. The jump from *magistros* to *protoproedros* is fortunately easy to place. Nicholas Skleros was *epi ton deeseon* with the rank of

Table 4.7 Normalized Seal Data, in Percentages, for the Titles of the *Epi ton Deeseon* c. 1066–c. 1133

Title/Date	Eleventh Century	
	Middle Third	Final Third
Protoproedros		37.6
Magistros and Vestes		18.8
Magistros		18.8
Vestarches, Praipositos and Patrikios	37	
Patrikios	12.6	12.4
Protospatharios	37.8	
None	12.6	12.4

Figure 4.3 Seal of John Solomon, *protoproedros* and *epi ton deeseon*. Dumbarton Oaks, Byzantine Collection, Washington, DC, BZS.1955.1.3324.
The obverse shows the Mother of God with a medallion of Christ.
Rev. +ΘK͞ER,Θ,|.ω͞ᾶΠΡΟΕΔΡ,|.ΕΠΙΤωΝΔΕ|ΗCΕωΝΤω|COΛΟΜωΝ|ΤΙ
Θεοτόκε βοήθει Ἰωάννῃ πρωτοπροέδρῳ καὶ ἐπὶ τῶν δεήσεων τῷ Σολομῶντι.
Theotokos, help your servant John Solomon, *protoproedros* and *epi ton deeseon*

magistros during the reign of Constantine X Doukas (1059–67).[95] Following Nicholas, we know of three men who held the rank of *protoproedros*, Constantine Iasites, John Solomon and Constantine Choirosphaktes, the last of whom can be firmly dated to the year 1088.[96] As the next firmly dated *epi ton deeseon* is John Taronites, a *kouropalates* in 1094, it is likely that the other two *protoproedroi* predated Choirosphaktes.[97] The change must thus have taken place either in the short regency of Eudokia (1067–8), the only slightly longer reign of Romanos IV Diogenes (1068–71), or, and this seems more likely, under Michael VII (1071–78). Moving from *magistros* to *protoproedros* would have allowed the office to maintain its status in the expanding hierarchy of the 1070s. When we see the post under the fully developed Komnenian system it was in the hands of John Taronites, as noted earlier, and it was accompanied by the even higher rank of *kouropalates*. John was one of an increasing number of men to hold the post of *epi ton deeseon* who hailed from families associated with the imperial family, such as the Kamateroi and the Kastamonitai, and also the Komnenoi themselves. As a result the office became increasingly linked with the imperial household.[98]

It is tempting to link the continually high prestige of the *epi ton deeseon* in the decade after 1050 to his position as a quasi-judicial official. At a time when the *droungarios tes viglas* was overseeing legal decisions made in the provinces and the *sekreton ton dikon* under the *epi ton kriseon* was collecting the copies of the judgements of the theme judges, it is not surprising that the office responsible for receiving and answering petitions to the emperor should itself become more important. On the other hand, the position of the *epi ton deeseon* was increasingly held by men linked to the imperial family and was, in a sense, absorbed into the imperial household. The evidence presented here suggests that the titles associated with the office became more elevated before the emperors began entrusting the position to close associates and family members; although the status of the *epi ton deeseon* increased rapidly once, its holders were exclusively drawn from the emperor's inner circle. However, this conclusion must be tentative. It is easier to assess who was a member of Alexios I's household because of ample documentation and the widespread use of family names. Earlier in the century

Table 4.8 Normalized Seal Data, in Percentages, for the Titles of the *Mystolektai* c. 1066–c. 1133

Title/Date	Eleventh Century		Twelfth Century
	Middle Third	Final Third	First Third
Protospatharios	70.8	44	
Primikerios	1.9	14	
None	27.3	42	100

neither of these things apply and we might be missing close links between the *epi ton deeseon* and the emperor of the day that would extend the relationship between the office and imperial household back even further.

4.2.6 The *mystolektes*

Σφραγὶς Ἰωάννῃ πρωτοσπαθαρίῳ ἐπὶ τοῦ Χρυσοτρικλίνου καὶ μυστολέκτῃ τῷ Βλαχερνίτῃ.

Seal of John Blachernites, protospatharios epi tou Chrysotriklinou and mystolektes.[99]

The last of the officials of the chancery presents a picture with which we are now very familiar: a gradual decline in the percentage of men with titles, and the devaluation of the titles that were still associated with the office. About half of the *mystolektai* from this period had a second office, invariably as a judge. The evidence for the *mystolektai* from the early twelfth century is scanty, and it is likely that, as with a number of other offices considered earlier, it ceased to exist around 1100.

4.3 The administration of Constantinople: A steady decline

4.3.1 The *eparch*

Ἔπαρχος ἐκ σοῦ καὶ πρόεδρος Παρθένε Ἐπιφάνιος Καματηρὸς ὅν σκέποις.

It is by your grace, Virgin, that Epiphanios Kamateros is eparch and proedros, and may you protect him.[100]

The last time that we saw the *eparch* of Constantinople he had cast off his long-held title of *protospatharios* and assumed the much more prestigious dignity of *magistros*. This happened at the same time that the office lost many of its responsibilities, and I argued that the two were not contradictory, but a sign of the importance that the imperial government attached to its capital. By c. 1060 the *eparchs* were mostly *magistroi* and *proedroi*, the lowest two titles in the top third of the hierarchy, dignities which would have placed them among the most powerful men in the empire. As we can see from Table 4.9, by the final third of the century the most frequently held title was that of *proedros*, with *protoproedros* coming in a close second. If these titles were held before the mid-1080s they would have granted the *eparchs* the same relative status as the earlier *magistroi* and *proedroi*. Their *rogai* would have fallen into an odd position depending exactly when they held office. The range of payments covered by the mid-eleventh-century titles of *magistros* and *proedros* was 16–28 pounds of *nomismata*, that of later *proedroi* and *protoproedroi* 28–30 pounds. Within these two ranges it is possible that an *eparch* could be either better or worse off than his predecessors of a generation earlier. The first third of the twelfth century presents a different picture. Continued advancement in spite of the rearrangements of the Komnenian system, actually took 22.7 per cent of the *eparchs* further into the elite of the empire, however, 77.3 per cent choose to display no title on their seals.

The obvious question is, Why did 77.3 per cent of the *eparchs* choose to omit their titles from their seals? There are a few possible answers to this. Metrical inscriptions composed of twelve-syllable verses were becoming an ever more popular form on seals. This trend led to the breakdown of the old formula for inscriptions of name, titles, offices, family name. Twelve-syllable verses were hard to compose; the syllables had to

Figure 4.4 Seal of Nicholas Mermentoulos, *nobelissimos* and *eparch*. Dumbarton Oaks, Byzantine Collection, Washington, DC, BZS.1958.106.5531.
Rev. + ΚΕΡΟΗΘ,|ΤШCШΔΉΛ,|ΝΙΚΟΛΑШΝШ|ΡΕΛΙCΙΜШC|ΕΠΑΡΧШΤШ|ΜΕΡΜΕΝ|ΤΟΥΛШ
Κύριε βοήθει τῷ σῷ δούλῳ Νικολάῳ νωβελισίμῳ καὶ ἐπάρχῳ τῷ Μερμεντούλῳ.
Lord, help your servant Nicholas Mermentoulos, *nobelissimos* and *eparch*.

Table 4.9 Normalized Seal Data, in Percentages, for the *Titles of the Eparchs* c. 1066–c. 1133

	Eleventh Century		Twelfth Century
Title/Date	Middle Third	Final Third	First Third
Protonobelissimos			9.1
Nobelissimos		8.8	13.6
Protoproedros		23.4	
Proedros	6	25.2	
Magistros and Vestarches	17.8		
Magistros	17.8		
Vestarches	14.9	13.6	
Vestes, Anthypatos and Patrikios	3	1.9	
Patrikios	11.9		
Protospatharios	6	1.9	
None	22.5	25.2	77.3

be divided between the words in the verse in a five–seven or seven–five split, with the accent on the penultimate syllable. It is easy to understand why this would lead to more creative inscriptions that might omit certain details to adhere to the rules and improve the composition. The other option is that the titles held by the *eparchs* simply did not matter anymore, so, just like many other offices that we have seen in this chapter, they saw no reason to include them on their seals. Considering the difference between the status of the *eparch* and, say, an *asekretis*, it might seem a little odd that they would be in the same boat. However, if we remember that titles from *protoproedros* down were effectively defunct by c. 1118, and that the only titles worth publicizing were those associated with the Komnenian elite, it makes sense that the only *eparchs* to include their titles on their seals were the *nobelissimoi* and *protonobelissimoi*, who made the cut. I suspect that many of the rest believed that their position as *eparch* was more significant than whatever second-rate honorific – and without *rogai* they were just honorifics – that the Komnenoi had bestowed upon them.

Piecing together evidence from seals and texts we can build a detailed picture of the changing status of the office of *eparch* in the last decades of the eleventh century. At the beginning of the period, possibly just before the Komnenian takeover, Epiphanios Kamateros and John Beriotes held the rank of *proedros*.[101] Sergios Hexamilites came next, a *protoproedros* between 1080 and 1085.[102] Basil Tzirithon was also a *protoproedros* in 1089, as was Michael Philokales, though he was raised to *protonobelissimos* by 1094.[103] A dip in status came around 1094 with John *proedros* (possibly John Skylitzes). After him Nicholas Mermentoulos began his tenure as *eparch* as *protoproedros* before receiving the rank of *nobelissimos* before 1100. Around the turn of the century there were five men with no recorded title, a member of the Xeros family in 1103, Basil in 1106, an anonymous Aristenos, and Leo Hikanatos.[104] The last *eparch* in our period was John Taronites, a life-long friend of Alexios I who was a *protokouropalates*.[105] This evidence suggests that the step up from *proedros* to *protoproedros* began around the same time as the reign of Alexios I. This was possibly an attempt to maintain the existing status of the office during the early years of the Komnenian reform of the hierarchy. *Protoproedros* continued as the regular rank throughout the 1080s and 1090s, though individuals could be raised up among the *nobelissimoi*. After that, the run of *eparchs* with no titles suggests that they were of the group holding lesser titles, to which *protoproedros* now belonged, the exception being John Taronites, who was connected to the imperial family. Taronites is also interesting because he is the only man in this group with a strong connection to Alexios I. Many of the rest, such as the Hexamilites, Tzirithon and Xeros, belonged to old families with a strong tradition of civilian service. For much of Alexios's reign it seems that the office of *eparch* was not important enough to grant to a member of the imperial family or allied clan, a decline for the office reflected in the lower titles awarded to its holders by comparison to their pre-Komnenian counterparts.

4.3.2 The *symponos*

Κύριε βοήθει Νικήτᾳ βασιλικῷ πρωτοσπαθαρίῳ βασιλικῷ νοταρίῳ καὶ συμπόνῳ πόλεως.

Lord, help Niketas, imperial protospatharios, imperial notarios, and symponos of the City.[106]

Table 4.10 Normalized Seal Data, in Percentages, for the Titles of the *Symponoi* c. 1066–c. 1133

Title/Date	Eleventh Century		Twelfth Century
	Middle Third	Final Third	First Third
Protoproedros		3.1	16.7
Magistros	1.7	4.1	
Protovestarches	1.7	10.2	
Vestarches	6.7	8.1	
Patrikios	15.1	6	
Hypatos	2.5		
Protospatharios	20.3	12.2	
Spatharokandidatos	5.1		
Spatharios	2.5		
None	44.3	56.3	83.3

In the later eleventh century, the *symponoi* continued their mixed trajectory. Over half placed no title on their seal, likely a sign that their titles were not worth advertising, while almost a quarter held exalted ranks ranging from *vestarches* in the upper middle of the hierarchy, to *protoproedros* in the upper third. The *protoproedroi* and *magistroi* were only *symponoi*, while the *protovestarchai* and *vestarchai* held other offices, but the placement of these on their seals indicates that *symponos* was the most important. For the first third of the twelfth century the evidence is less impressive. Far fewer seals have survived, but those that have present a compelling picture. Few *symponoi* possessed a title which they thought was worth mentioning, if they had a title at all. The office had clearly declined from its height in the mid-eleventh century. It was never held by members of elite families, falling to families such as the Anzas, Chytes, Varys and Bringas instead.

4.3.3 The *parathalassites*

Θεοτόκε βοήθει Βασιλείῳ κουροπαλάτῃ καὶ παραθαλασσίτῃ τῷ 'Αριστηνῷ.

Theotokos, help Basil Aristenos, kouropalates and parathalassites.[107]

I discussed all of the evidence for the office of *parathalassites* in the last section. The only point that needs reiterating here is that the two known *parathalassitai* from the last decades of the eleventh century held the titles of *protoproedros* and *kouropalates*, putting them on a par with contemporary *eparchs*, as they had been in the mid-eleventh century. This further demonstrates the importance of their now independent office and their role in the life of the capital, and by extension Constantinople itself.

4.3.4 The *praitor* of Constantinople

Λάτριν μάγιστρον Νικήταν τὸν 'Αργυροῦ Βυζαντίδος πραίτωρα, Παντάναξ, σκέποις.

Lord of all, may you protect your worshipper Niketas Argyros, magistros and praitor of Byzantium.[108]

In a similar position to the *parathalassites* is the *praitor*. All of the limited evidence has already been discussed in the previous section. A short discussion comparing it to the information for the *eparch* is in order however. From a point just below that of the *eparchs* the status of the *praitores* slipped until, as *magistroi* and *vestarchai*, they were noticeably in the second class, firmly in the middle of the hierarchy by c. 1070. They had to some degree preserved their status, but it was of a low enough level already that we must question the imperial commitment to it. I said in the last section that we are unsure what function the *praitores* performed, but that the creation of this new post in the eleventh century was another symptom of the significance of the capital within the empire. We must therefore conclude that the disappearance of the *praitor* by c. 1100 was an indication that the reverse was now the case.

4.4 Falling from Grace: The judiciary

For this reason the Roman world was afflicted and shaken by duplicitous intrigues, shrewd manoeuvring, a swarm of judicial proceedings, and official inquiries, with the result that the soldiers themselves set aside their weapons and terms of service and became parties to legal proceedings and eager participants in these machinations.[109]

4.4.1 The *koiaistor*

Χρῄζεις μαθεῖν; Γνώριζε κοιαίστωρά με κριτὴν Νικήταν τὸν Ξιφιλῖνον γένος.

Do you wish to know? Know that I am the koiaistor and judge Niketas, Xiphilinos by descent.[110]

The seals of the *koiastores* present further evidence for the idea that a mixture of new sigillographic fashions coupled with the devaluation of older dignities led an increasing number of men to choose not to place their title on their seals but to claim status through their offices. On the surface, the *koiaistores* did not experience a great deal of change to their position in the later eleventh century, or even under Alexios I. The consistency that had been a hallmark of the office for centuries continued unabated, with the *koiaistor* acting as one of the four chief judges of the empire into the twelfth century.[111] In terms of titles, a higher proportion of *koiasitores* than ever before held high rank, even as late as c. 1081 the 44.7 per cent of *koiaistores* with the rank of *proedros* or above were in the top tier of the hierarchy. That the numbers were so high is a sign that many *koiaistores* were promoted above the rate of title inflation. Discounting those with no title for now, the mean average *roga* of a *koiaistor* in the last third of the eleventh century was 10.37 pounds. of *nomismata*. The lowest figure, 9.38, is slightly lower than the highest figure for the preceding period of 10.37 pounds.

The figures quoted earlier need further examination. Usually dealing with a small number of individuals – and the *koiasitores* make up one of the smaller data sets suitable for analysis in this way – is a hindrance. However, with the *koiaistor*, an office held by

Table 4.11 Normalized Seal Data, in Percentages, for the Titles of the *Koiaistores* c. 1066–c. 1133

Title/Date	Eleventh Century		Twelfth Century
	Middle Third	Final Third	First Third
Protokouropalates			31.6
Protoproedros	11.8	14.9	15.8
Proedros	11.8	29.8	
Vestes	11.8	8.5	
Patrikios and Protospatharios	11.8		
Protospatharios	41.2		
None	11.8	46.8	52.6

Figure 4.5 Seal of Pekoules, judge and *koiaistor*. Dumbarton Oaks, Byzantine Collection, Washington, DC, BZS.1955.1.4040.
The bilateral metrical inscription on Pekoules' seal is a good example of the wordplay that became common in the eleventh century.
Rev. +|ΤΙϹΦΡΑ|Γ,ΕΝΓΡΑΜ|ΜΑϹΙΔΕΙ|ΚΝΥϹΙ|ΛΕΓΕ
Obv. ΚΡΙ|ΤΗΝΠΕ|ΚΥΛΗΝΚΟΙ|ΑΙϚΩΡΑ|ΠΡΟΓΡΑ|ΦΕΙ
τὶ σφραγὶς ἐν γράμμασι δείκνυσι, λέγε. κριτὴν Πεκούλην κοιαίστωρα προγράφει.
Read what the seal shows in its lettering. It announces the judge and *koiaistor* Pekoules.

one man at a time, it is beneficial, in that it is possible to put them in a rough order and attempt to see the circumstance of the office on either side of the accession of Alexios I in 1081. By combining the sigillographic and documentary evidence this is exactly what we shall now attempt. One thing becomes immediately clear: the *koiaistores* and *protoproedroi* of whose date we can be sure all lived after the Komnenian reforms were well underway post c. 1090. George Nikaeus is recorded as *koiaistor* and judge of the Velum in 1093, and the seals of Theodore Smyrnaios *protoproedros* and *koiaistor* are dated to 1095–1112.[112] I cannot make the same claim for the *proedroi*. They are mentioned only in seals, and these are dated to the final third of the eleventh century. It is possible that some held office under Alexios I up to c. 1090, but the *protoproedroi* seem to have been a part of his new system rather than the traditional eleventh-century hierarchy. Even if we take the above argument as accurate, it does not undermine the idea that the *koiaistores* of the period c. 1066–81 experienced an uptick in their fortunes, with more men than ever before finding themselves in the top third of the hierarchy.

4.4.2 The *Antigrapheus*

Κωνσταντίνῳ ἀσηκρῆτις καὶ ἀντιγραφεῖ.

Constantine *asekretis* and *antigrapheus*.[113]

The evidence for the *antigrapheis*, never plentiful, drops noticeably in the final third of the eleventh century. Half of the known *antigrapheis* were *hypatoi*, a quarter *protospatharioi* and a quarter recorded no title, as did all of their counterparts who lived in the early twelfth century. From *protospatharios* to *hypatos* was no promotion at all in this period: the latter was immediately above the former in the hierarchy, and both were firmly at the bottom of the title list. It does, however, represent a slight increase in *roga* from 72 *nomismata* to 144.

4.4.3 The *droungarios tes viglas*

Κύριε βοήθει Κωνσταντίνῳ πρωτοπροέδρῳ καὶ μεγάλῳ δρουγγαρίῳ τῆς βίγλας.

Lord, help Constantine, *protoproedros* and *megas droungarios* of the *vigla*.[114]

The judicial duties of the *droungarios tes viglas* remained constant throughout the eleventh and into the twelfth century. From the reign of Michael VII Doukas (1071–8), he was known as the *megas droungarios*, a sign of his continued importance within the imperial government.[115] At the same time he adopted a new position as president of the senate.[116] The earliest firmly dated seals after c. 1066 belonged to Constantine, the nephew of patriarch Michael Keroularios, who was *megas droungarios tes viglas* and *protoproedros* from 1074 until 1078, the last four years of the reign of Michael VII.[117] It is possible that his brother Nikephoros held the office with the same rank at roughly the same time; a man by this name has left behind four seals.[118] The only other *megas droungarios* from before the reign of Alexios I of whom I am aware was a certain Niketas *megas droungarios* and *magistros*.[119] He must date earlier than the two brothers, a conclusion which is supported by our earlier discussion of the *droungarios*, whom we left with the title of *magistros* towards the end of the middle third of the century. If Niketas is any indication, we can suppose that the title attached to the office of *droungarios* remained largely stable at the level of *magistros* in the decades leading up to the reign of Michael VII, when it increased to *protoproedros*. The tenure of the two Keroularios nephews marked the high point for the office of *megas droungarios*. Not only did they hold a title close to the top of the hierarchy, but it is likely that the office acted as a rung on the ladder that Constantine hoped would lead to the imperial throne.[120] That Constantine was a viable contender for the throne, and a threat to the unsteady Doukas dynasty, was the result of more than his position as *megas droungarios tes viglas*, but it certainly helped, giving him a position of great authority in government.[121]

We have little firm information about the *megas droungarios* during the reign of Nikephoros III Botaneiates (1078–81). It is possible that this was when Nikephoros, nephew of the patriarch, held the post, following on from his brother. We do know that under the first of the Komnenoi the office, while still prestigious, was not linked to the highest members of the court as it had been in earlier decades. In 1082, the *megas droungarios* was Michael, son of the earlier Constantine, *protokouropalates*, a dignity that just two years earlier would have made him one of the highest ranked men in the empire.[122] Under Alexios I's new regime, however, while still important, he was lower down the hierarchy. Nicholas Skleros is harder to date. We know that he was *droungarios* in the seventh indiction, which could have fallen in either 1084, 1099 or 1114.[123] As his title was not recorded, it does not matter for our analysis which of the three is correct.[124] John Thrakesios/Skylitzes was *droungarios* with the rather low title of *proedros* in 1090, although he became a *kouropalates* in 1092.[125] The next known holder of the office was Nicholas Mermentoulos, who appears in the account of the Synod of 1094 in the Blachernai, to whom we shall turn in more detail soon.[126] The final *megas droungarios* of the reign of Alexios I was a man who was a harsh critic of the emperor, John Zonaras.

Based on the evidence from seals and written materials, we can say that the office of *megas droungarios* was commonly associated with the title of *protoproedros* by the end of the reign of Nikephoros III Boataneiates in 1081, and that this pairing had been common for quite some time, since at least the reign of his predecessor Michael VII. As noted earlier, this was rather a jump from its earlier level. The first *droungarios* of the Komnenian era, and the third relation of the Keroularios family to hold the post in a decade, Michael, held the higher office of *kouropalates*, a slight elevation of the title held by his father and uncle. Although John Skylitzes began his tenure as a *proedros*, his elevation to the rank of *kouropalates* could make us think that this was the Komnenian title associated with the office, which by this point was operating at the lower end of the Komnenian elite.[127] The case of Nicholas Mermentoulos brings this conclusion into

Figure 4.6 Seal of Nikephoros *proedros* and 'first' of the judges. Dumbarton Oaks, Byzantine Collection, Washington, DC, BZS.1955.1.3734.
The obverse shows the Mother of God standing, flanked by two saints, identified in the reverse inscription as a martyr and a bishop. The reference to Nikephoros as 'first' of the judges probably means that he was *droungarios tes viglas*.
Rev. +CVNMH|TPICWTEP|MAPTVPIΘVH|ΠΟΛWCKEΠO..|ΠPOEΔPON...|.PITWNNI|KHΦOPON
Σὺν μητρί, Σῶτερ, μάρτυρι, θυηπόλῳ σκέποις πρόεδρον καὶ κριτῶν Νικηφόρον.
Savior, together with your Mother, the martyr, and the bishop, protect Nikephoros, *proedros* and "first" of the judges.

question. He appears in the text of the Synod of 1094 as Νικολάου πρωτοπροέδρου τῆς συγκλήτου καὶ μεγάλου δρουγγαρίου τῆς βίγλας τοῦ Μερμεντόλου.[128] His position as head of the senate is mentioned, but not his title. Gautier suggested that he was either *protokouropalates* or *kouropalates* in 1094.[129] This would make a certain amount of sense, as he falls between a *protokouropalates* and a *kouropalates* in the Blachernai document, and it would align with the observations just made about the pairing of that dignity with the office of *droungarios*. However, there is no other account of Nicholas Mermentoulos holding this title. Later in his career he became *eparch*, and we know from his seals that he held the title of *protoproedros* at this time, before being promoted to *nobelissimos* sometime later.[130] He cannot have stepped backwards, and his early seals struck as *eparch* make no mention of the senate or the *megas droungarios*, just the title of *protoproedros*. A possible solution is that his title was *protoproedros* in 1094, his title as president of the senate, and that his place in the order of precedence was elevated by the office that he held above the *kouropalatai* who would normally outrank him. This would make Nicholas the lone exception in a document which adheres to a strict hierarchy of title, office was largely irrelevant. However, it is the only solution that reconciles the sigillographic material with the documentary.

The evidence presented above suggests that the *megas droungarios tes viglas* remained one of the most important men in the imperial government throughout the late eleventh and early twelfth centuries. The addition of *megas* to the name of the office certainly implies as much. In terms of titles attached to the office, the move was from *magistros* to *protoproedros*, possibly when Constantine nephew of the patriarch Keroularios took the office in the early 1070s.[131] It remained at this level until incorporated into the Komnenian system, usually with the higher rank of *kouropalates*. One point of note is that this office was held by families with strong ties to the administration of the eleventh century even under the Komnenoi, such as Michael and Nicholas Skleros, as well new men such as John Skylitzes. Although Michael married into the Komnenian family, the rest did not, and at the very least John Zonaras identified with the pre-Komnenian elite rather than the extended clan around Alexios I. This office, then, offers us a glimpse at a group of bureaucrats, most strongly identified with the old Constantinopolitan order, who were admitted to the lower rungs of the new ruling class, but to some degree remained outsiders.

4.4.4 The judges of the Velum

Θεοτόκε βοήθει τῷ σῷ δούλῳ Ἐπιφανίῳ βεστάρχῃ καὶ κριτῇ τοῦ βήλου τῷ Ἐξαμιλίτῃ.

Theotokos, help your servant, Epiphanios Hexamilites, vestarches and judge of the Velum.[132]

We left the judges of the Velum with an improvement in their position both in terms of status and income from the end of the tenth century up until c. 1066. I argued at that point that their promotion was probably part of a change to the judicial system linked with the transformation of the *droungarios tes viglas* from a military commander into a

Table 4.12 Normalized Seal Data, in Percentages, for the Titles of the Judges of the Velum c. 1066–c. 1133

Title/Date	Eleventh Century		Twelfth Century
	Middle Third	Final Third	First Third
Protoproedros		1.4	
Proedros	1.6	6.1	
Magistros and Vestarches	1.6	1.9	
Magistros and Vestes	4.7	7.5	
Magistros	9.9	8	
Protovestarches	0.6	4.7	
Vestarches and Patrikios	0.3	0.9	
Vestarches and Hypatos	1.3	0.9	
Vestarches	10.6	17.8	
Vestes, Anthypatos, and Patrikios	1.9	1.4	
Vestes and Patrikios	0.9		
Vestes	9.2	17.5	
Anthypatos, Patrikios, and Hypatos	0.9	0.5	
Anthypatos and Patrikios	4.4	5.4	25
Patrikios and Hypatos	6.2	1.8	
Patrikios	12.4	6.1	
Dishypatos and Patrikios	0.9		
Dishypatos	0.3	0.5	
Hypatos and Protospatharios	2.5	0.5	
Hypatos	1.2	0.5	
Protospatharios	23	8.2	25
Spatharokandidatos	0.3		
None	5.3	8.5	50

judge. Which raises the question, how did they fair in the subsequent period, knowing what we now know about the fortunes of the *droungarios*? The answer is relatively well, but not excessively so. We have finally lost the majority of the *protospatharioi*, once the dominant title for judges of the Velum; it now accounted for just over 8 per cent of the total. Similarly, the titles close to *protospatharios* in the hierarchy saw an equal decline: there are no longer any *spatharokandidatoi*, and the number of *hypatoi* was down to under half of the previous total; there were half as many *patrikioi*. To a large extent the judges of the Velum had been promoted out of the bottom third of the hierarchy in the final third of the eleventh century. They had moved to ranks that by c. 1070 would be considered upper-middle positions, *vestes*, *vestarches*, *protovestarches* and *magistros*.[133] Some 7.5 per cent had even broken into the top third of the hierarchy.[134]

The status and income of the majority of the judges of the Velum had increased in the last third of the eleventh century broadly speaking, but it is possible to be more specific about the period before and after the coronation of Alexios I. One interesting phenomenon is that there were few men with seals recording no title in the period, although the figure does jump to 50 per cent for those seals whose date extends into the early twelfth century. I have argued earlier that this phenomenon was the result of the holders of offices not possessing a title of substance in the new era of the Komnenian hierarchy. How then, to explain the judges of the Velum with their almost universal inclusion of titles on their seals? I suspect that what we have is a case of them simply not striking seals once the reforms of Alexios had taken hold. This argument is borne out when we look at the seals that we can date most accurately. Fortunately, there are quite a few of these such as Basil Tzirithon, *protovestarches*, judge of the Velum and *krites* of the Kibyrraiotai, 1060–80, and Sergios Hexamilites, *protoproedros* and judge of the Velum.[135] Most of the seals with a date range beginning after 1060 were struck before 1080, somewhat fewer before 1090, and almost none dated to after this point. True, there are seals dated broadly to the last half, third, or quarter of the eleventh century, but where we can be sure of the date c. 1090 is our cut-off point. What seems to have happened is that the judges of the Velum ceased striking seals regularly and in large numbers in the 1090s. They continued to exist after this point, but like other, lower-ranking officials, they were not sealing their documents in lead.

The earlier conclusions are supported by the written sources, which also allow us to look further ahead into the reign of Alexios I. The three known judges from the 1070s held the titles of *patrikios* and *anthypatos*, later promoted to *proedros*, *disphypatos* and *protovestarches*.[136] Ten judges are known from the 1080s, all but two, one *vestarches* and one *protovestarches*, were *magistroi*.[137] From 1090 every judge for whom we have information was either a *protoproedros*, or a *kouropalates*; two had no known title.[138] Judge of the Velum was only the senior office for two these men: the two without titles. The rest were either *koiaistores* or *epi ton kriseon*, and in one case both. While sigillographic evidence proves that judges of the Velum could rise as high as *protoproedros* before the reign of Alexios I, once he began his reform of the hierarchy, the only time that they appear with titles is when they owe their rank to a different office. The judges of the Velum had risen to the upper middle of the hierarchy by c. 1070 and remained put in the turbulent decade that followed. There is some evidence of higher ranks, *proedroi* and *protoproedroi*, that we can perhaps assign to the mismanagement of the system and generous promotions attributed to Michael VII and particularly Nikephoros III, but the majority never moved higher than the most successful of their predecessors from the mid-eleventh century. The system was largely stable. The real change came in the second decade of the reign of Alexios I, by which time the judges of the Velum were certainly not members of the elite and did not feature in the Komnenian hierarchy of titles.

4.4.5 The judges of the Hippodrome

Μάρτυς βοήθει Δημητρίῳ πρωτοσπαθαρίῳ καὶ κριτῇ ἐπὶ τοῦ Ἱπποδρόμου τῷ Παμφίλῳ.

Martyr, help Demetrios Pamphilos, protospatharios and judge of the Hippodrome.[139]

The sigillographic evidence for the judges of the Hippodrome so far has presented a picture of an early-eleventh-century peak, followed by stagnation and decline, coupled with an increasing diversity of title. Exactly the same picture is presented for the final third of the eleventh century. While it is true that there had been a drop in the percentage of judges with the increasingly worthless dignity of *protospatharios*, they still accounted for nearly half of the total. If we take the total percentages of judges of the Hippodrome with titles in the bottom third of the hierarchy in c. 1060 and c. 1081, they account for 82.1 per cent and 71.4 per cent, respectively. When we add in the increase of 4.8 per cent of those with no title we begin to see that the situation for the judges of the Hippodrome in c. 1081 was not much different to that in c. 1060. The diversity of title offers some hints that this was not just a story of declining status and stagnant income. However, even here the figures disguise certain details that partly stifle that hope. While there were some judges who held their titles of *proedros*, *magistros* and *vestarches* with no other office, most were either theme judges or judges of the Velum, and it is difficult not to conclude that they held such high titles as a result. Furthermore, the seals of all of the *proedroi* from the final third of the eleventh century can be dated to the years after c. 1075, a period when the written sources tell us was one of liberal promotion. Could this explain why *proedroi* appear in larger numbers at this point, and perhaps the increased numbers of *vestai* and *anthypatoi* too?

Although the dating for the seals of the judges of the Hippodrome is not as refined as that for their counterparts of the Velum, I would make the same observation when discussing them that the rather low number of seals recording no title for the final third of the eleventh century suggests that the majority of these seals are dated to a point before the middle of the reign of Alexios I.[140] A number of judges of the Hippodrome are known from documentary evidence from the first half of Alexios's reign. In 1084, Michael Rodios was *protoanthypatos* and judge of the Hippodrome, John Melidones *protovestes*, *megas oikonomos* of the Oikoproateiou, and judge of the Hippodrome is recorded in 1085, three years later Nicholas Zonaras was *megas chartoularios* and judge of the Hippodrome with the title of *protovestarches*, and finally Michael Autoreianos

Table 4.13 Normalized Seal Data, in Percentages, for the Titles of the Judges of the Hippodrome c. 1066–c. 1133

Title/Date	Eleventh Century		Twelfth Century
	Middle Third	Final Third	First Third
Proedros	0.6	5.8	
Magistros	0.7	2.1	
Vestarches	1.5	3.2	
Protovestes	0.9		
Vestes, Anthypatos, and Patrikios	1.4	0.8	
Vestes and Hypatos	0.9		
Vestes	1.8	3.2	
Anthypatos and Patrikios	2	1.6	
Anthypatos	0.9		
Illoustrios	0.4	1.2	
Patrikios and Hypatos	3.2	2	33.3
Patrikios	5.3	10.7	33.3
Hypatos and Protospatharios	1.6	3.3	
Hypatos	4.1	2.4	
Protospatharios	64.1	48.5	33.3
Spatharokandidatos	3.8	3.3	
None	7.1	11.9	33.3

attended the Blachernai Synod in 1094 as *proedros* and judge of the Hippodrome.[141] The titles held by these men are all from the upper range found on the seals of the period, and could perhaps be further evidence that most of our seals date a little earlier than the 1080s. Whether the first three men mentioned achieved their rank during Alexios's reign or still held high titles granted under Nikephoros III is an intriguing question without an answer. We can say that only Michael Autoreianos held a title that was worth much in the Komnenian system, and even that would have dropped out of use by the end of the reign of Alexios I in 1118.

The judges of the Hippodrome had been fading for a generation before the 1070s, and in spite of a handful of highly ranked individuals the majority of judges saw a further decline in their fortunes. While the documentary evidence suggests that there may have been a late surge in their circumstances in the 1080s, the titles that they received had already been relegated to the second class and would soon be as much a mark of their exclusion from the imperial hierarchy as a valued mark of status.

4.4.6 The decline of the city judges

In closing it is worth taking a look at the judges of the Velum and judges of the Hippodrome together. From the point of virtual equality recorded in the *Taktikon Escorial*, the judges of the Velum had achieved a higher status than their colleagues of the Hippodrome since the early eleventh century, and they only drifted further apart in the following decades. That the two distinct categories of judges would eventually achieve different statuses is perhaps not surprising in the ever more complex judicial system of eleventh-century Byzantium. What must have been unforeseen was the effect that title inflation would have on the less prestigious judges of the Hippodrome. By the closing decades of the eleventh century their office had become a junior one, a mere stepping stone on the way to more valued positions. However, they continued to exist in large numbers. It is one of the most commonly found offices on seals, and as such remained an important part of the imperial system, even if one of increasingly low rank. As their position continually eroded, it is likely that the two offices merged into one judge of the Velum and Hippodrome in the twelfth century.[142] For the early part of the twelfth century they mostly appear alongside other officials in the sources as signatories ratifying copies of imperial documents.[143] While the *Ecloga Basilicorum* dated to the mid-twelfth century does not mention the judges of the Velum and Hippodrome explicitly, it does mention a board of twelve judges, which corresponds to a source from later in the century that explicitly connects this number with our judges.[144] As late as 1196 there were still judges of the Velum acting as judges.[145]

4.4.7 The *Epi ton kriseon*

> To the protoproedros and epi ton kriseon, who was very dear to me, but had acted in a rather jealous way.[146]

We discussed the only known seals of the men who held the post of *epi ton kriseon* in the previous section. The only new evidence for this period is from documentary evidence. We know that Constantine the nephew of Michael Keroularios held the post from 1074, likely first with the title of *protoproedros* then as *sebastos* from 1078.[147] As the first man to be granted the title of *sebastos* this could be taken as an interesting indication of the importance of the office of *epi ton kriseon*, and so it can, but in a roundabout way. Constantine was raised to his exalted dignity not because of the office he held, but because of his influence at court and probably his popularity in the capital, not to mention his successful career as one of the empire's most important bureaucrats.[148] The point is not that the office of *epi ton kriseon* made Constantine important, but that such an important man, with hopes of becoming *kaisar*, and presumably emperor, should partially express his power through a judicial post. Constantine was, however, an exception, and for the rule we must look elsewhere. After Constantine an anonymous *epi ton kriseon* is recorded in 1087 with the dignity of *protoproedros*, and later, in 1112, George Nikaeus filled the office as *kouropalates*.[149] These ranks were at the bottom of the contemporary elite hierarchy and make the office of *epi ton kriseon* comparable to that of *droungarios tes viglas*.

That the *epi ton kriseon* was such an important person throughout the eleventh century, finding a home among the elite of the empire for most of the period makes the lack of evidence for his existence puzzling. His contemporaries in status and position have all left behind much more sigillographic and documentary material than he. Even more than his importance, it is the intended role of the *epi ton kriseon* within the state that makes the lack of surviving seals so interesting. Constantine IX Monomachos created the post of *epi ton kriseon* to oversee the work of provincial judges. Seals of theme judges survive from this period in larger numbers than ever before, or after, yet the *epi ton kriseon* could almost slip by unnoticed. By the mid-twelfth century the *epi ton kriseon*, whatever his function in the eleventh century, was one of the seven most important judges of the empire.[150]

4.4.8 The *thesmophylax, thesmographos, exaktor* and *kensor*

> Βλάσιον ἐξάκτορα, ὦ μάρτυς, σκέποις.
>
> Martyr, may you protect the exaktor Blasios.[151]

The remaining judicial or pseudo-judicial offices can be dealt with as a group, as their story is by now familiar. For the *thesmophylax* and *thesmographos* the discussion is a simple one as they vanish from the sources in the middle of the eleventh century. Of course, this does not mean that the position ceased to exist at that point, just that their actions were not recorded and they did not use seals, both indications of their fading importance, and perhaps limited lifespan. For the *exaktores* and *kensores* there is sufficient sigillographic evidence for analysis, presented in the tables below.

From the data presented earlier it seems safe to conclude that the *exaktores* faded in the later eleventh century alongside so many of their lower-ranked colleagues. Even of those with titles, 40.8 per cent found themselves in the bottom third of the hierarchy by c. 1070, and those who were lucky enough to make it into the bottom ranks of the middle of the hierarchy did so because they held multiple offices of higher rank than *exaktor*, usually as judge of the Hippodrome or theme judge.

The *kensores* are a rather interesting group in that they exhibit an actual decline in title as well as in status. By c. 1066 the *vestarchai* and *vestai* were gone, leaving only

Table 4.14 Normalized Seal Data, in Percentages, for the Titles of the *Exaktores* c. 1066–c. 1133

	Eleventh Century	
Title/Date	Middle Third	Final Third
Vestes	2	6.2
Anthypatos and Patrikios	8	3.1
Illoustrios	2	6.3
Patrikios	2	3.1
Protospatharios	58.9	29.7
Spatharokandidatos	6	
None	21.1	51.6

Table 4.15 Normalized Seal Data, in Percentages, for the Titles of the *Kensores* c. 1066–c. 1133

	Eleventh Century		Twelfth Century
Title/Date	Middle Third	Final Third	First Third
Vestarches	9.5		
Vestes, Anthypatos, and Patrikios	4.7		
Illoustrios	6.4	4.1	
Protospatharios	22.1	10.8	50
None	57.3	85.1	50

illoustrioi and *protospatharioi*, but with an overwhelming majority recording no title at all, a sure sign of decline. As with a number of other offices, where we can more narrowly date the seals of the *kensores* the cut-off point is usually the 1070s, which makes one wonder for how long the office survived after this point.

4.5 The end of civilian government

If one regards the art of ruling as a science, a kind of supreme philosophy, the art of all arts, so to speak, and the highest science of all, then one would have to admire him as a scientist in a way and a leading thinker for having invented these imperial titles and functions … . Alexios, the master of the science of government, directed all his innovations towards the good of the empire itself, whether changes were effected in the allotment of duties or in the granting of titles.[152]

We began this chapter with three questions: Can we see any evidence of mismanagement and overpromotion, what did the bureaucracy inherited by Alexios I look like and how did he change it? There is no evidence of blanket, indiscriminate promotion among bureaucrats in this period. The holders of a few offices did receive titles far above those that their predecessors had held, such as the *mystikos* and the *epi ton deeseon*, both men privileged enough to have regular contact with the emperor. Where there is evidence of a move up the hierarchy of dignities it is for a gradual increase, not a sudden jump of multiple levels at once. This was the case with the *logothetes tou dromou*, the *epi tou kanikleiou* and the *epi tes sakelles*. The idea that everyone who wanted a promotion received a higher title would have been puzzling to mid- and lower-level bureaucrats. The vast majority of those who were *protospatharioi* in c. 1066 remained so until the 1080s, if they continued to hold a title at all. The same was true for the *mystographoi*, *mystolektai*, and for the majority of the judges of the Hippodrome. The only bureaus where subordinate positions did well was in the *sekreton* of the *epi ton oikeiakon* and in the treasuries of the *sakellion* and the *eidikon*, where some effort seems to have been made to help the *notarioi* overcome the worst effects of title inflation and currency devaluation. For most of the rest gradual promotion or stagnation was the order of the day. The dignity of *proedros* was frequently associated with those department heads who were not cast adrift, but who were no longer truly elite, such as the *logothetes tou genikou*, the *koiaistor* and the *eidikos*. Meanwhile the *logothetes tou stratiotikou* and the *epi tou vestiariou* fell behind with titles which perhaps preserved them at the level of their mid-century counterparts. The legal profession and the government of Constantinople continued to be highly valued up until c. 1080, and most of the trends observed in the preceding decades continued after c. 1066.

Alexios I inherited a system which was in the process of changing rapidly. The evidence that we have for lower-level bureaucrats declines significantly after c. 1066, that for humbler administrators with a title drops away even more precipitously. Even at the middle ranks, offices such as the *mystographoi* and *thesmographoi*, possibly had vanished before Alexios came to the throne. The end of *rogai* payments must have had something to do with this transformation. A state bureaucracy run on the concept of monetary compensation for service would melt away if the money dried up as it began to do in the 1070s, and it is easy to imagine that this would hit the average bureaucrat more than his superiors, as he would have less of an economic cushion. The treasuries were in an odd position, with the *eidikon* seemingly the most threatened by the disasters of the 1070s, seeing its chief the most consistently highly ranked of the three, and with the *vestiarion* languishing behind. Understandably, the *ephoros* was experiencing a difficult decade as the lands that he managed were overrun. Less easy to understand was the apparent success and continued high rank of the *epi ton oikeiakon*, who must have seen his fiscal lands suffer as well. Two areas of stability in the system inherited by Alexios were the government of Constantinople and the judiciary; the members of both had a more comfortable 1070s than most of their fellow bureaucrats.

While an unsuccessful decade and a half after c. 1066 usually meant a terrible time after c. 1081, better times earlier did not necessarily equal success under the Komnenoi. Almost every office which was not associated with the title of *proedros* more often than not suffered a demotion under Alexios I. This included the success stories of the eleventh century, the judges of the Velum and their lesser cousins, the judges of the Hippodrome. Still, they were luckier than some, such as the *sekreton* of the *stratiotikon*, the *eidikon* and the *ephoros*, none of which survived the first decade of Alexios's reign. While the creation of the *logothetes ton sekreton* had the effect of demoting everyone, some effort was made into the 1090s to incorporate the older higher-ranking offices such as the *eparch*, *koiaistor*, *droungarios* and *logothetes tou genikou* into the new Komnenian hierarchy. However, such moves did not last long. By the time of Alexios's death in 1118 most of the offices that had once been at the pinnacle of the Byzantine system were not even associated with titles worthy of record.

This does not mean that Alexios I had no interest in the system that he inherited. The creation of the *logothetes ton sekreton* and the two *megaloi logariastai* demonstrate that he was deeply concerned about the financial side of the bureaucracy, and the courts, of course, continued to function. However, after c. 1094, almost all of the titles with which we became familiar in the first eight decades of the eleventh century vanished, and the newly minted Komnenian titles were only rarely granted to bureaucrats. Equally important, men worthy of Komnenian titles rarely became bureaucrats either. It has been suggested that after 1094 office holding itself became a mark of status and rank, illustrated by the increasing number of men who only appear in records of the Komnenian court identified by their offices.[153] We have already noted this phenomenon on the seals of the period, and while I agree that it is possible that this was a sign that office holding became a sign of status to the exclusion of title, I suspect it is unlikely. It is much more likely that, excluded from the ranks that mattered, office-holders had no other mark of status to display. This continued to be so even with the creation of the lesser epithets *megalodoxotatos* and *megalepiphanestatos*. After all, if everyone had these titles why were they special? How did they help distinguish people? They did not, so people used their offices. The few exceptions, such as the occasional *eparch* or *droungarios* holding a high title, or offices linked to the emperor personally such as the *epi ton deeseon*, should not obscure the fact that the bureaucratic system that reached maturity in the opening decades of the eleventh century was effectively gone before 1100.

5

Changing priorities and an evolving government

5.1 The Byzantine hierarchy in the eleventh century

Using the data collected for this study it is possible to make a few general observations about the Byzantine hierarchy, both the *axiai dia logou* and the *axiai dia brabeion* as they pertained to the bureaucracy in the eleventh century. Firstly, we shall turn to the dignities, and look for patterns in their appearance over the century.

The system was largely stable c. 966–c. 1033. With few exceptions all of the changes of the early eleventh century look like the mild inflation that had been progressing steadily for at least the last two centuries. However, something changed in the middle decades of the eleventh century. Whereas before we could speak about the bottom, middle, and top of the hierarchy in terms of the relative position of titles, from the middle of the century there seems to have been a genuine perception that one moved definitively from one part of the hierarchy to another, or perhaps started at a certain level and did not leave it. The evidence for this comes from the way that titles were displayed alongside others on seals, shown in Table 5.1. From c. 966 to c. 1033 almost every title is found associated with every other title. High-ranking *magistroi* proclaimed their dignity of *protospatharios*, and even *spatharios*, and the whole system feels connected.[1] An important individual would present themselves as *magistros*, *anyhtpatos*, *patrikios* and *protospatharios*, such as the *genikos logothetes* Nicholas, who presumably started his career with the title of *protospatharios* and accumulated other dignities as he advanced through the ranks of the bureaucracy.[2]

From a point in the middle of the century, rather than a fully integrated system where the lowest and highest titles were proudly presented together, there developed a divided hierarchy, or at least the hierarchy was presented as divided. *Protospatharios* ceased to be associated with anything higher than *patrikios*, while *hypatos*, *patrikios* and *anthypatos* were only presented alongside titles up to *vestarches*, and *magistros* was matched with nothing lower than *vestes*. Above all this there were the new ranks from *proedros* up, which were never paired not only with lower dignities – there is no *proedros* and *vestes* – but also with their fellow top tier titles, no one boasted of being *kouropalates* and *protoproedros* for example. This seems to be evidence that the Byzantine bureaucracy, and perhaps Byzantine society, were becoming more stratified than had been the case earlier. It is likely that the different levels observed in the

Table 5.1 Titles Found Together on Seals

Title/Date	Tenth Century Final Third	Eleventh Century First Third	Eleventh Century Middle Third	Eleventh Century Final Third
Protospatharios	Magistros Anthypatos Patrikios	Magistros Anthypatos Patrikios Hypatos	Patrikios Dishypatos Hypatos	Patrikios Hypatos
Hypatos	N/A	Patrikios Protospatharios	Vestarches Vestes Anthypatos Patrikios Protospatharios	Vestarches Anthypatos Patrikios Protospatharios
Patrikios	Magistros Anthypatos Protospatharios	Magistros Vestes Anthypatos Hypatos Protospatharios	Vestarches Vestes Anthypatos Patrikios Protospatharios	Vestarches Vestes Anthypatos Patrikios Protospatharios
Anthypatos	Magistros Patrikios Protospatharios	Magistros Vestes Patrikios Protospatharios	Vestarches Vestes Hypatos Patrikios	Vestes Patrikios Hypatos
Vestes	Magistros	Magistros Anthypatos Patrikios	Magistros Vestarches Anthypatos Patrikios Hypatos	Magistros Vestarches Anthypatos Patrikios
Vestarches	N/A	Magistros	Magistros Vestes Anthypatos Patrikios Hypatos	Magistros Vestes Patrikios Hypatos
Magistros	Vestes Anthypatos Patrikios Protospatharios Spatharios	Vestes Anthypatos Patrikios Protospatharios Vestes	Vestarches Vestes	Vestarches Vestes

mid-eleventh-century hierarchy corresponded to the prospects of the men working in the bureaucracy. At the lowest level, a man starting life at or below the rank of *protospatharios* had no chance of moving beyond the rank of *patrikios*. The centre of the hierarchy remained more fluid, but those who had started there never progressed beyond the rank of *vestarches*. Only those who entered the system as *vestai* or *vestarchai* had a shot at becoming *magistroi* and presumably the more exclusive titles beyond. One example is John Beriotes who was a *vestes* around 1060, and a *proedros* then a *protoproedros* before the end of the century.[3] Where once a *protospatharios*, through a lifetime of imperial service, had the potential to progress to become a *magistros*, this was possibly not the case later. This is important for more than our understanding of the system of court dignities, because, as we have seen, titles were associated with offices. Never advancing beyond *patrikios* is another way of saying that there are jobs that a person could never hope to get. What the divided hierarchy likely meant was that in the late tenth and early eleventh century the Byzantine bureaucracy was more meritocratic than it was to become. Were an individual started, which was presumably had a great deal to do with family connections and wealth, dictated the outline of their career. While this was probably true throughout Byzantine history (and today for that matter) the stratification of the mid-eleventh century hierarchy, and the ceilings it seems to imply for career progression, mark a noticeable shift to a more graded and rigid system.

It is possible that the above analysis is too rigid and that people did move beyond their starting tier, but that once at a new level they ceased to mention their old ranks on their seals. We have seen that titles lower in the hierarchy were becoming devalued as the eleventh century progressed, especially the very common *protospatharios*. It is possible that once an individual progressed beyond the accepted limit of a title's reach it ceased to be of use to him. This may be why it was not uncommon to see a man stating that he was a *patrikios* and a *protospatharios*, yet while a *vestarches* would boast of his rank of *patrikios* he would never mention the rank of *protospatharios*, and a *magistros* was now so elevated that he would only mention the two ranks immediately below his senior title. If this is true then becoming a *proedros* took a man into an entirely new class, one where other titles were simply irrelevant in terms of prestige and self-promotion. There are plenty of examples of this phenomenon; Sergios Hexamilites held ranks ranging from *vestes* to *protoproedros* during his career, but only ever presented one title at a time on his seals, while Constantine Anzas presented *anthypatos* and *patrikios* together on his seals as judge of the Velum, but did not include the title of *protospatharios*, which he had held at an earlier point in his career as a judge of the Hippodrome.[4] I think it is possible that both explanations were at play, with attainment of high rank increasingly linked to ones initial title, and a devaluation of lower titles to the point that those who did manage to break out saw no benefit to their earlier ranks.

At the same time, there was a process in which the frequency with which certain titles were awarded changed. As we would expect from an ever-evolving system of dignities, different titles appeared on the seals at different times. While this statement is obvious when we consider new titles, it is perhaps more surprising to see certain fashions in the way that more established dignities were awarded over time. To help illustrate the following argument the same information is presented in two different ways: in Table 5.2 the seal data for the highest titles held by all bureaucrats has been normalized as a percentage to allow easy reference to for the importance of titles with relation to one another; Table 5.3 takes figures for title holders from Table 5.2 and assumes for the sake of comparison a pool of 200 bureaucrats working in the late tenth century, then uses the relative proportion of seals from each third of a century covered by this study to calculate the numbers in later periods as 344 bureaucrats in the first part, 398 in the middle and 248 in the final third of the eleventh century. This allows us to see how many holders of each title there would be per 200, 344, 398 and 248 bureaucrats working in Constantinople. By using the two tables we can compare percentages within a period to numbers across the century.

As can be seen in Table 5.2 in the final third of the tenth-century *magistros* was the highest title granted to bureaucrats and was thus rather rare. It became less common,

Table 5.2 Normalized Seal Data, in Percentages, for Highest Titles Held by Bureaucrats c. 966–c. 1133 with the Total Number of Holders in Parentheses

Title/Period	Tenth Century Final Third	Eleventh Century First Third	Eleventh Century Middle Third	Eleventh Century Final Third	Twelfth Century Final Third
Sebastophoros			0.1	0.2	
Nobelissimos				0.4	1.5
Protokouropalates					3
Kouropalates				0.6	1.5
Protoproedros			0.1	5.3	3
Proedros			1.6	5.7	3
Magistros	3.8	1.7	4.5	5	1.5
Protovestarches			0.1	1.1	
Vestarches		0.4	5.2 (5.9)	7.7 (8.3)	1.5
Protovestes			0.2		
Vestes	0.2 (0.8)	1.7 (2.3)	4.8 (6.4)	6.8 (8.4)	
Anthypatos	4.6 (5.8)	3.4 (4.7)	2.4 (3.9)	2.4 (2.9)	1.5
Illoustrios			0.3	0.4	
Patrikios	2.6 (7)	3.1 (7.7)	8.6 (12.5)	5.1 (8.1)	1.5 (3)
Dishypatos		0.1	0.3	0.1	
Hypatos		0.8 (1.1)	2.3 (5.3)	1.4 (2.7)	
Protospatharios	33.2 (36.7)	35.5 (38.2)	32 (33.7)	16.3 (17)	1.5
Spatharokandidatos	10.5	11.5	8.1	2.4	1.5
Spatharios	4.5 (4.7)	2.6 (2.7)	1.1	0.3	
Kandidatos	0.4		0.2		
Strator	0.7	0.1			
None	39.9	39	28.3	38.8	79.3

as a percentage of the whole, in the early eleventh century, only to exceed its former level in the mid-eleventh century and continue at roughly that level until the twelfth century. Percentages tell only part of the story in this case. From Table 5.3 we can see, the number of *magistroi* remained constant c. 966–c. 1033, the drop in the percentage of *magistroi* in the first decades of the tenth century was due to the vast increase in the number of holders of lower titles, notably *protospatharios*, and no title. The same forces are at work with the *anthpatoi* who declined as a percentage in the early eleventh century, but increased by half in absolute numbers. While the percentage of *protospatharioi* remained constant for the first century under consideration in terms of numbers the great expansion came in the first decades of the eleventh century. Psellos might claim that Constantine IX opened the senate (the lowest level of which were the *protospatharioi*) to the rabble of the marketplace, but when it came to the bureaucracy they more likely than not had Basil II to thank. Even though it was the gateway to senatorial status the devaluation of *protospatharios* is clear to see. There were twice as many in the opening decades of the eleventh century as there had been in the late tenth, but as a percentage of the whole they accounted for the same number. The reason was the rise in numbers of men holding titles higher than *protospatharios*, namely *patrikios*, *anthypatos* and *vestes*. This trend continued into the mid-eleventh

Table 5.3 Number of Titles Awarded in Proportion by Period Based on an Initial Size of 200 Bureaucrats

Title/Period	Tenth Century Final Third 200 bureaucrats	Eleventh Century		
		First Third 344 bureaucrats	Middle Third 398 bureaucrats	Final Third 248 bureaucrats
Sebastophoros				1
Nobelissimos				1
Kouropalates				2
Protoproedros				11
Proedros			6	12
Magistros	6	6	16	11
Protovestarches				2
Vestarches		1	21	20
Protovestes			1	
Vestes	2	8	22	19
Anthypatos	10	15	14	7
Illoustrios			1	1
Patrikios	14	23	45	19
Dishypatos			1	
Hypatos		3	19	6
Protospatharios	64	119	117	39
Spatharokandidatos	18	35	28	5
Spatharios	8	9	4	1
Kandidatos	1		1	
Strator	1	1		
Praipositos	1	1	1	1
Primikerios	3	1	2	1
Spatharokoubikoularios	3	2	2	1
None	69	120	97	88

century, but with the addition of *hypatos* and *vestarches*, and a significant increase in the numbers of *magistroi*. There were a lot more people with titles of a higher rank than *protospatharios* in c. 1050 than there had been in c. 966.

It could be said that there was a general readjustment up the hierarchy, which I have suggested through this book was at least as much the result of a realignment of the structures of imperial government as it was of an oversimplified view of title inflation. Possible pressure brought about by inflation as the result of devaluation might be visible at the bottom of the hierarchy. I have mentioned a number of times that the dignity of *protospatharios* became devalued as a result of the compartmentalization of the hierarchy. Yet, the overall proportion of title holders with this rank remained constant at about a third of the total. It is, in fact, the only low-level title not to experience a noticeable decline in this regard. Seals recording no title increased in almost exactly the same proportion as those of *protospatharioi* between the end of the tenth century and the beginning of the eleventh (see Table 5.3). However, while the number of *protospatharioi* remained constant as the bureaucracy grew in the middle of the century, the number of bureaucrats with no titles dropped by a sixth (Table 5.3), in percentage terms by a quarter (Table 5.2). By this point there were clearly more bureaucrats than ever and with higher titles than before. It is possible that as others were promoted above the level of *protospatharios*, for example the judges of the Velum, that there was an influx of these holders of lower office who replenished the depleted ranks of the *protospatharioi*, benefitting from the title's devaluation and, if not further devaluing it, cementing its third rate position. If there is any hint of Psellos's criticism of Constantine IX's expansion of the senate reflected in the seals of bureaucrats this is where we will find it, with a significant drop in both the numbers and percentage of sigilants with no title at the same time that the higher titles saw a vast increase in holders, and *protospatharios* held steady, presumably because those who previously had no title had moved up.

There is one final group to look at here, infrequently awarded titles. The heyday of the *anthypatoi* was the late tenth century; it was a respectable rank worth attaining in its own right and worth mentioning once higher dignities had been attained. After that the proportion of bureaucrats with this title dropped consistently across the following century, and it was no longer associated with *magistros*.[5] *Anthypatos* also seems to have been a victim of the new role of *vestes* and *vestarches* and the compartmentalization of the hierarchy; it fell on the wrong side of the dividing line and lost its role as the link between the middle and upper titles, becoming just another middling title and one which does not seem to have been frequently awarded. It is not the only title which is hard to see in the sigillographic evidence. Those like *spatharokandidatos*, *spatharios*, *kandidatos* and *strator* can be seen to drop out of the record as their value declined. But what of the titles supposedly introduced to meet the need of upward pressure and title inflation, *dishypatos*, *illoustrios*, *protovestes* and *protovestarches*? These titles were so infrequently awarded (see Tables 5.2 and 5.3) as to make one wonder whether they were ever really a regular part of the hierarchy at all. It is highly unlikely that the existence of a scattering of men with these dignities had much impact on how the Byzantines viewed their place in the hierarchy; to all intents and purposes a *vestarches* was directly below a *magistros*, for instance. Perhaps they were just occasional titles granted on a case-by-case basis to individuals who for some reason deserved special, but not too special, consideration? While this is a less than flattering way of viewing the *nomophylax* and future patriarch John Xiphilinos it does fit the evidence we have. If we accept these conclusions then the rather crowded hierarchy of sixteen titles awarded to bureaucrats found in the mid-eleventh century really consisted of ten titles (including the declining *anthypatos* and the newly minted *protoproedros*) plus two which were about to drop off the bottom (*spatharios* and *kandidatos*), and four infrequently awarded titles which were not regular dignities.

A few general conclusions before we move into the next period. In terms of numbers of bureaucrats holding offices we can see a continued move up the hierarchy as lower ranks and no title drop away and more bureaucrats held more, and higher titles. But this process does not necessarily equate with rampant inflation, and does not seem to be that different from that observable in the late tenth and early eleventh century, especially when we take into account the changes in the Byzantine government outlined in the preceding pages. The exception was what was happening at the bottom of the hierarchy as discussed earlier. The more radical development was the increasing complexity of the hierarchy, particularly the new relationship of one title to another.

The groupings of titles on seals suggest that we do not have people recording a lifetime's accumulation of titles but only those which continued to remain relevant to the holder as they moved up the hierarchy. It is also significant that certain titles were never paired with others. The lowest title acting as the senior partner with another was *hypatos*. No one was a *protospatharios* and *spatharokandidatos*, or a *spatharokandidatos* and a *spatharios*. At the other end of the spectrum none of the titles from *proedros* up are seen paired with another title, a change from earlier practice symbolic of the changes in the way that the Byzantines viewed the system of titles. Crossing the line from *magistros* to *proedros* must have had a significance, the meaning of which is now lost. I suspect that ranks at the top and bottom of the ladder superseded one another, for all that Philotheos tells us that titles were held for life. The new fractured system with exclusive titles held in isolation at the top and the bottom, a border rank of limited overlap with either end of the middle (*protospatharios* and *magistros*) and then a middle which continued the old pattern of associating titles with one another feels too symmetrical to have been accidental. Perhaps what appears to be a fracturing of the hierarchy was actually a move to a system where more and more titles superseded one another as the newly introduced titles, *proedros* and up, did. It is tempting to see the increasing sophistication of titles as related to the growing complexity of the state, and it is certainly possible that they were linked, although the specific relationship is now unknown.

All of which brings us to the closing decades of the eleventh century through to the death of Alexios I in 1118. This is the period when the hierarchy open to bureaucrats extended noticeably with small numbers of bureaucrats holding titles up to *nobelissimos*. At the same time there was an increase in the percentage of bureaucrats holding titles from *vestes* up (Table 5.2). Yet in terms of individuals (Table 5.3) there were roughly the same number of *vestai* and *vestarchai* as before, while there were double the *proedroi*, and a host of new *protoproedroi*. The numbers of men with dignities below this declined noticeably. We are perhaps seeing the end result of the gentle inflation of earlier decades in many cases, the drop in the number of *patrikioi* and *hypatoi* for example. An extreme case of this is the *protospatharioi*, the percentage of which halved, and which dropped to a third of the number found in the middle of the eleventh century. At the same time the percentage of bureaucrats with no title rose back to its former level of nearly 40 per cent (the numbers are roughly similar but the bureaucracy itself had shrunk). I suspect that there are two factors at work here: firstly, the continued devaluation of *protospatharios*-- the increased holding of which was likely the reason for the unusually low number of bureaucrats with no title in the mid-eleventh century – leading to it not being worth holding, or if held, not recording; secondly, the beginning of the effects of Alexios I's reform of the state which saw this phenomenon spread up the hierarchy. This last factor is clearly at work in the high percentage of seals dated after c. 1080 displaying no title. The large drop in the presence of all titles recorded on seals below the rank of *vestes* seen in Tables 5.2 and 5.3 is proof that they had become effectively worthless and unimportant as a means of identification and self-promotion. One final point: Alexios's new titles were not awarded in conjunction with one another, a man was either a *sebastokrator* or a *sebastos*; he was not both. In this regard Alexios's great innovation can be seen to have

Figure 5.1 Seal of Philaretos *illoustrios*, *exaktor* and judge of the East. Harvard Art Museums/Arthur M. Sackler Museum, Bequest of Thomas Whittemore, 1951.31.5.139. Philaretos was a rare example of a bureaucrat with the title *illoustrios*.
Obv. ΚΡ,ΤΗC|ΕѠΑCΦΙ|ΛΑΡΕΤ,C|ΕΖΑΚ|ΤѠΡ
Rev. .ΛΛΟΥ,|.ΤΡΙΟC|.CΥΜΡΟ|ΛΟΝΦΕ|.ΤΟΔΕ
Κριτὴς Ἑώας Φιλάρετος ἐξάκτωρ ἰλλούστριός τε σύμβολον φέρει τόδε.
The judge of the East, Philaretos, *exaktor* and *illoustrios*, bears this token.

been built on the foundations of the changes made to the hierarchy in the middle of the eleventh century, and it is perhaps no surprise that his new system preserved the equally exclusive titles, from *proedros* up. In many respects his new titles were an upward extension of this part of the hierarchy, the rest was jettisoned. He even followed the earlier tradition of awarding and elaborating once restricted imperial titles and granting them more widely seen in the 1060s and 1070s. The great change was in who received these titles and the implications that had for the Byzantine state.

5.2 Increasing numbers and growing complexity

If we believe that the bureaucracy expanded throughout the eleventh century, then it is easy to understand why we would see an increase in the percentage and numbers of low-level bureaucrats; most high-ranking members of the administration were supported by multiple low-level officials. When all of the sigillographic data for this study is combined, 16.5 per cent of the seals date to the last third of the tenth century, 28.3 to the first third of the eleventh, 32.8 to the mid-eleventh century, 20.4 to the final decades thereof and 2 per cent to the opening years of the twelfth century. Some of this will be down to luck, fashion and the availability of lead, but much of the higher percentage identified as early and mid-eleventh century must be the result of an increase in the number of seals being struck by bureaucrats in these decades.[6] The steep decline in numbers in the last third of the eleventh century is to be expected considering that the bureaucratic system ran smoothly for less than a decade before invasion, civil wars, and Alexios I changed things forever. That the number for these years is as high as it is, is further evidence of the size of the bureaucracy at this time.

Further evidence for the expansion of the number of men employed by the Byzantine bureaucracy in the tenth and eleventh century is the number of new positions that were created. It has already been noted that the *Escorial Taktikon* includes many officials not mentioned in earlier *taktika*, meaning that they must have come into existence in the preceding three decades or so, and even more offices came into existence in the eleventh century. This phenomenon is most striking in the areas of justice and land management. What is equally interesting is that it was not single officials, but entire departments which appear, such as that of the *euageis oikoi*, the *ephoros* or the *sekreton ton dikon*. Not only were new departments made from scratch; they also came about by the subdivision of older *sekreta*, usually by promoting a formerly subordinate official and giving him his own staff, such as the *oikistikos* and the *parathalassites*. What makes the creation of new departments even more interesting is that apart from the *megas kouratorikeion* there is no evidence that any existing bureaus were dissolved until the late 1080s. An increase in the percentage and numbers of low-level officials, higher numbers of seals being produced, and new departments of government: the evidence all points to an expansion of the bureaucracy beginning in earnest in the second half of the reign of Basil II.

Exactly how large the bureaucracy was at any one point is impossible to determine with any degree of accuracy. Attempts have been made to use the imperial feasts held in the Hall of the Nineteen Couches to estimate the number of bureaucrats resident in Constantinople, which occasionally included the sandal-wearing senate, those ranking below *protospatharios*. A problem with this approach is that the definition of the sandal-wearing senate is inconsistent at different points in the text.[7] Another is that many positions are not listed in both definitions. This last is in part related to the date of the text. The descriptions of these feasts come from the *Kletorologion of Philotheos*. The bureaucracy and empire of c. 1000 were different from that of 899. While Philotheos can provide a good starting point for any exploration of the later administration, he is not a reliable guide for eleventh-century realities, too much had changed in the intervening century.[8]

While not an exact record of the total number of bureaucrats, there is a good case to be made for the presence of an upper figure of 1,741 bureaucrats working in Constantinople in the century and a half covered by this study, with the majority of them concentrated before c. 1080. It is possible that the figure is somewhat lower. The seals of 1,741 men show a unique design with nothing to link them to another seal with a partially or wholly different design. In this way it is a cautious figure. It is tempting to assign various seals to the same person based on a shared office, but most such attempts are guesswork without a family name, particular or peculiar iconography, or an unusual combination of offices and titles. So, while it is perfectly reasonable that John *spatharokandidatos* and *notarios* went on to become John *vestes* and judge of the Velum, there is no proof. There will be individuals with multiple seal designs counted more than once in the grand total of 1,741. If we take another tack and assume that everyone who shared a name or names was actually the same person, clearly not the case (the 182 seals struck by a John are not the relics of a particularly productive and long-lived man with an incredible CV) then we arrive at the figure of 614.[9] The actual figure of known bureaucrats working in the central administration from c. 966 to c. 1120 is therefore between the impossibly low figure of 614 and a likely slightly inflated one of 1,741, in my opinion at a spot much closer to the latter than the former. These are the officials of whom we know. There must have been many more, particularly at the lower end of the spectrum who either did not seal in lead or simply did not require a seal to perform their duties. Then there are the seals which simply have not survived.

Figure 5.2 Basil II (976–1025) Nomisma Histamenon, 1005–25, Constantinople. Dumbarton Oaks, Byzantine Collection, Washington, DC, BZC.1948.17.3173.
This coin of emperor Basil II depicts a bust of Christ on the obverse and the two emperors Basil and his younger brother Constantine on the reverse.
Obv. +IhSXIREXREϟNΛNTIhM
Rev. +bΛSILCCONSZΛNTIbR
Jesus Christus Rex Regnantium, Jesus Christ King of Kings.
Basilios ce Constantinos basilis Romaion, Basil and Constantine, basileis of the Romans.

Expansion had to be paid for. It is impossible to know how much the Byzantine bureaucracy cost; however, we can make a rough calculation for the cost of the *rogai* given out to title holders. Although the absolute numbers of bureaucrats can never be known, if we use the figures in Table 5.3 as a starting point and add in the amounts paid in *roga* into the model of 200 bureaucrats working in the late tenth century, 344 in the early, 398 in the middle and 248 in the final third of the eleventh century, we can arrive at approximate figures. In pounds of *nomismata* and in parentheses number of coins, the figures for each third of a century are as follows: final third of the tenth, 330.3 (23,784); first third of the eleventh, 562 (40,464); middle eleventh, 1,465.7 (105,528); final third eleventh, 1,635.7 (117,768). The cost per bureaucrat in pounds of *nomismata* then coins was 1.65 (118.8), 1.63 (117.4), 3.68 (265), 6.60 (475.2). While the cost of the bureaucracy almost doubled during the reign of Basil II and his two successors, the amount paid out per bureaucrat actually decreased. The difference in the cost of the bureaucracy between the late tenth and early eleventh centuries was driven by an increase in the number of title holders up and down the hierarchy. There were twice as many *spatharokandidatoi* and *protospatharioi* in c. 1033 than there had been in c. 966, over one and a half times the number of *patrikioi* and *anthypatoi* and four times the *vestai*. The numbers of *magistroi* and *spatharioi* remained constant. By contrast the vast increase in cost between the first and second thirds of the eleventh century was driven by an increase in holders of mid- and upper-level titles only. The number of *magistroi* and *vestai* almost trebled, the *patrikioi* doubled, and there were vastly more *proedroi*. We must not forget the newly appearing *vestarchai*. In contrast the numbers of *protospatharioi* remained nearly constant, and there were fewer *spatharokandidatoi*. It was an increase in the numbers of bureaucrats with titles from the upper levels of the hierarchy that explains the high figure given for the final third of the eleventh century. Even though there were only a third of the *protospatharioi*, a sixth of the *spatharokandidatoi* a third of the *hypatoi*, half the *patrikioi*, *anthypatoi*, and only two-thirds of the *magistroi* than in the middle of the century, there were double the number of *proedroi* and a significant number of *protoproedroi* and *kouropalatai*. Such was the skewed nature of the *rogai* system that it took relatively few high-ranking officials to make up for a large drop in the numbers of lower-level title holders.

The eleventh century saw the progressive debasement of the Byzantine coinage, most spectacularly the *nomisma histamenon* in which the *rogai* of title holders were paid. There have been a number of studies, primarily by Philip Grierson and Cécile Morrisson examining the dropping fineness of Byzantine gold coins, and attempts to explain why such debasement occurred.[10] The debasement of the *nomisma histamenon*, started in the tenth century during the joint reign of Constantine VII and Romanos I Lekapenos (920–44), from a nominally pure coin to one consistently of 94.4 per cent purity, or 22.7 carats fineness.[11] With the exception of a blip in the middle of the reign of Basil II (976–1025), where the purity of the *nomisma histamenon* dropped to 90 per cent, the level of purity under Constantine VII was preserved into the eleventh century. The final issue of Basil II was 94.9 per cent gold.[12] The standard of Constantine VII was largely preserved throughout the first third of the eleventh century up to the reign of Michael IV who struck many coins of above average purity, but who also, produced *nomismata* of only 19 ½ carats, with a standard of about 90 per cent purity.[13] Constantine Monomachos oversaw a careful and systematic debasement of the gold coinage down to 18 carats, or 75 per cent, by the end of the reign, a standard that was maintained until 1069.[14] The final phase of debasement saw the purity of the *nomisma* drop to 70 per cent under Romanos IV Diogenes (1068–71), averaging about 14 carats under Michael VII Doukas (1071–8), 8 ½ carats under Nikephoros III Botaneiates (1078–81), and 2 ½, just 10.4 per cent, carats under Alexios I Komnenos until his reform of 1092.[15]

For the last third of the tenth and first thirds of the eleventh century it is fair to take an average of 94.4 per cent purity for the *nomisma*. For the subsequent period a range of 90–75 per cent, with most of the period falling under the latter figure is appropriate. For the final third of the eleventh century the range is approximately 70 per cent pure to about half that, 35.4 per cent. Using these figures it is possible to take the numbers of coins paid out to bureaucratic title holders and calculate the amount of gold required by the Byzantine state to make these payments. For each third century, accounting for the fluctuating number of bureaucrats, the figures in pounds of gold are, 311.8 for the late tenth century, 530.5 for the early eleventh, between 1,319.1 and 1099.3 for the middle of the century, and a range of 579–1,145 for the end. What is striking from these numbers is that for the *rogai* of bureaucrats, the Byzantine state did not save gold through debasing the coinage until the final phase of debasement. The figures are even more striking for gold per bureaucrat. The amount was roughly steady for the first two periods, 1.56 lbs. c. 966–c. 1000, and 1.54 lbs. c. 1000–c. 1033. As we would expect there was a large jump in the middle of the eleventh century, 3.3–2.76 lbs. It is the numbers for the last decades of the eleventh century that are the most surprising, 4.62–2.34 lbs. Even with the drastic debasement of the *nomisma* the cost in gold per bureaucrat remained higher than ever until the very end, and never dropped to the level seen at the beginning of the century. The reason has to be the increased number of bureaucrats with high titles. The push to move up the hierarchy had led to a dramatic increase in the cost of the imperial administration, one that the empire clearly struggled the bear as the eleventh century reached its end.[16]

The cost of the Byzantine administration increased greatly during the reign of Basil II and each generation thereafter until it collapsed, and that is without being able to account for the wages paid for holding an office, which included all those bureaucrats who did not have a title. Is this evidence of mismanagement? The expansion of government and the creation of new departments must have been one large factor in this development. It is easy to understand why the enlarged empire that came into being between c. 966 and the death of Basil II in 1025 should have seen across-the-board recruitment into an expanded bureaucracy. Similarly, the elevation of the judiciary under Basil and then increasingly in the mid-eleventh century initially added to the number of *protospatharioi*, and later was responsible for a significant proportion of the mid-eleventh-century explosion of the number of *patrikioi*, *vestai* and *vestarchai*. Yet we cannot discount title inflation as a cause for the increase in cost. This does not mean that we need to accept that the emperors were reckless in their handling of the system of titles; after all this process began under Basil II and no one considers that he mismanaged the empire. Simple expansion could explain a lot of the pressure placed on the system. Although the percentage of *protospatharioi* was roughly the same in the last-third of the tenth and the first-third of the eleventh centuries, in absolute numbers there were twice as many men with the title after c. 1000. If nothing else this must have made some of the ceremonial occasions detailed by Constantine VII rather crowded.[17] Twice as many people with your rank makes you half as special, and without a single piece of mismanagement or overpromotion, without anyone even mentioning the debasement of the currency, the seeds of a pressure for advancement leading inexorably to title inflation had been sown. Every new department, every readjustment of the workings of government must have had similar repercussions. The expansion of the membership of the senate made by Constantine IX and Constantine X must have had a similar affect, increasing the number men holding lower-level dignities and creating an upward pressure for titles.[18] The concentration of men around the title of *protospatharios* in the early and mid-eleventh century might be linked to the creation of new senators, but as we saw in the preceding pages there is no evidence of across-the-board promotions among bureaucrats.

The bureaucracy was not only expanding; it was becoming more specialized. While this was clearly not so at the level of the individual (many mid- and lower-level bureaucrats held a number of positions at once) it certainly was at a structural level. Where once one office had performed many tasks (those of the *eparch* and the *genikon* spring to mind) now their remits were streamlined and focused. Areas that had become too large for one *sekreton* to run efficiently, such as government property, were spun off into their own department. What was true for the late-tenth- and early-eleventh-century Byzantine army was true for the bureaucracy as well: specialization was a hallmark of sophistication. Much like the Byzantine army, specialization must have allowed the bureaucracy to perform its various tasks more efficiently, although, to switch analogies, much like specialized agriculture or industrial production it must have left the departments of government more vulnerable to the changing tides of history. Late casualties such as the *stratiotikon* fell afoul of alterations to the Byzantine military that left it without a function. Although not dissolved, the *sekreta* of the *ephoros* and the *megas oikonomos* were amalgamated by Alexios I into one department that must have looked like the less specialized *megas kouratorikion* that they had replaced over half a century earlier. To a certain degree the reforms of the bureaucracy by Alexios Komnenos were about undoing the expansion of the previous century, simplifying the administration of his smaller empire.

5.3 Imperial priorities

Between the death of Basil II in 1025 and the accession of Alexios I Komnenos in 1081 the Byzantines are sometimes accused of 'losing the peace'.[19] The accusation is that the Byzantines failed to maintain in peace time the vast empire that the previous century of warfare had brought them. In a similar vein, the failure is often seen as the result of the weak bureaucratic government that grew out of these decades of conflict-free bliss. The first question we should ask is, What is peace? The second question to be asked is, Was the government system that we have reconstructed in the previous chapters born from a period of calm abroad and stability at home? If we expand the initial parameters a little, to the end of the Bulgarian war in 1018, it is obvious that there was really no peace to lose. In the sixty-three years between the conquest of Bulgaria and the coronation of Alexios I the longest period without military activity that I can identify lasted for three years, 1026–8. In total, I can find thirteen years in which no violence occurred.[20]

If the new bureaucratic government of the eleventh century was not the result of a period of serene tranquillity, why did it appear when it did? The answer is simple, it didn't just appear. The *Escorial Taktikon* presents a whole range of offices in central government that did not exist when the *Taktikon Beneševič* was written forty years earlier. Government became more complex in the second half of the tenth century, during the wars of reconquest, and continued to develop along similar lines, with some adjustments in emphasis, into the eleventh century. When we look at the parallel development of provincial government, particularly the rising importance of the theme judges after c. 950, it becomes clear that it was the conquests themselves that were the driving factors behind the initial changes in the bureaucracy. The empire was larger and more complex than before, in numerous ways, territorially, in terms of population and social complexity, and economically, and it required a larger and more complex bureaucracy to run it. It was the spoils of war, even more so than the fruits of peace that led to the bureaucratic government we have explored here. The peace, such as it was, existed because of continued success and strength on the borders, hence the constant campaigning, which provided the core of the empire with as much security as possible.

Byzantium's successes in the late tenth and early eleventh century, the new realities of the 1000s, and the collapse of the territorial integrity of the empire each resulted in a series of different priorities for those in charge, and those priorities are reflected in the evolution of the Byzantine bureaucracy. These priorities become immediately

Figure 5.3 Romanos III Argyros (1028–34) Miliaresion, Constantinople. Harvard Art Museums/Arthur M. Sackler Museum, Bequest of Thomas Whittemore, 1951.31.4.1573.
The miliaresia of Romanos III depict the standing emperor on the reverse and the Mother of God on the obverse. Romanos was known for his particular devotion to the Virgin reflected here not only through her image, but in the inscription, a statement of faith in the powers of the Mother of God.
Obv. +ΠΑΡΘΕΝΕϹΟΙΠΟΛΥΑΙΝΕ
Rev. ΟϹΗΛΠΙΚΕΠΑΝΤΑΚΑΤΟΡΘΟΙ
Παρθένε σοι πολύαιωε ὅς ἤλιτικη πάντα κατορθοῖ
He who places his hope in you, O Virgin all-glorious, will prosper in all he does.

clear when we view the sigillographic evidence in aggregate. This is not the place for a repetition of the preceding pages, but a few areas of evidence from earlier in the text will help to illustrate this point.

From the *Escorial Taktikon* it is clear that Basil II inherited a government already more complex than it had been since late antiquity, but his stamp is discernible in certain areas. There was the general expansion described earlier, and while in terms of structure much of the administration remained static under his rule, some areas changed notably. The judiciary began their slow rise to prominence in his reign, which saw the generation prior to that of Eustathios Romaios bringing their profession into the sigillographic evidence in large numbers for the first time. There was also a gradual inflation of titles under Basil II: there were significantly more *spatharokandidatoi* and *protospatharioi* than a generation earlier. One of the biggest changes, and the one that is most easily tied to Basil's reign, is the increase in the number of bureaus concerned with land management and the elevation in the ranks of the men who worked in them. Thus, we have the appearance of the *epi ton oikeiakon* and the *ephoros* under Basil, as well as a reworking of the charitable institutions in the capital at least, and the beginning of the rise of the *oikistikos* to prominence. It is perhaps not surprising that a man who so concerned himself with the landed wealth of the empire, both crown and fiscal lands, and the properties of his subjects, should have left his greatest mark on the bureaucracy in this area. When one reviews the large number of cases in the *Peira* that concern questions over the ownership and exploitation of land it is hard not to wonder if the early stirrings of the new judicial elite were not in some way linked to Basil II's interest in the land of his empire.

Three traditionally maligned emperors – Romanos III Argyros, Constantine IX Monomachos and Constantine X Doukas – left their mark on the judiciary. Not all of these emperors were equal in their actions, but all deserve a mention here. Romanos

III, colleague of Eustathios Romaios, took the judiciary of which he had been a part and gave it a leading role in the Byzantine state. He did this in the most Byzantine way possible, by taking a declining military office, the *droungarios tes viglas*, and repurposing it as the head of the legal establishment, also giving its holder a place in the hierarchy equal to the most important men in the state. This was a monumental transformation, and one which I would suggest more than makes up for one failed campaign in Syria. Previously the chief legal official of the empire had been the *eparch*, a man with many other responsibilities. Now the judiciary were represented at the highest levels of Byzantine government by a man whose sole activity was as a judge. When we couple this with the continually rising status of the judiciary in general it is not hard to see that Romanos the jurist saw his former colleagues as integral to the administration of the empire. There was much more to Romanos than his biographer Psellos would have us believe. The same is certainly true of Constantine IX. He continued to reward the judiciary with high-status titles and preserved the position of the *droungarios tes viglas*. Importantly he also built on Romanos's work. The ephemeral law school was a good idea, but the *sekreton ton dikon* under the *epi ton kriseon* was almost as revolutionary as the earlier reforms of Romanos, which it complimented. When we look at the low-ranked judges of the Velum and judges of the Hippodrome of the *Escorial Taktikon*, it is difficult to imagine that within three generations they would be reorganized under a high magistrate and given the authority, and resources, to help monitor and overrule provincial judicial decisions. Finally, we come to Constantine X. He claimed to care deeply for the law and took a personal interest in its application, and there is nothing in the sigillographic record to indicate that he undermined or altered the good practices of his predecessors in any way. By comparison to Romanos III and Constantine IX this might seem like faint praise. On the other hand, Constantine X not undermining an area of his government was itself quite an achievement, as his commanders in the east could surely testify, and thus we must take it a sign of his imperial priorities.

Few other emperors stand out as individuals due to the broad strokes with which sigillographic evidence allows us to paint. The evolution of the government of Constantinople, for example, could have been just that, a slow process borne of the growth and enrichment of the capital, or it could have been the work of one or more emperors, just like the transformation of the judiciary. While it is certain that during the first third of the eleventh century the government of the capital became more elaborate and its leaders highly valued, the guiding hand or hands behind this transition are a mystery to us.

One emperor who is visible, for much the same reason as Basil II – he reigned for a long time – is Alexios I. As noted earlier his reign is partly clouded because of a change in sigillographic practices and our assessment is weakened by the end of *rogai* payments at the outset of his reign. However, the way that seals were used and the end of the *rogai* were in no small part Alexios's doing, reflecting his priorities as emperor just as surely as the creation of a *sekreton*. In another way the reign of Alexios I is visible for a reason which makes him different from Basil II, the prevalence of written material. From what we can see Alexios had two aims when it came to the bureaucracy, control and simplification. The former likely because he was all too aware of the fate of his two immediate predecessors, and control over all aspects of the empire, not just

Figure 5.4 Alexios I (1081–1118) Aspron Trachy Nomisma, 1092–3, Constantinople. Dumbarton Oaks, Byzantine Collection, Washington, DC, BZC.1969.8.
The obverse of this coin depicts Christ crowning John Komnenos, the reverse his parents Alexios I and Eirene. Struck to celebrate the coronation of the young junior emperor it also marked the beginning of a new phase of the Byzantine currency and a solidifying of the Komnenian control over the state.
Obv. IWΔECΠT+KEROHΘEI
Rev. +ΛΛΕΣΙWΔΕΕΙΡΗΝΛVΓU

the bureaucracy, must have been seen as a way to avoid their fate, or worse. The latter because in many respects his empire was a simplified version of that into which he had been born around 1048, and it did not need, and could not afford, the complex government machinery created in the tenth and eleventh centuries.

This is not the place to rehash the creation of a new Komnenian elite by Alexios, a gradual process visible from the beginning of his reign, largely established by the 1090s, and securely in control by his death in 1118, except to say that he used it to secure control of everything that mattered in the early years of crisis, the military and the chief strategic points of the empire.[21] There seems to have been some attempt into the 1090s to incorporate the old elite of Constantinople. We see the family of the patriarch Keroularios, and the odd Choirosphaktes, Tzirithon and Kamateros to name but a few, in positions of power and influence, but those not incorporated into the Komnenian elite gradually faded into the second tier of the hierarchy, as did the offices which they occupied. These were mostly those that were of an administrative nature. Alexios created a new Constantinopolitan elite from his family and its allies, and it was an elite of the court, which performed military or provincial governmental roles, and did not work in the bureaucracy. The old elite was still there and was still joined by ambitious young men from the provinces, but they were distinctly second-rate. Another aspect of the control Alexios desired was the creation of the *logothetes ton sekreton* and the two *megaloi logariastai* and their respective *sekreta*. This greatly reduced the direct reports that Alexios had and centralized control over the entire bureaucratic machinery into as few hands as possible.

Simplification has been proposed as the other priority of Alexios. The two of course tie together, as a smaller, less complex bureaucracy is easier to control. There is a certain amount of evidence that the administrative structure of 1081 was not what it had been even a decade earlier. The sigillographic evidence is less abundant and the picture that it paints is one of a system unable to fund much of its operation at a level that would have allowed its employees to maintain their income in troubled times. It is impossible to know the overall effects that this crisis of funding had on the bureaucracy. I would suggest that a system based on the practice of financial, monetary reward for service as the Byzantine government was would not long survive a period of sustained imperial fiscal retrenchment. Simply put, it is hard to envision the bureaucrats of Constantinople continuing to work for free for a protracted period of time. The bureaucracy was in danger, if not in the process, of collapsing when Alexios I took the throne, and I see no evidence that he tried to save or revive it. To some degree this is understandable, as his empire was significantly smaller than that which the system had been designed to rule. This was true not only in terms of territory. Initially Alexios ruled far fewer people than had even Michael VII or Nikephoros III. The empire of 1081 contained fewer areas operating a sophisticated economy, fewer significant urban centres and far less crownland than it had a decade before. Early in his reign Alexios also had other priorities, and it took him a decade to secure what remained of the empire. Only then did he turn to internal matters, and by that time the old system had been decaying for decades. Alexios did create one new *sekreton* under the *megas logariastes ton euagon sekreton*. While emphasizing the importance of the *euageis oikoi* on the one hand – with the loss of much other land they must have been particularly valuable – it also exemplifies the changes in the imperial system on the other. One of the chief duties of the new *sekreton* was to monitor the estates which were granted to the Komnenoi and their allies as the chief means through which they were enriched and raised above their subjects. This brings us back to priorities. The money was clearly there to fund an elite, but Alexios had no interest in spending it to support the old bureaucrats of Constantinople.

The changes that happened as a result of various imperial priorities can be summed up by comparing two documents, both records of church synods, one in 1029 and the other in 1094. As well as listing the ecclesiastics in attendance both of the documents detailing the proceedings of the synods also record the names, titles and offices of the secular officials who participated. The council of 1029 was attended by thirteen secular officials: three from the *logothesia*, the *logothetes tou dromou*, the *orphanotrophos* and the *epi ton oikeikon*; three from the chancery, the *mystikos*, *epi ton deeseon* and the *mystographos*; and at least nine judicial officials, the *droungarios tes viglas*, *koiaistor*, *kensor*, one judge of the Velum and five judges of the Hippodrome.[22] This was a sizeable secular contingent, particularly from the judiciary, and it has rightly been noted that this council was an early example of their increasingly exalted role in the operation of the state. By contrast the synod of 1094 was attended by forty secular officials: twenty-four of whom were members of the Komnenian elite with exalted titles but no office: five military officials, the *megas domestikos*, *protostrator*, *megas doux*, *megas hetaireiarchos* and *chartoularios tou stablou*; four men from the chancery, the *epi tou kanikleiou*, *mystikos*, *epi ton deeseon* and a *grammatikos*; three judges, the *megas droungarios tes viglas*, one judge of the Hippodrome, and a judge, and lastly, the *eparch*. One very much gets the impression that in 1029 many of the men who attended did so because of the office which they held, hence the largest contingent being that of judicial officials. In 1094, it seems rather that invitations were based on title, which is to say who one was, which explains why the military officials outnumbered the judges, and why the titled elite were most numerous of all.

A theme which runs through the imperial priorities outlined earlier is control. The bureaucracy increased in size and scope because after decades of conquest and internal growth the empire needed a different type of government from that developed over the preceding centuries. Basil enhanced his control over the empire through state run lands, and so the bureaucracy grew in this area. Constantine IX was in favour of standardization and centralization, and the judiciary grew to support his aims. Bureaucrats thus became the means through which emperors tried to extend their control. This gave them a privileged position in the empire and the titles and standing at court to match. This was the basis for the ascendency, such as it was, of the bureaucrats. While Basil II and his successors oversaw the transformation of the ninth-century government into something which allowed them to control the eleventh-century empire in a directed and thoughtful way, each and every one of them failed to do the same for the system of titles. The ad hoc addition of dignities over time to combat title inflation and accommodate the needs of an expanding state was the administrative equivalent of papering over a crack. While the new hierarchy worked in terms of prestige it created an increased economic burden. The scale of *rogai* payments had been created at a time when there were far fewer men drawing a stipend at each level.[23] Whether an empire secure in its territory and facing limited threats could have supported the new system indefinitely is unclear. Even with its increased cost it showed incredible resilience up until the 1060s, and to what degree the failings after that point were the result of internal politics, the mismanagement of the military by Constantine X, overwhelming external threats or just bad luck is a moot point. What we do know is that when the empire began to lose territory the system collapsed, and it played no part in how Alexios I secured control of the empire for himself. There is ample evidence that Alexios had a dislike of the existing elite of the capital before becoming emperor, and his actions once on the throne show that little changed.[24] Control for Alexios meant governing through a small group of men whom he could trust, and this included few bureaucrats. When he did turn his attention to the administration it was to create something small and manageable, befitting his new empire. Thus, almost simultaneously, the bureaucrats of Byzantium lost the empire of the eleventh century that had brought about their ascendency and their prime place in the imperial vision for government.

Appendix – *chartoularioi*, *notarioi* and *logariastai*

It is difficult to tell where the majority of the men involved in the basic book and record keeping tasks of the eleventh-century bureaucracy actually worked. The problem is that while they recorded their name, office and title if they had one on their seals, they did not always specify in which department they performed their tasks. Thus, we have far more seals of *notarioi* than we do *notarioi* of something. This lack could lead us into never-ending speculation. Are the seals vague because these men moved across departments, working wherever they were needed? Was there a pool of qualified men who were called up on an ad hoc basis to perform notarial or accounting tasks, but who otherwise were unattached to a particular department? Might they have worked outside of Constantinople? Is it possible that they chose not to place their specific department on their seals to avoid the expense of commissioning another *boulloterion* should they move to a different area of government? We can never know for sure, and all of the above might have been true, considering that we are talking about many men over a period somewhat longer than a century. There does not need to be one answer. I would suggest that the majority of the people who placed no jurisdiction on their seals were working in Constantinople. It seems that all of the reasons outlined earlier are more valid for the capital, with its dense grouping of various *sekreta*, treasuries, and other arms of government, than for the provinces. It is possible that some of the men discussed in the following pages actually worked in the themes, but I suspect not many.

The *chartoularioi*

Σφραγὶς Γρηγορίου χαρτουλαρίου τοῦ Χαλκίτου.

The seal of the chartoularios Gregory Chalkites.[1]

To aid in analysis the three different groups of *chartoularioi* will be considered separately, beginning with the *megaloi chartoularioi*, then the imperial *chartoularioi* and finally the *chartoularioi*.

The office of *megas chartoularios* is represented in the seals record by sixty-two seals struck in the names of forty-seven men. For the century after 966 the most common title held by the *chartoularioi* was *protospatharios*, with no title perpetually in second place. The two switched in the first third of the twelfth century. All but one of the *megaloi chartoularioi* (a *patrikios*) to hold a title higher than *protospatharios* were

Table 6.1 Normalized Seal Data, in Percentages, for the Titles of *Megaloi Chartoularioi* c. 966–c. 1133

Title/Period	Tenth Century Final Third	Eleventh Century		
		First Third	Middle Third	Final Third
Magistros		2.2	1.9	4
Vestarches				12.1
Vestes			3.8	3.9
Patrikios and Hypatos			9.4	3.9
Patrikios		2.2	1.9	4
Protospatharios	57.7	69.9	47.3	32.1
Spatharokandidatos		2.1	3.8	
None	42.3	23.4	31.9	40

also judges of the Velum or theme judges. Many of their *protospatharios* counterparts also held more than one office sometimes theme judges, judges of the Hippodrome, or *kourators*, often minor positions like *asekretis*. We know that *megaloi chartoularioi* were found in the department of the *genikon* from Philotheos, and in the *stratiotikon*, *orphanotropheion*, *oikeiaka*, from seals, so it is possible that the men discussed here worked in one of these departments. The seals without department display a similar preponderance of *protospatharioi* as those of the *genikon*, but with a far greater proportion recording no title. The distribution of titles, in fact, closely resembles that of the judges of the Hippodrome, mainly *protospatharioi*, but with a spread up to the upper-middle hierarchy when holding more than one office.[2]

There are very few pieces of evidence for imperial *chartoularioi*, only seven men are known from seals, and none from documents. Of those seven, four did not record a title on their seals; two from the late tenth or early eleventh century, one from the eleventh century, and one from the eleventh/twelfth century. Of the remaining three, a late-tenth-century imperial *chartoularios* was a *protospatharios*, a man living in the mid-eleventh century held the titles of *anthypatos* and *patrikios*, and from the last third of the eleventh century we have a *protovestes*. We are in a much better position when it comes to the *chartoularioi*, 120 seals recording the work of 106 men. The data from these seals is presented in Table 6.2. *Chartoularioi* were found across the government, in the *genikon*, *dromos*, *sakellion* and *vestiarion*, according to Philotheos, and we can add the *stratiotikon*, *orphanotropheion*, *euageis oikoi* and *eidikon* from the testimony of the seals. It is possible that the owners of the seals discussed here worked in any of the above departments, and also that they might have been assigned to the themes or the tagmata in the *sekreton* of the *stratiotikon*.

No title seems to have been the default for the regular *chartoularioi*. In this they were different from their counterparts who named their department who were predominantly *protospatharioi*. Holding extra offices does not seem to have been a factor in which title they held: all of the mid-century *patrikioi* were just *chartoularioi*, while one of the *protospatharioi* was a judge of the Velum. Whether the lower ranks held by these *chartoularioi* had anything to do with their seals not recording a department is difficult to conclude. Some of the reason could be that they were thematic or tagmatic *chartoularioi*, who ranked below their metropolitan brethren, but this cannot account for all of them. Perhaps it was considered more prestigious to be attached to a

Figure 6.1 Seal of John *notarios*. Dumbarton Oaks, Byzantine Collection, Washington, DC, BZS.1958.106.4610 John notarios.
John chose an unusual and humble inscription for the reverse of his seal, paired with an image of St. John Chrysostom.
Rev. CΦPA|ΓHCIWEV|TEΛUCNO|TAP,U
Σφραγὶς Ἰωάννου εὐτελοῦς νοταρίου.
Seal of John, worthless notarios.

Table 6.2 Normalized Seal Data, in Percentages, for the Titles of *Chartoularioi* c. 966–c. 1133

Title/Period	Tenth Century Final Third	Eleventh Century			Twelfth Century First Third
		First Third	Middle Third	Final Third	
Patrikios			7.2		
Protospatharios	14.8	16.4	14.5	6.1	
Spatharokandidatos		7.3	3.7	2	
Spatharios		5.5	2.4	2	
Spatharokoubikoularios			3.6		
None	58.2	70.8	68.5	89.8	100

department, hence the higher proportion of men with titles? Although based on very little evidence we could conclude that there was a difference between imperial and regular *chartoularioi* based on the observation that two of the imperial *chartoularioi* held titles above any known for a regular *chartoularios*, but two examples does not a pattern make.

The *notarioi*

As with the *chartoularioi* there were three classes of *notarioi*: *protonotrioi*, imperial *notarioi*, and *notarioi*, which shall be considered separately.

Γραφὰς βεβαιῶ Μιχαὴλ νοταρίου.

I secure the correspondence of the notarios Michael.[3]

The most well-known *protonotarios* is that of the *dromos*. Often, when a departmentless *protonotarios* is discussed in the written source it is taken for granted that the official meant was the *protonotarios tou dromou*. While the only *protonotarioi* recorded in Philotheos are the *protonotarios tou dromou* and the *protonotarioi* of the themes, we know from the sigillographic record that they were also on the staff of various charitable foundations, the *genikon*, *sakellion*, *stratiotikon*, *eidikon*, and working for the *ephoros* and the *koiaistor*. There are thus many more possible homes than the *dromos* for the sixty-five *protonotarioi* known from eighty-seven seals recorded in Table 6.3. The data presents a familiar picture of high percentages of seals throughout the period recording either no title, or that of *protospatharios*, with a smattering of seals in the titles to either side. The range of these is rather wide from the late tenth century, up to *vestes* and then *magistros*, perhaps indicating the higher prestige of being a *proto* as opposed to an imperial or regular *notarios*. The documentary evidence presents us with very limited data, two men with no title in 1055 and 1060, and a *protovestes* in 1088 who also happened to be *ek prosopou* of the *sakellion*.[4]

Imperial *notarioi* are rather rare beasts in the *taktika*. Philotheos records them in only the *vestiarion* and the *edikon*, though at the top of the hierarchy in those departments. Eventually the *oikistikos* was served by imperial *notarioi*, and they were to be found working for the *epi ton oikeiakon*, the *epi tes sakelles*, *ephoros*, *megas oikonomos*, in the *genikon*, *dromos*, the *asekretaion*, and for the *epi ton deeseon*. With so many opportunities it is perhaps not surprising that the imperial *notarioi*, even though they do not mention a department on their seals, are one of the most numerous groups in the database behind this study, 127 men known from 159 seals.

The imperial *notarioi* present a similar pattern to that observed for their superiors, the *protonotarioi*, but shunted down the hierarchy slightly. While the percentage of seals showing no title is similar between the two offices, the imperial *notarioi* had to wait until the early eleventh century to be more likely a *protospatharios* than a *spatharokandidatos*. Nor were they as likely to be *vestai* at this early stage. However, during the eleventh century the spread of titles given to imperial *notarioi* was very

Table 6.3 Normalized Seal Data, in Percentages, for the Titles of *Protonotarioi* c. 966–c. 1133

Title/Period	Tenth Century Final Third	Eleventh Century			Twelfth Century First Third
		First Third	Middle Third	Final Third	
Magistros			1.5	4.5	
Protovestarches				6.8	
Vestes	5.9	5.4	8	5.6	
Anthypatos	5.9	3.2			
Protospatharios	25.5	26.9	34.1	27	33
Spatharokandidatos	3.9	16	8.1	7.9	33
Spatharios		3.2	2.2		
Spatharokoubikoularios			4.3		
None	58.8	45.2	41.9	48.3	33

Table 6.4 Normalized Seal Data, in Percentages, for the Titles of Imperial *Notarioi* c. 966–c. 1133

Title/Period	Tenth Century Final Third	Eleventh Century First Third	Eleventh Century Middle Third	Eleventh Century Final Third	Twelfth Century First Third
Magistros		1	1.7	5.2	16.7
Protovestarches		0.9	0.8	2.3	
Vestarches			3.3	2.3	
Vestes	2.9	2.4	1.7	7	
Anthypatos			0.8	2.3	
Patrikios		0.9	2.1	8.7	
Patrikios and *Hypatos*		1.4		2.3	16.7
Patrikios and *Protospatharios*			1.7	1.8	16.7
Hypatos			6.6	1.1	
Protospatharios	18.2	31.1	43.5	33.1	
Spatharokandidatos	22.1	18.4	6.7	1.2	
Spatharios	8.7	3.3	3.3		
None	48.1	41.5	27.7	32.7	50

similar to that granted to *protonotarioi*, although with greater numbers in the lower part of the hierarchy. Every title up to *vestarches* appears on a seal which records the only office of its owner as *imperial notarios*, the *magistroi* all held another position, usually judge of the Velum. The impression from the seals is reinforced by the documentary evidence in which a wide range of titles are recorded. There is a *spatharokandidatos* (also *anagrapheus* and judge of Boleron, Strymon, and Thessaloniki) from 1042/3, an *anthypatos* and *patrikios* (also *anagrapheus* of the West and judge of the Velum) from 1059, a *dishypatos* (also *mystographos*) from 1077, a man with not title in 1085 (also a judge), another *dishypatos* in 1087, and finally a *vestes* in 1088.[5]

Notarios with no prefix are not recorded as belonging to a department in the *taktika*, although they do make more general appearances in these documents and in *De Ceremoniis*. From the seals we know that they worked in the *sakellion* and *genikon*. Exactly what distinguished them from their imperial colleagues is unknown. It cannot have been that they were employed by the state. They appear as civil servants on seals, and every time that they appear in texts it is as state officials, they are not to be mistaken for the modern notary, which although sharing a similar sounding name was an entirely different animal in Byzantium. One difference was the other offices that they held. Imperial *notarioi* are frequently found as various classes of judges, *asekretai*, *antiprosopoi*, and as *exaktores*, *mystographoi*, *mystolektes* and a *kensor*. Standard *notarioi* are only very rarely seen as judges, and slightly more frequently as *chartoularioi*. The majority, 126 out of the 146 men known from 164 seals, only held the office of *notarios*. These are the kinds of proportions only seen elsewhere at the very top of the bureaucracy.

The difference between the imperial *notarioi* and the *notarioi* is further demonstrated by the titles that they held. A *notarios* who was a *protospatharios* was doing very well indeed, and while the percentage with this dignity grew into the middle of the eleventh

Table 6.5 Normalized Seal Data, in Percentages, for the Titles of *Notarioi* c. 966–c. 1133

	Tenth Century Final Third	Eleventh Century			Twelfth Century First Third
Title/Period		First Third	Middle Third	Final Third	
Vestes, Anthypatos, and Patrikios		0.7	1	1.3	
Anthypatos			1	2.6	
Patrikios		0.7	1	1.3	
Protospatharios	3	5.9	8	6.6	
Spatharokandidatos	3	3	1	1.3	
Kandidatos	6.1				
None	87.9	89.6	87.9	86.9	100

Table 6.6 Normalized Seal Data, in Percentages, for the Titles of *Logariastai* c. 966–c. 1133

	Tenth Century Final Third	Eleventh Century			Twelfth Century First Third
Title/Period		First Third	Middle Third	Final Third	
Proedros				16.7	
Vestarches				8.3	20
Vestes, Anthypatos, and Patrikios			16.2		
Patrikios and Anthypatos			16.2		
Protospatharios			16.2		
Spatharokandidatos		13.8	11		
Spatharios	100				
None		86.2	40.5	75	80

century, most *notarioi* recorded no title on their seals. As they formed the lowest rung of the bureaucracy in Constantinople it is fair to say that there is no title on their seals because they had no title. This adds a certain weight to the conclusion drawn throughout this work that the majority of seals with inscriptions which do not mention a title belonged to a man with no title to record.

The *logariastai*

Γραφὰς σφραγίζω καὶ λόγους οὕς ἐκφέρει λογαριαστὴς Μιχαὴλ καὶ βεστάρχης.

I seal the letters and the words which the logariastes and vestarches Michael brings forth.[6]

We know of fewer *logariastai* from the seals than the other offices considered in this section, only twenty men from thirty-two seals. The office, a dedicated accountant, spread throughout the bureaucracy in the eleventh century, too late to appear in any of the *taktika*. We know from other sources that they were spread widely across the government serving the *oiksitikos, sakellarios, epi tes sakelles*, various charitable institutions, the *genikon*, and the *vestiarion*, in short, the majority of the departments that had something to do with the management or collection of the empire's resources. From the data in Table 6.6 it is clear that the *logariastai* were not high-ranking men. The single highest group of seals from all time periods records no title. The apparent rise in the importance of the office in the middle third of the eleventh century is the result of a higher than usual proportion of *logariastai* with other offices giving them access to a higher title. This is not the case with the *proedros* and *vestarches* from the late eleventh century. I suspect, but cannot prove, that the *proedros* at least, maybe the *vestarches* as well, were actually one of the two *megaloi logariastai* created by Alexios I in the early years of his reign. This hypothesis would explain why they held dignities so far above their fellow *logariastai*. This is likely true for the *logariastai* mentioned in documents dated to 1083, a *vestarches*, 1083, 1089, a *proedros*, and in 1112, a *protoproedros*.[7]

The ek prosopou

Κύριε βοήθει Κωνσταντίνῳ πρωτοσπαθαρίῳ καὶ ἐκ προσώπου.

Lord, help Constantine, protospatharios and ek prosopou.[8]

An *ek prosopou* was an agent of a higher-ranking official. They are known from the themes, both the civilian and military administrations, and even the church. As such it is not impossible that very few of the twenty-four men recorded in Table 6.7 actually worked in Constantinople. From other seals we know of the position in the *dromos* and the *sakellion*.

Table 6.7 Normalized Seal Data, in Percentages, for the Titles of *Ek Prosopou* c. 966–c. 1133

Title/Period	Tenth Century Final Third	Eleventh Century		
		First Third	Middle Third	Final Third
Protospatharios	28.6	27.4	16.9	60
Spatharokandidatos	42.9	50	33.4	20
Spathariokoubikoularios	7.1	6.8		
Kandidatos	14.3	4.4	11.3	
None	7.1	11.4	38.7	20

Notes

Chapter 1

1. Michael Psellos, *Chronographia* VII.1. ed. S. Impellizeri and trans. S. Ronchey, Michele Psello, *Imperatori di Bisanzio (Cronografia)*, 2 vols (Milan, 1984).
2. M. Angold, *The Byzantine Empire, 1025–1204: A Political History*, 2nd edn (London and New York, 1997); A. Kaldellis, *Streams of Gold, Rivers of Blood: The Rise and Fall of Byzantium, 955 A.D. to the First Crusade* (Oxford, 2017).
3. Yet sadly there will almost certainly never be an Anastasios, *patrikios* and *genikos logothetes*, the Revenue Shortfall Slayer or a Niketas, *proedros* and *epi ton kriseon*, the Ink-Stained Death of Provincial Judicial Corruption.
4. See in particular, J. Haldon, *Byzantium in the Seventh Century: The Transformation of a Culture* (Cambridge, 1990), pp. 173–253, 376–402; J. Haldon, *The Empire That Would Not Die: The Paradox of Eastern Roman Survival, 640–740* (Cambridge, MA and London, 2016), pp. 159–92; L. Brubaker and J. Haldon, *Byzantium in the Iconoclast Era, c. 680–850: A History* (Cambridge, 2011), pp. 573–615, 665–81, 709–22; F. Winkelmann, *Byzantinische Rang- und Ämterstruktur im 8. und 9. Jahrhundert*, Berliner byzantinistische Arbeiten 53 (Berlin, 1985) and *Quellenstudien zur herrschenden Klasse von Byzanz im 8. und 9. Jahrhundert*, Berliner byzantinistische Arbeiten 54 (Berlin, 1987).
5. For developments between the early Byzantine restructuring of the bureaucracy and imperial power structures and the period under consideration in this study, see Winkelmann, *Byzantinische Rang- und Ämterstruktur*, and *Quellenstudien zur herrschenden Klasse*.
6. *Scylitzes Continuatus*, ed. and trans., E. McGeer and J. Nesbitt, Chapter 6, section 27. 62.
7. Kaldellis, *Streams of Gold, Rivers of Blood*.
8. G. Weiss, *Oströmische Beamte im Spiegel der Schriften des Michael Psellos* (Munich, 1973).
9. As with his reassessment of the military policy of Constantine IX Monomachos, Anthony Kaldellis has forcefully argued that the idea of imperial military neglect should be applied to specific reigns, particularly Constantine X Doukas, rather than in general across the century. Kaldellis, *Streams of Gold, Rivers of Blood*, pp. 231–5. For the argument that it was the Byzantines's own actions following the Battle of Manzikert in 1071 not the defeat itself which resulted in the loss of Anatolia to the Turks, see J.-C. Cheynet, 'La résistance aux Turcs en Asie Mineure entre Mantzikert et la Première Croisade', *EYΨYXIA: Mélanges offerts à Hélène Ahrweiler* (Paris, 1998), pp. 131–47; J.-C. Cheynet, 'Mantzikert: un désastre militaire?', *Byzantion* 50 (1980), pp. 410–38; P. Frankopan, *The First Crusade: The Call from the East* (London, 2012). The only book to date to focus solely on the eleventh-century bureaucracy does so by almost exclusively using the testimony of Michael Psellos and considers the empire to have been falling apart from the inside not least because of the complex and unwieldy nature of the bureaucracy. Weiss, *Oströmische Beamte*, pp. 5–6.

10 John Skylitzes, *Synopsis of Histories*, ed. J. Thurn, *Ioannis Scylitzae Synopsis Historiarum* (Berlin and New York, 1973), p. 476.
11 George Kedrenos, *Historiarum Compendium*, ed. I. Bekker, 2 vols (Bonn, 1838, 1839), at Vol. II, p. 634.
12 See in particular J.-C. Cheynet, *Pouvoir et contestations à Byzance (963–1210)* (Paris, 1990); W. Kaegi, 'The Controversy about Bureaucratic and Military Factions', *Byzantinische Forshungen* 19 (1993), pp. 25–33. For factionalism in Byzantine Constantinople, see J.-C. Cheynet, 'Intrigues à la cour de Constantinople: le délitement d'une faction (1057–1081)', *Le saint, le moine et le paysan. Mélanges d'histoire byzantine offerts à Michel Kaplan* (Paris, 2016), pp. 71–84. For an interesting recent addition to this discussion, see D. Krallis, 'Urbane Warriors: Smoothing Out Tensions between Soldiers and Civilians in Attaleiates' Encomium to Emperor Nikephoros III Botaneiates', *Byzantium in the Eleventh Century Being in Between* (London and New York, 2017), pp. 154–68. For older or more traditional approaches, see A. A. Vasiliev, *A History of the Byzantine Empire* (Madison, 1928), p. 426; G. Ostrogorsky, *Pour l'histoire de la féodalité byzantine* (Brussels, 1954), *History of the Byzantine State,* revised edn (New Brunswick, 1969) and 'Observations on the Aristocracy in Byzantium', *Dumbarton Oaks Papers* 25 (1971), pp. 1–32; P. Lemerle, *Cinq études sur le XIe siècle byzantin* (Paris, 1977); A. P. Kazhdan and A. J. Wharton, *Change in Byzantine Culture in the Eleventh and Twelfth Centuries* (Berkley, 1985). For discussions of the aristocratization of the empire and political culture. See J.-C. Cheynet, 'Fortune et puissance de l'aristocratie (X-XII siècle)', *Hommes et richesses dans l'empire byzantin*, eds V. Kravari, J. Lefort and C. Morrisson (Paris, 1991), pp. 199–213; C. Holmes, 'Political Elites in the Reign of Basil II', *Byzantium in the Year 1000*, ed. P. Magdalino (Leiden, 2003), pp. 35–69. At the same time the significance of the private landed wealth of these men has come into question, and more emphasis placed on their position as officers within the Byzantine army. J.-C. Cheynet, *The Byzantine Aristocracy and Its Military Function* (London, 2006). For a recent, and forceful, summary of this argument with bibliography, see Kaldellis, *Streams of Gold, Rivers of Blood*, pp. 13–18.
13 Cheynet, *Pouvoir et contestations*, pp. 191–8.
14 Michael V was overthrown by the people of the city. Michael VI lost the support of powerful factions within the senate and from among the people during a military revolt, he had lost his capital before Isaac Komnenos arrived. That same Isaac Komnenos was deposed in strange circumstances by members of the very civilian establishment against which he rebelled, and later his fellow military man Romanos IV was ousted by the same group. Finally, Michael VII found himself in a similar situation to Michael VI.
15 Even the soldier emperor Isaac I did not oust his predecessor Michael VI through military might alone but as the leader of a widespread rebellion that incorporated elements of the military, mostly from the eastern provinces, and a part of the civilian elite of the capital, under the leadership of the patriarch Michael Keroularios. It was he who actually deposed Michael VI.
16 S. Vryonis, 'Byzantine Dēmokratia and the Guilds in the Eleventh Century', *Dumbarton Oaks Papers* 17 (1963), pp. 312–13.
17 Neatly summed up in M. Hendy, *Studies in the Byzantine Monetary Economy c. 300–1450* (Cambridge, 1985), pp. 570 with reference to Vryonis, 'Byzantine Dēmokratia', pp. 302–14 and Lemerle, *Cinq études*, pp. 287–93.
18 Michael Psellos, *Chronographia*, VI.29.

19 Hendy, *Studies*, p. 575.
20 Holders of dignities from *spatharokandidatos* and lower.
21 Hendy, *Studies*, p. 576.
22 Nikephoros Bryennios, *Nicephori Bryenii historiarum libri IV*, ed., P. Gautier (Brussels, 1975), IV.1, pp. 257, 259, trans. Hendy, *Studies,* p. 235.
23 This view of Byzantine decline was evocatively summed up at the end of the first part of Psellos's *Chronographia*, where he likened the empire to an ever-inflating body, being made more gross and distorted as successive emperors fed it fatty foods and added unnecessary limbs, while neglecting its health, by which he meant multiplied the number of useless salaried individuals, spent far too much money and neglected the army. Psellos, *Chronographia*, VII.52–59. While referring to the imperial administration as the first secular, disciplined, trained civil service in Europe Weiss, heavily influenced by Psellos, paints a picture of a bloated bureaucracy at the heart of a complex state that was slowly choking itself with procedures and paperwork, though he does admit that this was not all the fault of the bureaucrats themselves. Weiss, *Oströmische Beamte*, pp. 6, 155.
24 Psellos, *Chronographia*, VI.29.
25 While these individuals might be included under the general headings, civilian or Constantinopolitan elites, where a link to the centre is proven, without an office, they were not bureaucrats.
26 As noted in H.-G. Beck, 'Theorie und Praxis im Aufbau der byzantinischen Zentralverwaltung', *Bayerische Akademie der Wissenschaften. Philosophisch-Historische Klase Sitzunsberichte* 8 (1974), p. 4.
27 John Zonaras and T. Büttner-Wobst, *Ioannis Zonarae Epitome Historiarum libri XIII-XVIII, Corpus scriptiorum historiae Byzantinae* 49 (Leipzig, 1897), XVII.22.
28 Michael Psellus, *Orationes Forenses et Acta*, ed. G. T. Dennis (Stuttgart and Leipzig, 1994), p. 143. For a modern assessment of this case, see A. Kaldellis, *Mothers and Sons, Fathers and Daughters: The Byzantine Family of Michael Psellos* (Notre Dame, 2006), pp. 139–46.
29 While we cannot deny the importance of wealth, inherited or otherwise, and patronage to social and career advancement in Byzantium, the holding of a position was what gave an individual authority, and positions were not the de jure or de facto property of the well-connected or independently wealthy.
30 Two notable exceptions are H. Glykatzi-Ahrweiler, 'Recherhces sur l'administration de l'empire byzantin aux ixe-xie siècles', *Bulletin de correspondance hellénique* 84 (1960), pp. 1–111; N. Oikonomides, 'L'évolution de l'organisation administrative de l'empire byzantin au XIe siècle (1025–1118)', *Travaux et Memoires* 6 (Paris, 1976), pp. 125–52. See also, J.-C. Cheynet, 'Point de vue sur l'efficacité administrative entre les xe et xie siècles', *Byzantinische Forschungen* 19 (1993), pp. 7–16; R.-J. Lilie, 'Die Zentralbürokratie und die Provinzen zwischen dem 10. und dem 12. Jahrhundert. Anspruch und Realität', *Byzantinische Forschungen* 19 (1993), pp. 65–75; R. Morris, 'Travelling Judges in Byzantine Macedonia (10th-11th c.)', *Zbornik Radova Vizantološkog Instituta* 50 (2013), pp. 351–61; L. Neville, *Authority in Byzantine Provincial Society, 950–1100* (Cambridge, 2004); N. Oikonomides, 'L'organisation de la frontière orientale de Byzance aux xe-xie siècle et le taktikon de l'Escorial', *Actes du XIVe Congrès international des études byzantines* I (Bucharest, 1974), pp. 285–302.
31 See A. Kaldellis, 'The Manufacture of History in the Later Tenth and Eleventh Centuries: Rhetorical Templates and Narrative Ontologes', *Proceedings of the 23rd*

International Congress of Byzantine Studies (Belgrade, 22–27 August 2016): Plenary Papers (Belgrade, 2016), pp. 293–306.

32 This is not to argue that legal documents cannot be very useful for the study of the provinces with which they are concerned, it is just that very few of them speak of the capital, except to mention the odd bureaucrat from there currently serving in the themes.

33 It should also be remembered that seals could be attached to multiple copies of the same document. B. Caseau, 'Un aspect de la diplomatique byzantine: les copies de documents', *Recours à l'écrit, autorité du document, constitution d'archives au Moyen Âge. Orient et Occident,* XXXIXe Congrès de la SHMESP (Le Caire, 30 avril–5 mai 2008) (Paris, 2009), pp. 159–74.

34 G. Zacos, *Byzantine Lead Seals,* ed. J. W. Nesbitt, vol. II (Bern, 1984), no. 1012, also DO BZS.1958.106.5597 and BZS.1958.106.932.

35 One of the most interesting features of the eleventh century is the gradual shift from a power and hierarchy structure based on imperial service to one based on more aristocratic values of birth and relationship to the imperial family. Family names appear on seals with increasing frequency in our period, though this was less so among bureaucrats. Even in Byzantine society as a whole the move from state-centred inscriptions to family centric ones does not affect the majority of seals until well into the twelfth century.

36 This pattern is present on seals as early as the sixth century and remained largely consistent to the end of the eleventh century with the exception of the introduction of family names beginning in the latter half of the tenth century.

37 Constantine VII, *De Ceremoniis aulae byzantinae,* ed., J. J. Reiske (Bonn, 1829–30), p. 707. Also, N. Oikonomides, *Les listes de préséance byzantines des IXe et Xe siècles* (Paris, 1972), p. 87.

38 Constantine VII, *De Ceremoniis,* p. 707. Also, Oikonomides, *Listes,* p. 89.

39 F. Bernard and C. Livanos, eds. and trans., 'On the Golden Bull of the Lavra', *The Poems of Christopher of Mytilene and John Mauropous* (Cambridge, MA and London, 2018), no. 46, p. 409.

40 Oikonomides, *Listes,* pp. 24–9.

41 N. Oikonomides, 'Chrysobull', in *The Oxford Dictionary of Byzantium* (Oxford University Press, 1991). Retrieved 31 July 2019, from https://www-oxfordreference-com.ezp-prod1.hul.harvard.edu/view/10.1093/acref/9780195046526.001.0001/acref-9780195046526-e-1090

42 Oikonomides, *Listes,* pp. 258–61. The surviving manuscript dates to the eleventh century.

43 Ibid., pp. 45–7, 81, 240–3. For the earlier dating of the *Taktikon Uspenskij,* see T. Živkovič, 'Uspenskij's Taktikon and the Theme of Dalmatia', Σύμμεικτα 17 (2005), pp. 49–85.

44 Ibid., p. 292. *Zoste patrikia* was the only title reserved for a woman, ibid., p. 293.

45 That the title of *anthypatos* was still awarded regularly at the time that the *Taktikon Escorial* was written is not in doubt, the reason for its omission from this text is a mystery, but it seems likely to be a simple error either in the original composition or at some time in the manuscripts transmission, perhaps when the surviving version of the text was copied in the eleventh century. The dignity of *vestes* was created during the reign of Nikephoros II Phokas, 963–9, and thus made its first appearance in the *Taktikon Escorial,* ibid., p. 294.

46 Ibid.

47 Psellos, *Orationes forenses et acta,* pp. 176–81.

48 Oikonomides, 'L'évolution', p. 126.
49 Discounting the exceptional use of the title *sebaste* for the mistress of Constantine IX Monomachos, the first recorded use of *sebastos* as a title used for an individual other than the emperor is the case of Constantine Keroularios who possessed the title before 1078. Within a few years the brothers Isaac and Alexios Komnenos would also be granted the title by Nikephoros III Botaneiates. Ibid., pp. 126–7.
50 This observation does not include the title *protospatharios* which dates to at least the early eighth century.
51 Ibid.
52 J.-C. Cheynet, 'Dévaluation des dignités et dévaluation monétaire dans la seconde moitié du XIe siècle', *Byzantion* 53 (1983), p. 474. It should be noted that many of the newer titles appear less frequently than the traditional ones on seals. For instance, *illoustrios* and *hypatos* are quite rare; *dishypatos* is by no means common; however, *vestes*, *vestarches* and *proedros* are comparatively common. The effect that this had on how the Byzantines viewed their place in the hierarchy is unknown, and as they were a part of that hierarchy they are included here.
53 A. H. M. Jones, *The Later Roman Empire, 284–602*, vol. 1 (Oxford, 1964), pp. 528–30.
54 His brothers Isaac, Adrian and Nikephoros received the new titles of *sebastokrator*, *protosebastos*, *pansebastos* respectively, Michael Taronites, his brother-in-law was also made a *protosebastos*. Oikonomides, 'L'évolution', p. 127.
55 Oikonomides, 'L'évolution', p. 127.
56 Michael Taronites would eventually hold this more exalted dignity. P. Magdalino, *The Empire of Manuel I Komnenos* (Cambridge, 1993), p. 181.
57 Oikonomides, 'L'évolution', p. 127.
58 Unpublished translation of *Scylitzes Continuatus*, E. McGeer and J. Nesbitt, p. 25.
59 See for example, Michael Attaleiates, *History*, ed. and trans. A. Kaldellis and D. Krallis (Washington, DC, 2012), pp. 30–1, 498–505.
60 Attaleiates, *History*, pp. 108–10.
61 Psellos, *Chronographia*, VI.3.
62 Liutprand of Cremona, *legatio Constantinopolitana*; ed. J. Becker (*Die Werke Liudprands von Cremona*) (Hanover and Leipzig, 1915), p. 158. These payments were carefully counted out into bags before being secured by a seal to ensure the safety of the salary and guarantee its value. P. Magdalino, 'Apokomnion', in *Oxford Dictionary of Byzantium*, ed. A. Kazhdan (Oxford, 1991), pp. 135–6.
63 Ibid., p. 157 ln. 29–158 ln. 34 (158. 17–21 for these titles and *rogai*).
64 Psellus, *Orationes forenses et acta*, pp. 143–55, at pp. 145–6.
65 Ibid., pp. 169–75.
66 Ahrweiler recorded in Lemerle, '"Roga" et rente d'Etat aux Xe – XIe siècles', *Revue des etudes byzantines* 25 (1967), p. 94. This is contrary to the proposals made by H. Antoniadis-Bibicou, 'Démographie, salaires et prix à Byzance au XIe siècle', *Annales. Économies, Sociétés, Civilisations* 27, no. 1 (1972), pp. 215–46.
67 Cheynet, 'Dévaluation', p. 474.
68 As Paul Lemerle pointed out, this document, when taken alongside the dispute between Elpidios Kenchres and Michael Psellos, and the example from the reign of Leo VI demonstrates that the *roga* associated with the dignity of protospatharios remained steady at 1 pound of gold coins for almost two centuries. Lemerle, 'Roga et rente', pp. 77–100.
69 Constantine VII, *Constantine Porphyrogenitus, De Administrando Imperio*, ed. Gy. Moravcsik and trans. R. J. H. Jenkins (Washington, DC, 1967), p. 244.

70 Lemerle, 'Roga et rente', pp. 95–6 for discussion, for the *chrysobull*, see F. Dölger and P. Worth, *Regesten Der Kaiserurkunden des Oströmischen Reiches von 565-1453*, 2nd edn (Munich: C. H. Beck, 1977), no. 865; I. and P. Zépos, eds, *Jus graecoromanum*, vol. 1 (Athens, 1931; rp. Aalen, 1962), p. 628; K. N. Kanellakis, Χιακὰ ἀνάλεκτα (Athens, 1890), p. 541.
71 Ibid., p. 96, for the *chrysobull*, see Dölger and Worth, *Regesten*, no. 1030; Zépos, *JGR* 1, pp. 643–4, Kanellakis, Χιακὰ ἀνάλεκτα, p. 578; F. Miklosich and J. Müller, *Acta et diplomata graeca medii aevi sacra et profana*, vol. 5 (Vienna, 1860–90), no. 6, pp. 8–10.
72 N. Oikonomides, 'Title and Income at the Byzantine Court', in *Byzantine Court Culture from 829 to 1204*, ed. H. Maguire (Washington, DC, 1997), pp. 199–215, at pp. 205, 208, referencing *Peira* 38.74, and Lemerle, 'Roga et rente', pp. 89–90.
73 Lemerle, 'Roga et rente', p. 90.
74 Hendy also discusses two passages in Psellos and Kekaumenos which possibly reference devaluation. Hendy, *Studies*, p. 510. In the case of Kekaumenos I am inclined to agree with Hendy. About Psellos I am less sure as in describing Michael VII's understanding of the use of a touchstone he could simply have been referring to the everyday practices of the mint and marketplace rather than to measures made necessary through inflation. For the silence on earlier developments, see C. Morrisson, 'La devaluation de la monnaie byzantine au XIe siècle: essai d'interprétation', *Travaux et Mémoires* 6 (1976), p. 13.
75 Antoniadis-Bibicou, 'Démographie, salaires et prix à Byzance au XIe siècle', pp. 215–46, at pp. 227–33; Morrisson, 'La devaluation de la monnaie byzantine', pp. 18–20; D. M. Metcalf, *Coinage in South-Eastern Europe 820–1396* (London, 1979), p. 68; J.-C. Cheynet, É. Malamut and C. Morrisson, 'Prix et salaires à Byzance (Xe-XVe siècle)', *Hommes et richesses dans l'Empire byzantin*, 2 (1991), pp. 339–74, at p. 373.
76 Antoniadis-Bibicou, 'Démographie, salaires et prix', pp. 231–3; Cheynet, et al., 'Prix et salaires', pp. 361–3.
77 C. Morrisson, 'Byzantine Money: Its Production and Circulation', in *Economic History of Byzantium*, ed. A. E. Laiou (Washington, DC, 2002), pp. 909–66, at pp. 931, 944.
78 C. Morrisson, 'Le Michaèlaton et les noms de monnaies de la fin du XIe siècle', *Travaux et Mémoires* 3 (1968), pp. 369–74.
79 A. E. Laiou and C. Morrisson, *The Byzantine Economy* (Cambridge, 2007), p. 149. Morrisson, 'les noms de monnaies de la fin du XIe siècle', p. 370. Not all of these were related to the major phases of debasement in the eleventh century, the *helioselenaton* was a coin of Basil II. Morrisson, 'La devaluation de la monnaie byzantine', p. 14.
80 DO BZS.1947.2.646.
81 See N. Oikonomides, *A Collection of Dated Byzantine Lead Seals* (Washington, DC, 1986), for an early attempt to systematize the dating of seals which, although modified in the subsequent decades, still forms the foundation for sigillographic dating today.
82 A list of the catalogues and publications consulted for this study can be found in the bibliography.
83 The increased viability of statistical analysis when dealing with large numbers of seals is also a point in favour of date ranges which are not too narrow, as dividing the seals among too many small boxes would make them far less useful.
84 And as Haldon notes, Isaac I soon became a proponent of the strongly bureaucratic central government against which he had rebelled. J. Haldon, 'Social Élites, Wealth, and Power', *A Social History of Byzantium*, ed. J. Haldon (Chichester, 2009), p. 185.

Chapter 2

1. V. Laurent, *Le corpus des sceaux de l'Empire byzantin, vol. 2, L'administration centrale* (Paris, 1981), no. 145.
2. DO BZS.1958.106.243.
3. For discussions of the iconographic choices made by the Byzantines for their seals, see J.-C. Cheynet and C. Morrisson, 'Texte and image sur les sceaux byzantins: les raisons d'un choix iconographique', *Studies in Byzantine Sigillography* 4 (1995), pp. 9–32; J. Cotsonis, 'Onomastics, Gender, Office and Images on Byzantine Lead Seals: A Means of Investigating Personal Piety', *Byzantine and Modern Greek Studies* 32, no. 1 (2008), pp. 1–37.
4. Cotsonis, J., 'The Contribution of Byzantine Lead Seals to the Study of the Cult of Saints (Sixth-Twelfth Centruy)', *Byzantion* 75 (2005), Chart II, p. 391. The time periods Cotsonis uses do not align perfectly with those in this study, so it has been necessary to amalgamate the periods of both to allow for comparison.
5. B. Caseau, 'Saint Mark, a Family Saint? The Iconography of the Xeroi Seals', in *Ἠπειρόνδε (Epeironde), Proccedings of the 10th International Symposium of Byzantine Sigillography (Ioannina, 1–3 October 2009)*, eds Ch. Stavrakos and B. Papadopoulou (Leiden, 2011), pp. 81–109.
6. Cheynet and Morrisson and later Seibt observed a preference among members of families associated with the civilian bureaucracy for civilian saints. The data I have presented does not break down in quite the same way being concerned with office holding rather than family, although it does seem to suggest that military saints were less popular among this group than in the general population. See Cheynet and Morrisson, 'Texte and Image', pp. 30–2; W. Seibt, 'Zwischen Identifizierungsrauch und -verweigerung: Zur Problematik synchroner homonymer Siegel', *Siegel un Siegler: Akten des 8 Internationalen Symposions für Byzantinische Sigillographie*, ed. C. Ludwig (Berlin, 2005), pp. 141–50, at p. 143.
7. Cotsonis, 'Cult of Saints', p. 468.
8. Ibid., p. 457.
9. Ibid., p. 461.
10. Ibid.; J.-C. Cheynet, 'Par St Georges, par St Michel', in *Travaux et Mémoires* 14 (2002), pp. 114–34, at pp. 119–24.
11. Costonis, 'Cult of Saints', pp. 417–18.
12. Ibid., pp. 442–6, see particularly fns 213, 218–25 for bibliography.
13. Cotsonis, 'Cult of Saints', p. 446. He was also hardly ever depicted in military attire in this period. Cotsonis, 'Cult of Saints', p. 445.
14. Cotsonis, 'Cult of Saints', pp. 442, 445.
15. Ibid., p. 427.
16. Ibid., pp. 431–3.
17. For Cotsonis's conclusions, see J. Cotsonis, 'Onomastics, Gender, Office and Images', pp. 5–10 for homonymous seals and pp. 21–33 for family and occupation.
18. Laurent, *Corpus* II, no. 1026.
19. P. Stephenson, 'A Development in Nomenclature of the Seals of the Byzantine Provincial Aristocracy in the Late Tenth Century', *Revue des Études Byzantines* 52 (1994), pp. 187–211.
20. Wassiliou and Seibt, *Bleisiegel* II, p. 287.
21. Šandroskaja and Seibt, *Eremitage*, p. 68.

22 Ibid., p. 104.
23 Wassiliou and Seibt, *Bleisiegel* II, p. 43.
24 Ibid., p. 32.
25 M. Campagnolo-Pothitou and J.-C. Cheynet, *Sceaux de la collection Georges Zacos au Musée d'art et d'histoire de Genève* (Geneva, 2016), p. 357.
26 V. S. Šandrovskaja and W. Seibt, *Byzantinische Bleisiegel der Staatlichen Eremitage mit Familiennamen, vol. 1, Sammlung Lichačev—Namen von A bis I* (Vienna, 2005), p. 85.
27 Ibid., p. 83.
28 Wassiliou and Seibt, *Bleisiegel* II, p. 38. A. Kazhdan, 'Iasites', in *The Oxford Dictionary of Byzantium* (Oxford University Press, 1991). http://www.oxfordreference.com.ezp-prod1.hul.harvard.edu/view/10.1093/acref/9780195046526.001.0001/acref-9780195046526-e-2399
29 Wassiliou and Seibt, *Bleisiegel* II, p. 38.
30 The earliest known Gymnos was a late-tenth-century monk in Calabria. Šandroskaja and Seibt, *Eremitage*, p. 108.
31 A family likely of Armenian origin. The name refers to the *tagma* of the *Hikanatoi* founded by Nikephoros I in 809. Wassiliou and Seibt, *Bleisiegel* II, p. 214.
32 A. Kazhdan and A. Cutler, 'Philokales', in *The Oxford Dictionary of Byzantium*. http://www.oxfordreference.com.ezp-prod1.hul.harvard.edu/view/10.1093/acref/9780195046526.001.0001/acref-9780195046526-e-4304
33 Skylitzes, *Synopsis of Histories*, p. 198; Laurent, *Corpus* II, no. 396; R. Janin, *Constantinople byzantine*. (Paris, 1964), p. 390; Idem., *Églises,* p. 553; Wassiliou and Seibt, *Bleisiegel* II, p. 178. A. Kazhdan, 'Kyparissiotes', in *The Oxford Dictionary of Byzantium*. http://www.oxfordreference.com.ezp-prod1.hul.harvard.edu/view/10.1093/acref/9780195046526.001.0001/acref-9780195046526-e-2968
34 The Choirosphaktes family, for example, originated in the Peloponnese, but had been resident in Constantinople since at least the late ninth century. Wassiliou and Seibt, *Bleisiegel* II, p. 216.
35 Wassiliou and Seibt, *Bleisiegel* II, p. 195.
36 Campagnolo-Pothitou and Cheynet, *Geneva*, p. 415.
37 Cheynet, 'Pouvoir', p. 363, n. 26. Wassiliou and Seibt, *Bleisiegel* II, p. 257.
38 Wassiliou and Seibt, *Bleisiegel* II, p. 178.
39 Ibid., p. 38.
40 Ibid., p. 40.
41 J. Nesbitt and W. Seibt, 'The Anzas Family: Members of the Civil Establishment in the Eleventh, Twelfth, and Thirteenth Centuries', *Dumbarton Oaks Papers* 67 (2013), pp. 189–207.
42 A.-K. Wassiliou, 'Die Familie Hexamilites. Ein Beitrag zur Byzantinischen Prosopographie', Ἑλληνικά 52 (2002), pp. 234–61.
43 A. Kazhdan, 'Pepagomenos', in *The Oxford Dictionary of Byzantium*. http://www.oxfordreference.com.ezp-prod1.hul.harvard.edu/view/10.1093/acref/9780195046526.001.0001/acref-9780195046526-e-4214
44 For the Argyroi, see J.-C. Cheynet, *La société byzantine. L'apport des sceaux* II (Paris, 2008), pp. 525–62.
45 J.-C. Cheynet and J.-F. Vannier, 'Les Argyroi', *Zbornik Radova Vizantološkog Instituta* 40 (2003), p. 79; Niketas, ibid., p. 81.
46 Campagnolo-Pothitou and Cheynet, *Geneva*, p. 357.
47 Wassiliou and Seibt, *Bleisiegel* II, pp. 96–7.

48 Ibid., p. 216.
49 Campagnolo-Pothitou and Cheynet, *Geneva*, pp. 368, 414.
50 There must have been many more men with a personal or family history in trade or craftsmanship among the men recording no family name on their seals.
51 For example, Michael Machetarios, Wassiliou and Seibt, *Bleisiegel* II, no. 10; Michael Choirosphaktes, Laurent, *Corpus* II, no. 114. Cf. Wassiliou and Seibt, *Bleisiegel* II, p. 307, n. 374.
52 F. Bernard and Livanos, *Christopher of Mytilene and John Mauropous*, no. 66 'On Someone Who Was Suddenly Promoted', pp. 455–6.
53 Dennis, *Orationes, Forenses et Acta*, p. 145. *PBW* Elpidios 2101.
54 Dennis, *Orationes, Forenses et Acta*, pp. 147–8. Note that Psellos could not simply acquire and give the title of *patrikios* to Elpidios as he had with that of *protospatharios*.
55 *PBW* Konstantinos 120.
56 For the career of Constantine nephew of Michael Keroularios, see M. Jeffreys, 'Constantine, Nephew of the Pariarch Keroularios, and His Good Friend Michael Psellos', *The Letters of Psellos: Cultural Networks and Historical Realities* ed. M. Jeffreys and M. D. Lauxtermann (Oxford, 2016), pp. 59–88.
57 Miklosich and Müller V, no. 2 (1045); Ch. Stavrakos, *Die byzantinischen Bleisiegel mit Familiennamen aus der Sammlung des Numismatischen Museums Athen* (Wiesbaden, 2000), no. 257; Konstantopoulos, Βυζαντιακὰ μολυβδόβοθλλα τοῦ ἐν Ἀθήναις Ἐθνικοῦ Νομισματικοῦ Μοθσείου (Athens, 1917), no. 483; Laurent, *Legendes*, pp. 473–7, no. 2; Šandrovskaja, 'Sfragistika', no. 747; Laurent, *Corpus* II, no. 1032. For a summary of Basil's entire career see the commentary in Stavrakos , *Familiennamen*, p. 381 and Jordanov, *Bulgaria* 3, no. 1175. *PBW* Basileios 214.
58 *PBW* Nikolaos 20149.
59 Wassiliou, 'Hexamilites', no. 14; *PBW* Ioannes 20422.
60 Wassiliou, 'Hexamilites', pp. 253–6, no. 17; *PBW* Sergios 105.
61 Laurent, *Corpus* II, no. 1033; Ch. Stavrakos, *Familiennamen*, no. 270; *PBW* Michael 20229.
62 *DO Seals* 4.32.6.
63 Cheynet and Morrisson, *Seyrig*, no. 155.
64 *DO Seals* 1.43.8; see Jordanov, *Bulgaria* 3, no. 1178A for further bibliography.
65 Zarnitz Kestner, no. 65; Jordanov, *Bulgaria* 3, no. 1175.
66 *DO Seals* 2.59.7; Wassiliou and Seibt, *Bleisiegel* II, no. 191; Šandrovskaja, 'Sfragistika', no. 721; Konstantopoulos, Νομισματικοῦ Μουσείου, no. 483; Laurent, *Legendes*, pp. 473–77, no. 2; Šandrovskaja, 'Sfragistika', no. 747; Laurent, *Corpus* II, no. 1032.
67 Much of his career is outlined in Wassiliou and Seibt, *Bleisiegel* II, p. 178; *PBW* Konstantinos 20304.
68 *DO Seals* 3.86.27; Hirsch 183.1799. cf. Wassiliou and Seibt, *Bleisiegel* II, p. 178, n. 238.
69 *DO Seals* 3.86.36; Cheynet et al., *Istanbul*, no. 311a and b.
70 Zarnitz Kestner, no. 75. Cf. Seibt, *Bleisiegel* I, p. 303, n. 10 and II, p. 178, n. 228. V. S. Šandrovskaja, 'Sfragistika', *Iskusstvo Vizantii v sobranijach SSSR (Katalog vystavki)*, vol. 2 (Moscow, 1977), no. 713. Cf. Wassiliou and Seibt, *Bleisiegel* II, p. 178, n. 227; *DO Seals* 4.1.19; Wassiliou and Seibt, *Bleisiegel* II, p. 178, n. 228.
71 Wassiliou and Seibt, *Bleisiegel* II, nos. 172a and b; *DO Seals* 3.86.25 a, b and c.
72 Šandrovskaja, 'Sfragistika', no. 712.
73 Laurent, *Corpus* II, no. 809, cf. Wassiliou and Seibt, *Bleisiegel* II, p. 39, n. 65; Šandrovskaja and Seibt, *Ermitage*, p. 68, n. 47.

74 H. Hunger, 'Zehn unedierte byzantinische Beamtensiegel und in sonstigen Belegen', *Studies in Byzantine Sigillography* 5 (1998), pp. 1–28, no. 8; Wassiliou and Seibt, *Bleisiegel* II, no. 11; Šandrovskaja and Seibt, *Ermitage*, p. 68, n. 46 and 48.
75 V. Laurent, 'Sceaux byzantins inedits', *Byzantinische Zeitschrift* 33 (1933), pp. 331–61, at p. 347; Laurent, *Corpus* II, no. 341; *DO Seals* 4.11.14; Campagnolo-Pothitou and Cheynet, *Geneva*, no. 46; and Zacos, *Lead Seals* II, no. 681b.
76 *PBW* Theodoros 20127.

Chapter 3

1 Partial list of civilian bureaucrats attending the Patriarchal Synod of 1029. G. Ficker, *Erlasse des Patriarchen von Konstantinopel Alexios Studites* (Kiel, 1911), pp. 20–1.
2 Constantine VII, *De Ceremoniis*, pp. 3–5.
3 Salač, A., *Novella constitutio saec. XI medii, quae est de schola iuris Constantinopoli constituenda et legum custode creando, a Ioanne Mauropode conscripta, a Constantino IX Monomacho promulgata. Textum De Lagardianum latine vertit, notis* illustravit (Prague, 1954); translated in Z. Chitwood, *Byzantine Legal Culture and the Roman Legal Tradition, 867–1056* (Cambridge, 2017), pp. 193–203.
4 Of course, some might argue that government moulded the more weak-willed emperors in its image.
5 At no point do I intend to give the impression that the jurisdictional divisions were as neat as the sub-chapters of this book. I have included the *eparch* of Constantinople in the section of the government of the capital, but he also chaired a tribunal for example. I have tried to place each official into the section in which I believe the majority of their duties fell.
6 The exceptions were the *chartoularioi* of the *sakellion* and the *vestiarion*. The earliest recorded form of *sekreton* is as *secretarium*, a tribunal for investigating Christian activities dated to 303. It was later applied to courts, and to the imperial *consistorium*, and from this could be used as a blanket term for the elite bureaucrats of the empire. Kazhdan, A. 'Sekreton', *The Oxford Dictionary of Byzantium* (Oxford, 1991).
7 G. T. Dennis, *Three Byzantine Military Treatises* (Washington, DC, 2009), p. 217.
8 Hendy, *Studies*, pp. 410–12. For a discussion of the process by which the departments and sub-departments were transformed into the *sekreta* of the Middle Byzantine period, likely in the reign of Heraclius (610–41), see Haldon, *Seventh Century*, pp. 183–94. Cf. N. Oikonomides, 'The Role of the Byzantine State in the Economy', *The Economic History of Byzantium*, ed. A. E. Laiou (Washington, DC, 2002), pp. 988–95. For a discussion of the following period, see Winkelmann, *Rang- und Ämterstruktur*.
9 J. B. Bury, *The Imperial Administrative System in the Ninth Century with a Revised Text of the Kletorologion of Philotheos* (London, 1911), pp. 78–83.
10 The earliest record of *chartoularioi* dates to 326. The eariest *chartoularios* attached to a *logothesion* is from the early seventh century.
11 This was a far cry from their origins in the late Roman period where they had been important officials on the staff of the praetorian prefects. Kazhdan, A. 'Kankellarios', *The Oxford Dictionary of Byzantium* (Oxford, 1991).

12 Oikonomides, 'L'évolution', p. 140; R. Guilland, 'Études sur l'histoire administrative de l'empire byzantin'. Le logariaste, ὁ λογαριαστής; le grand logariaste, ὁ μέγας λογαριασ τής', *Jahrbuch der Österreichischen Byzantinistik* 18 (1969), pp. 101–8.
13 P. Lemerle, ed., *Actes de Kutlumus* (Paris, 1945–1946), no. 5.
14 Oikonomides, 'Role of the Byzantine State', p. 994.
15 Oikonomides, *Listes*, p. 107.
16 DO BZS.1955.1.2923.
17 For the early development of the post of the *sakellarios*, see Haldon, *Seventh Century*, pp. 183–6. Cf. Oikonomides, 'Role of the Byzantine State', pp. 988–9. Contrary to Bury, *Administrative System*, pp. 84–6.
18 Oikonomides, *Listes*, p. 312.
19 Ibid., p. 113.
20 Ibid., p. 269.
21 The percentages for the total number of seals belonging to the *sakellarioi* are as follows: last third of the tenth century, 48.3, first third of the eleventh century, 41.4, middle third of the eleventh century 3.5, final third of the eleventh century, 4.3, first third of the twelfth century, 2.6.
22 Oikonomides, *Listes*, pp. 113–15.
23 Theophanes, *Chronographia*, pp. 367, 369. This particular reference is actually to a financial official serving in the caliphate, Sergios son of Mansur, under 'Abd al-Malik. The first Byzantine recorded was Theodotos, *genikos logothetes* in 694/5. For the history of the *genikon* and the officials who worked there see Oikonomides, *Listes*, p. 313; Bury, *Administrative System*, pp. 86–90; F. Dölger, *Beiträge zur Geschichte der byzantinischen Finanzverwaltung, besonders des 10. und 11. Jahrhunderts* (Leipzig, 1927), pp. 19–21, 47; D. A. Xanalatos, *Beiträge zur Wirtschafts- und Sozialgeschichte Makedoniens im Mittelalter, hauptsächlich auf Grund der Briefe des Erzbischofs Theophylaktos von Achrida* (Speyer a. Rh.,1937), p. 40; G. Millet, 'L'origine du logothète général', *Mélanges d'histoire du Moyen Age offerts à M. F. Lot* (Paris, 1925), pp. 563–73; E. Stein, 'Untersuchungen zum Staatsrecht des Bas-Empire', *Zeitschrift der Savigny-Stifung für Rechtsgeschichte, Romanistische Abteilung* 41 (1920), pp. 195–251, at pp. 33–4; R. J. Guilland, *Les logothetes: études sur l'histoire administrative de l'Empire byzantin* (Paris, 1971), pp. 11–24.
24 Hendy, *Studies*, p. 411, with further bibliography.
25 Dölger, *Finanzverwaltung*, pp. 14ff, 47.
26 Oikonomides, *Listes*, pp. 113–15. For the *megaloi chartoularioi tou sekretou*, see ibid., p. 313; Dölger, *Finanzverwaltung*, pp. 101–3; N. G. Svoronos, *Recherches sur le cadastre byzantin et la fiscalité aux 11. et 12. siècles: le cadastre de Thèbes* (Athens, 1959), p. 58; for the *chartoularioi ton arklon*, see Hendy, *Studies*, p. 429; Dölger, *Finanzverwaltung*, pp. 69, 103; for the *epoptai ton thematon*, see Oikonomides, *Listes*, p. 313; Dölger, *Finanzverwaltung*, pp. 79–80; for the *kometes hydaton*, see Oikonomides, *Listes*, p. 314; Bury, *Administrative System*, p. 87; Dölger, *Finanzverwaltung*, p. 90, n. 9; Mentioned in Attaleiates, *History*, p. 167; for the *oikistikos* see below; for the *o tes kouratias*, see Oikonomides, *Listes*, p. 313; for the *komes tes lamias*, see Oikonomides, *Listes*, p. 314; J. Haldon, 'Comes horreorum – komēs tēs Lamias?', *Byzantine and Modern Greek Studies* 10 (1986), pp. 203–9; for the *dioiketes*, see Oikonomides, *Listes*, p. 313; Dölger, *Finanzverwaltung*, p. 70; Svoronos, *Cadastre*, p. 56; for the *komentianos*, see Bury, *Administrative System*, p. 90. For the provincial officials and their function, see Oikonomides, 'Role of the Byzantine State', p. 991.

27 E. Stepanova, 'New Seals from Sudak', *Studies in Byzantine Sigillography* 6 (1999), no. 19.
28 Oikonomides, *Listes*, p. 269.
29 DO BZS.1958.106.5505.
30 Note judge of the Hippodrome, not the more prestigious judge of the Velum like the *megaloi chartoularioi*.
31 Stephen, *protospatharios epi tou Chrysotriklinou* and *protonotarios* of the *genikon*, V. Laurent, *Corpus* II, no. 387; Leo, *protospatharios* and *protonotarios tou genikou*, *Peira* 61.6.
32 No title: Harvard Art Museums 1951.31.5.2696; Laurent, *Corpus* II, no. 395; J.-C. Cheynet, T. Gökyıldırım and V. Bulgurlu, *Les sceaux byzantins du Musée archéologique d'Istanbul* (Istanbul, 2012), no. 2.139 *Spatharios*: Laurent, *Corpus* II, no. 392. *Spatharokandidatos*: Campagnolo-Pothitou and Cheynet, *Geneva*, no. 125; Laurent, *Corpus* II, no. 396. *Protospatharios*: Harvard Art Museums 1951.31.5.3115.
33 E. McGeer, J. W. Nesbitt and N. Oikonomides, *Catalogue of Byzantine Seals at Dumbarton Oaks and in the Fogg Museum of Art, 4: The East* (Washington, DC, 2001), no. 22.22; J. W. Nesbitt, 'The Office of the *oikistikos*: Five Seals in the Dumbarton Oaks Collection', *Dumbarton Oaks Papers* 29 (1975), p. 342, no. 4.
34 Oikonomides, *Listes*, pp. 113, 155, 233.
35 Ibid., p. 273.
36 Nesbitt, '*Oikistikos*', p. 343.
37 For example, the *chrysobull* of Constantine IX Monomachos for his Nea Mone, Miklosich and Müller, V no. 2, p. 4.
38 Nesbitt, '*Oiksitikos*', pp. 343–4.
39 None, I. Jordanov, *Corpus of Byzantine Seals from Bulgaria*, 3 vols (Sofia, 2003–9), vol. 3, no. 834; *Spatharios*, Cheynet et al., *Istanbul* no. 2.143; *Protospatharios*, *DO Seals* 4.1.17, Nesbitt '*Oikistikos*', no. 2; *Vestes*, W. Seibt and M. L. Zarnitz, *Das byzantinische Bleisiegel als Kunstwerk: Katalog zur Ausstellung* (Vienna, 1997), no. 1.2.6; *Protovestes*, Nesbitt, '*Oikistikos*', no. 4.
40 Nesbitt, '*Oikistikos*', no. 1.
41 Ibid., no. 5. The Dumbarton Oaks seal is damaged, but likely matches a seal recorded in G. Schlumberger, *Sigillographie de l'Empire byzantin* (Paris, 1884), p. 557, in the name of David. Nesbitt, '*Oikistikos*', p. 343.
42 Nesbitt, '*Oikistikos*', p. 343.
43 Ibid., no. 4; B. A. Pančenko, *Kollekcii Russkago Archeologičeskago Instituta v Konstantinopolě: Katalog molivdovulov* (Sofia, 1908), p. 50; Laurent, *Corpus* II, no. 400; *PBW* Stephanos 20169, Michael 20285.
44 Oikonomides, *Listes*, p. 115.
45 Hendy, *Studies*, p. 412; Bury, *Administrative System*, p. 90.
46 Constantine VII, *De Ceremoniis*, p. 698.
47 Oikonomides, *Listes*, p. 314; Bury, *Administrative System*, pp. 90–1; Dölger, *Finanzverwaltung*, pp. 21–2, 60; Xanalatos, *Beiträge*, pp. 44–52; Glykatzi-Ahrweiler, 'Recherches', pp. 10, 43; I. Ševčenko, 'Poems on the Deaths of Leo VI and Constantine VII in the Madrid Manuscript of Scylitzes', *Dumbarton Oaks Papers* 23/24 (1969/70), p. 216; Guilland, *Logothetes*, pp. 25–31.
48 J. Haldon, *Byzantine Praetorians: An Administrative, Institutional and Social Survey of the Opsikion and Tagmata, c. 580–900* (Bonn, 1984), pp. 314–18.
49 Oikonomides, *Listes*, pp. 114–15. For the *chartoularioi ton thematon*, see Glykatzi-Ahrweiler, 'Recherches', p. 43; Dölger, *Finanzverwaltung*, pp. 21f. For the *optiones*, see Oikonomides, *Listes*, p. 314; Bury, *Administrative System*, p. 91; Jones, *Later Roman*

Empire II, pp. 626–7. Although not working in Constantinople, and therefore not strictly covered by this study, it is interesting to note that the *chartoularioi* of the themes and the tagmata are the only such officials not in charge of a department to appear in the *Escorial Taktikon* suggesting their importance, and by extension that of the *sekreton tou stratiotikou* to the running of the empire.

50 DO BZS.1955.1.1576.
51 Hendy, *Studies*, p. 413; Chronicon Paschale, ed. L. Dindorf, 2 vols (Bonn, 1832), p. 721.
52 Laurent, *Corpus* II, no. 557.
53 DO BZS.1958.106.3958.
54 Oikonomides, *Listes*, pp. 311–12; Bury, *Administrative System*, pp. 91–3; Dölger, *Finanzverwaltung*, pp. 22–3; F. Dölger, *Byzantinische Diplomatik* (Ettal, 1956), p. 61; L. Bréhier, *Les institutions de l'empire byzantin* (Paris, 1949), pp. 300, 328; D. A. Miller, 'The Logothete of the Drome in the Middle Byzantine Period', *Byzantion* 36 (1966), pp. 438–70; Hendy, *Studies*, p. 608 and n. 240.
55 Oikonomides, 'Role of the Byzantine State', p. 993.
56 Laurent, *Corpus* II, pp. 195–261 for a catalogue of seals demonstrating this point.
57 Wassiliou and Seibt, *Bleisiegel*, p. 84.
58 Hendy, *Studies*, pp. 607–8.
59 Oikonomides, *Listes*, pp. 117, 311–12.
60 Ibid., p. 273.
61 Laurent, *Corpus* II, no. 435.
62 Oikonomides described the *logothetes tou dromou* as the 'logothetes par excellence'. Oikonomides, *Listes*, p. 311.
63 Constantine VII, *De Ceremoniis*, p. 520.
64 Ibid., pp. 138, 568.
65 Ficker, *Alexios Studites*, p. 19. This still placed him in the top third of the contemporary hierarchy. *PBW* Eustathios 116.
66 *PBW* Niketas 107.
67 For John, see Zonaras, *Epitome Historiarum* III, pp. 649–50 and DO BZS.1947.2.1308. For Niketas Xylinites, see J. W. Nesbitt and N. Oikonomides, *Catalogue of Byzantine Seals at Dumbarton Oaks and in the Fogg Museum of Art, 2: South of the Balkans, the Islands, South of Asia Minor* (Washington, DC, 1994), no. 44.9; DO BZS.1958.106.3238, and Skylitzes, *Synopsis of Histories*, p. 479.
68 Skylitzes, *Synopsis of Histories*, p. 480.
69 Laurent, *Corpus* II, no. 483.
70 J. Haldon, 'Theory and Practice in Tenth-Century Military Administration: Chapters II, 44 and 45 of the Book of Ceremonies', *Travaux et Mémoires* 13 (2000), p. 232.
71 Oikonomides, *Listes*, p. 121.
72 Haldon, *Seventh Century*, p. 181; Hendy, *Studies*, p. 412; Bury, *Administrative System*, pp. 84–5.
73 Oikonomides, *Listes*, p. 121. For the relationship between the central bureaus and the provinces, and between the representatives of different departments in the themes, see Glykatzi-Ahrweiler, 'Recherches', p. 43.
74 Oikonomides, *Listes*, pp. 121, 271.
75 DO BZS.1958.106.4734.
76 Laurent, *Corpus* II, no. 806.
77 DO BZS.1955.1.2479, BZS.1955.1.2480, BZS.1955.1.2481, BZS.1955.1.2482, and BZS.1955.1.2483.
78 DO BZS.1955.1.1574.

79 DO BZS.1958.106.2240.
80 *Spatharokandidatos*, Laurent, *Corpus* II, no. 810. *Protospatharioi*, Jordanov, *Bulgaria* 3, no. 885; Laurent, *Corpus* II, no. 812, *PBW* Methodios 20102; DO BZS.1958.106.5145. No title, Zacos, *Lead Seals* II, no. 710, Laurent, *Corpus* II, no. 811, Cheynet et al., *Istanbul*, no. 2.141, DO 1958.106.2240, *PBW* Stephanos 20174.
81 Oikonomides, *Listes*, p. 121.
82 Hendy, *Studies*, p. 412; Bury, *Administrative System*, pp. 95–7; Haldon, *Seventh Century*, p. 181.
83 Bury, *Administrative System*, pp. 95–7; Dölger, *Finanzverwaltung*, pp. 27–31; J. Ebersolt, 'Sur les fonctions et les dignités du Vestiarium byzantin', in *Mélanges Diehl, II, Histoire* (Paris, 1930), pp. 83–4; L. Bréhier, *Les institutions de l'empire byzantine* (Paris, 1970), p. 267; Oikonomides, *Listes*, p. 316.
84 Constantine VII, *De Ceremoniis*, pp. 672, 676.
85 Oikonomides, *Listes*, p. 121. For the *archon tes charages* who was likely synonymous with the *chrysepsetes*, see Hendy, *Studies*, p. 427, n. 245; Oikonomides, *Listes*, p. 316; Bury, *Administrative System*, pp. 96; Dölger, *Finanzverwaltung*, p. 28. For the *exartistes*, see Oikonomides, *Listes*, p. 316; Bury, *Administrative System*, p. 97. For the *chosbaitai*, see Oikonomides, *Listes*, p. 316; Constantine VII, *De Ceremoniis*, pp. 234, 269, 344.
86 Laurent, *Corpus* II, no. 704.
87 Oikonomides, *Listes*, p. 271.
88 Ibid., p. 123.
89 Hendy, *Studies*, p. 411.
90 Haldon, *Seventh Century*, p. 182; Bury, *Administrative System*, pp. 98–9.
91 E. Stein, *Studien zur Geschichte des byzantinischen Reiches vornehmlich unter den Kaisern Justinus II. u. Tiberius Constantinus* (Stuttgart, 1919), pp. 149–50; Dölger, *Finanzverwaltung*, pp. 19–20, 35–9; and Hendy, *Studies*, pp. 628–9.
92 For the history of the *eidikon*, see Hendy, *Studies*, 412; Oikonomides, *Listes*, pp. 316–7; Bury, *Administrative System*, pp. 98–100; Dölger, *Finanzverwaltung*, pp. 35–9; Bréhier, *Institutions*, pp. 267–8. Bury argues that despite the name of the treasury, that the *eidikon* was not related to the Late Antique *res privata*, but that the term might derive from εἴδη, a term used to mean taxes in kind. Bury, *Administrative System*, pp. 98–9. It is possible to imagine a situation where the treasury which held taxes paid in kind would take over the responsibility for housing the products of imperial workshops, and eventually management of the workshops themselves.
93 Lemerle, 'Roga et rente', pp. 95–6; Oikonomides, *Listes*, p. 316, n. 170.
94 Oikonomides, *Listes*, p. 317. In the tenth century it also held fake uniforms used for spies working in the Arab lands on the eastern border.
95 See Haldon, 'Theory and Practice'.
96 Haldon, *Byzantine Praetorians*, pp. 316–17, 320–2.
97 Laurent, *Corpus* II, no. 612.
98 Of these *epi tou eidikou logou* is the most descriptive, the one in charge of the accounts of the *eidikon*.
99 *Protospatharios*, Konstantopoulos, Νομισματικοῦ Μουσείου, no. 513; Laurent, *Corpus* II, no. 620; *patrikios* and *hypatos*, Laurent, *Corpus* II, no. 616; *vestes*, Konstantopoulos, Νομισματικοῦ Μουσείου, no. 340; Laurent *Corpus* II, no. 618 and no. 617; *vestarches*, Laurent, *Corpus* II, no. 619.
100 Miklosich-Müller, 5, no. 1, p. 1. dated to 1045 records that the *eidikos* Eustathios held the dignity of *vestarches*.
101 Zacos, *Lead Seals* II, no. 1053.

102 Laurent, *Corpus* II, no. 624, Konstantopoulos, Νομισματικοῦ Μουσείου, no. 597a, *PBW* Ioannes 20392.
103 Campagnolo-Pothitou and Cheynet, *Geneva*, no. 41.
104 For the growth, distribution and uses of crown estates, see J. D. Howard-Johnston, 'Crown Lands and the Defence of Imperial Authority in the Tenth and Eleventh Centuries', *Byzantinische Forschungen* 21 (1995), pp. 75–100. For a different approach, based on clients and tribute rather than estates, see C. Holmes, *Basil II and the Governance of Empire* (Oxford, 2005), pp. 373–7.
105 See, for example, Howard-Johnston, 'Crown Lands', pp. 93–4. They could also be distributed to loyal servants or foreign magnates and rulers entering the empire. While this process does not directly concern us here, once the lands passed out of state hands our bureaucrats ceased to manage them, it is further indication of the importance of crown lands and the efficient management thereof. Ibid., pp. 94–7.
106 *DO Seals* 4.12.2
107 The name of the bureau was also occasionally shortened by omitting *oikon*. Oikonomides, 'L'évolution', pp. 138–9. W. Seibt, 'Prosopographische Konsequenzen aus der Umdatierung von Grumel, Regestes 933 (Patriarch Eustathios anstelle von Eustratios)', *Jahrbuch der Österreichischen Byzantinistik* 22 (1973), pp. 103–15, at pp. 108–9. For the appearance of *oikonomos*, see G. A. Ralles and M. Potles, Σύνταγμα τῶν θείων καὶ ἱερῶν κανόνων, 6 vols (Athens 1852–1859, repr. 1966), at vol. V, p. 364; Dölger, *Finanzverwaltung*, pp. 40–1, believed that the *megas oikonomos* was the successor of the *megas kourator* as superintendent of the crownlands, the two terms being synonyms. While this is certainly true, it does not explain why the crownlands would be termed *euageis oikoi*, or account for the *ephoros*.
108 For *chartoularioi* and *notarioi*, see Oikonomides, *Listes*, pp. 61, 183, 197; *Peira* 15.12; Oikonomides, 'L'évolution', p. 138. For the remainder see the following pages.
109 Early *protospatharioi*: Seibt and Zarnitz, *Kunstwerk*, no. 2.1.7, Speck, *Berlin* I, no. 114; *DO Seals* 4.11.2, R. M. Harrison, *Excavations at Saraçhane in Istanbul* I (Washington, DC and Princeton, NJ, 1986), no. 738. Later seals: Zacos, *Lead Seals* II, nos. 881 and 469; DO BZS.1958.106.1443; DO BZS.1958.106.3243; DO BZS.1958.106.5730; Zacos, *Lead Seals* II, no. 882.
110 Oikonomides, 'L'évolution', pp. 138, 140; Oikonomides, 'Role of the Byzantine State', p. 995. For the tax status of the *euageis oikoi*, see *Peira* 9.7 and 15.12.
111 George Kedrenos, *Historiarum Compendium*, ed. I. Bekker, 2 vols (Bonn, 1838, 1839), at vol. II, p. 645; Zonaras, *Epitome Historiarum* III, p. 670. See also, N. Oikonomides, 'St. George of the Mangana, Maria Skleraina and the "Malyj Sion" of Novgorod', *Dumbarton Oaks Papers* 34–35 (1980–81), pp. 239–46.
112 Zacos, *Lead Seals* II, no. 562.
113 Oikonomides, 'L'évolution', p. 136. See P. Lemerle, A. Guillou and N. Svoronos, *Actes de Lavra. Première partie: Des origines à 1204, Archives de l'Athos V* (Paris, 1970), no. 11.
114 Oikonomides, 'Role of the Byzantine State', p. 992; 'L'évolution', p. 136. See also, Dölger, *Finanzwaltung*, pp. 43–5 and Guilland, *Logothetes*, p. 95.
115 Previously to Basil's reform lands which ended up as possessions of the fisc had been sold off as quickly as possible at bargain prices. Oikonomides, 'L'évolution', pp. 136–7. I reject the idea that the *epi ton oikeiakon* was in some way a replacement for the *eidikos*. Not only are Oikonomides's arguments more convincing, but the sigillographic evidence discussed earlier shows that the *sekreton tou eidikou* was alive and well at the point when these changes were taking place.

116 The Dumbarton Oaks Collection alone includes 192 seals once owned by an *epi ton oikeiakon*.
117 These also account for a tiny fraction – two – of the seals bearing the inscription *epi ton oikeiakon* in our period.
118 Codice Diplomatico Barese IV, no. 21, DO BZS.1955.1.1931.
119 Campagnolo-Pothitou and Cheynet, *Geneva*, no. 47.
120 Laurent, *Orghidan*, no. 79; Zacos, *Lead Seals* II, no. 629.
121 *Vestes*, Zacos, *Lead Seals* II, no. 532; I. G. Leontiades, 'Acht Siegel aus dem Museum für Byzantinische Kultur in Thessalonike', *Studies in Byzantine Sigillography* 9 (2006), no. 40; and DO BZS.1955.1.2450. *Vetarches*, Jordanov, *Bulgaria* 3, no. 833 (Sofia Archaeological Museum 50); Šandrovskaja, 'Sfragistika', no. 725; *Magistros*, Zacos, *Lead Seals* II, no. 510.
122 Wassiliou-Seibt and Seibt, *Sammlung Zarnitz Museum Kestner*, no. 65.
123 *Protospatharios*, Zacos, *Lead Seals* II, nos. 562 and 1051, Cheynet, *Theodorides*, no. 54. No title, DO BZS.1958.106.4924 and Jordanov, *Bulgaria* 3, no. 832.
124 Schlumberger, *Sigillographie*, p. 586; Laurent, *Corpus* II, no. 1139; Šandrovskaja and Seibt, *Eremitage*, p. 50, n. 169; Cheynet-Vannier, 'Argyroi', p. 79.
125 Haldon, *Seventh Century*, p. 183, n. 32.
126 Oikonomides, 'Role of the Byzantine State', p. 994; Dölger, *Finanzverwaltung*, p. 40.
127 DO BZS.1958.106.5509.
128 Rather more have survived that were owned by the managers of provincial estates.
129 Oikonomides, 'L'évolution', p. 138.
130 Sometimes known as simply the *ephoros*, or as a department as the *sekreton tou ephorou*. Oikonomides, 'L'évolution', p. 138; Dölger, *Finanzverwaltung*, p. 45; Bury, *Administrative System*, pp. 100–102.
131 *Patrikios*, Laurent, *Corpus* II, no. 1135; *Vestes*, Laurent, *Orghidan*, no. 309; *Magistros*, Cheynet 'Par St. George', p. 121; and *vestes*, Laurent, *Corpus* II, no. 1136; *Proedros*, Campagnolo-Pothitou and Cheynet, *Geneva*, no. 41 and Laurent, *Corpus* II, no. 1138.
132 DO BZS.1955.1.2094.
133 *Protonotarioi*, Laurent, *Corpus* II, nos. 1142 and 1141; *Domestikos*, Campagnolo-Pothitou and Cheynet, *Geneva*, no. 33 and Laurent, *Corpus* II, no. 1140. Imperial *notarioi*, Schlumberger, *Sigillographie*, p. 586; Laurent, *Corpus* II, no. 1139; Cheynet-Vannier, 'Argyroi', p. 79; Šandrovskaja and Seibt, *Eremitage*, p. 50, n. 169; J. Lefort, N. Oikonomides, D. Papachryssanthou, H. Métrévéli and V. Kravari, *Actes d'Iviron, Actes de l'Athos XIV and XVI* (Paris, 1985–1990), vol. 2, no. 35, p. 102 (c. 1062); and *Actes de Docheiariou, Archives de l'Athos XIII*, ed. N. Oikonomides (Paris, 1984), no. 1, p. 53 (dated 1037).
134 List of officials from the chrysobull for the Nea Mone on Chios issued by Constantine IX Monomachos (1045). Miklosich-Müller 5, no. 2, p. 4.
135 H. Ahrweiler, *Byzance et la mer: la marine de guerre, la politique, et les institutions maritimes de byzance aux VIIe-XVe siècles* (Paris, 1966), pp. 200–2.
136 Oikonomides, *Listes*, pp. 121–3.
137 DO BZS.1958.106.3613.
138 For a discussion of the office of *epi tou kanikleiou*, see Oikonomides, *Listes*, p. 311; Bury, *Administrative System*, p. 117; Dölger, *Diplomatik*, pp. 50–65; Dölger and Karayannopulos, *Byzantinische Urkundenlehre. 1, Die Kaiserurkunden* (München, 1968), pp. 62, 126, 131–2.
139 Oikonomides, *Listes*, p. 271.

140 In *Peira* 9.10 an unnamed *epi tou kanikleiou* acted as a judge. This is not evidence that the *epi tou kanikleiou* had regular judicial duties, but that any official could be ordered to act as a judge at the whim of the emperor.
141 Bury, *Administrative System*, p. 117.
142 Oikonomides, *Listes*, p. 311. Being a member of the imperial staff brought access to great wealth as well as power. As a part of the ceremonies during which men received titles from the emperor they had to distribute customary gifts to the members of the imperial household and palace staff among others. Philotheos records that the *epi tou kanikleiou* received 32 *nomismata* from every new *magistros*, 16 *nomismata* from *patrikioi* and 8 from each *anthypatos*. Oikonomides, *Listes*, p. 95.
143 Within a decade of John's time *vestes* would be slip further down the rankings into the middle of the hierarchy.
144 Michael Psellos describing service in the *asekreteion*. K. Sathas, Μεσαιωνική Βιβλιοθήκη 5. Μιχαὴλ Ψελλοῦ ἱστορικοὶ λόγοι, ἐπιστολαὶ καὶ ἄλλα ἀνέκδοτα (Paris, 1876), pp. 248–9.
145 The structure of the *asekreteion* was outlined by Philotheos, Oikonomides, *Listes*, p. 123. I am inclined to agree with Oikonomides that the *notarioi* in this *sekreton* were not led by a *protonotarios* who was simply overlooked by Philotheos. The *notarioi* were technically of the same function as the *asekretai*, just of a different grade. The *protoasekretis* thus fulfilled the functions of the *protonotarios*. Oikonomides, *Listes*, p. 311, n. 130. For arguments to the contrary, see Dölger, *Byzantinische Urkundenlehre*, p. 125, n. 51 and Bury, *Administrative System*, p. 98.
146 DO BZS.1958.106.1450.
147 For the most recent study on the *protoasekretis* and the *asekretai*, see A. Gkoutzioukostas, 'Η εξέλιτξη του θεσμού των ἀσηκρῆτις και του πρωτοασηκρῆτις στο πλαίσιο της αυτοκρατορικής γραμματείας', *Βυζαντινά* 23 (2002–2003), pp. 47–93. The most significant pieces of older literature are, Oikonomides, *Listes*, p. 310; Bury, *Administrative System*, pp. 96–8; Dölger, *Diplomatik*, pp. 62–4 and *Urkundenlehre*, p. 124; Bréhier, *Institutions*, pp. 167–8.
148 *Le Liber pontificalis*, ed. L. Duchesne, 3 vols (Paris 1886–1957), 1.452.12. Laurent, *Corpus* II, nos. 3–4. Oikonomides, *Listes*, p. 310; Gkoutzioukostas, A., *Ο θεσμός του κοιαίστωρα του ιερού παλατίου : η γένεση, οι αρμοδιότητες και η εξέλιξή του* (Εταιρεία Βυζαντινών ερευνών 18) (Thessaloniki, 2001), pp. 130–1.
149 Dölger, *Diplomatik*, p. 62; Dölger and Karayannopulos, *Byzantinische Urkundenlehre*, p. 65.
150 Oikonomides, *Listes*, p. 310. *Peira* 9.10 records that the *protoasekretis* Peter acted as a judge. Knowing the future responsibilities of the office, see next section, it is tempting to view this as an early example of the *protoasekretis* assuming judicial functions. However, this was the same case mentioned earlier where the other judge was an anonymous *epi tou kanikleiou* and, like him, it is more likely that Peter was selected by the emperor to judge this case as part of an ad hoc arrangement.
151 DO BZS.1958.106.2416 (Constantine), DO BZS.1958.106.1155 (Theo…), Harvard Art Museums 1951.31.5.3082 (Eustathios), DO BZS.1955.1.1487 (John), DO BZS.1958.106.1889 (Theodore), Harvard Art Museums 1951.31.5.2659 (Konst…), DO BZS.1958.106.1450 (Leo Chrysobalantites), and (Constantine) I. Koltsida-Makri, *Byzantina molyvdoboulla sylloges Orphanide–Nikolaïde Nomismatikou Mouseiou Athenon* (Athens, 1996), no. 101.
152 *Protospatharios*: DO BZS.1958.106.2416, DO BZS.1955.1.1487, DO BZS.1958.106.1889. *Patrikios* and *protospatharios*: Koltsida-Makre, *Orphanide–Nikolaïde*, no. 101, DO BZS.1958.106.1155.

153 *Peira* 14.1.
154 DO BZS.1958.106.5402.
155 Oikonomides, *Listes*, p. 310 with bibliography on the early *asekretai*.
156 For discussion of the date, see *ODB* and Oikonomides, *Listes*, p. 310, with reference to Procopius, who felt the need to explain the function of the *asekretai* to his readers. Procopius, *Secret History*, 14.4, *Wars* 2.7. For early seals of the *asekretai*, see Laurent, *Corpus* II, nos. 9–13. For the *Kathisma*, see R. Guilland, *Études de topographie de Constantinople byzantines*, 2 vols (Amsterdam, 1969). See also, Dölger, *Urkundenlehre*, pp. 59–65.
157 DO BZS.1958.106.737 and BZS.1958.106.757.
158 For Christmas, see Oikonomides, *Listes*, pp. 169, 181, 189. For Easter, see pp. 203, 205. For a discussion of the sandaled-senate, see A. P. Kazhdan and M. McCormick, 'The Social World of the Byzantine Court', *Byzantine Court Culture from 829 to 1204*, ed. H. Maguire (Washington, DC, 1997), pp. 167–98, at pp. 180–1 and Oikonomides, *Listes*, p. 168, n. 147.
159 Elsewhere in *De Ceremoniis* the distinction between the *notarioi* in various departments is made clear with a discussion of 'the *asekretai* and *notarioi* of the *asekreteion* and those of the *sekreta*'. Constantine VII, *De Ceremoniis*, p. 575. Their official dress for important ceremonies was also recorded here, *kamisia* and *chlamyses* with purple *tablia*.
160 While it is possible that, as by 258 men I mean 258 distinct seal designs that there were fewer individual *asekretai*, one man possibly owning more than one seal during his career, there is no way to be certain of this, and I think that it is better to err on the side of caution rather than arbitrarily lump seals struck by men with the same first name together where there is no other indication of a unique identity such as a family name or rare iconographic choice.
161 Constantine VII, *De Ceremoniis*, p. 693.
162 Oikonomides, *Listes*, pp. 123, 311; Dölger, *Urkundenlehre*, p. 125; Bury, *Administrative System*, p. 98; Bréhier, *Institutions*, pp. 166–7.
163 Jordanov, *Bulgaria* 3, pp. 273–4.
164 Seibt, *Bleisiegel* I, no. 60.
165 For the most recent study of the office of *mystikos* with a discussion of the earlier literature, see A. Gkoutzioukostas, Το αξίωμα του μυστικού. Θεσμικά και προσωπογραφικά προβλήματα (Thessaloniki, 2011).
166 R. Guilland, 'Études sur l'Histoire administrative de l'empire byzantin. Le mystique, ὁ μυστικός', *Revue des études byzantines* 26, no. 1 (1968), pp. 279–96; Oikonomides, *Listes*, p. 324; Gkoutzioukostas, Το αξίωμα του μυστικού, pp. 57–64.
167 Oikonomides, *Listes*, pp. 249, 271.
168 For an early proponent of this argument, see Dölger, *Diplomatik*, p. 64. See also, Dölger and Karayannopulos, *Byzantinische Urkundenlehre*, p. 62; Guilland, 'Le mystique, ὁ μυστικός', pp. 279–96; Laurent, *Corpus* II, p. 50; A. Christophilopoulou, Το πολίτευμα και οι θεσμοί της βυζαντινής αυτοκρατορίας 324–1204. Κράτος, διοίκηση, οικονομία, κοινωνία (Athens, 2004), p. 384.
169 Oikonomides suggested that this was why the *mystikos* had not appeared in the *Kletorologion of Philotheos*, because he was either subordinate to or somehow linked to the *protoasekretis*, becoming independent by the time of the later *taktika*. Oikonomides, *Listes*, p. 324.
170 Oikonomides, *Listes*, p. 324; Oikonomides, 'St George of Mangana', pp. 239–46, at p. 245.

171 For the later evolution of the *mystikos*, particularly in the reign of Manuel I Komnenos (1143–1180), see P. Magdalino, 'The Not-So-Secret Functions of the Mystikos', *Revue des études byzantines* 42 (1984), pp. 228–40.
172 Constantine VII, *De Ceremoniis*, p. 587. During a different ceremony recorded earlier in the same document the *mystikos* stood alongside the *logothetes tou dromou*, the *raiktor*, the *protoasekretis* and the *protospatharioi* of the Chrysotriklinos. In this list I would suggest that it is the *logothetes* who was the odd man out, the rest falling under the label of household or palatine staff.
173 Gkoutzioukostas, *Η απονομή δικαιοσύνης στο Βυζάντιο*; A. Gkoutzioukostas, *To αξίωμα του μυστικού. Θεσμικά και προσωπογραφικά προβλήματα* (Thessalonike, 2011); A. Gkoutzioukostas, 'Administrative Structures of Byzantium During the 11th Century: Officials of the Imperial Secretariat and Administration of Justice', *Travaux et Mémoires* 21/2, ed. B. Flusin and J.-C. Cheynet (Paris, 2017), pp. 561–80, at pp. 567–9.
174 Given the bouncing around between departments and holding of multiple jobs in different *sekreta* that was a hallmark of the Byzantine system, I am not convinced that we can look at the other offices held by the *mystikoi* and deduce their area of specialization and responsibility. In the case of the *mystikoi* the seals are very little help in this regard as the majority only record the office of *mystikos*. Of those that mention another office two are judicial, one a straight judge (Wassiliou and Seibt, *Bleisiegel* II, no. 59), another a judge of the Velum (Harvard Art Museums 1951.31.5.2184), one palatine (Laurent, *Corpus* II, no. 121), and the final seal owner also served as *eparch* (Konstantopoulos, *Νομισματικού Μουσείου*, no. 415; Stavrakos, *Familiennamen*, no. 270; Laurent, *Corpus* II, no. 1033). Three different areas of authority all paired with the *mystikos*.
175 *Protospatharioi*, Harvard Art Museums 1951.31.5.2184; DO BZS.1958.106.1304; Wassiliou and Seibt, *Bleisiegel* II, no. 59, Laurent, *Corpus* II, no. 120, *PBW* Basileios 20174; Jordanov, *Bulgaria* 3 no. 739. *Patrikios*, Laurent, *Corpus* II, no. 121, *PBW* Ioannes 20275. *Vestes*, Wassiliou and Seibt, *Bleisiegel* II, no. 60, Laurent, *Corpus* II, no. 119, *PBW* Nikolaos 20151.
176 Demetrios Polemarchios, Kekaumenos, *Consilia et Narrationes* 29; Eustathios Romaios, Oikonomides, 'Peira', p. 172; Abramios, Ficker, *Alexios Stoudites*, p. 20. *PBW* Abramios 102.
177 Oikonomides, 'St. George of the Mangana', pp. 239–46.
178 *Actes de Saint Pantéléèmôn*, no. 5 (1057), pp. 58.
179 For dismissing and reassigning the *proto* prefix, see Dölger, *Diplomatik*, p. 64, n. 299. For equating *protomystikos* and *protoasekretis*, see Laurent, *les sceaux byzantins du Médaillier Vatican (Medagliere della Biblioteca Vaticana* 1) (Vatican, 1962), p. 113, nos. 2–3. For the *protomystikos* as the chief of the *mystoi*, see Gkoutzioukostas, 'Seals of Byzantine Officials Connected with the Administration of Justice', *Jahrbuch der Österreichischen Byzantinistik*, 62 (2012), p. 17.
180 Gkoutzioukostas, 'Administration of Justice', p. 17. *PBW* Konstantinos 20458.
181 For the Xeroi, see J.-C. Cheynet, 'Les Xèroi, administrateurs de l'Empire', *Studies in Byzantine Sigillography* 11 (2011), pp. 14–15. *PBW* Ioannes 433.
182 DO BZS.1958.106.5496.
183 H. Grégoire, *Recueil des inscriptions grecques-chrétiennes d'Asie Mineure. 1,* Paris 1922 (repr. Amsterdam 1968), no. 302.
184 Oikonomides, *Listes*, p. 271.
185 That the two offices were listed separately in the *Escorial Taktikon* debunks the theory expressed by Dölger and Karaiannopoulos that they were one and the

same. Dölger, *Diplomatik*, p. 64. For the most recent study on the *mystographoi*, see A. Gkoutzioukostas, 'Mystographos-Mystolektes', with a discussion of older scholarship.

186   A. Gkoutzioukostas, 'Some Remarks on *mystographos* and *Mystolektes*', in Ἠπειρόνδε *(Epeironde) Proceedings of the 10th International Symposium of Byzantine Sigillography (Ioannina, 1–3 October 2009)*, ed. Ch. Stavrakos and B. Papadopoulou (Ioanina, 2011), pp. 191–219, at pp. 197–9.

187   Ibid., p. 200.

188   The *Peira* notes that the *mystographos* judged a case, which led Oikonomides to conclude that he also had judicial duties. *Peira*, 7.15, Oikonomides, *Listes*, p. 325. There is really not enough evidence to conclude this with a certainty, and this is more likely to have been an example of the ad hoc granting of judicial power by the emperor to the *mystographos* than evidence for a regular duty. For a different take on the judicial functions of the *mystographos*, see P. Magdalino, 'Justice and Finance in the Byzantine State, Ninth to Twelfth Centuries', *Law and Society in Byzantium: Ninth-Twelfth Centurires*, ed. A. E. Laiou and D. Simon (Washington, DC, 1994), p. 104. For further discussion of the link between the *mystikos*, *mystographos* and *mystolektes*, see A. Gkoutzioukostas, Το αξίωμα του μυστικού. Θεσμικά και προσωπογραφικά προβλήματα (Thessaloniki, 2011), pp. 117–25, 127–31.

189   Basil and Ficker, *Alexios Stoudites*, p. 21, *PBW* Basileios 229; Nikephoros, Nea Mone Miklosich and Müller 5, no. 1, p. 1, *PBW* Nikephoros 229; Elpidios was, however, later promoted to *patrikios*, Dennis, *Orationes, Forenses et Acta*, p. 148.

190   Harvard Art Museums 1951.31.5.2229.

191   R. Morris, 'What Did the epi tôn deêseôn Actually Do?', in *La pétition à Byzance*, ed. D. Feissel and J. Gascou (Paris, 2004), pp. 125–40, at p. 126; Bury, *Administrative System*, pp. 77–8. Bréhier, *Institutions*, pp. 167, 226–7; Jones, *Later Roman Empire* I, pp. 367–68, 504–5; R. Guilland, 'Études sur l'histoire administrative de l'Empire byzantine: Le Maître des Requêtes', *Byzantion* 35 (1965), pp. 97–118; and Oikonomides, *Listes*, p. 322.

192   Morris, 'epi tôn deêseôn', pp. 130, 136–8.

193   Ibid., p. 135.

194   Ibid., p. 126.

195   J.-C. Cheynet and C. Morrisson, 'Lieux de trouvaille et circulation des sceaux', *Studies in Byzantine Sigillography* 2 (Washington, DC, 1990), pp. 105–36, at pp. 111, 118, 123.

196   Oikonomides, *Listes*, p. 322. The *epi ton deeseon*, as the *o tou deeseos*, was listed as a legal official by Philotheos. While I do not wish to contradict the Byzantiness's own definition of their offices, receiving, reviewing and answering petitions seems to fit better with our modern understanding of the chancery, or with those officials close to the emperor who also form a part of this chapter. Oikonomides, *Listes*, p. 107.

197   Laurent, *Corpus* II, no. 230. Seals also record the existence of provincial *epi ton deeseon*, but whether these were a permanent fixture of provincial life or were sent out from the capital, either periodically or in response to a particular petition, is unknown. Oikonomides, *Listes*, p. 322.

198   Oikonomides, *Listes*, p. 271.

199   C. Will, *Acta et scripta quae de controversiis ecclesiae graecae et latinae saeculo undecimo composita extant* (Leipzig and Marburg, 1861), pp. 165–6. An earlier document dated to 1029 tallies with the earlier seals recording as it does the presence of Leo *protospatharios* and *epi ton deeseon* and judge of the Hippodrome, Ficker, *Alexios Stoudites*, p. 21.

200   DO BZS.1958.106.1505.

201 Laurent thought that the *mystolektes* was a report writer and messenger for the chancery. He was followed in this opinion by Werner Seibt, Ermitage no. 11, and with slight modifications placing more emphasis on the emperor than the chancery by Gkoutzioukostas, 'Mystographos-Mystolektes', p. 202. Oikonomides and Magdalino argued that he was a judicial official. 'L'évolution', p. 54; Magdalino, 'Justice and Finance', pp. 93–115, at p. 104. While all of these arguments are based on very little evidence, the meaning of a title or a single document, it seems to me that the *mystolektes* was likely an elite messenger, perhaps with scribal duties attached, and thus he finds his home in a discussion of the secretarial officers of the state.
202 Michael Psellos describing service in the *asekreteion*. Sathas, Μεσαιωνικὴ Βιβλιοθήκη 5, p. 249.
203 I have already discussed the gifts given to the *epi tou kanikleiou*. The *protoasekretis* received twenty-four *nomismata* from *stratelates* of the themes, six from every *hypatos* and *dishypatos*. Oikonomides, *Listes*, pp. 89, 91.
204 Ceremony for appointing a new eparch. *Constantine Porphyrogennetos: The Book of Ceremonies*, trans. A. Moffatt and M. Tall (Leiden and Boston, 2012), p. 264.
205 For the revival, see P. Magdalino, ed., 'Constantine V and the Middle Age of Constantinople', in *Studies on the History and Topography of Byzantine Constantinople* (Aldershot, 2007); P. Magdalino, 'Constantinople and the Outside World', in *Strangers to Themselves: The Byzantine Outsider*, ed. D. C. Smythe (Aldershot, 2000), pp. 149–62.
206 Magdalino, 'Constantinople and the Outside World', p. 151; D. Ostler, 'From Periphery to Center: The Transformation of Late Roman Self-Definition in the Seventh Century', in *Shifting Frontiers in Late Antiquity*, eds R. W. Mathisen and H. S. Sivan (Aldershot, 1996), pp. 93–101; J. Haldon, *The Empire That Would Not Die*, pp. 146, 194; and P. Magdalino, 'Byzantium=Constantinople', in *A Companion to Byzantium*, ed. L. James (Malden, MA, 2010), pp. 43–54.
207 Hendy, *Studies*, pp. 561–4; Laiou and Morrisson, *The Byzantine Economy*, pp. 130–42.
208 Michael Attaleiates, *Diataxis*, trans. A.-M. Talbot, '*Attaleiates: Rule* of Michael Attaleiates for His Almshouse in Rhaidestos and for the Monastery of Christ Panoiktirmon in Constantinople', in *Byzantine Monastic Foundation Documents: A Complete Translation of the Surviving Founders' Typika and Testaments*, eds J. Thomas and A. Constantinides Hero, vol. 1 (Washington, DC, 2000), p. 333. For original Greek, see Michael Attaleiates, *Diataxis*, ed. and trans. P. Gautier, 'La Diataxis de Michel Attaliate', *Revue des études byzantines* 39 (1981), pp. 19–20. Attaleiates was, as his name implies, almost certainly from Attaleia, and thus a Byzantine. He was alien to Constantinople, but still a Byzantine. His attitude towards the capital speaks volumes about the Byzantine conception of Constantinople and its place in the imperial order.
209 For the ceremony surrounding the appointment of the *demarchs*, see Constantine VII, *De Ceremoniis*, pp. 269–71.
210 Oikonomides, *Listes*, p. 271.
211 Liudprand, *Antapodosis*, 5.21.
212 Skylitzes, *Synopsis of Histories*, XIII.7, p. 257; Leon the Deacon, *Leonis diaconi Caloënsis Historiae libri decem*, ed. C. B. Hase (Bonn, 1828), Book III.7; Constantine VII, *De Ceremoniis*, pp. 435–9.
213 See A. Kaldellis, *The Byzantine Republic: People and Power in New Rome* (Cambridge, MA, 2015), esp. pp. 118–64; D. Krallis, '"Democratic" Action in Eleventh-Century

Byzantium: Michael Attaleiates' "Republicanism" in Context', *Viator* 40, no. 2 (2009), pp. 35–53.

214 For the background of Michael IV, see Psellos, *Chronographia*, IV.10; Skylitzes, *Synopsis of Histories*, XVIII.17, pp. 389–90; for the overthrow of Michael V and the involuntary elevation of Theodora, see Psellos, *Chronographia*, V.16, Attaleiates, *History*, pp. 18–29; Skylitzes, *Synopsis of Histories*, XX, pp. 417–21; for the revolt of Tornikios, see Psellos, *Chronographia*, VI.104–8; Attaleiates, *History*, pp. 40–9; Skylitzes, *Synopsis of Histories*, XXI.8, pp. 439–40; for the coup against Michael VI, see Psellos, *Chronographia*, VII.35–6; Attaleiates, *History*, pp. 100–107; Skylitzes, *Synopsis of Histories*, XXIII.12, pp. 497–9.

215 By ruling well or vice versa I mean in the opinion of Constantinople's citizens rather than by any impartial rubric.

216 DO BZS.1947.2.543.

217 For the acclamation of the *eparch* as Father of the City, see Constantine VII, *De Ceremoniis*, pp. 527–8. For the ceremonial appointment and acclamation of an *eparch*, see Constantine VII, *De Ceremoniis*, pp. 265–8.

218 J. Koder, ed. *Das Eparchenbuch Leons des Weisen*, CFHB 33 (Vienna, 1991). The *Peira* also mentions the *eparch*'s authority over the guilds of Constantinople. *Peira*, 51.29.

219 For the most recent discussion of the judicial duties of the *eparch* with relevant references to the law codes of the ninth century, see A. Gkoutzioukostas, *Η απονομή δικαιοσύνης στο Βυζάντιο (9ος–12ος αι.). Τα δικαιοδο-τικά όργανα και δικαστήρια της πρωτεύουσας* (Βυζαντινά Κείμενα και Μελέται 37) (Thessaloniki, 2004), pp. 103–7. For examples of records of cases involving the *eparch*, see *Peira*, 44.1, 49.4 (which took place in the Covered Hippodrome in the Great Palace) and 51.31.

220 K. E. Zachariä von Lingenthal, ed. *Collectio librorum juris graeco-romani ineditorum Ecloga Leonis et Constantini, epanagoge Basilii Leonis et Alexandri* (Leipzig: 1852); Epanagoge, 11.7, p. 89; Zepos, *JGR* II, p. 260. 'The decision of the eparch is not subject to appeal, except to that of the emperor alone.' Translation from Chitwood, *Byzantine Legal Culture*, p. 60, n. 62.

221 Ibid.

222 Bury, *Administrative System*, pp. 69–73; L. Bréhier, *Les institutions de l'empire byzantin* (Paris, 1949), pp. 186–92; Oikonomides, *Listes*, pp. 319–20; Oikonomides, 'L'évolution', p. 133; Gkoutzioukostas, *Η απονομή δικαιοσύνης στο Βυζάντιο*, pp. 103–5. R. Guilland, 'Études sur l'histoire administrative de l'Empire Byzantin-L'Eparque I. L'éparque de la ville', *Byzantinoslavica* 41 (1980), pp. 17–32, 145–80 and 'Etudes sur l'histoire administrative de l'Empire Byzantin-L'Eparque II. Les éparques autres que l'éparque de la ville', *Byzantinoslavica* 42 (1981), pp. 186–96.

223 Oikonomides, *Listes*, p. 113.

224 Ibid., pp. 319–20, including a full list of the known offices subordinate to the *eparch* as described in the ninth- and tenth-century *taktika*. See also, Bury, *Administrative System*, pp. 70–3.

225 For examples where Eustathios Romaios as *droungarios* of the *Vigla* overturned the decisions of the *eparchs* Leo and Nicholas, see *Peira*, 51.21 and 51.31.

226 Oikonomides, 'L'évolution, p. 133. For the *eparch* supervising the guilds in 1112/13, see a Novel of Alexios I, *JGR* I, pp. 645–6.

227 Oikonomides, *Listes*, p. 265.

228 Five, in fact. Three specify their owner as *eparch* of the City (Marianos, Harvard Art Museums 1951.31.5.607; Peter, Laurent, *Vatican* no. 87; Leo, DO BZS.1955.1.1520, DO BZS.1955.1.1521), one as *eparch* of Constantinople (*DO Seals* 5.22.6 Harvard Art

Museums 1951.31.5.2886, DO BZS.1947.2.543), and one as *eparch* of the Queen of Cities (Leo, Zacos, *Lead Seals* II, no. 1001).

229 J.-C. Cheynet, 'L'éparque: Corrections et additions', *Byzantinoslavica* 45 (1984), fasc. 1, pp. 50–4.

230 *Protospatharios*: Sisinnios in 963, *Théodore Daphnopatès, Correspondance*, ed. and trans., J. Darrouzès and L. G. Westerink (Paris, 1978), Letter 33 (*PBMZ* no. 27115), Peter in 1026, A. Schmink, 'Vier eherechtliche Entscheidungen aus dem 11. Jahrhundert', *Fontes Minores* 3 (1979), pp. 221–79, at no. 1; Sergios in 1029, Fickler, *Alexios Stoudites*, p. 20. *Patrikios*: Sisinios in 967, Skylitzes, *Synopsis of Histories* 275; Romanos Argyros in 1025–8, 'Histoire de Yaḥyā ibn Saīd d'Antioche, Continuateur de Said-Ibn-Bitriq' *Patrologia Orientalis* 47, no. 4, ed. and trans. F. Micheau and G. Troupeau (1997), pp. 371–559, at pp. 484–9. Leo in 1033, Eustathios Romaios 51.21; Nicholas in 1033, *Peira* 51.31; Anastasios in 1042, Skylitzes, *Synopsis of Histories*, p. 418; Attaleiates, *History*, pp. 22–3.

231 Based on the available sigillographic evidence it is highly likely that the *eparchs* who were *protospatharioi* in the middle third of the eleventh century were in office at the beginning of that period.

232 Attaleiates, *History*, p. 26.

233 When John Tzimiskes seized power by murdering his uncle Nikephoros II in 969 his first appointments were the men in charge of guarding the palace, the fleet and the prisons of Constantinople. Securing the capital was still the priority, but the means by which this was achieved had changed.

234 Harvard Art Museums 1951.31.5.3643.

235 Book of the Eparch VI.4, p. 32, XI.9, p. 45, XII.9, p. 47, XIII.2, p. 48, XIX.4, p. 56 (weights of measures, *stathmia e metra*; balances, *kampanoi, zygia, bolia*; marked with his seal, *te tou eparkhou esphragismena boulle*) Coin weights, *hexagia*, Book of the Eparch XIII.5, p. 48.

236 Book of the Eparch, VIII.3, p. 37; Oikonomides, *Listes*, p. 13.

237 Oikonomides, *listes*, p. 320; Gkoutzioukostas, *Η απονομή δικαιοσύνης στο Βυζάντιο*, pp. 105–6, n. 429.

238 Oikonomides, *listes*, p. 113.

239 Sjuzjumov and Nicole advanced the theory that each guild was monitored by a separate *symponos* in contrast to Bury, *Administrative System*, pp. 70–1, who argued that there was usually only a single *symponos*. Oikonomides, *Listes*, p. 320, agreed with Bury. Certainly, Philotheos only mentions *symponos* in the singular when describing the *eparch*'s staff.

240 Bernard and Livanos, *Christopher of Mytilene and John Mauropous*, no. 15 'On the Patrician and Parathalassites Melias', p. 27.

241 Oikonomides, *Listes*, p. 113. Ahrweiler, *Mer*, p. 144; H. Ahrweiler, 'Fonctionnaires et bureaux maritimes a Byzance', *Revue des études byzantines*, 19 (1961), p. 249 claimed that the *parathalassites* moved from the staff of the *eparch* to that of the *logothetes tou dromou* at some point after the *Kletorologion of Philotheos* was written in 899. This assertion was challenged, quite convincingly, in Laurent, *Corpus* II, no. 625.

242 H. Ahrweiler, *Études sur les structures administrative et sociales de Byzance* (London, 1971), p. 246; Lemerle, 'Notes sur l'administration byzantine à la veille de la IVe croisade, d'après deux documents inédits des archives de Lavra', *Revue des études byzantines* 19 (1961), p. 258. Oikonomides, *Listes*, p. 321.

243 *Peira*, 51.29.

244 Oikonomides, *Listes*, p. 321; Bernard and Livanos, *Christopher of Mytilene and John Mauropous*, no. 15, p. 27. For the Parathalassites' judicial duties, see Gkoutzioukostas, Η απονομή δικαιοσύνης, pp. 193–4.
245 Theodosios Monomachos, Laurent, *Corpus* II, no. 1126, see Cheynet, 'Par St. Georges', p. 121, *PBW* Theodosios 20112; John, Laurent, *Corpus* II, no. 1127, *PBW* Ioannes 20455.
246 Some of the officials in the new department of the *parathalassites* are described in the *chrysobull* issued for the monastery of the Lavra on Mount Athos in 1102, *Lavra* I, no. 55, pp. 285–6. It was suggested by Hélène Ahrweiler that the *parathalassites* had moved from the department of the *eparch* to that of the *logothetes tou dromou* at some point in the tenth century. Ahrweiler, *Mer*, p. 144. While this does not seem as likely his remaining in the office of the *eparch*, as argued by V. Laurent, Laurent, *Corpus* II, no. 625, all agree on his eleventh century independence. For the extension of the jurisdiction of the *parathalassites*, see Oikonomides, 'L'évolution', p. 133, n. 44; Ahrweiler, 'Fonctionnaires et bureaux maritimes a Byzance', pp. 246–9.
247 DO BZS.1958.106.1880.
248 For the most recent discussion of this office, see A. Gkoutzioukostas, 'The Praitor Mentioned in the History of Leo the Deacon and the Praitor of Constantinople: Previous and Recent Considerations', *Byzantiaka* 25 (2005–6), pp. 105–15.
249 *Leonis diaconi Caloënsis Historiae libri decem*, ed. C. B. Hase (Bonn, 1828), IV.7, p. 65.
250 Glykatzi-Ahrweiler, 'Recherches', pp. 1–109, at p. 44.
251 Oikonomides, 'L'évolution', p. 133, n. 43; Oikonomides, *Listes*, p. 113.
252 Gkoutzioukostas, 'Praitor and Praitor', p. 109.
253 Ibid., p. 114.
254 Ibid. Cf. a restatement of his original argument in 'Administrative Structures', pp. 572–3. The use of the word *praitor*, which at the time was also applied to the judges in the themes, adds weight to the conclusion that the *praitor* of Constantinople was primarily a judicial office. Ahrweiler, 'Administration', p. 74; Gkoutzioukostas, 'Praitor and Praitor', p. 112. A *praitor* is mentioned as a judicial official in the *Peira*, and is likely the *praitor* of Constantinople. See *Peira*, 51.29. For relevant argument, see Gkoutzioukostas, Η απονομή δικαιοσύνης στο Βυζάντιο, p. 192.
255 *D. O. Seals* 5.28.4.
256 This seal is DO BZS.1947.2.1280 which belonged to George Spanopoulos. First Laurent, Laurent, *Corpus* II, no. 1144, and then Dumbarton Oaks, *D. O. Seals* 5.28.1, identified George as a *praitor* of Constantinople, and I have followed their lead here, but, as Werner Seibt noted, there is no guarantee that this was the case. Werner Seibt, REVIEW *Byzantinische Zeitschrift* 99, no. 2 (2006).
257 *D. O. Seals* 5.28.3; *PBW* Theodoros 20225.
258 Stephen, DO BZS.1958.106.1880 (*D. O. Seals* 5.28.2), *PBW* Stephanos 20221; Niketas, Zacos, *Lead Seals* II, no. 649, Spink 127:72, *PBW* Niketas 20150; Niketas Argyros, Laurent, *Corpus* II, no. 1145, Cheynet-Vannier *Argyroi* p. 81, *PBW* Niketas 20206; Leo, Laurent, *Orghidan*, no. 188, Laurent, *Corpus* II, no. 1146, *PBW* Leon 20257.
259 Chitwood, makes the apt comparison with the governors of Roman provinces.
260 Kekaumenos, *Consilia et Narrationes* (SAWS edn, 2013), p. 78.24–7.
261 Psellos, *Chronographia*, V.15–16; Skylitzes, *Synopsis of Histories*, p. 417.
262 For Monomachos's actions during the Russian attack on Constantinople, see Psellos, *Chronographia*, VI.93; Attaleiates, *History*, pp. 32–4; Skylitzes, *Synopsis of Histories*,

pp. 431; For a very visible Constantine IX during the revolt of Tornikios, see Psellos, *Chronographia*, VI.106; Attaleiates, *History*, p. 40. For his part, the rebel Tornikios thought that Constantinople would fall quickly into his hands precisely because Constantine IX was disliked by the people. Psellos, *Chronographia*, VI.104, yet in the end failed to take the city because it was he who did not have the support of its citizens. Psellos, *Chronographia*, VI.109–10.

263 Psellos, *Chronographia*, VI.117, 130. Compare this attidue of sovereign to people and vice versa with the story of Basil II, who took part in a ceremonial procession through the empty streets of Constantinople not long before his death in 1025, the people of the city were too frightened to watch him on parade. Aristakes of Lastivert, *Ré cit des malheurs de la nation arménienne*, trans. M. Canard and H. Berbérian according to the edn and trans. (Russian) by K. Yuzbashian (Brussels, 1973), p. 25.

264 Attaleiates, *History*, p. 102; Skylitzes, *Synopsis of Histories*, pp. 497–8. In the end, it was to be Michael's reliance on the people that would be his undoing when they switched sides, either because they believed that he was forcing them to perjure themselves by insisting that they swear never to recognize the rebel Isaac Komnenos as emperor, then making a deal with him, or at the instigation of the elite of the city and the patriarch Keroularios. See also, Psellos, *Chronographia*, VII.36. It should come as no surprise that the people were easily swayed from their support of Michael VI; he had been a seen as a joke in the city since his coronation when the populace dubbed him the Old Man. Even his attempts at urban renewal were mocked. When he ordered the late antique paved square of the Strategion cleared of centuries of accumulated waste in search of the paving underneath, it was suggested that he was looking for a toy he had lost there as a child. Skylitzes, *Synopsis of Histories*, p. 483.

265 Psellos, *Chronographia*, VII.45–6.

266 As we have seen Michael V fell afoul of the sentiments of the people of the marketplace and the workshops in favour of the last surviving members of the Macedonian dynasty Zoe and Theodora. Michael VI lost the support of the senate and people. There is no reason to believe that if Constantinople had remained loyal, that Isaac Komnenos's rebellion would have succeeded. The precedent of Constantine IX alone, who survived two military revolts because the capital remained loyal, even through a siege, suggests that Kekaumenos was correct to say that 'the emperor in Constantinople always wins'. Isaac I was becoming unpopular with at least a section of the people of the capital in 1059 and was removed in a coup by the leading elements of the Constantinopolitan elite. Psellos in the *Chronographia* and the government of Constantine X in a proclamation to the provinces tried incredibly hard to make it seem as if Isaac had not been overthrown, I think that the strength of their protest is telling to say the least. Psellos, *Chronographia*, VII.74–92.

267 Trans., Chitwood, *Byzantine Legal Culture*, p. 193.

268 For a recent discussion of the legislative agenda of the early Macedonians, including an assessment of their motives and methods, see Chitwood, *Byzantine Legal Culture*, chapter 1, from which much of the following section is taken.

269 K. E. Zachariä von Lingenthal, ed., *Imperatorum Basilii, Constantini et Leonis prochiron* (Leipzig: 1837); Zepos *JGR* II, pp. 107–228, 395–410.

270 A. Schminck, *Studien zu mittelbyzantinischen Rechtsbüchern* (Frankfurt am Main, 1986), proem, lines 45–51.

271 Chitwood, *Byzantine Legal Culture*, pp. 29–32. Not least the sections concerning patriarchal power and authority.

272 Chitwood, *Byzantine Legal Cutlure*, pp. 32–5 for the early history of the *Basilika*. The earliest recorded use of the term *Basilika* is believed to date from 1039 and has been attributed to John Xiphilinos, later to be Constantine IX's *nomophylax* in charge of legal education, and later patriarch. Schminck, *Rechtsbüchern*, pp. 30–2.

273 For a discussion of this theory complete with an amusing anecdote about the misspelling of *rex*, see Chitwood, *Byzantine Legal Culture*, pp. 19–22.

274 Chitwood, *Byzantine Legal Culture*, p. 35.

275 Ibid., p. 36.

276 Ibid., pp. 38–42.

277 E. McGeer, *The Land Legislation of the Macedonian Emperors* (Toronto, 2000).

278 Of course, the first piece of land legislation was not issued by a Macedonian as such, but by Romanos I Lekapenos (920–944) who seized the throne from the regency council set up to govern for the infant Constantine VII, Leo VI's son. As we know it ended well for Constantine who was married to Romanos's daughter Helena, and eventually took the throne in 944. Constantine issued his own piece of land legislation, the first to be concerned with military lands. This law was superseded by one issued by another interloper, Nikephoros II Phokas. Finally, Basil II issued two laws regarding the lands of the poor and the powerful.

279 See Chitwood, *Byzantine Legal Cutlure*, pp. 26, 30; *Imperatorum Basilii, Constantiniet Leonis. Prochiron*, ed. K. E. Zachariä von Lingenthal (Leipzig: 1837), p. 5; Zepos, *JGR* II, p. 115; Zachariä von Lingenthal, *Collectio librorum, Epanagoge*, p. 61; Zepos *JGR* II, p. 236. The *Novel* of Romanos I Lekapenos issued in September 934 is a particularly powerful example of the blending of the legal authority of the emperor and the divine nature of justice. N. Svoronos, *Les Nouvelles des empereurs macédoniens concernant la terre et les stratiotes*, ed. Paris Gounaridis (Athens, 1994), pp. 72–93; Zépos, *JGR* I, pp. 205–14. For commentary and translation, see McGeer, *The Land Legislation of the Macedonian Emperors*, pp. 49–60.

280 In 966/7 Nikephoros II Phokas summed up this connection in a *novel* aimed to restrict the practice whereby the powerful bought the lands of the poor thus,

> A just father who tends to all his children in equal measure, a scale of justice, a straight line and an accurate measuring rod, the Lord our God, unbiased, honoured not for inequity but for the care He exercises for all alike, created heaven and earth and the things contained therein for the sake of all. Accordingly, it is incumbent upon those to whom the rulership has fallen to follow His example all the more, both to preserve equality among all those under their power and to see to the welfare of all in common, since they have been called by the lawgivers of old legal authorities and a blessing in common and equitable.

Translation from McGeer, *Land Legislation*, pp. 99. Svoronos, *Nouvelles*, pp. 177–81; Zépos, *JGR* I, pp. 253–55. Similar sentiments can be found in the *Novella constitutio* of Constantine IX Monomachos issued in 1047, where the law, which is gift from God, is the guide of just imperial rule. Chitwood, *Byzantine Legal Culture*, p. 194.

281 Constantine X and Michael VII.

282 Chitwood, *Byzantine Legal Culture*, chapter 4.

283 Ibid., p. 130.

284 For the *Peira* and the career of Eustathios Romaios, see L. Burgmann, 'Zur diplomatischen Terminologie in der Peira', in *Zwischen Polis, Provinz un Peripherie: Beiträge zur byzantinischen Geschichte und Kultur*, ed. L. M. Hoffmann (Wiesbaden, 2005), pp. 457–67; L. Burgmann, 'Turning Sisinnios against the Sisinnians: Eustathios Romaios on a Disputed Marriage', in *Byzantium in the Year 1000*, ed. P. Magdalino (Leiden and Boston, 2003), pp. 161–81; J. Howard-Johnston, 'The *Peira*

and Legal Practices in Eleventh-Century Byzantium', in *Byzantium in the Eleventh Century Being in Between*, eds M. D. Lauxtermann and M. Whittow (London and New York, 2017), pp. 63–76; A. d' Emilia, 'L'applicazione pratica del diritto bizantino secondo il titolo della Πεῖρα Εὐσταθίου τοῦ Ρωμαίου relative alla compravendita', *RSBN* n.s. 2–3[12–13] (1965–6), pp. 33–80; A. d'Emilia, 'L'applicazione pratica del diritto bizantino secondo la c.d. "Peira d'Eustazio Romano"', *RSBN* n.s. 4[14] (1967), pp. 71–94; H. Köpstein, 'Sklaven in der "Peira"', *Fontes Minores* 9 (1993), pp. 1–33; A. E. Laiou, 'Οικονομικά ζητήματα στη "Πείρα' Ευσταθίου Ρωμαίου" in *Η αυτοκρατορία σε κρίση? Το Βυζάντιο τον Ιιο αιώνα, 1025*, ed. V. N. Vlysidou (Athens, 2003), pp. 179–89; N. Oikonomides, 'The "Peira" of Eustathios Rhomaios: An Abortive Attempt to Innovate in Byzantine Law', *Fontes Minores* 7 (1986), pp. 169–92; E. S. Papagiane, Το έγκλημα της 'φθοράς' και η αγωγή 'περί ύβρεως' στο χωρίο 49.4 της Πείρας', in *Κατεθόδιον: in memoriam Nikos Oikonomides*, ed. S. N. Troianos (Athens and Komotene: 2008), pp. 81–106; A. Schmink, 'Zur Einzelgesetzgebung der 'makedonischen' Kaiser', *Fontes Minores* 11 (2005), pp. 249–68; D. Simon, 'Das Ehegüterrecht de Pira. Ein systematischer Versuch', *Fontes Minores* 7 (1987), pp. 193–238; D. Simon, *Rechtsfindung am byzantinischen Reichsgericht* (Fankfurt am Main, 1973); D. Tsourka-Papasthante, 'Vente d'office: observations sur la Πεῖρα Ευσταθίου του Ρωμαίου 38.74', in *Byzantine Law: Proceedings of the International Symposium of Jurists, Thessaloniki, 10–13 December 1998*, ed. C. Papatathis (Thessaloniki, 2001), pp. 229–34; S. Vryonis, 'The *Peira* as a Source for the History of Byzantine Aristocratc Society in the First Half of the Eleventh Century', in *Near Eastern Numismatics, Iconography, Epigraphy and History: Studies in Honor of George C. Miles*, ed. Dickran K. Kouymjian (Beirut, 1974), pp. 279–84; G. Weiss, 'Hohe Richter in Konstantinopel. Eustathios Rhomaios und seine Kollegen', *Jahrbuch der Österreichischen Byzantinistik* 22 (1973), pp. 117–43.
285 Oikonomides, 'Peira', p. 175; Weiss, 'Hohe Richter', p. 118, has reconstructed 276 cases from the fragments scattered throughout the chapters of the *Peira*. On the structure of the *Peira*, see Howard-Johnston, 'The *Peira* and Legal Practices', pp. 64–9 and p. 76, n. 40 for the date of the *Peira*.
286 Demonstrated in *Peira*, 51.29.
287 DO BZS.1955.1.2149.
288 Oikonomides, *Listes*, pp. 139, 249, 269.
289 For cases involving wills and questions of inheritance, see *Peira* 14.11, 16.13, 51.29; *Iviron*, 2, nos. 44, 46, 47. For family law, see *Peira* 16.5, 16.13, 16.20, 51.21, 58.4. For cases involving property, see Gautier, 'diataxis', 27. For criminal cases, see *Peria* 66.1, 66.2. For the position of the *koiaistor* as an important judicial official, see Zachariä von Lingenthal, *Collectio librorum*, epanagoge, 11.8, p. 89; Zepos, *JGR* II, p. 260.
290 In the late ninth century, and probably into the eleventh, the decisions of the *koiaistor* could only be appealed before the emperor. Zachariä von Lingenthal, *Collectio librorum*, epanagoge, 11.8, p. 89; Zepos, *JGR* II, p. 260, 'The decision of the quaestor is not subject to appeal but is also only scrutinized by the emperor alone.' Translation from Chitwood, *Byzantine Legal Culture*, p. 60, n. 62.
291 Oikonomides, 'L'évolution', p. 135. In fact, the consistency lasted even longer. The *koiaistor* appears as the chair of a permanent tribunal in the 1166 novel of Manuel I Komnenos (1143–1180) and the mid-twelfth century *Ecloga Basilicorum*. It still existed in the fourteenth century, but by this point the position of *koiaistor* was a purely ceremonial position. The *koiaistor* of the eleventh century was an important judicial official, with a large staff, who presided over his own court. Oikonomides,

Listes, pp. 321–2; *Oxford Dictionary of Byzantium*, pp. 1765–6; Laurent, *Corpus* II, no. 605; Jordanov, *Bulgaria*, 3, no. 343; R. Guilland, 'Études sur l'histoire administrative de l'empire byzantin. Le Questeur: ö Κοιασοτοπ, quaestor', *Byzantion* 41 (1971), pp. 78–104; Gkoutzioukostas, *Η απονομή δικαιοσύνης στο Βυζάντιο*: 105–9, pp. 185–6; A. Gkoutzioukostas, *Ο θεσμός του κοιαίστωρα του ιερού παλατίου : η γένεση, οι αρμοδιότητες και η εξέλιξή του* (Εταιρεία Βυζαντινών ερευνών 18) (Thessalonike, 2001).
292 *Protospatharios*: Romanos Argyros (before 1028), *Peira* 58.4; Sergios (1028 and 1029), *Peira* 66.1, 66.2, Ficker, *Alexios Stoudites*, p. 20; Myron (1033), *Peira* 16.13. *Anthypatos* and *patrikios*: Peter (1027), *Peira* 51.21; Peter (1029), Ficker, *Alexios Stoudites*, p. 19. *Vestes*, *anthypatos*, and *patrikios*: Eustathios Romaios (1030), Oikonomides, 'Peira', p. 173.
293 DO BZS.1955.1.1514.
294 Oikonomides, *Listes*, pp. 321–2.
295 Laurent, *Corpus* II, no. 888.
296 The first attestation of the *droungarios* of the *Vigla* was in 791.
297 Oikonomides, *Listes*, pp. 331, 269.
298 The last recorded *droungarios* to serve in a military function was the eunuch Symeon during the reign of Constantine VIII (1025–1028). Oikonomides, 'L'évolution', p. 133; Guilland, *Recherches sur les institutions byzantines* (Berlin and Amsterdam, 1967), p. 573.
299 For a discussion of this older issue, see Gkoutzioukostas, *Η απονομή δικαιοσύνης στο Βυζάντιο*, pp. 124–38 with reference to older bibliography.
300 For examples of cases involving property, see *Peria* 7.6, 8.34, 9.9, 15.12, 15.14, 15.17, 15.9, 19.16, 33.1, 38.12, 42.19, 50.6, 51.24. For cases concerning the rights of women, including questions related to dowries, see 17.5, 17.19, 25.36, 25.65, 49.25, 64.5, 65.1, 49.10. For issues of inheritance, see 14.12, 14.16, 14.22, 14.5, 16.13, 16.9, 25.25, 25.65, 31.5, 41.9, 43.5, 43.8, 45.11, 65.5. For crimes of a violent nature and those involving theft, see 17.17, 28.6, 42.11, 42.17, 51.25, 63.1, 66.27.
301 For records of the *droungarios* of the *Vigla* overruling other judges, see *Peira*, 16.13 (*koiaistor*), 51.21 and 51.31 (*eparch*). Examples where the tribunal of the *droungarios* acted as a court of appeal, or where the *droungarios* overruled another judge can be found at *Peira*, 7.12, 7.15, 7.16, 7.18 51.31, 52.29, 58.4, 66.27, 74.2. Other judges also came to the *droungarios* for help in deciding a point of law, see 23.6.
302 For examples of cases concerning matters outside of Constantinople, see *Peira* 7.16, 9.9, 15.17, 23.3, 26.27, 42.18, 43.5, 51.24, 58.1, 66.24, 9.10.
303 Weiss, 'Hohe Richter', pp. 131–6, noted that when the emperor attended the court, which he did in eleven cases recorded in the *Peria*, that the plaintiffs were always office or title holders. However, Eustathios Romaios showed a remarkable understanding of the poor and the difficulties that they faced in getting access to justice, not least their fear of more powerful neighbours.
304 H. Saradi, 'The Byzantine Tribunals: Problems in the Application of Justice and State Policy (9th–12th C.)', *Revue des études byzantines* 53 (1995), pp. 173–4. Oikonomides, 'L'évolution', pp. 133–4; Jordanov, *Bulgaria*, 3, nos. 346–7; Bury, *Administrative System*, pp. 60–2; Guilland, *Recherches*, pp. 563–87; Oikonomides, *Listes*, p. 331; Gkoutzioukostas, *Η απονομή δικαιοσύνης στο Βυζάντιο*, p. 106.
305 A sixteenth could be Niketas, *magistros* and *mega droungarios* who was the owner of DO BZS. 1951.31.5.3362, however, the seal is badly damaged and it is impossible to determine of what he was *megas droungarios*. While it is likely that it was the *Vigla* as I cannot be certain I have not included him in the analysis of this office.

306 The number gleaned from the written sources is actually higher, but Constantine, nephew of patriarch Michael Keroularios, Nicholas Mermentoulos, and in all likelihood, John Skylitzes are known from both the sigillographic and written record.
307 Damian, DO 1958.106.4649; Theodore, Harvard Art Museums 1951.31.5.762. Interestingly, all of the seals dated to this period record individuals who held more than one title. In this period, the title of *anthypatos* was in the third place in the hierarchy, *patrikios*, held the fourth place, and *protospatharios*, the fifth place.
308 Kyriakos, Laurent, *Corpus* II, no. 889a, Harvard Art Museums 1951.31.5.2462; Jordanov, *Bulgaria* 3, nos. 1042–4, *PBW* Kyriakos 20103; *PBW* Theophylaktos 20118.
309 *PBW* Eustathios 61. Zacos, *Lead Seals* II, no. 142; Laurent, *Corpus* II, no. 888.
310 Oikonomides 'Peira', p. 174. *Peira* 63.1 for Eustathios and *magistros* and *droungarios*.
311 Anonymous *magistros* and *vestarches*, Laurent, *Corpus* II, no. 890, *PBW* Anonymous 2229.
312 Oikonomides, 'Peira', p. 174.
313 Skylitzes, *Synopsis of Histories*, p. 479; *PBW* Manuel 103.
314 Kekaumenos, *Consilia et Narrationes* (SAWS edition, 2013), p. 6.8–12.
315 For the most recent study of the tribunal with an excellent exploration of the secondary scholarship around the judges of the Hippodrome and Velum, see Gkoutzioukostas, *Η απονομή δικαιοσύνης στο Βυζάντιο*, pp. 119–81. For an alternate view see Oikonomides, 'Peira', pp. 169–92. For the first appearance of the judges of the Hippodrome and Velum in Byzantine sources see Oikonomides, *Listes*, p. 273; for further discussion see Oikonomides, *Listes*, p. 322–3.
316 *Ecloga Basilicorum*, B. 2.3.70, p. 112.
317 Gkoutzioukostas, *Η απονομή δικαιοσύνης στο Βυζάντιο*, p. 159. It is not even entirely clear that they were either of the types of judge under discussion.
318 The *Ecloga* in particular has been the source of differing opinions as to whether the twelve judges were judges of the Velum, see Oikonomides 'Peira', *Listes*, p. 323 and Gkoutzioukostas, *Η απονομή δικαιοσύνης στο Βυζάντιο*, p. 164, who reviews the entire debate pp. 159–65, for judges of the Hippodrome and judges of the Velum together, see Zachariä von Lingenthal, *Geschichte*, p. 360.
319 It is not even universally agreed that the *Ecloga Basilicorum* even refers to judges, might it mean notaries instead? Christophilopoulou, *Τα βυζαντινά δικαστήρια κατά τους 10ο-11ο αιώνες*, p. 171.
320 The various opinions have been collected and recounted by Gkoutzioukostas, *Η απονομή δικαιοσύνης στο Βυζάντιο*, pp. 138–59. Among the most recent commentators, Oikonomides. *Listes*, p. 323, using Balsamon for the number of judges of the Velum and promotion from the Hippodrome, and Psellos, Sathas, *Μεσαιωνική Βιβλιοθήκη* 5, p. 206 for promotion at the order of the emperor, was of the opinion that the judges of the Velum and judges of the Hippodrome belonged to two distinct groups, with the Velum superior to the Hippodrome, a position with which Laurent agreed. Cheynet, 'Devaluation', p. 459 argues that they were effectively the same thing.
321 For a collection of scholarship from the last century on this issue, see Gkoutzioukostas, *Η απονομή δικαιοσύνης στο Βυζάντιο*, pp. 138–59.
322 For different tribunals, see Oikonomides, 'Peira', p. 188, Christophilopoulou, *Βυζαντινά δικαστήρια*, pp. 168–72; Saradi, 'Byzantine Tribunals', p. 172. D. Simon thought that they were the same. Gkoutzioukostas, *Η απονομή δικαιοσύνης στο Βυζάντιο*, p. 138.

323 Theophanes, *Chronographia*, p. 493. The earliest known case considered at a court in the Covered Hippodrome dates to 908. D. Papachryssanthou, *Actes du Prôtaton, Archives de l'Athos VII* (Paris, 1975), no. 2, pp. 181–5. In *De Ceremoniis*, p. 507, Constantine VII makes it very clear that the Hippodrome and the Covered Hippodrome were different structures in his description of the triumph of Emperor Theophilos in 831. The exact location of the Covered Hippodrome and even the form that it took are unknown. For a survey of the scholarship on this topic, see Andreas Gkoutzioukastas, *Η απονομή δικαιοσύνης στο Βυζάντιο*, pp. 119–24.

324 There is also debate over whether more than one court met in the Covered Hippodrome, and if so, how many. See Weiss, 'Hohne Richter', p. 119.

325 Oikonomides, *Listes*, p. 323.

326 Gkoutzioukostas, *Η απονομή δικαιοσύνης στο Βυζάντιο*, pp. 135–6. It first appears in a letter of Michael Psellos, Kurtz and Drexl, *Scripta minora* 2, no. 100, then later in the reign of Alexios I under the authority of the *droungarios* of the Vigla John Thrakesios, in 1092, Zepos, *JGR* I, p. 319.

327 Oikonomides, *Listes*, p. 323.

328 For the curtain as a barrier between the judges and the public, see J. A. B. Montreuil, *Histoire du droit byzantin, ou du droit romain dans l'Empire d'Orient, depuis la mort de Justinien jusqu'à la prise de Constantinople en 1453* (Paris, 1843), pp. 89–90 and Oikonomides, *Listes*, p. 323. For the division of the courtroom using a curtain, see Christophilopoulou, *Βυζαντινά δικαστήρια*, p. 171.

329 Gkoutzioukastas, *Η απονομή δικαιοσύνης στο Βυζάντιο*, p. 150 notes that no source mentions the velum, but that there was a curtain in all of the courts, so why this particular one was important enough to give its name to the judges of the Velum us a mystery.

330 Weiss, 'Hohe Richter', p. 119. As noted earlier the *Peira* does not always give people their full titles. It is possible, even likely, that many of the men described as a 'judge' in the *Peira* were actually judges of the Velum, but that it was not necessary to make any such distinction in the text. As such the omission of the judges of the Velum from the *Peira* is less revealing than we might have hoped.

331 Oikonomides, 'Peira', pp. 187–8.

332 Oikonomides, 'Peira', p. 188. Contrary to the opinion of S. Troianos, *Οι Πηγές του Βυζαντινού Δικαίου, Τρίτη έκδοση συμπληρωμένη* (Athens, 2011), pp. 215–16, who despite the rather convincing evidence presented by Oikonomides, does not consider the *Peira* to be discussing the *droungarios* and his court. L. Burgmann, 'Zur Organisation der Rechtsprechung in Byzanz (mittelbyzantinische Epoche)', in *Ausgewählte Aufsätze zur byzantinischen Rechtsgeschichte*, ed. L. Burgmann (Frankfurt, 2015), pp. 259–84; Christophilopoulou, *Βυζαντινά δικαστήρια*, pp. 168–71 also doubt the link between the courts of the Hippodrome and Velum and the *droungarios* of the *Vigla*. For a discussion of the various arguments, see Gkoutkioukostas, *Η απονομή δικαιοσύνης στο Βυζάντιο*, pp. 124–30.

333 For Michael Ophrydas, see Šandrovskaja, 'Sfragistika', p. 802; Lichačev Molivdovuly LXVIII, 15. For Leo Thylakas, see Oikonomides, 'Peira', p. 175.

334 Gkoutzioukostas, 'Thessaloniki', pp. 1–2. Gkoutzioukostas, *Η απονομή δικαιοσύνης στο Βυζάντιο*, pp. 154–5.

335 *Ecloga Basilicorum*. For the various categories of judges see B.2.2.207, p. 68, B.7.8.2 + 4, p. 286.

336 Gkoutzioukostas, *Η απονομή δικαιοσύνης στο Βυζάντιο* notes this, p. 131. See Zépos, *JGR* I, p. 630, Dölger – Wirth, *Regesten* no. 868.

337 To a large degree, and perhaps primarily, the theme judges were administrators of their provinces, not judicial officials although their job encompassed judicial duties. When we look past the fact that the two groups were designated by the same word, *krites*, judge, and look at what they actually did, there is less contradiction between the idea that the theme judge, as a governor, held a higher status than the city judges, but that as a legal expert and judicial official his pronouncements were less valued.
338 Chitwood, *Byzantine Legal Culture*, chapter 2, specifically pp. 58–9.
339 Zepos, *JGR* I, pp. 218–21, 227–9.
340 Zepos, *JGR* I, p. 220. Translation Chitwood, *Byzantine Legal Culture*, p. 59.
341 Chitwood, *Byzantine Legal Culture*, pp. 59–60.
342 Weiss, 'Hohe Richter', p. 119; Oikonomides, 'Peira', p. 188.
343 A great deal has been written on this topic, admirably and patiently presented by Gkoutioukostas, *Η απονομή δικαιοσύνης στο Βυζάντιο*, pp. 124–30. Much of the debate about the place of the *droungarios* of the *Vigla* and the Court of the Hippodrome is based on far too little evidence to ever be resolved. One note of interest, Gkoutzioukostas explains that the *Peira*, which presents much of our evidence for a court chaired by the *droungarios*, only mentions the Covered Hippodrome and a court sitting therein three times. Gkoutzioukostas, *Η απονομή δ ικαιοσύνης στο Βυζάντιο*, p. 132. While this is so, the *Peira* mentions many things by terms presumably well known at the time. Eustathios Romaios is referred to by his title, *magistros* far more often than by name or office, and this makes one wonder where the many courts mentioned in the *Peira* took place.
344 This procedure was an innovation not found in earlier law codes. Weiss, 'Hohe Richter', p. 126.
345 Oikonmides, 'Peira', p. 188 referencing *Peira* 61.16.
346 Unfortunately, we do not have sources that describe the operation of the tribunals of the *eparch* and the *koiaistor*. It is possible that on these older courts the city judges had less of a voice than on the new creation of the court of the *droungarios*, but it is equally likely that all three functioned the same way.
347 Oikonomides, 'Peira', p. 172.
348 A. Gkoutzioukostas, 'Judges of the Velum and Judges of the Hippodrome in Thessalonike (11th c.)', *Byzantina Symmeikta* 20 (2010), pp. 67–84.
349 Laurent, *Corpus* II, no. 838.
350 Oikonomides, *Listes*, p. 273.
351 *Protospatharios*, Ficker, *Alexios Stoudites*, p. 20 and Miklosich-Müller 5. no. 1, p. 1. *Vestes*, *anthypatos*, and *patrikios* in Miklosich-Müller 5. no. 1, p. 2. Hypatos Iviron 2. no. 31, pp. 79, 80 and *Iviron* 2. no. 34, p. 98; no. 35, p. 104. *Anthypatos* and *patrikios* in *Iviron*, no. 32, p. 87. *Dishypatos* in Nicolas Oikonomides, *Actes de Esphigmenou, Archives de l'Athos VI* (Paris, 1968), no. 4, p. 52.
352 While not as useful for assessing the body of judges of the Velum, the figures for the range of payments made to them is interesting. These were 0.94 to 5.67 lbs., 0.46–0.47 to 25.76–26.46 lbs. and 0.37–0.45 to 20.97–25.2 lbs. in the late tenth, early and mid-eleventh century respectively. Not only is the variety of titles clearly on display, so is the huge wealth that came with the higher dignities.
353 DO BZS.1955.1.1394.
354 Oikonomides, *Listes*, p. 273.
355 The only *judges* with higher status in c. 1060 than the majority had held in c. 966 were the 10.7 per cent with titles of *anthypatos* and above.

356 The *protospatharioi*, Ficker, *Alexios Stoudites*, pp. 20–1 (1029); Miklosich-Müller 5, no. 1, pp. 1–2 (1045); Psellos, *Orationes forenses et acta*, pp. 145–6 (1053); the *hypatoi*, Iviron 2, no. 34, p. 98; no. 35, p. 104 (1062); *Dionysiou*, no. 1, p. 41 (1056); Iviron 2, no. 31, p. 79, 80 (1056); the *anthypatos* and *patrikios*, Iviron no. 32, p. 87 (1059); the *illoustrios* Novella constitutio 8. Chitwood, *Byzantine Legal Culture*, p. 196.
357 Howard-Johnston, 'The *Peira* and Legal Practices', p. 70; Weiss, 'Hohe Richter', p. 119.
358 Nicolas Oikonomides, 'Peira', pp. 171–2.
359 He was likely made *vestes* between the end of 1028 and May 1030. Oikonomides, 'Peira', p. 182.
360 For an outline of Eustathios's career, see Oikonomides, 'Peira', pp. 171–6. For a slightly different account, see Weiss, 'Hohe Richter', pp. 119–21. A number of seals possibly belonging to Eustathios are known, Zacos, *Lead Seals* II, no. 142, Eustathios *anythypatos, patrikios*, and *vestes, droungarios* of the *Vigla*; Laurent, *Corpus* II, no. 888, Eustathios *magistros* and *droungarios* of the *Vigla*; Zacos, *Lead Seals* II, no. 145 Eustathios *protospatharios* judge of the Hippodrome and *anagrapheus* of Paphlagonia; and DO 1947.2.702 Eustathios *protospatharios*, judges of the Hippodrome, and *epi tou mystikou domou*.
361 The case is recorded in a court summary (*hypomnema*) Dennis, *Orationes, Fortenses et Acta*, pp. 143–54. Psellos thought that Elpidios had betrayed the terms of the engagement, by proving himself an unworthy husband and son-in-law, and wished to break it. The dispute was over whether this was justified, and what would become of Euphemia's dowry. For recent scholarship on the question of the authorship of the summary as well as a discussion of the text, see Kaldellis, *Mothers and Sons*, pp. 139–46.
362 Dennis, *Michaelis Pselli Orationes*, pp. 145, 151.
363 Elpidios, perhaps vindicating Psellos' opinion of him, left no such legacy.
364 Presumably the drop in both figures in the final third of the eleventh century was the result of their being the same number of judges of the Velum and the Hippodrome, but increasingly fewer provinces.
365 Zacos, *Lead Seals* II, no. 1013.
366 K. E. Zachariä von Lingenthal, *Geschichte des griechisch- romischen Rechtes*, 3rd edn (Berlin, 1892), p. 374.
367 For a review of this debate with relevant bibliography, see Gkoutzioukostas, *Η απονομή δικαιοσύνης στο Βυζάντιο*, pp. 202–7 and the recent study by S. Antonov, 'The Byzantine Office of ἐπὶ τῶν κρίσεων and Its Holders (in the Light of Sphragistic Evidence and Written Sources)', *Studia Ceranea* 7, (2017), pp. 9–25.
368 For oversight of the decisions of theme judges, see Oikonomides, 'L'évolution', p. 134, Oikonomides believed that the impetus behind the creation of the review process for provincial judicial decisions was the result of the growing number of *theme* judges who were not trained jurists. For wide-ranging authority over the theme judges see Chondridou, *Κωνσταντίνος Θ᾿ Μονομάχος*, pp. 127–40. For collecting and storing provincial judicial decisions and the extension of central authority, see Christophilopoulou, *Βυζαντινά δικαστήρια*, p. 174–5. For administrative oversight, see Ahrweiler, 'Administration', pp. 70–1; For provincial administrative coordination, see Angold, *The Byzantine Empire 1025–1204*, p. 114.
369 Attaleiates, *History*, p. 37.
370 Psellos, *Orationes, Forenses, et Acta*, p. 143.
371 Iviron 2, no. 35.
372 *Πάτμου* 1, no. 5, p. 44.

373 *Actes d'Iviron* 2, no. 44 for the will, no. 46 for 1112 copy of the original certification.
374 We know that by the mid-twelfth century that the *epi ton kriseon* chaired one of the four permanent courts in the capital as one of the empire's great judges, being listed after the *droungarios* of the *Vigla*, and before the *koiaistor* and the *eparch*. Oikonomides, 'L'évolution', pp. 134–5. However, this reveals little about the functions of the office in the eleventh century, and as we have seen the duties of officials could change rather quickly, let alone over a century.
375 Appeal of the decisions of provincial judges to the central authority of the emperor, *eparch* and *koiaistor* is mentioned in the Zachariä von Lingenthal, *Collectio librorum, epanagoge*, 11.9, p.89; Zepos *JGR* II, p. 260–1, where it is assumed that distance from Constantinople will lead to mistakes in verdicts that would require appeal and retrial. It should be noted that the court of the *epi ton kriseon* reviewed provincial cases, but was itself not a court of appeal. Oikonomides, 'L'évolution', p. 134.
376 More seals, at least sixteen belonging to five individuals, have been identified as belonging to an *epi ton kriseon* by earlier scholars. However, I am inclined to agree with Andreas Gkoutzioukostas that unless a seal specifically mentions the office of *epi ton kriseon*, rather than κρίσεις, judgements, that we cannot be certain that the sigilant was not a simple judge. Gkoutzioukostas, 'Seals of Byzantine Officials Connected with the Administration of Justice', pp. 10–18, 16.
377 Michael, Laurent, *Corpus* II, no. 899; Zacos, *Lead Seals* II, no. 1013, *PBW* Michael 20193; Niketas, Zacos, *Lead Seals* II, no. 654; Laurent, *Corpus* II, no. 900, *PBW* Niketas 20154.
378 *Iviron*, no. 35, p. 102.
379 *DO Seals* 4.11.13.
380 My special thanks to Lain Wilson for his insight into this office.
381 Oikonomides, *Listes*, p. 271.
382 For a discussion of the *thesmophylax* as guardian of the laws, and the *nomophylax*, also guardian of the laws, see P. Christophilopoulos, 'Νομοφύλακες και Θεσμοφύλακες', Πλάτων 20 (1968), pp. 134–43.
383 Weiss, 'Hohe Richter', p. 119 for the policeman, Gkoutzioukostas, *Η απονομή δικαιοσύνης στο Βυζάντιο*, p. 200 for the record keeper or judge, and Oikonomides, *Listes*, p. 326 for subordination to the *droungarios* of the *Vigla*.
384 Laurent, *Corpus* II, no. 1079; Zacos, *Lead Seals* II, no. 978.
385 Gkoutzioukostas, 'Administration of Justice', p. 10.
386 *Thesmophylax*, DO BZS.1955.1.2196 and Konstantopoulos *Νομισματικοῦ Μουσείου*. 598. *Thesmophylax* and *tribunos*, Laurent, *Corpus* II, no. 915. *Thesmophylax* of the *kriseis*, and *symponos*, Laurent, *Corpus* II, no. 1079 and Zacos, *Lead Seals* II, no. 978. *Thesmophylax*, *asekretis*, and judge, Cheynet and Theodorides, *Theodorides*, no. 86. *Thesmophylax*, judge of the Hippodrome, and judge of Thrakesion, Cheynet, 'Selçuk', no. 24. *Thesmophylax*, judge of the Hippodrome, and judge of the *Boukellarion*, *DO Seals* 4.1.16. *Thesmophylax* and judge of Thrakesion, *DO Seals* 3.2.29.
387 Oikonomides, *Listes*, p. 326.
388 Gkoutzioukostas, *Η απονομή δικαιοσύνης στο Βυζάντιο*, p. 200 has argued that because Elpidios Kenchres obtained the office of *thesmographos* after that of judge of the Velum, and that this must have represented a promotion, that the *thesmographoi* must necessarily rank higher than the judges. That this was not the case is suggested by the sigillographic material, where an ever-increasing number of the judges of the Velum held titles higher than *protospatharios*, which was, as far as we can tell, never

the case for the *thesmographoi*. We are forced to conclude that Kenchres accumulated positions in a non-hierarchically dependent fashion.

389 These offices are remenicent of the *mystikos*, *mystographos* and *mystolektes* in that their names share a common root, which also happens to be the main clue as to their function.

390 Gkoutzioukostas, 'Administrative Structures', p. 574 proposes the possible translation of *thesmographos* as 'notary of justice'.

391 See *DO Seals* 4.32.10, judge of the Hippodrome and judge of Chaldia. Cheynet, Morrisson and Seibt, *Seyrig*, no. 197, judge of the Hippodrome and judge of Boleron, Strymon and Thessaloniki. Zacos, *Lead Seals* II, no. 740 and Laurent, *Corpus* II, no. 866, judge of the Hippodrome.

392 Psellos, *Orationes, Forenses et Acta*, pp. 150–1; Gkoutzioukostas, 'Administrative Structures'; *PBW* Michael 2101, Gabriel 2101.

393 For the *exaktor* as a fiscal official, see Gkoutzioukostas, *Η απονομή δικαιοσύνης στο Βυζάντιο*, p. 190; Weiss, 'Hohe Richter', p. 120. For the *exaktores* as fiscal judges, see Magdalino, 'Justice and Finance', pp. 104–5, Seibt and Zarnitz, *Kunstwerk*, 2.2.1. For the *exaktor* as a high-ranking jurist, see Oikonomides, *Listes*, p. 325.

394 In the *Escorial Taktikon* the *exaktor* came 148/125 in the hierarchy.

395 John Tzetzes, *Ioannis Tzetzae Chiliades*, ed. P. A. M. Leone (Naples, 1968), pp. 190–1.

396 Oikonomides, *Listes*, p. 325.

397 Magadlino, 'Justice and Finance', p. 104, and more generally for the idea of fiscal judicial offices and tribunals in Byzantium. The case was *Peira* 36.18.

398 *Peira* 36.18, translation from Magdalino, 'Justice and Finance', p. 104. The word translated here as 'substance' could equally mean property.

399 See *Peira* 16.11, 25.8, and 44.1.

400 Oikonomides, *Listes*, p. 325 decided that this did not mean that the *exaktor* was a fiscal official, while Gkoutzioukostas, *Η απονομή δικαιοσύνης στο Βυζάντιο*, pp. 190–1, came to exactly the opposite conclusion. Cf. Gkoutzioukostas, 'Administration of Justice', pp. 14–15 and Gkoutzioukostas, 'Administrative Structures', pp. 575–6.

401 Oikonomides, *Listes*, p. 271.

402 *Peira*, 63.5.

403 In this conclusion I differ from Gkoutzioukostas, *Η απονομή δικαιοσύνης στο Βυζάντιο*, p. 194, who, working from a smaller sample of seals, concluded that the majority of secondary offices were of a financial nature. See also a development of this argument in Gkoutzioukostas, 'Administrative Structures', pp. 574–5.

404 J.-C. Cheynet and D. Theodorides, *Sceaux byzantins de la collection D. Theodorides. Les sceaux patronymiques* (Paris, 2010), pp. 68, 194.

405 Thus, I find myself in the enviable position of agreeing with Oikonomides, *Listes*, p. 325, who considered the *kensor* to be a judicial official, and J.-C. Cheynet, 'Sceaux byzantines des musees d'Antioche et de Tarse', *TM* 12 (1994), pp. 414–15 who concluded that the *kensores* were judges of the same level as the Hippodrome and Velum.

406 *DO Seals* 4.43.4 for the *vestarches*, DO BZS.1958.106.4947 for the *vestes*, *anthypatos* and *patrikios*, and Cheynet et al., *Istanbul*, no. 2.99 and Sode, *Berlin* II, no. 353 for the *illoustrios*.

407 Type one, Laurent, *Corpus* II, no. 1155, Šandrovskaja, 'O dvuch pečatjach vizantinijskich juristov', *ADSV* 41 (2013), pp. 153–7, 159; Schlumberger, 'Sceaux inédits', p. 340, no. 255. Type two, Laurent, *Corpus* II, no. 1156. For a discussion of

these seals, see W. Seibt, 'Katechanas – ein lange verkannter mittelbyzantinischer Bei- bzw. Familienname', *Byzantinische Zeitschrift* 110, no. 3 (2017), pp. 749–54.
408 Constantine IX Monomachos, *Novella constitutio*, trans. Chitwood, *Byzantine Legal Culture*, p. 197.
409 The exact date at which the law school was founded is uncertain. Chitwood, *Byzantine Legal Culture*, p. 168, A. Markopoulos, 'Education', in *The Oxford Handbook of Byzantine Studies*, eds M. Jeffreys, J. Haldon and R. Cormack (Oxford, 2008), pp. 785–95, at p. 790; and J. Lefort, 'Rhétorique et politique: trois discours de Jean Mauropous en 1047', *TM* 6 (1976), pp. 265–303, at pp. 279–84 argue for a date of 1047, E. Follieri, 'Sulla Novella promulgata da Costantino IX Monomaco per la restaurazione della Facoltà giuridica a Costantinopoli', *Studi in onore di Edoardo Volterra* II (Milan, 1971), pp. 647–64 and Weiss prefer a date of 1043, while Dölger, *Regesten*, pp. 207–11 opted for 1045.
410 Chitwood, *Byzantine Legal Culture*, p. 197ff.
411 Ibid., p. 168.
412 Sathas, Βιβλιοθήκη 4, pp. 421–46, at pp. 427–33. Oikonomides, 'Peira', p. 189, Kaldellis, *Streams of Blood, Rivers of Gold*, p. 190, n. 1 for references to similar conplaints elsewhere in Psellos's writings about the decline of education. As Weiss, 'Hohe Richter', p. 122 points out the case of Eustathios Romaios and the *Peira* is firm evidence that there was a flourishing and knowledgeable cadre of judges working in Constantinople without the need for Xiphilinos' instruction.
413 Chitwood, *Byzantine Legal Culture*, pp. 194–5.
414 Ibid., pp. 174–7
415 Oikonomides, 'Peira', p. 190 pointed out that the law school of John Xiphilinos was the first diploma issuing educational institution in Europe.
416 Chitwood, *Byzantine Legal Culture*, p. 199.
417 See Oikonomides, 'Peira', p. 190 for much of what follows.
418 Oikonomides, 'Peira', p. 190 referencing Sathas, Μεσαιωνικὴ Βιβλιοθήκη, 4 pp. 431, 433; V, p. 182.
419 Chitwood, *Byzantine Legal Culture*, p. 198.
420 Sathas, Μεσαιωνικὴ Βιβλιοθήκη, 5, pp. 181–96.
421 *Peira*, 16.9, 19.5, 51.16.
422 For the dispute between the aged judge and Xiphilinos, Lemerle, *Cinq études*, pp. 211–XXX; W. Wolska-Conus, 'Les écoles de Psellos et de Xiphilin sous Constantin IX Monomaque', *Travaux et Mémoires* 6 (1976), pp. 238–42, who dates the attack to c. 1050, and the possibility that Eustathios Romaios may have been behind the quarrel, see Oikonomides, 'Peira', p. 176.
423 For a discussion of this event, including an dismissive take on Psellos's defence of his friend, see Weiss, *Oströmische Beamte*, pp. 84–5, who reaches the conclusion that the complaints of Ophrydas about the young, self-trained Xiphilinos were likely entirely reasonable.
424 Chitwood, *Byzantine Legal Culture*, p. 193.
425 At least, if the emperors had made a big deal out of creating the position of *thesmophylax* then no evidence of it has survived.
426 For the case of Alexios Stoudites and the Church of the East, see Chitwood, *Byzantine Legal Culture*, pp. 141–8. In this chapter Chitwood puts forward the excellent argument that in using the assembled legal minds of the capital to construct his attacks on heretics Alexios Stoudites both recognized them as the highest legal authorities in the empire, and helped to cement their position as such. The

only qualms that I have about Chitwood's argument are that I would place slightly more emphasis on the recognition than the cementing, and I would not consider Eustathios et al as the first generation of jurists, but perhaps the second behind those who had risen to equal prominence by c. 975 at the latest.
427 *Novella constitutio*, trans., Chitwood, *Byzantine Legal Culture*, p. 203.

Chapter 4

1 Attaleiates, *History*, p. 139,
2 Ibid., p. 391.
3 P. Gautier, 'Le synode des Blachernes (fin 1094). Étude prosopographique', *Revue des Études byzantines* 29, (1971), pp. 213–84, at p. 217.
4 His next appearance was in *Lavra* I, no. 43, p. 240. See also, Oikonomides, 'L'évolution', p. 132; Stein, 'Untrsuchungen', p. 34; C. M. Diehl, 'Un haut fonctionnaire byzantin: le logothète "tôn sékrétôn"', in *Mélanges N. Jorga* (Paris, 1933), pp. 217–29; Brehier, *Institutions*, pp. 270–1; Ahrweiler, *Mer*, pp. 200–204; Guilland, *Logothètes*, pp. 75–84.
5 Wassiliou, 'Hexamilites', no. 17; J. Gouillard, 'Le proces officiel de Jean l'Italien: les actes et leurs sous-entendus', *Travaux et Mémoires* 9 (1985), pp. 133–69, *PBW* Sergios 105. Anonymous, *Docheiariou*, no. 2, p. 59. *PBW* Anonymous 676.
6 Gautier, 'Blachernes', p. 217; Anna Komnene, *Alexiad*, p. 87; *Lavra* I, no. 58, p. 302, *PBW* Michael 122.
7 *PBW* Gregorios 105.
8 P. Magdalino, 'Innovations in Government', in *Alexios I Komnenos. 1, Papers of the Second Belfast Byzantine International Colloquium, 14–16 April 1989*, eds M. Mullett and D. Smythe (Belfast, 1996), pp. 146–66, at pp. 153–5.
9 For the evolution of this office after our period, see Gkoutzioukostas, 'Administrative Structure', pp. 578–80.
10 DO BZS.1958.106.4080.
11 Michael Jeffreys makes a powerful argument in favour of the earlier date. Jeffreys, 'Constantine Nephew of the Patriarch'. For the latter option, see Wassiliou-Seibt, A.-K., 'Die Neffen des Patriarchen Michael I. Kerullarios (1043-1058) und ihre Siegel. Ikonographie als Ausdrucksmittel der Verwandtschaft', *Bulgaria Mediaevalis* 2 (2012), pp. 107-19, at p. 109.
12 Jeffreys, 'Psellos and the Nephew of the Patriarch'.
13 Oikonomides, 'L'évolution', p. 135. Miklosich and Müller V, 5, no. 6, p. 9.
14 As Oikonomides noted the epithet of *megas* was not consistently applied to the *sakellarios*. Oikonomides, 'L'évolution', p. 135. It is possible that it was given out as a mark of distinction to certain individuals rather than applied to the office itself, in contrast to the *megas droungarios*. Even so, it seems an unlikely action to occur if an office was being phased out.
15 Attaleiates, *History*, pp. 506–8.
16 Oikonomides, 'Role of the Byzantine State', p. 992 and 'L'évolution', p. 135. I agree with Oikonomides that there is no evidence that the *sakellarios* lost his preeminent position over the bureaucracy when the *megas logariastes* appeared. For this argument, see Dölger, *Finanzverwaltung*, pp. 17–18.
17 *PBW* Michael 195.

18 Oikonomides, 'L'évolution', p. 135. Miklosich-Müller V, no. 6, p. 9.
19 Laurent, *Corpus* II, no. 807 (with different dating), *PBW* Michael 20298.
20 Oikonomides, 'L'évolution', pp. 140–1; R. Guilland, 'Études sur l'histoire administrative de l'empire byzantine. Le logariaste, ὁ λογαριαστής; le grand logariaste, ὁ μέγας λογαριαστής', *Jahrbuch der Österreichischen Byzantinistik* 18 (1969), pp. 101–8.
21 Oikonomides, 'Evolution', pp. 140–1; Dölger and Wirth, *Regesten*, no. 1175; *Lavra* I, nos. 67, 68.
22 Schlumberger, *Sigillographie*, p. 715; Šandrovskaja, 'Sfragistika', no. 743; Laurent, *Corpus* II, no. 327; Wassiliou and Seibt, *Bleisiegel* II, p. 188, n. 284.
23 Oikonomides, 'Role of the Byzantine State', p. 992 and 'L'évolution', p. 135.
24 See Nesbitt, 'Oikistikos'.
25 Oikonomides, 'L'évolution', p. 135.
26 Theodore tou Aktouariou held the title of *magistros*, a dignity which does not appear on any seals known to me, in 1088. Vranousis and Nystazopoulou-Pelekidou, *Πάτμου* 1, no. 48, p. 338.
27 No title, *Πάτμου*, 1, no. 48, p. 339. *Dishypatos*, *Πάτμου*, 1, no. 46, p. 330. *Vestarches*, *Πάτμου*, 1, no. 46, p. 330. *Magistros*, *Πάτμου* 1, no. 49, p. 346, 1, no. 48, p. 339. *Protoproedros*, *Πάτμου* 1, no. 8, p. 338.
28 Campagnolo-Pothitou and Cheynet, *Geneva*, no. 28.
29 Oikonomides, 'L'évolution', pp. 135–6. Final mention Miklosich and Müller VI, no. 14, pp. 50–1.
30 *PBW* Michael 20288, 20287.
31 *Πάτμου* 1. nos. 48, p. 339, 49, p. 346, *PBW* Niketas 157.
32 Oikonomides, 'L'évolution', pp. 135–6.
33 Beriotes, Laurent, *Corpus* II, no. 809. See also, Wassiliou and Seibt, *Bleisiegel* II, p. 39, n. 65 and Šandroskaja and Seibt, *Eremitage*, p. 68, n. 47, *PBW* Ioannes 20402; Chrysoberges, *Πάτμου* 1, no. 48, p. 339, *PBW* Ioannes 360.
34 Adramytenos, Campagnolo-Pothitou and Cheynet, *Geneva*, no. 28; Matzoukes, *Πάτμου* 1, no. 48, p. 339, no. 49, p. 346, *PBW* Anastasios 107.
35 Wassiliou and Seibt, *Bleisiegel* II, no. 56.
36 Oikonomides, 'L'évolution', p. 131, n. 35.
37 Ibid., p. 131.
38 John *proedros* second half of the eleventh Konstantopoulos, Νομισματικοῦ Μουσείου, no. 407, *PBW* Ioannes 20383. Michael Aristenos last third, no title. Laurent, *Corpus* II, no. 439, Wassiliou and Seibt, *Bleisiegel* II, no. 56; Jordanov, *Bulgaria*, 2, no. 57, *PBW* Michael 20286. Theodore *proedros* second half eleventh, Konstantopoulos, *Stamoules*, no. 95; Zacos, *Lead Seals* II, no. 735, *PBW* Theodoros 20167.
39 Nikephoritzes, *hypersebastos*, 1072 onwards, Attaleiates, *History*, p. 330; Bryennios, *Historiarum Libri IV*, IV.1, p. 143; Sathas, Μεσαιωνικὴ Βιβλιοθήκη, 5, p. 378. He was possibly the last of the traditionally powerful *logothetai tou dromou*.
40 For John, see *Lavra* I, no. 48, p. 258. For Andronikos Skleros, see Gautier, 'Blachernes', p. 217, *PBW* Andronikos 102.
41 Laurent, *Corpus* II, no. 447, *PBW* Georgios 20139.
42 Sathas, Μεσαιωνικὴ Βιβλιοθήκη, 5, p. 372; Gouillard, 'Le proces officiel de Jean l'Italien', I.160, II 159–60, *PBW* Eustratios 101, Konstantinos 126.
43 For comparison it is interesting that the only known *protonotarios* of the *genikon* from this period, 1088 to be exact, was a *patrikios*. *Πάτμου* 1, no. 49, p. 345.

44 Schlumberger, *Sigillographie*, p. 603, no. 8; Werner Seibt, *Die Skleroi* (Vienna, 1976), p. 88, n. 318.
45 Oikonomides, 'L'évolution', p. 137.
46 Ibid.
47 Miklosich-Müller, VI, no. 13, p. 48.
48 Oikonomides, 'Role of the Byzantine State', pp. 993, 1021 and 'L'évolution', p. 137. The implied requirement to dip into various pots of money to fund the empire's expenses is further suggestion that the *sakellarios* retained some overarching responsibilities up to 1079.
49 *PBW* Konstantinos 20230, 20582, 20280.
50 For Constantine, second half of the eleventh century, see Laurent, *Corpus* II, no. 622. For Constantine Mytlienaios, 1070–90, see Campagnolo-Pothitou and Cheynet, *Geneva*, no. 36 and Stavrakos, *Familiennamen*, no. 178. For Constantine Blachernites, 1070–95, see Laurent, *Corpus* V.3, no. 1651.
51 For the *epi tes sakelles*, see Gregory, Campagnolo-Pothitou and Cheynet, *Geneva*, no. 42 and Laurent, *Corpus* II, no. 800. Niketas Cheynet et al., *Istanbul*, no. 2.72. John, Zacos, *Lead Seals* II, no. 522; Campagnolo-Pothitou and Cheynet, *Geneva*, no. 43, Laurent, *Corpus* II, no. 802; Theophylaktos, Wassiliou and Seibt, *Bleisiegel* II, no. 16; George Promoundenos in 1088, Πάτμου 1, no. 49, p. 345, and John Radenos in 1088, Πάτμου 1, no. 48, p. 340. For the *epi tou vestiariou*, see Pothos *vestes* Zacos, *Lead Seals* II, no. 681b and Campagnolo-Pothitou and Cheynet, *Geneva*, no. 46.
52 *Sakellion*, Nicholas Anzas, Wassiliou and Seibt, *Bleisiegel* II, p. 93, n. 432; Nicholas Tzanzes, Campagnolo-Pothitou and Cheynet, *Geneva*, no. 127. *Eidikon*, Anonymous, Seyrig, no. 113; Niketas Zacos, *Lead Seals* II, no. 649; Nicholas Artabasdos, V. Bulgakova, *Byzantinische Bleisiegel in Osteuropa: Die Funde auf dem Territorium Altrusslands* (Wiesbaden, 2004), no. 1.2.10.
53 Their titles were not the result of higher offices held concurrently with that of imperial *notarios*. While Nicholas held the lowest rank of the three, *protospatharios*, his seals place his position as imperial *notarios* after that of *mystographos*, implying that it was the more important office. Niketas was also *praitor* of Constantinople, an office which did not affect his titles.
54 Oikonomides, 'L'évolution', p. 137.
55 Not least the mint.
56 From the chrysobull of Alexios I issued in 1099 containing the first mention of the *megas logariastes ton euagon sekreton*. Miklosich-Müller VI, no. 22, p. 95.
57 DO BZS.1958.106.3655.
58 Šandroskaja and Seibt, *Eremitage*, no. 48; Wassiliou and Seibt, *Bleisiegel* II, p. 39, n. 67; Šandroskaja and Seibt, *Eremitage*, p. 67, n. 44.
59 Πάτμου 1, no. 46, p. 329, no. 48, p. 338, *PBW* Theoktistos 106.
60 Πάτμου 1, no. 48, p. 338, no. 49, p. 344, *PBW* Basileios 205.
61 No title, Πάτμου 1, no. 46, p. 329 (1087), no. 48, p. 338 (1088), no. 49, p. 344 (1088). *Vestes*, Πάτμου 1, no. 46, p. 329 (1087), no. 48, p. 338 (1088), no. 49, p. 344 (1088), *Lavra* I, no. 40, pp. 222, 223 (1079), *Iviron* 2, no. 46, p. 169 (1080–4), Šandrovskaja and Seibt, *Eremitage*, no. 54. *Dishypatos*, Πάτμου 1, no. 49, p. 344. *Protovestarches*, Πάτμου 1, no. 48, p. 338.
62 The *dishypatos* was not so lucky.
63 Oikonomides, 'L'évolution', p. 137.
64 Cheynet, 'Les sceaux byzantins de Londres', *Studies in Byzantine Sigillography* 8 (2003), p. 88, n. 15.

65 Campagnolo-Pothitou and Cheynet, *Geneva*, no. 40.
66 Šandrovskaja, 'Sfragistika', no. 802.
67 The *oikos* of the Hebdomon founded by Basil II went to Nikephoritzes under Michael VII, Attaleiates, *History*, p. 201; Kedrenos, *Historiarum Compendium*, II, p. 714. Later Nikephoros III gave the deposed empress Maria of Alania the same property along with the Mangana specifically so that she could live in royal state, Zonaras, *Epitome Historiarum*, III, p. 733. The same emperor did something similar for yet another deposed empress Eudokeia Makrembolitissa, Attaleiates, *History*, p. 304. Alexios I made a gift of the Myrelaion to his mother Anna.
68 Oikonomides, 'L'évolution', p. 140. The Seyrig collection includes a seal of N. Argyros *protospatharios*, who among other duties was *oikonomos* of the West, dated to the second third of the eleventh century. J.-C. Cheynet, C. Morrisson and W. Seibt, *Sceaux byzantins de la collection Henri Seyrig* (Paris, 1991): no. 81. See also, Šandroskaja and Seibt, *Eremitage*, p. 50, n. 172.
69 *Antiprosopon*, J.-C. Cheynet, 'Les sceaux byzantins de Londres', p. 88, n. 15, *PBW* Thomas 20115. *Deuteros*, Wassiliou and Seibt, *Bleisiegel* II, no. 36, p. 64, n. 242, *PBW* Georgios 20187. *Chartoularios*, Wassiliou and Seibt, *Bleisiegel* II, no. 83 and A. Szemioth and T. Wasilewski, 'Sceaux byzantins du Musée National de Varsovie', *Studia Źródłoznawcze, Commentationes* 11 (1966), pp. 1–38 and 14 (1969), pp. 63–89, no. 10, *PBW* Michael 20374. *Notarioi*, Stavrakos, *Familiennamen*, p. 179; Jordanov, *Bulgaria* 2, p. 173; Campagnolo-Pothitou and Cheynet, *Geneva*, no. 66, *PBW* Gregorios 20144, Nikolaos 1101.
70 Miklosich-Muller VI, no. 13, p. 48. Oikonomides, 'L'évolution', p. 141.
71 Miklosich-Muller VI, no. 22, p. 95; *Lavra* I, nos. 67, 69. Oikonomides, 'L'évolution', p. 141 dates this reform to the period after Alexios I stabilized the military situation in the Balkans, meaning that it could have taken place as early as 1091.
72 The *sekreton* is last recorded in 1145. Dölger, *Finanzverwaltung*, p. 42.
73 Description of John Taronites who held the post of *epi ton deeseon* under Alexios I Komnenos. Anna Komnene, *The Alexiad*, trans. E. R. A. Sewter. Revised by P. Frankopan (London, 2009), pp. 357–8.
74 DO BZS.55.1.4060.
75 Oikonomides, 'L'évolution', p. 131.
76 N. Oikonomides, 'Ho megas droungarios Eustathios Kymineianos kai he sphragida tou (1099)', *Byzantina* 13, no. 2 (1985), pp. 899–907; *Dated Lead Seals*, no, 106, *PBW* Gregorios 20136, Eustathios 15001.
77 Sathas, Μεσαιωνικὴ Βιβλιοθήκη, 5, pp. 331–2; Πάτμου 1, no. 5, p. 44, *PBW* Basileios 2103, Manuel 104; Gautier, 'Blachernes', p. 217. Eustathios Kymineianos also appears in Komnene, *Alexiad*, p. 353, and presumably held the office after Manuel Philokales.
78 Sathas, Μεσαιωνικὴ Βιβλιοθήκη, 5, p. 251.
79 Laurent, *Corpus* II, no. 8.
80 Oikonomides, 'L'évolution', p. 131. Laurent, *Corpus* II, p. 5; Magdalino, 'Justice and Finance', pp. 93–115, at pp. 108–9. There is a significant gap of some decades, perhaps six, between the final attestation of the *protoasekretis* as head of the chancery and his appearance as a judge. Exactly when in the intervening years the switch occurred is unknown. Gkoutzioukostas has suggested that the *protoasekretis* never left the imperial secretariat, but continued to work in that department while also acting as a senior judge, citing evidence from the reign of Manuel I Komnenos (1143–80), Gkoutzioukostas, 'Ἡ εξέλιξη του θεσμοῦ των σηκρῆτις και του πρωτοασηκρῆτις στο πλαίσιο της αυτοκρατορικής γραμματείας', Βυζαντινά 23 (2002–2003), pp. 86–7.

However, there is somewhat of a gap between Manuel's time and the last mention of the *protoasekretis* as a chancery official in 1106 (Dölger & Wirth, Regesten, no. 1231).
81　Laurent, *Corpus* II, no. 7; see, Seibt, *Bleisiegel* I, pp. 291–2; *PBW* Ioannes 20268.
82　E. Kurtz and F. Drexl, *Michaelis Pselli Scripta minora magnam partem adhuc inedita II* (Milan, 1941), no. 148, *PBW* Anonymous 2300.
83　For Eustratios Choirosphaktes, see Attaleiates, *History*, p. 302 and *Skylitzes Continuatus*, p. 152, *PBW* Eustratios 101. For John, see J. Bompaire, J. Lefort, V. Kravari and C. Giros, *Actes de Vatopédi I. Des origines à 1329, Archives de l'Athos XXI* (Paris, 2001), no. 11, p. 117, *PBW* Ioannes 426.
84　P. Gautier, *Théophylacte d'Achrida, II. Lettres*, Corpus fontium historiae Byzantinae 16/2 (Thessalonike 1986), p. 571. Gregory also appeared with this post in 1094 in the records of the synod held that year, but his title was not recorded.
85　For the career of Gregory Kamateros, see *PBW* Gregory 105.
86　DO BZS.1958.106.5651. Cf. A.-K. Wassiliou-Seibt, *Corpus der byzantinischen Siegel mit metrischen Legenden* I (Vienna, 2011), no. 207.
87　For Constantine, see *Lavra* I, no. 56, p. 293, *PBW* Konstantinos 240. For John, see *Lavra* I, no. 56, p. 293.
88　I freely admit that it is perhaps unlikely that similar evidence would explain a mere *anagrapheus* holding this title either.
89　Laurent, *Orghidan*, no. 78; Laurent, *Corpus* II, no. 122.
90　Magdalino, 'Mystikos', pp. 237–8.
91　Michael was promoted to *protoproedros* around 1080 when he became *eparch* of Constantinople, a rank that had been increased to *protonobelissimos* by 1094. Gautier, 'Blachernes', p. 217, *PBW* Michael 20229.
92　Laurent, *Corpus* II, no. 149.
93　The *mystographos* was Theodore, the son of Michael Attaleiates, the author of the document that records his rank. Gautier, 'diataxis', pp. 29, 35, 117.
94　DO BZS.1955.1.3324.
95　Cheynet, 'Devaluation', p. 462. He has left behind a number of seals, *PBW* Nikolaos 2104.
96　Πάτμου 1, no. 6, p. 60, no. 48, p. 337, no. 49, p. 343, *PBW* Konstantinos 20271, Ioannes 15019, Konstantinos 126.
97　Gautier, 'Blachernes', p. 217, *PBW* Ioannes 118.
98　Morris, 'epi tôn deêseon', pp. 132–3, 139. Constantine Choirosphaktes, while not related to Alexios I was a close supporter. See also, *Oxford Dictionary of Byzantium*, *epi ton deeseon*. This trend continued into the twelfth century. See, for example, *PBW* Andronikos 112 (Andronikos Doukas Kamateros), Konstantinos 216 (Constantine Tornikios) and Michael 20240 (Michael Kamateros).
99　Stavrakos, *Familiennamen*, no. 40; Laurent, *Corpus* II, no. 154; Konstantopoulos, Νομισματικοῦ Μουσείου, no. 598b.
100　Laurent, *Corpus* II, no. 1028.
101　Kamateros, Bees, N., 'Zur Sigillographie der byzantinischen Themen Peloponnes und Hellas', *Vizantijskij Vremennik* 21 (1914), pp. 90–110 and 192–235, at p. 219; Konstantopoulos, Νομισματικοῦ Μουσείου, no. 345; Laurent, 'Un sceau inédit du protonotaire Basile Kamatéros', *Byzantion* 6 (1931), pp. 253–72, at p. 264; Laurent, *Bulles metriques*, no. 130; Laurent, *Corpus* II, no. 1028; Lichačev, 'Molivdovuly', p. 163, no. 14; Stavrakos, *Familiennamen*, no. 102. Beriotes, Wassiliou and Seibt, *Bleisiegel* II, no. 11.
102　Laurent, *Corpus* II, no. 1031, see also, Wassiliou, 'Hexamilites', no. 17(vi).

103 Tzirithon, *Lavra* I, no. 49, p. 261; Philokales, *Protoproedros*, Laurent, *Corpus* II, no. 1033; *Protonobelissimos*, Gautier, 'Blachernes', p. 217.
104 Xeros, Anna Komnene, *Alexiad*, p. 373, *PBW* Anonymous 15093; Basil, Anna Komnene, *Alexiad*, p. 368, *PBW* Basileios 233; N. Aristenos, Wassiliou and Seibt, *Bleisiegel* II, no. 13; Jordanov, *Bulgaria* 3, no. 925, *PBW* Anonymous 20241; and Leo Hikanatos, Laurent, *Corpus* II, no. 1037, *PBW* Leon 20251.
105 Anna Komnene, *Alexiad*, p. 384, *PBW* Ioannes 118.
106 DO BZS.1951.31.5.2909.
107 W. Seibt, 'Die Darstellung der Theotokos auf Byzantinichen Bleisiegeln besonders im 11. Jahrhundert', *Studies in Byzantine Sigillography* 1 (1987), pp. 35–56, no. 14.
108 Laurent, *Corpus* II, no. 1145.
109 *Scylitzes Continuatus*, ed. and trans. E. McGeer and J. Nesbitt, chapter 2, section 2.
110 Laurent, *Corpus* II, no. 1116.
111 See especially R. Macrides, 'Competent Court'.
112 For George Nikaeus, see *Iviron* 2, no. 44, p. 156, *PBW* Georgios 140. For Theodore Smyrnaios, see Wassiliou and Seibt, *Bleisiegel* II, p. 75, n. 313, *PBW* 109. We know that Theodore was not yet *koiaistor* in 1094 because of the records of the synod held at Blachernai in that year. He was *hypatos ton philosophon*. Gautier, 'Blachernes', p. 218.
113 Wassiliou and Seibt, *Bleisiegel* II, no. 1.
114 Laurent, *Corpus* II, no. 891; Lichačev, 'Molivdovuly', p. 150, no. 14.
115 On the evolution of the office and the use of the epithet *megas*, see Oikonomides, 'L'évolution', p. 134. See also, Magdalino, 'Justice and Finance' and Macrides, 'Competent Court'.
116 Guilland, *Recherches sur les institutions byzantines* I, pp. 573–5.
117 Laurent, *Corpus* II, no. 891; Lichačev, 'Molivdovuly', p. 150, no. 14; Cheynet, Morrisson and Seibt, *Seyrig*, no. 96; *PBW* Konstantinos 120.
118 Laurent, *Corpus* II, no. 892; Wassiliou and Seibt, *Bleisiegel* II, no. 93; Birch, *British Library*, no. 17776; *PBW* Nikephoros 20171.
119 Harvard Art Museums 1951.31.5.3362.
120 For the most recent exploration of the fascinating career of Constantine, see Jeffreys, 'Constantine, Nephew of the Patriarch', pp. 59–88.
121 That Constantine was a threat to the Doukas dynasty was voiced by the dying emperor Constantine X Doukas who forced his wife Eudokia, Constantine's cousin, to take a vow before becoming regent which included a clause never to entrust either of her cousins with the administration of the empire. Jeffreys, 'Constantine, Nephew of the Patriarch', p. 72. See also, Oikonomides, 'Le serment de l'impératrice Eudocie (1067): Un episode de l'histoire dynastique de Byzance', *Revue des études byzantines* 21 (1963), pp. 101–28.
122 Zachariä, *JGR* III, p. 343; Dölger, *Regesten*, no. 1283; See Gautier, 'Blachernes', p. 249. By the time of the Blachernai Synod of 1094 Michael had changed careers becoming *logothetes tou sekreta* with the title of *sebastos*, an interesting indication about the new position of the judiciary in the imperial government.
123 Zachariä, *JGR* III, p. 410; Dölger, *Regesten*, no. 1113; See Gautier, 'Blachernes', p. 249.
124 The Skleroi did not join the Komnenian elite and faded from prominence in the twelfth century. For the history of the Skleros family, see Seibt, *Skleroi*.
125 Seibt, *Skleroi*, p. 81. For older bibliography, see Gautier, 'Blachernes', p. 249, n. 77, *PBW* Ioannes 110.
126 *PBW* Nikolaos 104.

127 Two seals likely belonging to John Skyltizes from this time survive: Campagnolo-Pothitou and Cheynet, *Geneva*, no. 34 and I. Koltsid-Makrè, Ἡ συλλογή μολυβδοβούλλων Δημητρίου Δούκα', *Hypermachos. Studien zu Byzantinistik, Armenologie und Georgistik: Fetschrift für Werner Seibt zum 65. Geburtstag*, eds Ch. Stavrakos, A.-K. Wassiliou and M. K. Krikorian (Wisbaden, 2008), pp. 139–52, no. 9.
128 Gautier, 'Blachernes', p. 217.
129 Ibid., p. 249.
130 *Protoproedros*, Wassiliou and Seibt, *Bleisiegel*, p. 40, n. 80; Laurent, *Corpus* II, no. 1031; Wassiliou, 'Hexamilites' no. 17(vi); Wassiliou and Seibt, *Bleisiegel* II, p. 73, n. 301, DO BZS.1958.106.3222. *Nobelissimos*, Laurent, *Corpus* II, nos. 1040, 1042; Wassiliou and Seibt, *Bleisiegel* II, no. 12. For a reconstruction of Nicholas's career including a stint in the provinces, see Wassiliou and Seibt, *Bleisiegel* II, p. 40.
131 He was already *protoproedros* at this point. Jeffreys, 'Constantine, Nephew of the Patriarch', p. 79.
132 Wassiliou, 'Hexamilites', no. 18a; Laurent, *Vatican*, no. 83 and *Corpus* II, no. 846.
133 These four titles alone accounted for 60.6 per cent of the judge of the Velum at this time.
134 The *proedroi* and *protoproedroi*.
135 For Basil Tzirithon, see Wassiliou and Seibt, *Bleisiegel* II, no. 191. For Sergios Hexamilites, see Wassiliou and Seibt, *Bleisiegel* II, p. 73 n. 300 and Wassiliou, 'Hexamilites', no. 17(v).
136 Gautier, 'diataxis', pp. 19, 83, 103; J. Lefort, *Actes d'Esphigménou, Archives de l'Athos VI* (Paris, 1973), no. 4, p. 52.
137 All are known from the same source. The *vestarches*, Thomas Chalkoutzes, Πάτμου 1, no. 46, p. 330. The *protovestarches*, Basil Gorgonites, Πάτμου 1, no. 48, p. 338. The *magistroi*, Basil Chalkoutzes, Πάτμου no. 46, p. 330, Basil Kamateros, Πάτμου 1, no. 48, p. 338, Epiphanios Hexamilites, Πάτμου 1, no. 48, p. 340, no. 49, p. 345, George Promoundenos Πάτμου 1, no. 49, p. 345, Leo Hexamilites, Πάτμου 1, no. 48, p. 339, no. 49, p. 346, Leo Karamallos, Πάτμου 1, no. 49, p. 346, Nicholas Beriotes, Πάτμου 1, no. 48, p. 340.
138 No title, Niketas Anzas *Iviron* 2, no. 48, p. 188. *Protoproedros*, George Nikaeus *Iviron* 2, no. 44, p. 156, later *kouropalates*, *Iviron* 2, no. 46, 169.
139 DO BZS.1958.106.5457.
140 Where more accurate dating is possible the cut-off date is usually 1080, with significantly fewer seals falling into a wider date range extending later.
141 Michael Rodios, *Lavra* I, no. 46, p. 250, *PBW* Michael 252. John Melidones, *Iviron* 2, no. 43, pp. 146, 149, *PBW* Ioannes 182. Nicholas Zonaras, Πάτμου 1, no. 49, p. 346, *PBW* Nikolaos 205. Michael Autoreianos, Gautier, 'Blachernes', p. 218, *PBW* Michael 127.
142 Gkoutzioukostas, *Η απονομή δικαιοσύνης στο Βυζάντιο*, pp. 164, 174. Mention is made here of the examples of Monasteriotes, Basil Liparites and Constantine Kaisarites who were all judges of the Velum and Hippodrome in 1108, and all recorded no titles. Dölger, *Regesten*, no. 1243a.
143 See Gkoutzioukostas, *Η απονομή δικαιοσύνης στο Βυζάντιο*, pp. 172–6 for a discussion of this function of the judges. As signatories they usually appear as either the lowest or second lowest-ranked office, ahead only of the *mystikos*.
144 *Ecloga Basilcorum* B.7.2.1–2, pp. 237–8. For a discussion of these sources and the possible numbers of judges, see Gkoutzioukostas, *Η απονομή δικαιοσύνης στο Βυζάντιο*, pp. 159–65.

145 *Lavra* I, no. 68, p. 355, records eleven *judges*.
146 P. Gautier, 'Quelques lettres de Psellos inédites ou déjà éditées', *Revue des études Byzantines* 44 (1986), pp. 111–97, no. 21, translation from Jeffreys, 'Constantine, Nephew of the Patriarch', p. 86.
147 Sathas, Μεσαιωνικὴ Βιβλιοθήκη, 5, no. 157; Kurtz and Drexl, *Scripta minora*, no. 214. For a discussion of Constantine's career and his rank of *sebastos*, see Jeffreys, 'Psellos and the Nephew of the Patriarch', pp. 79–84.
148 Ibid.
149 Πάτμου 1, no. 5, p. 44; *Iviron*, 2, no. 46, p. 169, *PBW* Georgios 140.
150 Of the seven judges mentioned in the twelfth century, *Ecolga Basilicorum* the *epi ton kriseon* comes fifth in terms of number of appearances in the text behind the *droungarios*, *eparch*, *dikaiodotes* and *koiaistor*, but ahead of the *protoasekretis* and *katholikos*. R. J. Macrides, 'The Competent Court', *Law and Society in Byzantium: Nonth-Twelfth Centuries* eds A. E. Laiou and D. Simon (Washington, DC, 1994), pp. 117–29, at p. 120.
151 DO BZS.1955.1.3592. Cf. Wassiliou-Seibt, *Siegel mit metrischen Legenden* I, no. 205.
152 Komnene, *Alexiad*, trans. Sewter, pp. 87–8.
153 Magdalino, *Manuel*, p. 183.

Chapter 5

1 The exception was *vestarches*, which is only ever found associated with *magistros*.
2 DO BZS.1958.106.4951.
3 Wassiliou and Seibt, *Bleisiegel II*, no. 11, also p. 39, fn. 65.
4 Nesbitt and Seibt, 'The Anzas Family', pp. 189–207; Wassiliou, 'Hexamilites', no. 17. See also, Wassiliou and Seibt, *Bleisiegel II*, p. 73.
5 Its performance was equally lacklustre when we look at absolute numbers in Table 5.3.
6 See, N. Oikonomides, 'The Lead Blanks Used for Byzantine Seals', *Studies in Byzantine Sigilloraphy* 1 (1987), pp. 100, n. 11 and G. Vikan and J. Nesbitt, *Security in Byzantium: Locking, Sealing, Weighing* (Washington, DC, 1980), p. 25 for questions about the availability of lead in the eleventh century.
7 Oikonomides, *Listes*, p. 169 lists *asekretai*, and *chartoularioi* and imperial *notarioi* of the great *sekreta*. The grand total is 168 men. Ibid., p. 181 mentions *asekretai*, *chartoularioi* of the *genikon* and *stratiotikon*, the *antigrapheis* of the *koiaistor*, the *symponos*, the *logothetes tou praitoriou*, judges of the regions of Constantinople, and *notarioi* of the *sakellion*, *vestiarion*, and *eidikon*.
8 Weiss, *Oströmische Beamte*, p. 107 favoured a total of 170 men of senatorial rank in total.
9 It is equally unlikely that every seal recording a matching first and family name belonged to the same man in an age when cousins frequently shared names which ran in families and could appear in quick succession even within the same branch of the family, certainly close together enough to cause confusion.
10 P. Grierson, 'The Debasement of the Bezant in the Eleventh Century', *Byzantinishce Zeitschrift* 47 (1954), pp. 379–94, and 'Notes on the Fineness of the Byzantine Solidus', *Byzantinische Zeitschrift* 54 (1961), pp. 91–7, restated and emended in, P. Grierson, *Catalogue of the Byzantine Coins in the Dumbarton Oaks Collection and in the Whittemore Collection*, Vol. 3, Part 1(Washington, DC, 1973), pp. 40–2; C. Morrisson,

'La devaluation de la monnaie byzantine au XIe siècle: essai d'interprétation', *Travaux et Mémoires* 6 (1976), pp. 3–48, and 'Numismatique et histoire, l'or monnayé de Rome à Byzance : purification et altérations', *Comptes rendus des séances de l'Académie des Inscriptions et Belles-Lettres* 126, no. 2 (1982), pp. 203–23, with a summary in C. Morrisson, 'Byzantine Money: Its Production and Circulation', in *The Economic History of Byzantium from the Seventh through the Fifteenth Centuries*, ed. A. E. Laiou, pp. 909–66, and Laiou and Morrisson, *The Byzantine Economy*, pp. 88, 147–50; C. Kaplanis, 'The Debasement of the "Dollar of the Middle Ages"', *Journal of Economic History* 63, no. 3 (September 2003).

11 Morrisson, 'l'or monnayé', p. 216 and 'Byzantine Money', pp. 931–2. As Morrisson points out the period of debasement began at the same time as, and could well have been intended to finance, a period of sustained warfare in the East under the *domestikos ton Scholon* John Kourkouas, which would lead to the campaigns of Nikpehoros Phokas and John Tzimiskes.

12 Morrisson, 'La devaluation de la monnaie byzantine', p. 6.

13 The range is from 81.5 per cent to 97.0 per cent. See Morrisson, 'La devaluation de la monnaie byzantine au XIe siècle', pp. 6, 35–6 for her findings on the beginning of the decline in the gold content of the nomismata histamenon in the eleventh century.

14 Ibid., p. 7.

15 For a consolidated table of Morrisson's findings, see C. Morrisson, *Byzance et sa monnaie (IVe-XVe siècle)* (Paris, 2015), pp. 80–1.

16 I have left aside the question of purchasing dignities in Byzantium. Figures for the purchase of some dignities are provided by Constantine VII in *De Ceremoniis*, for a time just before the start of our period in the reign of his father Leo VI. The dignity of *spatharokandidatos* could be purchased for 6 pounds of gold, and that of *protospatharios* for 12 or 18 pounds. No matter what the rank, if a *roga* was desired, that added 4 pounds to the purchase cost, and if the buyer wished to become a member of the *Chrysotriklinos*, the imperial throne room, that added a further 4 pounds to the price. Constantine VII, *De Ceremoniis*, p. 693. There are a great many individuals who record the dignity of *protospatharios epi tou Chrysotriklinou* on their seals. While we do not know whether these figures held steady from Constantine's time into the eleventh century, they probably provide a rough guide for the cost of certain dignities in the imperial system. Elpidios Kenchres's dignity of *protospatharios*, with *roga*, was bought for him by his father-in-law-to-be Michael Psellos for 20 pounds of gold. Psellos, *Orationes*, pp. 143–54. The financial return on this investment was usually lower than the standard interest rate at the time. Moreover, the initial payment was lost, given to the state in return for the dignity. While it is possible that some of the outlay would have been recovered from exceptional payments at special feasts or in the form of accessional donatives, gifts given out when a new emperor was crowned, it is likely that the investor spent more than he received in *roga*, the driving motive in purchasing these titles must have been the status that they conferred. Oikonomides, 'Title and Income', pp. 205–8. Thus, it has been proposed that far from bankrupting the empire, the liberal granting of dignities by the eleventh-century emperors, and the opening of the senate to groups previously disbarred from membership by Constantine IX Monomachos and Constantine X Doukas, was in fact a shrewd move to access the hoarded wealth of the Byzantine elite. Ibid., p. 208, Lemerle *Cinq études*, pp. 287 ff. While this could certainly be true, we must keep in mind that there is no evidence for the sale of any title above the rank of *protospatharios*. Oikonomides, 'Title and Income', p. 205. All higher dignities were

a gift of the emperor, a mark of favour or a reward for service, yet as we have seen they came with high annual salaries. Thus, to a certain extent the imperial policy of selling lower-level titles would have contributed to the empire's financial woes despite payments from the newly entitled, because of the upward pressures of title inflation created by a host of new title holders. This effect was doubly damaging when coupled with the free distribution of titles undertaken by other emperors.

17 Basil II had 'thrown open the doors of the senate' long before Constantine IX, but he opened it to low-level bureaucrats rather than merchants and artisans, so perhaps that was less objectionable.

18 This pressure is alone, enough to explain the desire for higher titles without having to turn to an explanation based on a decreased value of the *rogai* due to debasement.

19 After 1081 there was no peace to be lost for most of Alexios's reign.

20 1019–20, 1023–4, 1026–8, 1030–1, 1035, 1044, 1046 and 1057.

21 Recently Peter Frankopan has argued that Alexios I did not rule through his family noting their absence from the chief positions of state, particularly after the attempted coup of the Diogenes brothers in the mid-1090s. While this argument is a thought-provoking correction to the usual assumptions about Alexios's government, I would note that a prioritization of the imperial family and granting them the highest offices in the empire are not necessarily the same thing. Alexios granted exalted titles and vast state resources to his family, an act which put them in a position of great power and influence even if they did not hold every military office. One thing that he did not do was to make them, or any of his closest followers, bureaucrats. P. Frankopan, 'Re-interpreting the Role of the Family in Comnenian Byzantium: Where Blood Is Not Thicker than Water', in *Byzantium in the Eleventh Century Being in Between*, eds M. D. Lauxtermann and M. Whittow (London and New York, 2017), pp. 181–96.

22 Ficker, *Alexios Stoudites*, pp. 19–21. Also listed are an unspecified number of city judges.

23 The two obvious solutions would have been to restructure the scale of the *rogai*, cutting their value, or to move the threshold at which men were expected to purchase their title. It is easy to see why neither of these options was attractive; they would have created considerable resentment among the very people on whom the emperors relied.

24 For a discussion of the actions of the troops of Alexios I after his capture of Constantinople, Alexios's cancelling of payments to senators, downgrading of mercantile senators, and the reaction to these, see Hendy, *Studies*, pp. 582–5.

Appendix – Chartoularioi, notarioi and logariastai

1 DO BZS.1955.1.3986.

2 There are two references in the documentary sources for the *megas chartoularios*. Both date to the early years of the Komnenian regime, so it difficult to be sure whether they reflect the result of the accelerated title inflation of the late 1070s, or the new system implemented by Alexios in 1081. They record a *megas chartoularios* and *magistros* in 1089, who was also an *anagrapheus*, two *protovestarchai*, one 1087, this was his only recorded office, and one 1088, who was also a judge of the Hippodrome. Πάτμου 2, no. 54, p. 79, 1, no. 47, p. 334, 1, no. 49, p.346.

3 DO BZS.1958.106.4198. Cf. Wassiliou-Seibt, *Siegel mit metrischen Legenden* I, no. 301.

4 No Title, A. Karpozilos, 'Δύο ἀνέκδοτες ἐπιστολὲς τοῦ Μιχαὴλ Ψελλοῦ', *Δωδώνη 9* (1980), pp. 299–310, no. 1 and I. Bekker, *Michaelis Glycae Annales, Corpus scriptorum historiae Byzantinae* 21 (Bonn, 1836), pp. 599. *Protovestes*, Πάτμου, 1, no. 49, p. 345.
5 *Lavra* I, no. 39, p. 223 (1042–3), Πάτμου, 1, no. 47, p. 334 (1087), Attaleiates, *Diataxis*, 117.1613, 29.204, 35.289 (1077), (1059), Πάτμου 1, no. 49, p. 345 (1088), *Lavra* I, no. 47, p. 254 (1085).
6 The absence of the *eidikon* is puzzling.
7 *Lavra* I, no. 45, p. 246; no. 49, p. 262; *Iviron* 2, no. 52, p. 211; *Docheiariou*, no. 3, p. 68.
8 Zacos, *Lead Seals* II, no. 431.

Bibliography

Primary sources

Actes de Dionysiou, Archives de l'Athos IV, ed. N. Oikonomides (Paris, 1968).
Actes de Docheiariou, Archives de l'Athos XIII, ed. N. Oikonomides (Paris, 1984).
Actes d'Esphigménou, Archives de l'Athos VI, ed. J. Lefort (Paris, 1973).
Actes d'Iviron, Actes de l'Athos XIV and XVI, ed. J. Lefort, N. Oikonomides, D. Papachryssanthou, H. Métrévéli and V. Kravari (Paris, 1985–1990).
Actes de Kutlumus, Archives de l'Athos 2, ed. P. Lemerle (Paris, 1945–1946).
Actes de Lavra. Première partie: Des origines à 1204, Archives de l'Athos 5, eds. P. Lemerle, (Paris, 1970).
Actes de Saint Pantéléèmôn, Archives de l'Athos XII, ed. P. Lemerle, G. Dagron and S. Ćircović (Paris, 1982).
Actes de Vatopédi I. Des origines à 1329, Archives de l'Athos XXI, ed. J. Bompaire, J. Lefort, V. Kravari and C. Giros (Paris, 2001).
Actes de Xéropotamou, Archives de l'Athos III, ed. J. Bompaire (Paris, 1964).
Actes du Prôtaton, Archives de l'Athos VII, ed. D. Papachryssanthou (Paris, 1975).
Aristakes of Lastivert, *Ré cit des malheurs de la nation arménienne*, trans. M. Canard and H. Berbérian according to the edn and trans. (Russian) by K. Yuzbashian (Brussels, 1973).
Attaleiates, Michael, *Diataxis*, trans., A.-M. Talbot, '*Attaleiates: Rule* of Michael Attaleiates for His Almshouse in Rhaidestos and for the Monastery of Christ *Panoiktirmon* in Constantinople', in *Byzantine Monastic Foundation Documents: A Complete Translation of the Surviving Founders' Typika and Testaments*, eds J. Thomas and An. Constantinides Hero, vol. 1 (Washington, DC, 2000).
Attaleiates, Michael, *History*, ed. and trans. A. Kaldellis and D. Krallis (Washington, DC, 2012).
Bernard, F. and Livanos, C. eds and trans., *The Poems of Christopher of Mytilene and John Mauropous* (Cambridge, MA and London, 2018).
Bryennios, Nikephoros, *Materials for a History*, ed. and trans. P. Gautier, *Nicephori Bryennii Historiarum libri quattuor (Nicéphore Bryennios: Histoire)* (Bruxelles, 1975).
Chronicon Paschale, ed. L. Dindorf, 2 vols (Bonn, 1832).
Constantine Porphyrogennetos: The Book of Ceremonies, trans. A. Moffatt and M. Tall (Leiden and Boston, 2012).
Constantine VII, *De Ceremoniis aulae byzantinae*, ed. J. J. Reiske (Bonn, 1829–30).
Constantine VII, *Constantinus Porphyrogenitus, De Administrando Imperio*, ed. Gy Moravcsik and trans. R. J. H. Jenkins (Washington, DC, 1967).
Dennis, G. T., *Three Byzantine Military Treatises* (Washington, DC, 2009).
Dölger, F. and Worth, P., *Regesten Der Kaiserurkunden des Oströmischen Reiches von, 565–1453*, 2nd edn (Munich: C. H. Beck, 1977).
Ecloga Basilicorum, ed. L. Burgmann (Frankfurt, 1988).
Ficker, G., *Erlasse des Patriarchen von Konstantinopel Alexios Studites* (Kiel, 1911).

Gautier, P., 'La diataxis de Michel Attaliate', *Revue des Etudes Byzantines* 39 (1981), pp. 5-143.
Gautier, P., 'Quelques lettres de Psellos inédites ou déjà éditées', *Revue des Etudes Byzantines* 44 (1986), pp. 111-97.
Gautier, P., *Théophylacte d'Achrida, II. Lettres*, Corpus fontium historiae Byzantinae 16/2 (Thessalonike, 1986).
Gouillard, J., 'Le proces officiel de Jean l'Italien: les actes et leurs sous-entendus', *Travaux et Mémoires* 9 (1985), pp. 133-69.
'Histoire de Yaḥyā ibn Saīd d'Antioche, Continuateur de Said-Ibn-Bitriq', *Patrologia Orientalis* 47, no. 4, ed. and trans. F. Micheau and G. Troupeau (1997).
Imperatorum Basilii, Constantini et Leonis prochiron, ed. K. E. Zachariä von Lingenthal (Leipzig: 1837).
Kanellakis, K. N., Χιακὰ ἀνάλεκτα (Athens, 1890).
Karpozilos, A. 'Δύο ἀνέκδοτες ἐπιστολὲς τοῦ Μιχαὴλ Ψελλοῦ', Δωδώνη 9 (1980), pp. 299-310.
Kedrenos, George, *Historiarum Compendium*, ed. I Bekker, 2 vols (Bonn 1838, 1839).
Kekaumenos, *Cecaumeni Strategicon et incerti scriptoris de officiis regii libellus*, ed. B. Vasilievskij and V. Jernstedt, (St. Petersburg, 1896).
Kekaumenos, *Consilia et Narrationes* (SAWS edition, 2013), www.ancientwisdoms.ac.uk/library/kekaumenos-consilia-et-narrationes/.
Koder, J., ed., *Das Eparchenbuch Leons des Weisen* CFHB 33 (Vienna, 1991).
Kurtz, E. and Drexl, F., *Michaelis Pselli Scripta minora magnam partem adhuc inedita II* (Milan, 1941).
Le Liber pontificalis, ed. L. Duchesne, 3 vols (Paris 1886-1957).
Leo the Deacon, *Leonis diaconi Caloënsis Historiae libri decem*, ed. C. B. Hase (Bonn, 1828).
Liutprand of Cremona, *legatio Constantinopolitana*; ed. J. Becker (*Die Werke Liudprands von Cremona*) (Hanover and Leipzig, 1915).
McGeer, E., *Land Legislation of the Macedonian Emperors* (Toronto, 2000).
Michaelis Glycae Annales, Corpus scriptorum historiae Byzantinae 21, ed. I. Bekker (Bonn, 1836).
Miklosich, F. and Müller, J., *Acta et diplomata graeca medii aevi sacra et profana*, 6 vols (Vienna, 1860-90).
Oikonomides, N., *Les Listes de préséance byzantines des IXe et Xe siècles* (Paris, 1972).
Peira = 'Πεῖρα ἤγουν διδασκαλία ἐκ τῶν πράξεων τοῦ μεγάλου κυροῦ Εὐσταθίου τοῦ Ῥωμαίου', *Jus Graecoromanum* 4, Practica ex actis Eustathii Romani. Epitome legume, eds P. Zepos and I. Zepos, (Athens, 1931, reprinted, Aalen, 1962), pp. 1-260.
Psellos, Michael, *Chronographia*, ed. S. Impellizeri and trans. S. Ronchey, *Michele Psello, Imperatori di Bisanzio (Cronografia)*, 2 vols (Milan, 1984).
Psellos, Michael, *Orationes forenses et acta*, ed. G. T. Dennis (Stuttgart-Leipzig, 1994).
Ralles, G. A. and Potles, M., Σύνταγμα τῶν θείων καὶ ἱερῶν κανόνων, 6 vols (Athens, 1852-1859, repr. 1966).
Salač, A., *Novella constitutio saec. XI medii, quae est de schola iuris Constantinopoli constituenda et legum custode creando, a Ioanne Mauropode conscripta, a Constantino IX Monomacho promulgata. Textum De Lagardianum latine vertit, notis illustravit* (Prague, 1954).
Sathas, E. N., Μιχαὴλ Ψελλοῦ Ἐπιτάφιοι λόγοι εἰς τοὺς πατριάρχας Μιχαὴλ Κηρουλλάριον, Κωνσταντῖνον Λειχούδην καὶ Ἰωάννην Ξιφιλῖνον, Μεσαιωνικὴ Βιβλιοθήκη 4 (Paris, 1874), pp. 421-46.

Sathas, E. N., Μεσαιωνικὴ Βιβλιοθήκη 5. Μιχαὴλ Ψελλοῦ ἱστορικοὶ λόγοι, ἐπιστολαὶ καὶ ἄλλα ἀνέκδοτα (Paris, 1876), pp. 219–523.
Schmink, A., 'Vier eherechtliche Entscheidungen aus dem 11. Jahrhundert', Fontes Minores 3 (1979), pp. 221–79.
Skylitzes, John, Synopsis of Histories, ed. J. Thurn, Ioannis Scylitzae Synopsis Historiarum (Berlin and New York, 1973).
Théodore Daphnopatès, Correspondance, ed. and trans., J. Darrouzès and L. Gerrit Westerink (Paris, 1978).
Tzetzes, John, Ioannis Tzetzae Chiliades, ed. P. A. M. Leone (Naples, 1968)
Vranousis, E. and Nystazopoulou-Pelekidou, M., Βυζαντινὰ ἔγγραφα τῆς μονῆς Πάτμου 1. Αὐτοκρατορικά (Athens, 1980).
Vranousis, E. and Nystazopoulou-Pelekidou, M., Βυζαντινὰ ἔγγραφα τῆς μονῆς Πάτμου 2. Δημοσίων λειτουργῶν (Athens, 1980).
Will, C., Acta et scripta quae de controversiis ecclesiae graecae et latinae saeculo undecimo composita extant (Leipzig and Marburg, 1861)
Zachariä von Lingenthal, K. E., ed., Collectio librorum juris graeco-romani ineditorum Ecloga Leonis et Constantini, epanagoge Basilii Leonis et Alexandri (Leipzig, 1852).
Zépos, I. and Zépos, P., eds, Jus graecoromanum, 8 vols (Athens, 1931; rp. Aalen, 1962).
Zonaras, John, Ioannis Zonarae Epitome Historiarum libri XIII–XVIII, Corpus scriptiorum historiae Byzantinae 49, ed. T. Büttner-Wobst (Leipzig, 1897).

Secondary sources

Ahweiler, H., 'Recherches sur l'administration de l'empire byzantin aux IXe-XIe siècles', Bulletin de Correspondance Hellénique 84 (1960), pp. 1–111.
Ahweiler, H., 'Fonctionnaires et bureaux maritimes à Byzance', Revue des études byzantines, 19 (1961), pp. 246–9.
Ahweiler, H., Byzance et la Mer: La marine de guerre, la politique, et les institutions maritmes de Byzance aux VIIe-XVe siècles (Paris, 1966).
Angold, M., The Byzantine Empire, 1025-1204: A Political History, 2nd edn (London and New York, 1997).
Antoniadis-Bibicou, H., 'Démographie, salaires et prix à Byzance au XIe siècle', Annales. Economies, Sociétés, Civilisations 27, no. 1 (1972), pp. 215–46.
Antonov, S., 'The Byzantine Office of ἐπί τῶν κρίσεων and Its Holders (in the Light of Sphragistic Evidence and Written Sources)', Studia Ceranea 7 (2017), pp. 9–25.
Beck, H.-G., 'Theorie und Praxis im Aufbau der byzantinischen Zentralverwaltung', Bayerische Akademie der Wissenschaften. Philosophisch-Historische Klase Sitzunsberichte 8 (1974), pp. 3–33.
Bréhier, L., Les institutions de l'empire byzantin (Paris, 1970).
Brubaker, L. and Haldon, J., Byzantium in the Iconoclast Era, c. 680–850: A History (Cambridge, 2011).
Burgmann, L., 'Turning Sisinnios against the Sisinnians: Eustathios Romaios on a disputed marriage', in Byzantium in the Year 1000, ed. P. Magdalino (Leiden and Boston, 2003), pp. 161–81.
Burgmann, L., 'Zur diplomatischen Terminologie in der Peira', in Zwischen Polis, Provinz und Peripherie: Beiträge zur byzantinischen Geschichte und Kultur, ed. L. M. Hoffmann (Wiesbaden, 2005), pp. 457–67.

Burgmann, L., 'Zur Organisation der Rechtsprechung in Byzanz (mittelbyzantinische Epoche)', in *Ausgewählte Aufsätze zur byzantinischen Rechtsgeschichte*, ed. L. Burgmann (Frankfurt, 2015), pp. 259-84.

Bury, J. B., *The Imperial Administrative System in the Ninth Century with a Revised Text of the Kletorologion of Philotheos* (London, 1911).

Caseau, B., 'Un aspect de la diplomatique byzantine: les copies de documents', *Recours à l'écrit, autorité du document, constitution d'archives au Moyen Âge. Orient et Occident*, XXXIXe Congrès de la SHMESP (Le Caire, 30 avril-5 mai 2008) (Paris, 2009), pp. 159-74.

Caseau, B., 'Saint Mark, a Family Saint? The Iconography of the Xeroi Seals', in *Ἠπειρόνδε (Epeironde), Proccedings of the 10th International Symposium of Byzantine Sigillography (Ioannina, 1-3 October 2009)*, eds Ch. Stavrakos and B. Papadopoulou (Leiden, 2011), pp. 81-109.

Cheynet, J.-C., 'Mantzikert: un désastre militaire?', *Byzantion* 50 (1980), pp. 410-38.

Cheynet, J.-C., 'Dévaluation des dignités et dévaluation monétaire dans la seconde moitié du XIe siècle', *Byzantion* 53 (1983), pp. 453-77.

Cheynet, J.-C., 'L'éparque: Corrections et additions', *Byzantinoslavica* 45 (1984), fasc. 1, pp. 50-4.

Cheynet, J.-C., *Pouvoir et contestations à Byzance (963-1210)* (Paris, 1990).

Cheynet, J.-C., 'Fortune et puissance de l'aristocratie (X-XII siècle)', *Hommes et richesses dans l'Empire byzantin*, eds V. Kravari, J. Lefort and C. Morrisson (Paris, 1991), pp. 199-213.

Cheynet, J.-C., 'Point de vue sur l'efficacité administrative entre les xe et xie siècles', *Byzantinische Forschungen* 19 (1993), pp. 7-16.

Cheynet, J.-C., 'La résistance aux Turcs en Asie Mineure entre Mantzikert et la Première Croisade', *ΕΥΨΥΧΙΑ: Mélanges offerts à Hélène Ahrweiler* (Paris, 1998), pp. 131-47.

Cheynet, J.-C., 'Par St Georges, par St Michel', in *Travaux et Mémoires* 14 (2002), pp. 114-34.

Cheynet, J.-C., *The Byzantine Aristocracy and Its Military Function* (London, 2006).

Cheynet, J.-C., 'Les Xèroi, administrateurs de l'Empire', *Studies in Byzantine Sigillography* 11 (2011), pp. 14-15.

Cheynet, J.-C., 'Intrigues à la cour de Constantinople: le délitement d'une faction (1057-1081)', *Le saint, le moine et le paysan. Mélanges d'histoire byzantine offerts à Michel Kaplan* (Paris, 2016), pp. 71-84.

Cheynet, J.-C. and Morrisson, C., 'Lieux de trouvaille et circulation des sceaux', *Studies in Byzantine Sigillography* 2 (1990), pp. 105-36.

Cheynet, J.-C. and Morrisson, C., 'Texte et image sur les sceaux byzantins: les raisons d'un choix iconographique', *Studies in Byzantine Sigillography* 4 (1995), pp. 9-32.

Cheynet, J.-C. and Vannier, J.-F., 'Les Argyroi', *Zbornik Radova Vizantološkog Instituta* 40 (2003), pp. 57-90.

Cheynet, J.-C. Malamut, É. and Morrisson, C., 'Prix et salaires à Byzance (Xe-XVe siècle)', in *Hommes et richesses dans l'Empire byzantin*, 2 (1991), pp. 339-74.

Chitwood, Z., *Byzantine Legal Culture and Roman Legal Tradition, 867-1056* (Cambridge, 2017).

Christophilopoulou, A., Τα βυζαντινά δικαστήρια κατά τους αιώνες Ι΄-Α΄, *Δίπτυχα* 4, (1986-87), pp. 163-77.

Christophilopoulou, A., *Το πολίτευμα και οι θεσμοί της βυζαντινής αυτοκρατορίας 324-1204. Κράτος, διοίκηση, οικονομία, κοινωνία* (Athens, 2004).

Christophilopoulos, P., 'Νομοφύλακες και Θεσμοφύλακες', *Πλάτων* 20 (1968), pp. 134–43.
Cotsonis, J., 'The Contribution of Byzantine Lead Seals to the Study of the Cult of Saints (Sixth-Twelfth Centruy)', *Byzantion* 75 (2005), pp. 383–497.
Cotsonis, J., 'Onomastics, Gender, Office and Images on Byzantine Lead Seals: A Means of Investigating Personal Piety', *Byzantine and Modern Greek Studies* 32, no. 1 (2008), pp. 1–37.
d' Emilia, A., 'L'applicazione pratica del diritto bizantino secondo il titolo della Πεῖρα Εὐσταθίου τοῦ Ῥωμαίου relative alla compravendita', *Rivista di studi bizantini e neoellenici* n.s. 2–3[12–13] (1965–6), pp. 33–80.
d' Emilia, A., 'L'applicazione pratica del diritto bizantino secondo la c.d. "Peira d'Eustazio Romano"', *RSBN* n.s. 4[14] (1967), pp. 71–94
Diehl, C. M., 'Un haut fonctionnaire byzantin : le logothète "tôn sékrétôn"', *Mélanges N. Jorga* (Paris, 1933), pp. 217–29.
Dölger, F., *Beiträge zur Geschichte der byzantinischen Finanzverwaltung, besonders des 10. und 11. Jahrhunderts* (Leipzig, 1927).
Dölger, F., *Byzantinische Diplomatik* (Ettal, 1956).
Dölger, F., *Byzantinische Urkundenlehre* (München, 1968).
Ebersolt, J., 'Sur les fonctions et les dignités du Vestiarium byzantin', *Mélanges Diehl, II, Histoire* (Paris, 1930), pp. 81–9.
Follieri, E., 'Sulla Novella promulgata da Costantino IX Monomaco per la restaurazione della Facoltà giuridica a Costantinopoli', *Studi in onore di Edoardo Volterra* II (Milan, 1971), pp. 647–64.
Frankopan, P., *The First Crusade: The Call from the East* (London, 2012).
Frankopan, P., 'Re-interpreting the Role of the Family in Comnenian Byzantium: Where Blood Is Not Thicker than Water', in *Byzantium in the Eleventh Century Being in Between*, eds M. D. Lauxtermann and M. Whittow (London and New York, 2017), pp. 181–96.
Gautier, P., 'Le synode des Blachernes (fin 1094). Étude prosopographique', *Revue des études byzantines* 29, (1971), pp. 213–84.
Gkoutzioukostas, A., *Ο θεσμός του κοιαίστωρα του ιερού παλατίου : η γένεση, οι αρμοδιότητες και η εξέλιξή του* (Εταιρεία Βυζαντινών ερευνών 18) (Thessaloniki, 2001).
Gkoutzioukostas, A., "Η εξέλιτξη του θεσμού των ἀσηκρῆτις και του πρωτοασηκρῆτις στο πλαίσιο της αυτοκρατορικής γραμματείας', *Βυζαντινά* 23 (2002–2003), pp. 47–93.
Gkoutzioukostas, A., *Η απονομή δικαιοσύνης στο Βυζάντιο (9ος-12ο αιώνες): Τα κοσμικά δικαιοδοτικά όργανα και δικαστήρια της πρωτεύουσας* (Thessalonike, 2004).
Gkoutzioukostas, A., 'The Praitor Mentioned in the History of Leo the Deacon and the Praitor of Constantinople: Previous and Recent Considerations', *Byzantiaka* 25 (2005–6), pp. 105–15.
Gkoutzioukostas, A., 'Judges of the Velum and Judges of the Hippodrome in Thessalonike (11th c.)', *Byzantina Symmeikta* 20 (2010), pp. 67–84.
Gkoutzioukostas, A., 'Some Remarks on *mystographos* and *Mystolektes*', in *Ἠπειρόνδε (Epeironde) Proceedings of the 10th International Symposium of Byzantine Sigillography (Ioannina, 1–3 October 2009)*, ed. Ch. Stavrakos and B. Papadopoulou (Ioanina, 2011), pp. 191–219.
Gkoutzioukostas, A., *Το αξίωμα του μυστικού. Θεσμικά και προσωπογραφικά προβλήματα* (Thessaloniki, 2011).
Gkoutzioukostas, A., 'Seals of Byzantine Officials Connected with the Administration of Justice', *Jahrbuch der Österreichischen Byzantinistik*, 62 (2012), pp. 9–18.

Gkoutzioukostas, A., 'Administrative Structures of Byzantium During the 11th Century: Officials of the Imperial Secretarit and Administration of Justice', *Travaux et Mémoires* 21/2, ed. B. Flusin and J.-C. Cheynet (Paris, 2017), pp. 561–80.

Glykatzi-Ahrweiler, H., 'Recherches sur l'administration de l'empire byzantin aux IXe-XIe siècles', *Bulletin de correspondance hellenique* 84 (1960), pp. 1–111.

Grégoire, H. *Recueil des inscriptions grecques-chrétiennes d'Asie Mineure. 1*, Paris 1922 (repr. Amsterdam 1968).

Grierson, P., 'The Debasement of the Bezant in the Eleventh Century', *Byzantinische Zeitschrift*, 47 (1954), pp. 379–94.

Grierson, P., 'Notes on the Fineness of the Byzantine Solidus', *Byzantinische Zeitschrift* 54 (1961), pp. 91–7.

Grierson, P., *Catalogue of the Byzantine Coins in the Dumbarton Oaks Collection and in the Whittemore Collection*, vol. 3, Part 1 (Washington, DC, 1973).

Guilland, R. J., *Recherches sur les institutions byzantines* I (Berlin and Amsterdam, 1967).

Guilland, R. J., 'Études sur l'Histoire administrative de l'empire byzantin. Le mystique, ὁ μυστικός', *Revue des études byzantines* 26, no. 1 (1968), pp. 279–96.

Guilland, R. J., 'Études sur l'histoire administrative de l'Empire byzantin: Le Maître des Requêtes', *Byzantion* 35 (1965), pp. 97–118.

Guilland, R. J., *Études de topographie de Constantinople byzantines*, 2 vols (Amsterdam, 1969).

Guilland, R. J., 'Études sur l'histoire administrative de l'empire byzantin. Le logariaste, ὁ λ ογαριαστής; le grand logariaste, ὁ μέγας λογαριαστής', *Jahrbuch der Osterreichischen Byzantinistik* 18 (1969), pp. 101–8.

Guilland, R. J., 'Études sur l'histoire administrative de l'empire byzantin. Le Questeur : ὁ κοιαίστωρ, quaestor', *Byzantion* 41 (1971), pp. 78–104.

Guilland, R. J., *Les logothetes: études sur l'histoire administrative de l'Empire byzantin* (Paris, 1971).

Guilland, R. J., 'Etudes sur l'histoire administrative de l'Empire Byzantin-L'Eparque I. L'éparque de la ville', *Byzantinoslavica* 41 (1980), pp. 17–32, 145–80.

Guilland, R. J., 'Etudes sur l'histoire administrative de l'Empire Byzantin-L'Eparque II. Les éparques autres que L'éparque de la ville', *Byzantinoslavica* 42 (1981), pp. 186–96.

Haldon, J., *Byzantine Praetorians: An Administrative, Institutional and Social Survey of the Opsikion and Tagmata, c. 580–900* (Bonn, 1984).

Haldon, J., 'Comes horreorum – komēs tēs Lamias?', *Byzantine and Modern Greek Studies* 10 (1986), pp. 203–9.

Haldon, J., *Byzantium in the Seventh Century: The Transformation of a Culture* (Cambridge, 1990).

Haldon, J., 'Theory and Practice in Tenth-Century Military Administration: Chapters II, 44 and 45 of the Book of Ceremonies', *Travaux et Mémoires* 13 (2000), pp. 201–352.

Haldon, J., 'Social Élites, Wealth, and Power', in *A Social History of Byzantium*, ed. J. Haldon (Chichester, 2009), pp. 168–211.

Haldon, J., *The Empire That Would Not Die: The Paradox of Eastern Roman Survival, 640–740* (Cambridge, MA and London, 2016).

Hendy, M. F., *Studies in the Byzantine Monetary Economy c. 300–1450* (Cambridge, 1985).

Holmes, C., 'Political Elites in the Reign of Basil II', in *Byzantium in the Year 1000*, ed. P. Magdalino (Leiden, 2003), pp. 35–69.

Holmes, C., *Basil II and the Governance of Empire* (Oxford, 2005).

Holmes, C., 'Byzantine Political Culture and Compilation Literature in the Tenth and Eleventh Centuries: Some Preliminary Inquiries', *Dumbarton Oaks Papers* 64 (2010), pp. 55–80.

Howard-Johnston, J. D., 'Crown Lands and the Defence of Imperial Authority in the Tenth and Eleventh Centuries', *Byzantinische Forschungen* 21 (1995), pp. 75–100.

Howard-Johnston, J. D., 'The *Peira* and Legal Practices in Eleventh-Century Byzantium', in *Byzantium in the Eleventh Century Being in Between*, eds M. D. Lauxtermann and M. Whittow (London and New York, 2017), pp. 63–76.

Janin, R., *Constantinople byzantine. Développement urbain et Répertoire topographique* (Archives de l'Orient latin, 4) (Paris, 1950).

Janin, R. *La Géographie Ecclésiastique de L'empire Byzantin, Vol. 1, Le Siège de Constantinople et Le Patriarcat Oecuménique, Pt. 3, Les Églises et Les Monastères*, 2nd ed. (Paris, 1969).

Jeffreys, M., 'Constantine, Nephew of the Pariarch Keroularios, and His Good Friend Michael Psellos', in *The Letters of Psellos: Cultural Networks and Historical Realities*, ed. M. Jeffreys and M. D. Lauxtermann (Oxford, 2016), pp. 59–88.

Jones, A. H. M., *The Later Roman Empire, 284–602*, vol. 1 (Oxford, 1964).

Kaegi, W., 'The Controversy about Bureaucratic and Military Factions', *Byzantinische Forshungen* 19 (1993), pp. 25–33.

Kaldellis, A., *Mothers and Sons, Fathers and Daughters: The Byzantine Family of Michael Psellos* (Notre Dame, 2006).

Kaldellis, A., *The Byzantine Republic: People and Power in New Rome* (Cambridge, MA, 2015).

Kaldellis, A., 'The Manufacture of History in the Later Tenth and Eleventh Centuries: Rhetorical Templates and Narrative Ontologes', *Proceedings of the 23rd International Congress of Byzantine Studies (Belgrade, 22-27 August 2016): Plenary Papers* (Belgrade, 2016), pp. 293–306.

Kaldellis, A., *Streams of Gold, Rivers of Blood: The Rise and Fall of Byzantium, 955 A.D. to the First Crusade* (Oxford, 2017).

Kaplanis, C., 'The Debasement of the Dollar of the Middle Ages', *Journal of Economic History* 63, no. 3 (September, 2003), pp. 768–801.

Kazhdan, A. P. and Wharton, A. J., *Change in Byzantine Culture in the Eleventh and Twelfth Centuries* (Berkley, 1985).

Kazhdan, A. P. and McCormick, M., 'The Social World of the Byzantine Court', in *Byzantine Court Culture from 829 to 1204*, ed. H. Maguire (Washington, DC, 1997), pp. 167–98.

Köpstein, H., 'Sklaven in der 'Peira', *Fontes Minores* 9 (1993), pp. 1–33.

Krallis, D., '"Democratic" Action in Eleventh-Century Byzantium: Michael Attaleiates' "Repulicanism" in Context', *Viator* 40, no. 2 (2009), pp. 35–53.

Krallis, D., 'Urbane Warriors: Smoothing Out Tensions between Soldiers and Civilians in Attaleiates' Encomium to Emperor Nikephoros III Botaneiates', *Byzantium in the Eleventh Century Being in Between* eds M. D. Lauxtermann and M. Whittow (London and New York, 2017), pp. 154–68.

Laiou, A. E., Ὀικονομικά ζητήματα στη 'Πείρα' Ευσταθίου Ρωμαίου', in *Η αυτοκρατορία σε κρίση? Το Βυζάντιο τον ΙΙο αιώνα, 1025*, ed. V. N. Vlysidou (Athens, 2003), pp. 179–89.

Laiou, A. E. and Morrisson, C., *The Byzantine Economy* (Cambridge, 2007).

Lefort, J., 'Rhétorique et politique: trois discours de Jean Mauropous en 1047', *TM* 6 (1976), pp. 265–303.

Lemerle, P., 'Notes sur l'administration byzantine à la veille de la IVe croisade, d'après deux documents inédits des archives de Lavra', *Revue des études byzantines* 19 (1961), pp. 258–72.

Lemerle, P., '"Roga" et rente d'État aux Xe-XIe siècles', *Revue des études byzantines* 25 (1967), pp. 77–100.

Lemerle, P., *Cinq études sur le XIe siècle byzantin* (Paris, 1977).

Lilie, R.-J., 'Die Zentralbürokratie und die Provinzen zwischen dem 10. und dem 12. Jahrhundert. Anspruch und Realität', *Byzantinische Forschungen* 19 (1993), pp. 65–75.

Magdalino, P., 'The Not-So-Secret Functions of the Mystikos', *Revue des études byzantines* 42 (1984), pp. 228–40.

Magdalino, P., *The Empire of Manuel I Komnenos 1143–1180* (Cambridge, 1993).

Magdalino, P., 'Justice and Finance in the Byzantine State, Ninth to Twelfth Centuries', in *Law and Society in Byzantium: Ninth-Twelfth Centuries*, eds D. Simon and A. Laiou (Washington, DC, 1994).

Magdalino, P., 'Innovations in Government', in *Alexios I Komnenos. 1, Papers of the Second Belfast Byzantine International Colloquium, 14–16 April 1989*, eds M. Mullett and D. Smythe (Belfast, 1996), pp. 146–66.

Magdalino, P., 'Constantinople and the Outside World', in *Strangers to Themselves: The Byzantine Outsider*, ed. D. C. Smythe (Aldershot, 2000), pp. 149–62

Magdalino, P., 'Constantine V and the Middle Age of Constantinople', in *Studies on the History and Topography of Byzantine Constantinople*, ed. P. Magdalino (Aldershot, 2007).

Magdalino, P., 'Byzantium=Constantinople', in *A Companion to Byzantium*, ed. L. James (Malden, MA, 2010), pp. 43–54.

Markopoulos, A., 'Education', in *The Oxford Handbook of Byzantine Studies*, ed. M. Jeffreys, J. Haldon and R. Cormack (Oxford, 2008), pp. 785–95.

Miller, D. A., 'The Logothete of the Drome in the Middle Byzantine Period', *Byzantion* 36 (1966), pp. 438–70.

Millet, G., 'L'origine du logothète général', *Mélanges d'histoire du Moyen Age offerts à M. F. Lot* (Paris, 1925), pp. 563–73.

Montreuil, J. A. B., '*Histoire du droit byzantin, ou du droit romain dans l'Empire d'Orient, depuis la mort de Justinien jusqu'à la prise de Constantinople en 1453* (Paris, 1843).

Morris, R., 'What Did the epi tôn deêseôn Actually Do?', in *La pétition à Byzance*, ed. D. Feissel and J. Gascou (Paris, 2004), pp. 125–40.

Morris, R., 'Travelling Judges in Byzantine Macedonia (10th–11th c.)', *Zbornik Radova Vizantološkog Instituta* 50 (2013), pp. 351–61.

Morrisson, C., 'La devaluation de la monnaie byzantine au XIe siècle: essai d'interprétation', *Travaux et Mémoires* 6 (1976), pp. 3–48.

Morrisson, C., 'Numismatique et histoire, l'or monnayé de Rome à Byzance : purification et altérations', *Comptes rendus des séances de l'Académie des Inscriptions et Belles-Lettres* 126, no. 2 (1982), pp. 203–23.

Morrisson, C., 'Byzantine Money: Its Production and Circulation', in *The Economic History of Byzantium from the Seventh Through the Fifteenth Centuries*, ed. A. E. Laiou (Washington, DC, 2002), pp. 909–66.

Morrisson, C., 'Le Michaèlaton et les noms de monnaies de la fin du XIe siècle', *Travaux et Mémoires* III (1968), pp. 369–74.

Morrisson, C., *Byzance et sa monnaie (IVe-XVe siècle)* (Paris, 2015).

Nesbitt, J. W., 'The Office of the *oikistikos*: Five Seals in the Dumbarton Oaks Collection', *Dumbarton Oaks Papers* 29 (1975), pp. 341–4.

Nesbitt, J. and Seibt, W., 'The Anzas Family: Members of the Civil Establishment in the Eleventh, Twelfth, and Thirteenth Centuries', *Dumbarton Oaks Papers* 67 (2013), pp. 189–207.

Neville, L., *Authority in Byzantine Provincial Society, 950–1100* (Cambridge, 2004).
Oikonomides, N., 'Le serment de l'impératrice Eudocie (1067): Un episode de l'histoire dynastique de Byzance', *Revue des études byzantines* 21 (1963), pp. 101–28.
Oikonomides, N., 'L'organisation de la frontière orientale de Byzance aux xe-xie siècle et le taktikon de l'Escorial', in *Actes du XIVe Congrès international des études byzantines* I (Bucharest, 1974), pp. 285–302.
Oikonomides, N., 'L'évolution de l'organisation administrative de l'empire byzantin au XIe siècle (1025–1118)', *Travaux et Mémoires* 6 (1976), pp. 125–52.
Oikonomides, N., 'St. George of the Mangana, Maria Skleraina and the "Malyj Sion" of Novgorod', *Dumbarton Oaks Papers* 34–35 (1980–81), pp. 239–46.
Oikonomides, N., 'The "Peira" of Eustathios Romaios: An Abortive Attempt to Innovate in Byzantine Law', *Fontes Minores* 7 (1984), pp. 162–92.
Oikonomides, N., 'Ho megas droungarios Eustathios Kymineianos kai he sphragida tou (1099)', *Byzantina* 13, no. 2 (1985), pp. 899–907.
Oikonomides, N., *A Collection of Dated Byzantine Lead Seals* (Washington, DC, 1986).
Oikonomides, N., 'The Lead Blanks Used for Byzantine Seals', *Studies in Byzantine Sigillography* 1 (1987), pp. 97–103.
Oikonomides, N., 'Title and Income at the Byzantine Court', in *Byzantine Court Culture from 829–1204*, ed. H. Maguire (Washington, DC, 1997), pp. 199–215.
Oikonomides, N., 'The Role of the Byzantine State in the Economy', in *The Economic History of Byzantium*, ed. A. E. Laiou, 3 vols (Washington DC, 2002), pp. 973–1058.
Ostler, D., 'From Periphery to Center: The Transformation of Late Roman Self-Definition in the Seventh Century', in *Shifting Frontiers in Late Antiquity*, ed. R. W. Mathisen and H. S. Sivan (Aldershot, 1996), pp. 93–101.
Ostrogorsky, G., *Pour l'histoire de la féodalité byzantine* (Brussels, 1954).
Ostrogorsky, G., *History of the Byzantine State,* revised edn (New Brunswick, 1969).
Ostrogorsky, G., 'Observations on the Aristocracy in Byzantium', *Dumbarton Oaks Papers* 25 (1971), pp. 1–32.
Oxford Dictionary of Byzantium, ed. A. Kazhdan (Oxford, 1991).
Papagiane, E. S., 'Το έγκλημα της 'φθοράς' και η αγωγή 'περί ύβρεως' στο χωρίο 49.4 της Πείρας', in *Κατεθόδιον: In Memoriam Nikos Oikonomides*, ed. S. N. Troianos (Athens and Komotene: 2008), pp. 81–106.
Saradi, H., 'The Byzantine Tribunals: Problems in the Application of Justice and State Policy (9th–12th C.)', *Revue des études byzantines* 53 (1995), pp. 165–204.
Schminck, A., 'Zur Einzelgesetzgebung der "makedonischen" Kaiser', *Fontes Minores* 11 (2005), pp. 249–68.
Schminck, A., *Studien zu mittelbyzantinischen Rechtsbüchern* (Frankfurt and Main, 1986).
Seibt, W., 'Prosopographische Konsequenzen aus der Umdatierung von Grumel, Regestes 933 (Patriarch Eustathios anstelle von Eustratios)', *Jahrbuch der Österreichischen Byzantinistik* 22 (1973), pp. 103–15.
Seibt, W., *Die Skleroi* (Vienna, 1976).
Seibt, W., 'Zwischen Identifizierungsrauch und -verweigerung: Zur Problematik synchroner homonymer Siegel', in *Siegel un Siegler: Akten des 8 Internationalen Symposions für Byzantinische Sigillographie*, ed. C. Ludwig (Berlin, 2005), pp. 141–50.
Ševčenko, I., 'Poems on the Deaths of Leo VI and Constantine VII in the Madrid Manuscript of Scylitzes', *Dumbarton Oaks Papers* 23/24 (1969/70), pp. 185, 187–228.
Simon, D., *Rechtsfindung am byzantinischen Reichsgericht* (Fankfurt am Main: 1973).
Simon, D., 'Das Ehegüterrecht de Pira. Ein systematischer Versuch', *Fontes Minores* 7 (1987), pp. 193–238.

Stein, E., *Studien zur Geschichte des byzantinischen Reiches vornehmlich unter den Kaisern Justinus II. u. Tiberius Constantinus* (Stuttgart, 1919).
Stein, E., 'Untersuchungen zum Staatsrecht des Bas-Empire', *Zeitschrift der Savigny-Stifung für Rechtsgeschichte, Romanistische Abteilung* 41 (1920), pp. 195–251.
Stephenson, P., 'A Development in Nomenclature of the Seals of the Byzantine Provincial Aristocracy in the Late Tenth Century', *Revue des études byzantines* 52 (1994), pp. 187–211.
Svoronos, N. G., *Recherches sur le cadastre byzantin et la fiscalité aux 11. et 12. siècles: le cadastre de Thèbes* (Athens, 1959).
Troianos, S., *Οι Πηγές του Βυζαντινού Δικαίου, Τρίτη έκδοση συμπληρωμένη* (Athens, 2011).
Tsourka-Papasthante, D., 'Vente d'office: observations sur la Πεῖρα Εὐσταθίου τοῦ Ῥωμαίου 38.74', in *Byzantine Law: Proceedings of the International Symposium of Jurists, Thessaloniki, 10–13 December 1998*, ed. C. Papatathis (Thessaloniki, 2001), pp. 229–34.
Vasiliev, A. A., *A History of the Byzantine Empire* (Madison, 1928).
Vikan, G. and Nesbitt, J., *Security in Byzantium: Locking, Sealing, Weighing* (Washington, DC, 1980).
Vryonis, S., 'Byzantine Dēmokratia and the Guilds in the Eleventh Century', *Dumbarton Oaks Papers* 17 (1963), pp. 287–314.
Vryonis, S., 'The *Peira* as a Source for the History of Byzantine Aristocratc Society in the First Half of the Eleventh Century', in *Near Eastern Numismatics, Iconography, Epigraphy and History: Studies in Honor of George C. Miles*, ed. D. K. Kouymjian (Beirut, 1974), pp. 279–84.
Wassiliou, A.-K., 'Die Familie-Hexamilites. Ein Beitrag zur byzantinischen Prosopographie', *Hellenika* 52/2 (2002), pp. 243–58.
Wassiliou-Seibt, A.-K. 'Die Neffen des Patriarchen Michael I. Kerullarios (1043–1058) und ihre Siegel. Ikonographie als Ausdrucksmittel der Verwandtschaft', *Bulgaria Mediaevalis* 2 (2012), pp. 107–19.
Weiss, G., 'Hohe Richter in Konstantinopel. Eustathios Rhomaios und seine Kollegen', *Jahrbuch der Österreichischen Byzantinistik* 22 (1973), pp. 117–43.
Weiss, G., *Oströmische Beamte im Spiegel der Schriften des Michael Psellos* (Munich, 1973).
Winkelmann, F., *Byzantinische Rang- und Ämterstruktur im 8. und 9. Jahrhundert*. Berliner byzantinistische Arbeiten 53 (Berlin, 1985).
Winkelmann, F., *Quellenstudien zur herrschenden Klasse von Byzanz im 8. und 9. Jahrhundert*. Berliner byzantinistische Arbeiten 54 (Berlin, 1987).
Wolska-Conus, W., 'Les écoles de Psellos et de Xiphilin sous Constantin IX Monomaque', *Travaux et Mémoires* 6 (1976), pp. 238–42.
Xanalatos, D. A., *Beiträge zur Wirtschafts- und Sozialgeschichte Makedoniens im Mittelalter, hauptsächlich auf Grund der Briefe des Erzbischofs Theophylaktos von Achrida* (Speyer a. Rh.,1937).
Zachariä von Lingenthal, K. E., *Geschichte des griechisch- romischen Rechtes*, 3rd edn (Berlin, 1892).
Živkovič, T., 'Uspenskij's Taktikon and the Theme of Dalmatia', *Σύμμεικτα* 17 (2005), pp. 49–85.

Catalogues of Byzantine seals

Bulgakova, V., *Byzantinische Bleisiegel in Osteuropa: Die Funde auf dem Territorium Altrusslands* (Wiesbaden, 2004).

Campagnolo-Pothitou, M. and Cheynet, J.-C., *Sceaux de la collection Georges Zacos au Musée d'art et d'histoire de Genève* (Geneva, 2016).

Cheynet, J.-C., 'Sceaux byzantins des musées d'Antioche et de Tarse', *Travaux et Mémoires* 12 (1994), pp. 391–478.

Cheynet, J.-C., 'Les sceaux byzantins du Musée de Manişa', *Revue des études byzantines* 56 (1998), pp. 261–7.

Cheynet, J.-C., 'Les sceaux byzantins du musée de Selçuk', *Revue Numismatique* 155 (1999), pp. 317–52.

Cheynet, J.-C., *Sceaux de la collection Zacos (Bibliothèque nationale de France) se rapportant aux provinces orientales de l'Empire byzantine* (Paris, 2001).

Cheynet, J.-C., 'Les sceaux byzantins de Londres', *Studies in Byzantine Sigillography* 8 (2003), pp. 85–100.

Cheynet, J.-C., 'Sceaux de la collection Khoury', *Revue Numismatique* 159 (2003), pp. 419–56.

Cheynet, J.-C., *Sceaux byzantins de la collection D. Theodoridis: les sceaux patronymiques* (Paris, 2010).

Cheynet, J.-C. and Sode, C., *Studies in Byzantine Sigillography* 8 (2003).

Cheynet, J.-C. and Sode, C., *Studies in Byzantine Sigillography* 10 (2010).

Cheynet, J.-C., Morrisson, C. and Seibt, W., *Sceaux byzantins de la collection Henri Seyrig* (Paris, 1991).

Cheynet, J.-C., Gökyıldırım, T. and Bulgurlu, V., *Les sceaux byzantins du Musée archéologique d'Istanbul* (Istanbul, 2012).

Davidson, G. R., *The Minor Objects [= Corinth XII]* (Princeton, 1952).

De Gray Birch, W., *Catalogue of Seals in the Department of Manuscripts in the British Museum* (London, 1989).

Harrison, R. M., *Excavations at Saraçhane in Istanbul* I (Washington, DC and Princeton, NJ, 1986).

Hunger, H., 'Zehn unedierte byzantinische Beamtensiegel', *Jahrbuch der Österreichischen Byzantinistik* 17 (1968), pp. 179–88.

Hunger, H., 'Die Makremboliten auf byzantinischen Bleisiegeln und in sonstigen Belegen', *Studies in Byzantine Sigillography* 5 (1998), pp. 1–28.

Jordanov, I., *Corpus of Byzantine Seals from Bulgaria*, 3 vols (Sofia, 2003–9).

Koltsida-Makrè, I., *Byzantina molyvdoboulla sylloges Orphanide–Nikolaïde Nomismatikou Mouseiou Athenon* (Athens, 1996).

Koltsida-Makrè, I., 'Ἡ συλλογή μολυβδοβούλλων Δημητρίου Δούκα', in *Hypermachos. Studien zu Byzantinistik, Armenologie und Georgistik: Fetschrift für Werner Seibt zum 65. Geburtstag*, eds Ch. Stavrakos, A.-K. Wassiliou and M. K. Krikorian (Wisbaden, 2008), pp. 139–52.

Konastantopoulos K. M., *Βυζαντιακὰ μολυβδόβουλλα τοῦ ἐν Ἀθήναις Εθνικοῦ Νομισματικοῦ Μουσείου* (Athens, 1917).

Konstantopoulos, K. M., *Βυζαντιακὰ μολυβδόβουλλα (Συλλογὴ Κ. Π. Σταμούλη)* (Athens, 1930).

Laurent, V., 'Un sceau inédit du protonotaire Basile Kamatéros', *Byzantion* 6 (1931), pp. 253–72.

Laurent, V., *Les bulles métriques dans la sigillographie byzantine* (Athens, 1932).
Laurent, V., 'Sceaux byzantins inédits', *Byzantinische Zeitschrift* 33 (1933), pp. 331–61.
Laurent, V., 'Sceaux byzantins inédits', *Echos d'Orient* 32 (1933), pp. 35–53.
Laurent, V., *La collection C. Orghidan* (Paris, 1952).
Laurent, V., *Les sceaux byzantins du Médailler Vatican* (Vatican City, 1962).
Laurent, V., *Le corpus des sceaux de l'Empire byzantin, vol. 2, L'administration centrale* (Paris, 1981).
Leontiades, I. G., 'Acht Siegel aus dem Museum für Byzantinische Kultur in Thessalonike', *Studies in Byzantine Sigillography* 9 (2006), pp. 23–31.
Likhachev, N. P., *Molivdovuly grecheskogo vostoka*, ed. V. S. Šandrovskaja (Moscow, 1991).
McGeer, E., Nesbitt, J. W. and Oikonomides, N., *Catalogue of Byzantine Seals at Dumbarton Oaks and in the Fogg Museum of Art, 4: The East* (Washington, DC, 2001).
McGeer, E., Nesbitt, J. W. and Oikonomides, N., *Catalogue of Byzantine Seals at Dumbarton Oaks and in the Fogg Museum of Art, 5: The East Continued* (Washington, DC, 2005).
Metcalf, D. M., *Byzantine Leas Seals from Cyprus* (Nicosia, 2004–14).
Nesbitt, J. W. and Oikonomides, N., *Catalogue of Byzantine Seals at Dumbarton Oaks and in the Fogg Museum of Art, 1: Italy, North of the Balkans, North of the Black Sea* (Washington, DC, 1991).
Nesbitt, J. W. and Oikonomides, N., *Catalogue of Byzantine Seals at Dumbarton Oaks and in the Fogg Museum of Art, 2: South of the Balkans, the Islands, South of Asia Minor* (Washington, DC, 1994).
Nesbitt, J. W. and Oikonomides, N., *Catalogue of Byzantine Seals at Dumbarton Oaks and in the Fogg Museum of Art, 3 West, Northwest, and Central Asia Minor and the Orient* (Washington, DC, 1996).
Nesbitt, J. W., Wassiliou-Seibt, A.-K. and Seibt, W., *Highlights from the Robert Hecht, Jr., Collection of Byzantine Seals* (Thessaloniki, 2009).
Nitti di Vitto, F., ed., *Codice diplomatico Barese IV: Le pergamene di S. Nicola di Bari (939–1071)* (Bari, 1900).
Oikonomides, N., ed., *Studies in Byzantine Sigillography* 3 (1993).
Oikonomides, N., ed., *Studies in Byzantine Sigillography* 5 (1998).
Oikonomides, N., ed., *Studies in Byzantine Sigillography* 6 (1999).
Pančenko, B. A., *Kollekcii Russkago Archeologičeskago Instituta v Konstantinopolě*: Katalog *molivdovulov* (Sofia, 1908).
Schlumberger, G., *Sigillographie de l'Empire byzantin* (Paris, 1884).
Seibt, W., 'Die Darstellung der Theotokos auf Byzantinischen Bleisiegeln besonders im 11. Jahrhundert', *Studies in Byzantine Sigillography* 1 (1987), pp. 35–56.
Seibt, W., 'Katechanas – ein lange verkannter mittelbyzantinischer Bei- bzw. Familienname', *Byzantinische Zeitschrift* 110, no. 3 (2017), pp. 749–54.
Seibt, W. and Wassiliou, A.-K., *Die byzantinischen Bleisiegel in Österreich, vol. 2, Zentral- und Provinzialverwaltung* (Vienna, 2004).
Seibt, W. and Zarnitz, M. L., *Das byzantinische Bleisiegel als Kunstwerk: Katalog zur Ausstellung* (Vienna, 1997).
Šandrovskaja, V. S., 'Sfragistika', in *Iskusstvo Vizantii v sobranijach SSSR (Katalog vystavki)*, vol. 2 (Moscow, 1977).
Šandrovskaja, V. S., 'Eparchi Konstantinopolja XI-XII vv', *Antichnaja drevnost i srednie veka* 26 (1992), pp. 62–77.

Šandrovskaja, V. S., "Pečati predstavitelej armjanskogo roda Machetariev", in *Patmamanasirakan Handes-Istoriko-filologiceskij Zurnal* 162 (2003).

Šandrovskaja, V. S. and Seibt, W., *Byzantinische Bleisiegel der Staatlichen Eremitage mit Familiennamen, vol. 1, Sammlung Lichačev—Namen von A bis I* (Vienna, 2005).

Sode, C., *Byzantinische Bleisiegel in Berlin, vol. 2* (Bonn, 1997).

Speck, P., *Byzantinische Bleisiegel in Berlin (West)* (Bonn, 1986).

Stavrakos, Ch., *Die byzantinischen Bleisiegel mit Familiennamen aus der Sammlung des Numismatischen Museums Athen* (Wiesbaden, 2000).

Stepanova, E., 'New Seals from Sudak', in *Studies in Byzantine Sigillography* 6 (1999), pp. 47-58.

Szemioth, A. and Wasilewski, T., 'Sceaux byzantins du Musée National de Varsovie', *Studia Źródłoznawcze, Commentationes* 11 (1966), pp. 1-38 and 14 (1969), pp. 63-89.

Veis, N., 'Zur Sigillographie der byzantinischen Themen Peloponnes und Hellas', *Vizantijskij Vremennik* 21 (1914).

Wassiliou-Seibt, A.-K., *Corpus der byzantinischen Siegel mit metrischen Legenden* I (Vienna, 2011).

Wassiliou-Seibt, A.-K. and Seibt, W., *Der byzantinische Mensch in seinem Umfeld: weitere Bleisiegel der Sammlung Zarnitz im Museum August Kestner* (Rahden, 2015).

Zacos, G., *Byzantine Lead Seals*, ed., J. W. Nesbit, vol. 2 (Bern, 1984).

Zacos, G. and Veglery, A., *Byzantine Lead Seals*, vol. 1 (Basel, 1972).

Index

Aboudemos, Basil   65
Abydinos   29
Adramytenos   29
Adramytenos, Nikephoros, *patrikios*,
   hypatos, and imperial *chartoularios*
   of the *stratiotikon*   131
Agallianos, Michael, *magistros* and
   imperial *protonotarios* of the *megas*
   sakellarios   127–8
Akapnes, Nicholas, *asekretis*, judge of
   Hellas, *mystolektes*, *kensor*, judge of
   Tarsos and Seleukeia   34
Akropolites   30
Alexios I Komnenos   1, 2, 3, 35, 135, 137,
   140, 147, 149, 152, 153, 154–5, 157,
   168, 173, 178
   bureaucratic reforms of   6, 126, 148,
      158–9, 175–8
   cancelling *roga* payments   20, 175
   droungarios tes viglas and   150–1
   epi tou kanikleiou and   137
   epi ton kriseon and   110
   hierarchy and   6, 13–17, 125, 145,
      159, 167
   imperial family and   138–9, 145, 150,
      177, 225 n.98, 230 n.21
   imperial household and   137, 138–9,
      142
   logothetes ton sekreton and   69, 126,
      176
   megas logariastes ton euagon sekreton
      and   176, 177, 185
   megas logariastes ton sekreton
      and   128, 176, 185
   protoasekretis and   138–9
   reform of the coinage   20, 171
   sekreton tou dromou and   132
   state properties and   173
Alopos   30, 31
Anagoures, Nicholas, imperial
   protospatharios epi tou
   Chrysotriklinou and imperial
   sakellarios   44

Andreas, imperial *protospatharios*
   and *epi tou Chrysotriklinou*
   and *chartoularios* of the *oxys*
   dromos   57
Anthemiotes   30
Antigrapheus   94, 96, 149
Antiochites   29
Antiprosopon
   ephoros   67
   euageis oikoi   136
   oikeiakon   66
Anzas   31, 146
Anzas, Constantine, *protospatharios*
   and judge of the Hippodrome,
   anythpatos and *patrikios* and judge
   of the Velum   163
Arabantenos   29
Areobindenos, Constantine,
   spatharokandidatos epi tou
   Chrysotriklinou and imperial
   notarios of the *genikon*   48
Areobindos/enos   30
Argyros   32, 38
Argyros, John, *protospatharios epi tou*
   Chrysotriklinou, imperial *notarios*
   of the *sekreton* of the *ephoros*
   32, 66
Argyros, Niketas, *magistros* and *praitor* of
   Constantinople   32, 90, 146
Aristenos, Basil, *kouropalates* and
   parathalassites   146
Aristenos, Michael, *logothetes* of the
   dromos   132
Aristenos, N. *eparch*   145
Aristenos, N. *vestarches* and
   protoasekretis   138, 145
Artabasdos   30, 32
Asekretai   37, 69, 71, 72–4, 80–1, 139,
   145, 180
   origins and duties of   72
Asekreteion   71, 138, 202 n.145, *see also*
   asekretis; chancery; *notarioi*;
   protoasekretis

Attaleiates, Michael   8, 23, 93, 140, 206 n.208
  career of   32, 82
  on the decline/mismanagement of the empire   3, 125, 128, 130
  epi ton kriseon and   109–10
  sekreton ton dikon and   110
  Theodora's seizure of government and   85–6
Autoreianos, Michael, *proedros* and judge of the Hippodrome   154–5

Basil, *eparch* of Constantinople   145
Basil, imperial *protospatharios* and judge   21
Basil, imperial *protospatharios epi tou Chrysotriklinou*, judge of the Hippodrome, judge of the Velum, *epi tes basilikes sakelles*, and *mystographos*   25
Basil, *protospatharios epi tou Chrysotriklinou*, imperial *notarios* of the *eidikos logothetes*, *mystographos*, and judge of the Hippodrome   78–9
Basil, *spatharokandidatos* and *protonotarios* of the *sakellion*   60
Basil, *vestarches* and *epi tou kanikleiou*   137
Basil I   31, 122
  kouratorikion of the Mangana and   66
  legal reforms of   92, 121, 123
  megas kourator and   66
  Mystikos and   74
Basil II   1, 2, 7, 22, 30, 39, 40, 66, 70, 82, 173, 210 n.263
  coinage and debasement under   171
  cost of the bureaucracy under   170, 172
  expansion of government under   123, 164, 169, 172, 174, 178, 230 n.17
  fiscal lands and   65, 174, 178
  judiciary under   123, 174
  title inflation under   174
Basilika   92–3, 211 n.272
Beriotes   29
Beriotes, John, *proedros*, judge of the Velum, and *eparch*   145

protoproedros and *epi ton oikeiakon*   135, 162
vestes, judge of the Hippodrome, *megas logothetes tou stratiotikou*, and imperial *notarios* of the *sakellion*   37
vestes, *megas chartoularios* of the *stratiotikon*, judge of the Velum, and imperial *notarios* of the *sakellion*   131, 133
Blachernai Synod (1094)   11, 17, 151, 177
Blachernites   30
Blachernites, Constantine, *proedros* and *eidikos*   133
Blachernites, John, *protospatharios epi tou Chrysotriklinou* and *mystolektes*   143
Botaneiates   30
Bringas   30, 91, 146
Bringas, Joseph   82
Bryennios, Nikephoros   8
  on Alexian coinage reform   20
  on mismanagement of empire   5
bureaucracy   7
  size of   163–5, 169, 172
  specialization of   172
bureaucrats   6–7
  careers of   33–8 (*see also* Kenchres, Elpidios; Promoundenos, Constantine; Romaios, Eustathios; Tzirithon, Basil)
  family names   29–33
  holding multiple offices   37–8, 105
  origins of   29–31

centralization of government   178, *see also epi ton kriseon*; judiciary; *sekreton ton dikon*
Chalkoprateites   30
Chalkoutzes   32
chancery   74, 78, 136, 177, 224 n.80, *see also asekreteion*; *asekretis*; *mystikos*; *mystographos*; *mystolektes*; *notarioi*; *protoasekretis*
  connection to the imperial household   81
  origins, composition, and duties of   69
  status of   80–1

Charsianites 29
Chartoularioi 42, 43–4, 180–1, 195 n.10
  dromos 42, 57, 58
  euageis oikoi 136
  genikon 46, 49–50, 130
  sakellion 42
  stratiotikon 52, 53–4
  vestiarion 42, 60;
Chersonites 29
Chiotes 29
Choirosphaktes 30, 32–3, 176, 193 n.34
Choirosphaktes, Constantine,
  protoproedros and *epi ton deeseon* 142, 225 n.98
  protoproedros and *protonotarios tou dromou* 132
Choirosphaktes, Eustratios, *magistros* and *protoasekretis* 138
  magistros and *protonotarios tou dromou* 132
Choirosphaktes, Leo, *mystikos* 74, 75
Christopher, imperial *protospatharios* and *epi tou Chrysotriklinou* and judge of the Hippodrome 105
Chryselios 30
Chrysobalantites 33
Chrysobalantites, Leo, *protoasekretis* and *chartoularios* 71
Chrysoberges 30
Chrysoberges, John, *vestarches* and *megas chartoularios tou genikou* 131
Chrysobulls 11, 12
  of 1081 126
  epi tou kanikleiou and 70
  protoasekretis and 71
  for Robert Guiscard 18–19
Chrysos 30
Chytes 146
coinage
  debasement of 20–1, 171
  inflation 20–1, 191 n.74
Constantine, *anthypatos, patrikios, protospatharios*, and *oikistikos* 50
Constantine, *asekretis* and *antigrapheus* 149
Constantine, *kouropalates, asekretis*, and *anagrapheus* 139
Constantine, *magistros* and *protomystikos* 76

Constantine, nephew of the patriarch Keroularios 34, 104, 127, 128, 149, 150, 151, 155–6, 226 n.121
Constantine, *proedros*, judge and *logothetes tou dromou* 54
Constantine, *proedros* and *eidikos* 133
Constantine, *protospatharios* and *ek prosopou* 185
Constantine IX Monomachos 7, 19, 27, 57, 64, 69, 75, 76, 93, 99, 190 n.49
  centralization under 109–11, 178
  Constantinople and 82–3, 90–1, 210 n.266
  decline/mismanagement of empire under 3, 8, 229 n.16
  devaluation of the coinage under 21, 171
  epi ton kriseon and 109–11, 123, 156, 175
  expansion of the senate under 4–5, 33, 118, 164, 166, 172, 229 n.16, 230 n.17
  judiciary and 39, 98, 121, 122–3, 174–5, 178
  law school and 110, 118–21, 123, 175
  nomophylax didaskalos and 118–21
  rehabilitation of 3
  sekreton ton dikon and 109–11, 123, 175
Constantine X Doukas 142
  Constantinople and 82
  debasement of the currency under 21
  expansion of the senate under 5, 82, 118, 172, 229 n.16
  judiciary and 174–5
  mismanagement of the empire under 178, 229 n.16
Constantinople 7, 20, 32, 81–3, 158, 175, 176, 208 n.233, *see also eparchoi* of Constantinople; guilds of Constantinople; *parathalassites*; *praitores* of Constantinople; senate; *symponoi*
  economy of 82, 128
  families from 30
  political importance of 4, 82–3, 90–1, 209–10 n.262, 210 n.263, 210 n.266
Court of the *eparch*, *see eparchikon bema*

Court of the Hippodrome 97, 100, 102, 216 n.343
Court of the Velum 100, 108

Dalessene, Anna 126
debasement, *see* coinage
De Ceremoniis 39, 55, 62, 75
Dekapolites, Theodore, imperial *protospatharios epi tou Chrysotriklinou* and *koiaistor* 94
Deuteroi (*euageis oikoi*) 136
Diabatenos 30
Diernergon of the *sekreton* of the *oikeiakon* 135
dignity, *see* titles
Domestikoi (*ephoros*) 67
Dromos 54–8, *see also chartoularioi; logothetai; notarioi; protonotarioi*
    origins, composition, and duties of 54
Droungarios tes viglas 84, 96–9, 123, 149–51, 158, 175, 213 n.298, 228 n.150
    origins and duties of 96–8, 213, n.296
    relationship to the *nomophylax didaskalos* 120

Ecloga Basilicorum 99, 101, 155
Eidikoi 62–3, 68–9, 133, 158
Eidikon 61–3, 133, 134, 158, *see also eidikoi; kankellarioi; notarioi; protonotarioi*
    last mention of 133
    origin, composition, and duties of 61–2, 199 n.92
Eisagoge 92
Elegmites, Constantine, *protospatharios* and *mystographos* 77, 140
Elesbaam, John 36
Eparchikon bema 83
Eparchoi of Constantinople 83–6, 90, 143–5, 158
    origins, staff and duties of 83–4
Ephoroi ton basilikon kouratorion 67, 68, 135–6, 158, 174
    final mention of 136
Epi tes sakelles 59, 68, 133–4, 158
Epi ton deeseon 69, 78–9, 141–3, 157
    connection to the imperial household 142, 159

    origin and duties of 78, 205 nn.196–7
Epi ton kriseon 112, 155–6, 175
    origin and duties of 109–11, 119–20, 218 nn.374–5, 228 n.150
Epi ton oikeiakon 65–6, 135, 158, 174
Epi tou kanikleiou 69, 70–1, 80, 136–7, 158
    connection to the imperial household 81, 137
    origin and duties of 70, 202 n.140, 202 n.150
Epi tou vestiariou 61, 68, 133–4, 158
Epoptai 46
Escorial Taktikon 11–12, 40, 122–3, 173–4
Euageis oikoi 63, 64, *see also antiprosopon; chartoularioi; deuteroi; megaloi logariastai; notarioi; oikonomoi ton euagon oikon*
Eustathios, *symponos* 86
Exaktores 115–16, 156–7
    duties of 112, 114–15, 121–2

Galaton 29
Galaton, Niketas 32
Garidas 30, 31
Genikon 46–50, 129, 130, *see also chartoularioi; epoptai; kankellarioi; megaloi chartoularioi; notarioi; oikistikoi; protokankellarioi; protonotarioi*
    origin, composition, and duties of 42, 46
George, *patrikios*, judge of the Velum, *thesmophylax*, and *symponos* 113
George, *protospatharios epi tou Chrysotriklinou* and *megas kourator* of the imperial monastery 66
George, *vestarches, hypatos*, judge of the Velum, and *deuteros* of the charitable foundations 136
Gorgonites, Basil, *protovestarches* and *megas chartoularios* of the *sekreton* of the *oikeiaka* 135
Guilds of Constantinople 4, 33, 65, 75, 81–3, 84–6, 117–18
Guiscard, Robert 12, 18
Gymnos 30

Helladikos 29
Hexamilites 31, 35, 38, 127, 145
Hexamilites, Epiphanios, *vestarches* and judge of the Velum 151
Hexamilites, Sergios 35, 163
   protoproedros and *eparch* 145
   protoproedros and judge of the Velum 153
   protoproedros and *logothetes ton sekreton* 126
Hikanatos 30
Hikanatos, Leo, *eparch* 145

Iasites 30
Iasites, Constantine, *protoproedros* and *epi ton deeseon* 142
imperial household 137, 140, 142–3
inflation, *see* coinage; titles

John, *kouropalates*, *asekretis*, and *anagrapheus* 139
John, *magistros*, *anthypatos*, *patrikios*, and imperial *spatharios* 56
John, *magistros* and *epi ton deeseon* 79
John, *mystikos* and *praipositios epi tou koitonos* 140
John, *notarios* 181
John, *patrikios*, imperial *notarios*, judge of the Velum, and of the Kibyrraiotai 26
John (possibly Skylitzes), *proedros* and *eparch* 145
John, *proedros* and *ephoros* 63
John, *protoproedros* and *logothetes tou dromou* 132
John, *protoproedros* and *protoasekretis* 138
John, *protospatharios*, *mystolektes*, judge of the Velum and of the Armenian themes 79
John, *vestarches* and *logothetes tou dromou* 57
John, *vestes*, *anthypatos*, *patrikios*, and *parathalassites* 88
judges of the Hippodrome 93–4, 105–8, 121–2, 153–5, 158
   duties and tribunals of 100–3, 108
   number of 99–100, 108
   provincial duties of 108–9

judges of the Velum 103–5, 121–2, 123, 151–3, 155, 158
   duties and tribunals of 100–3, 108
   number of 99–100, 108
   provincial duties of 108–9
judiciary 91–4, 121–3, 174–5, *see also antgrapheis*; *droungarioi tes viglas*; *epi ton kriseon*; *exaktores*; judges of the Hippodrome; judges of the Velum; *kensores*; *koiaistores*; law school; *nomophylakes didaskalos*; *sekreton ton dikon*; *thesmographoi*; *thesmophylakes*

Kamaterios, Epiphanios, *proedros* and *eparch* 143, 145
Kamateros 31, 38, 142, 176
Kamateros, Gregory, *nobelissimos* and *logothetes ton sekreton* 127
   nobelissimos and *protoasekretis* 138–9
Kamateros, Gregory, *protospatharios*, *mystographos*, and judge of the Hippodrome 136
Kankellarioi 43–4, 60
Karamallos, Theodore, *protospatharios*, *oikonomos* of the pious foundations, and *anagrapheus* of Paphlagonia 64
Karianites 29
Kastamonites 29, 142
Katakalon 30
Katechanas, Nicholas, *protospatharios*, *thesmographos*, *primikerios* of the advocates 117–18
Kekaumenos (author) 91, 93, 102, 191 n.74, 210 n.266
Kekaumenos (family) 30
Kenchres, Elpidios 33–4, 100, 107–8
   court case against Michael Psellos 18, 107, 110, 217 n.361
   protospatharios, *mystographos*, judge of the Velum, *thesmographos*, and *exaktor* 77–8
   roga of 18, 229 n.16
   thesmographos 114, 218 n.388
Kensores 93, 116–17, 156–7
   duties of 112, 117, 122
Kephallonites 29
Keroularios 150

Kibyrraiotes 30
Kibyrraiotes, George, *proedros* and
    protonotarios of the *dromos* 31,
    132
Kletorologion of Philotheos 11, 40–1, 72,
    75, 167, 169
Koiaistores 94–6, 147–8, 158, 212 n.290
    origins and duties of 94–5, 212 n.291
Komnene, Anna 8
    logothetes ton sekreton creation of 126
Komnenian elite 38, 142, 145, 176–7
Komnenian hierarchy 16–17, 145, 159
    bureaucrats' place in 132, 134, 137,
    138, 142, 144, 150–1, 153, 158–9
Komnenian reforms 159, *see also*
    logothetai ton sekreton; *megaloi
    logariastai ton euagon sekreton*;
    megaloi logariastai ton sekreton
Kymineianos, Eustathios, *epi tou
    kanikleiou*, *ethnarch*, and *megas
    droungarios* 136–7
Kyparissiotes 30

Laktentitzes, Nikephoros, imperial
    *protospatharios epi tou
    Chrysotriklinou*, *mystographos*, and
    chartoularios of the *stratiotikon
    logothesion* 53
law school 110–11, 118–21
Leo, *epi tou kanikleiou* 70
Leo, imperial *protospatharios* and *epi tou
    kanikleiou* 70
Leo, imperial *protospatharios epi tou
    Chrysotriklinou* and *epi tou
    vestiariou* 61
Leo, *magistros*, *vestarches*, judge of
    the Velum, and *praitor* of
    Constantinople 90
Leo, *protoproedros* and *koiaistor* 25
Leo, *protospatharios* and imperial *notarios
    ton oikeiakon* 65
Leo, *spatharokandidatos* and
    antigrapheus 96
Leo, *spatharokandidatos* and *protonotarios*
    of the *sakellion* 60
Leo VI 92, 121, 123
    logothetes tou dromou and 55
Leontios, *protospatharios*, judge of
    the Hippodrome, and *epi ton
    deeseon* 39

Libellisios, John, *vestes*, *anthypatos*,
    patrikios, and *epi tou
    kanikleiou* 70–1, 136–7
Logariastai 43–4, 184–5
    oikistikon 51
Logothetai, *see also epi ton oikeiakon*
    dromos 55–7, 69, 132, 158
    genikon 46, 47–8, 129–30, 158
    stratiotikon 52–3, 131, 158
    ton sekreton 69, 126–7, 159, 176

Macedonian legal reforms 92–3, 211 n.278
Machetarios 30
Machetarios, Michael, *vestarches* and
    eparch 29, 30, 31
Makrembolites 30, 38
Makrembolites, George 36
Maleinos 30
Mandatores 43–4, 60
Manuel, *droungarios tes viglas* 99
Matzoukes, Anastasios, *protovestes*
    and *megas chartoularios tou
    genikou* 131
Matzoukes, Nicholas, imperial *notarios*
    of the charitable foundations and
    exaktor 136
Megaloi chartoularioi 42, 179–80
    genikon 42, 46, 48–50, 130
    oikeiakon 135
    stratiotikon 42, 52, 53, 131
Megaloi droungarioi tes viglas,
    see droungarioi tes viglas
Megaloi kouratores 66–7
Megaloi logariastai
    ton euagon sekreton 136, 159, 176–7
    ton sekreton 128–9, 159, 176
Megaloi oikistikoi, *see oikistikoi*
Megaloi oikonomoi ton euagon oikon,
    see oikonomoi ton euagon oikon
Megaloi sakellarioi, *see sakellarioi*
Megas kouratorikion 66–7, *see also
    megaloi kouratores*
Melidones, John, *protovestes*, *megas
    oikonomos* of the Oikoproateiou,
    and judge of the Hippodrome 154
Mermentoulos 31
Mermentoulos, Nicholas, *droungarios tes
    viglas* 150–1
    nobelissimos and *eparch* 144, 145
Michael, *logothetes tou dromou* 9

Michael, *magistros*, *vestes*, and *epi ton kriseon*   109, 112
Michael, *notarios*   181
Michael, *patrikios*, judge of the Hippodrome, and *chartoularios* of the charitable foundations   136
Michael, *patrikios* and *eparch*   83
Michael, *proedros* and *logariastes ton oikistikon*   51
Michael, *protospatharios*, judge of the Velum, and *epi ton oikeiakon*   39
Michael, *thesmographos*   114
Michael, *vestarches*, and *logariastes*   184
Michael, *vestarches*, *vestes*, *anthypatos*, *patrikios*, and *logothetes tou stratiotikou*   131
Michael, *vestes*, judge of the Velum, and *epi tes basilikes sakelles*   27, 59
Michael VII Doukas   125, 128, 132, 142, 149, 150, 177
   chrysobull for Robert Guiscard   11, 12, 18
   debasement of the coinage under   21, 171, 191 n.74
Michael Hexamilites, *kensor* and judge of Paphlagonia   112
Michael of Neokaisarea, *megas sakellarios*   128
Michael son of Constantine nephew of the patriarch, *kouropalates* and *droungarios tes viglas*   150-1, 226 n.122
   sebastos and *logothetes ton sekreton*   126, 127
military administration, *see stratiotikon*
Monomachos   27, 30, 38
Monomachos, Theodosios, *protospatharios* and *parathalassites*   88
Mousele   30
Mystikos   69, 74-7, 140, 157
   origin and duties of   74-5
Mystographos   69, 77-8, 80-1, 140-1, 158
   duties of   77
Mystolektes   69, 79-80, 143, 158
   connection to the imperial household   81
Mytilenaios   30
Mytilenaios, Constantine, *proedros* and *eidikos*   133

Nicholas, *anthypatos*, *patrikios*, *vestes*, and *mystikos*   74
Nicholas, *hypatos*, judge of the Hippodrome, and *symponos*   87
Nicholas, *protospatharios* and *asekretis*   73
Nicholas Mystikos   75
Nikaeus, George, *epi ton kriseon*   110-11, 156
   koiaistor and judge of the Velum   148
Nikephoros, imperial *protospatharios* and *protonotarios* of the *sakellion*   60
Nikephoros, *protospatharios*, judge of the Hippodrome, and *mystographos*   39, 77
Nikephoros III Botaneiates   4, 19, 125, 128, 149, 150
   debasement of the coinage under   171
   mismanagement of the empire under   5, 130
   suspension of *roga* payments under   20, 125, 133
Nikephoros nephew of the patriarch, *protoproedros* and *droungarios tes viglas*   149, 150
Niketas, *anthypatos*, *patrikios*, imperial *notarios* of the *eidikon* and *praitor* of Constantinople   89-90
Niketas, *anthypatos*, *patrikios*, imperial *protospatharios*, and *logothetes tou genikou*   47
Niketas, *anthypatos*, *patrikios*, imperial *protospatharios* and *logothetes tou stratiotikou*   52
Niketas, *magistros* and *droungarios tes viglas*   149
Niketas, *magistros* and *logothetes tou stratiotikou*   131
Niketas, *proedros* and *epi ton kriseon*   111-12
Nomismata, *see* coinage
Nomophylakes didaskalos   118, 120-1
Notarioi   42, 43-4, 179, 182-4
   asekreteion   74, 203 n.159
   dromos   42-3, 58
   eidikon   42-3, 62, 63, 134, 158
   ephoros   67
   euageis oikoi   136
   genikon   50
   oikeiakon   66, 135

oikistikon 50–1
sakellarios 42–3
sakellion 42–3, 58, 60, 134, 158
vestiarion 42–3, 60
Novella constitutio 118–22, 123

Oikeiakoi, see epi ton oikeiakon
Oikeiakon 65–6, 135, 158, see also antiprosopon; epi ton oikeiakon; megaloi chartoularioi; notarioi
Oikisitkoi 46, 50–1, 174
Oikonomoi ton euagon oikon 64, 68, 136
final mention of 136
Ophrydas, Michael, vestes, judge of the Velum, and imperial notarios of the ephoros 101, 120, 136
Ouranos, Nikephoros, magistros, vestes, and epi tou kanikleiou 70–1
Ouranos, Symeon, vestarches and kensor 117
Oxys dromos, see dromos

Pamphilos 30
Pamphilos, Demetrios, protospatharios and judge of the Hippodrome 153
Parathalassites 83–4, 88, 146
origin and duties of 88, 90
Peira 93
Peter, protospatharios and protoasekretis 72, 202 n.150
Philaretos, Epiphanios, magistros and protoasekretis 138
Philaretos, Illoustrios, exaktor, and judge of the East 168
Philokales 30
Philokales, Manuel, protonobelissimos and epi tou kanikleiou 137
Philokales, Michael, proedros and mystikos 140
protoproedros, protonobelissimos, mystikos, and eparch of Constantinople 35, 145
Philokales Setes, Constantine, asekretis 139
Phokas 30
Phokas, Leo, logothetes tou dromou 55–6, 57
Phokas, Nikephoros, vestes, anthypatos, patrikios, and kensor 117

Praitores of Constantinople 89–90, 146–7
origin and duties of 89
Primikerioi of the Advocates 117–18
Prochiron 92
Promoundenos 30, 38
Promoundenos, Constantine 35, 36–7
Proteuon, Theodore 37
patrikios and judge of the Velum 103
Protoasekretai 69, 71–2, 80, 138–9
connection to the imperial household 81, 139
origin and duties of 71
Protokankellarioi 43, 60
Protokensores 117
Protomandatores 43
Protomystikos 76–7
Protonotarioi 42–3, 182
dromos 43, 54–5, 58, 132
eidikon 63
ephoros 67
genikon 50
sakellion 58, 60, 134
stratiotikon 53
Psellos, Michael 18–19, 23, 33–4, 107, 110, 114, 229 n.16
on decline/mismanagement of the empire 3, 6, 8, 44, 125, 188 n.23
on expansion of the senate 4, 90–1, 164, 166
on fiscal land 65
on legal reform 93, 119–20, 175
protoasekretis 72

Radenos 30
Radenos, John, protospatharios and eidikos 62
Radenos, Michael, magistros, vestarches, and logothetes tou stratiotikou 131
Rodios, Michael, protoanthypatos and judge of the Hippodrome 154
Rogai
augmentation of 20
cost of 170–2
debasement of coinage and 20–1
end of 20, 158
evidence for 17–20
protospatharaton 19
Romaios 30

Romaios, Eustathios 120, 122, 174, 175
  career of 102, 107
  droungarios tes viglas 96, 97–8, 101, 108, 113, 207 n.225
  exaktor 115
  logothetes tou dromou 56–7
  mystikos 75
  Peira 93
  provincial office of 36
Romanos, *protospatharios epi tou theophylaktou koitonos* and *kensor* 39
Romanos III Argyros 91, 107
  debasement of the currency under 21
  droungarios tes viglas and 98, 108, 122–3, 174–5
  eparch of Constantinople 32, 93
  mismanagement of the empire under 3

St. Basil 26, 27, 28
St. George 26–7
St. John Chrysostom 26–9
St. John Prodromos 26–8
St. Michael 26, 28–9
St. Nicholas 26, 29, 35
St. Theodore 26–8
Sakellarioi 44–5, 69, 127–8, *see also mandatores*; *notarioi*
  origins and duties of 44
Sakellion 58–60, 132–3, 134, 140, 158
  origins, composition, and duties of 58–9
Sapanopolos 33
Saronites 30, 31
Sekreton ton dikon 109–11, 119, 175
Sekreton ton oikeiakon, *see oikeiakon*
Sekreton tou dromou, *see dromos*
Sekreton tou ephorou, *see antiprosopon*; *domestikoi*; *ephoroi*; *notarioi*; *protonotarioi*
Sekreton tou genikou, *see genikon*
Sekreton tou stratiotikou, *see stratiotikon*
Senate 5, 19, 82, 85, 88, 149, 150, 187 n.14, 210 n.266, 230 n.24, *see also* Constantine IX Monomachos; Constantine X Doukas
  sandaled 72, 169
Skleros 30
Skleros, Andronikos, *protonobelissimos* and *logothetes tou dromou* 132

Skleros, Leo, *magistros* and *epi tou vestiariou* 132
Skleros, Nicholas, *magistros* and *epi ton deeseon* 141–2
Skylitzes, John, *droungarios tes viglas* 150, 151
  on decline/mismanagement of empire 3, 8
  proedros and *eparch* 145
Smyrnaios 30, 32
Smyrnaios, Theodore, *protoproedros* and *koiaistor* 148
Solomon, John, *protoasekretis* 138
  protoproedros and *epi ton deeseon* 141–2
state finances, *see* coinage; Constantine IX Monomachos; Constantine X Doukas; *rogai*; treasuries
state properties, *see euageis oikoi*; *megaloi kouratores*; *megaloi logariastai ton euagon sekreton*; *oikeiakon*; *sekreton tou ephorou*
Stephen, *asekretis* and *protonotarios* of the *sakellion* 60
Stephen, *patrikios* and *praitor* of Constantinople 89
Stephen, *protovestes*, *oikistikos ton neon orthoseon* and judge of the Armeniakoi 50–1
Stratiotikon 52–4, 198 n.49, *see also chartoularioi*; *logothetai*; *megaloi chartoularioi*; *protonotarios*
  final mention of 131
  origin, composition, and duties of 52
Symeon Logothetes, *magistros* and *logothetes tou dromou* 56
Symponoi 83, 86–8, 90, 145–6
  origins and duties of 86
Synod (1029) 122, 177, 220 n.426

Taktika, *see Escorial Taktikon*; *Kletorologion of Philotheos*; *Taktikon Beneševič*; *Taktikon Uspenskij*
Taktikon Beneševič 11, 121, 173
Taktikon Uspenskij 11
Taronites, John 136
  kouropalates and *epi ton deeseon* 142
  protokouropalates and *eparch* 145

Theodore, *anthypatos, patrikios*, and *droungarios tes viglas* 98
Theodore, *patrikios*, imperial *notarios* of the *eidikon*, and *praitor* of Constantinople 89
Theodore, *patrikios* and *ephoros* 67
Theophylaktos, *anthypatos, patrikios, protospatharios* and *droungarios tes viglas* 98
Theophylaktos, *vestarches*, judge, *megas oikonomos*, and *gerokomos* 51
Thesmographos 114, 156, 158
  duties of 112, 114
Thesmophylakes 113–14, 156
  duties of 112, 113, 121–2
Thrakesios, John, *see* Skylitzes, John
Thylakas, Leo, judge of the Hippodrome 101
titles 6, 11, 163–8, *see also* Alexios I Komnenos; Komnenian hierarchy; *rogai*
  cost of 170–2
  expansion of 12–13
  hierarchy of 11–17, 161–3
  inflation of 5, 12, 67–8, 81, 90, 161, 165–7, 172, 174, 178, 229–30 n.16, 230 n.2
Tornikios 30
Treasuries, *see eidikon; sakellion; vestiarion*
Tzetzes, John, description of the function of *exaktores* 114
Tzirithon 31, 176
Tzirithon, Basil 36
  anthypatos, patrikios, and *antiprosopon* of the *epi ton oikeiakon* 66
  protoproedros and *eparch* 145

protovestarches, judge of the Velum, and judge of the Kibyrraiotai 34, 153

Varys 31, 146
Vestiarion 60–1, 133, *see also chartoularioi; epi tou vestiariou; mandatores; notarioi*
  origins, composition, and duties of 60
Vlangas 30

Xeros 26
Xeros, Basil, *proedros* and *genikos logothetes* 129
Xeros, John, *magistros, vestes*, and *protoasekretis* 138
Xeros, John, *protomystikos* 77
Xeros, Thomas, *hypatos, patrikios*, and *antiprosopon* of the *oikonomos* of the charitable foundations 135–6
Xiphilinos 30
Xiphilinos, John, *exaktor* 115
  nomophylax didaskalos 118–21, 166
  provincial origins of 32
Xiphilinos, Niketas, *koiaistor* and judge 147
Xylinites 31, 38
Xylinites, Niketas 31
  proedros and *logothetes tou dromou* 55–7, 99, 132

Zonaras, John, Alexios I and 8
  droungarios tes viglas 150, 151
Zonaras, Nicholas, *protovestarches, megas chartoularios* and judge of the Hippodrome 154